CONVIVIAL CONSERVATION

From Principles to Practice

Published by Mayfly Books. Available in paperpack
and free online at www.mayflybooks.org in 2023.

ISBN (Print)   978-1-906948-65-8
ISBN (PDF)   978-1-906948-66-5
ISBN (ebook) 978-1-906948-67-2

Cover art work by Ink & Water who retains the image copyright.

Layout by Jess Parker.

may f l y

CONVIVIAL CONSERVATION

From Principles to Practice

Edited by Kate Massarella, Judith E. Krauss, Wilhelm A. Kiwango
and Robert Fletcher

Table of Contents

Part IV: Alternative Governance and Financing Mechanisms

Contributor Biographical Information

Christine Ampumuza is a senior lecturer in the Department of Tourism and Hospitality at Kabale University Uganda.

Paolo Bocci is a cultural anthropologist and STS scholar. He is a former faculty at Duke University and currently works as design researcher at IBM.

Séverine van Bommel is an interdisciplinary social scientist working with rural communities on the co-construction of meaning in interaction in environmental communication and extension, gender issues and co-design of technologies. Taking an interpretive approach, she has studied and contributed to a number of innovative research methodologies for multi-level, multi-stakeholder and multi-species research.

Susan Boonman-Berson is an independent animal-geography researcher and speaker at 'Bear at Work', based in Nijmegen, the Netherlands. Her topic of interest is cohabitation between humans and wild animals.

Bram Büscher is chair of Development Sociology at Wageningen University and visiting professor at the University of Johannesburg. He published widely on the relations between nature, development and political-economy. His most recent book on environmentalism in the era of post-truth and platform capitalism was published by *University of California Press*.

Valentina Fiasco is a PhD researcher at the Sustainability Research Institute of the University of Leeds as part of the ESRC White Rose DTP program. She is an interdisciplinary scholar interested in studying human-wildlife coexistence, drawing insights from the natural and social sciences and the humanities.

Robert Fletcher is associate professor of Sociology of Development and Change at Wageningen University in the Netherlands. His most recent book is *Failing Forward: The Rise and Fall of Neoliberal Conservation* (UC Press, 2023).

George Holmes is professor of Conservation and Society in the Sustainability Research Institute, University of Leeds. His work studies the structures, practices and values of conservationists, and the interactions between conservation projects and local people.

Elaine (Lan Yin) Hsiao is an assistant professor at the Kent State University School of Peace and Conflict Studies and chairs the International Union for the Conservation of Nature (IUCN) Commission on Environment, Economics, and Social Policy (CEESP) Theme on Environment and Peace. Much of her work seeks to address conflicts in conservation, conservation in places of conflict, and conflict resolution through conservation (i.e., environmental peacebuilding).

George Iordăchescu is a political ecologist interested in wildlife conservation, rewilding politics, and European environmental governance. He is currently researching illegal wildlife trade in European species as part of the Beastly Business project at the University of Sheffield.

Wilhelm Kiwango is a lecturer and researcher from the Department of Geography and Environmental Studies, the University of Dodoma. His research interests include decentralised Environmental Governance and Conservation Social Sciences.

Judith Krauss is a lecturer at the University of York's Department of Politics/Interdisciplinary Global Development Centre. She works on decoloniality and justice in conservation as well as sustainable global value chains.

Mathew Bukhi Mabele is a lecturer and conservation social scientist, working in the Department of Geography and Environmental Studies at the University of Dodoma, Tanzania. He teaches and researches on the governance of human-environment interactions in tropical ecosystems.

Kate Massarella is an environmental social scientist and lecturer at Tilburg University in the Netherlands. Her work combines political ecology, science and technology studies, and justice theory to explore practices and processes of environmental interventions, and to understand barriers and opportunities for transformations to sustainability.

Claire Quinn is an environmental social scientist and chair in Natural Resource Management in the Sustainability Research Institute, University of Leeds. Her research focuses on socio-ecological systems, specifically livelihood vulnerability, adaptation and resilience; and knowledge and governance for sustainable management of natural resources.

Revati Pandya is faculty in the School of Development at Azim Premji University, Bengaluru, India. Her work is centred on intersectional community dynamics, access and equity in conservation and natural resource governance spaces.

Hanna Pettersson is a conservation social scientist based at the Leverhulme Centre for Anthropocene Biodiversity, University of York, where she studies human-wildlife interactions, (re)wilding and conservation governance.

Steven Sait is an ecologist in the School of Biology, University of Leeds, whose research interests focus on the impacts of environmental change on trophic interactions, and the multi-scale processes and associated trade-offs that affect biodiversity and food sustainability in farming landscapes.

Svetoslava Toncheva is assistant professor in the Comparative Folklore Studies Department of the Institute of Ethnology and Folklore Studies in the Ethnographic Museum, Bulgarian Academy of Sciences. Her research focuses on human-nonhuman interactions, convivial conservation, multispecies ethnography and large carnivores.

Esther Turnhout is a professor and chair of Science, Technology, and Society at the University of Twente, the Netherlands. Her research focuses on the interactions between science, technology, policy and society, particularly in the context of environmental governance and sustainability transformations.

Acknowledgements

This edited volume is based primarily on a special issue published in the journal Conservation and Society (volume 20, issue 2) in 2022, entitled 'Exploring Convivial Conservation in Theory in Practice'. Contributions to this special issue have been republished here thanks to the journal editors' kind permission as well as the Creative Commons licence under which the journal is published. Other chapters are also based on previously published articles, which are similarly republished due to gracious consent from the original publishers. Support for both the Conservation and Society collection and this volume has been provided by the NORFACE and Belmont Forum Transformations to Sustainability (T2S) Joint Research Programme Project #949 'Towards Convivial Conservation: Governing Human-Wildlife Interactions in the Anthropocene' (CONVIVA). We would like to extend our gratitude to all contributors to this volume for their hard work and patience, as well as the management and editorial teams at Conservation and Society, the Journal of Political Ecology, and Biological Conservation. We would also like to thank all of the other participants in the CONVIVA project for their convivial collaboration these past years. Finally, grateful acknowledgments to the editors and production team at MayFly Books for taking on this book project and guiding it through to completion.

Kate Massarella, Judith E. Krauss, Wilhelm A. Kiwango, and Robert Fletcher
January 2023

PART I

Introduction

Chapter 1:

Exploring Convivial Conservation in Theory and Practice

By Kate Massarella, Judith E. Krauss, Wilhelm A. Kiwango, and Robert Fletcher

Introduction: Transformative Change and Convivial Conservation

We are living in a time of widespread anxiety about the state of our planet, in relation to issues including climate change, social injustices, ecosystem degradation and biodiversity loss. These issues are largely driven by human activity, leading to many labelling the current epoch 'the Anthropocene' (Lorimer 2015). Growing concerns about global biodiversity loss have led many in the conservation community—conservationists, academics, governments officials, and civil society groups—to call for radical transformation in biodiversity conservation policy and practice (IPBES 2019; Wyborn et al. 2020). Transformation can be defined as a 'substantial, profound and fundamental change, which requires a paradigm shift in how we relate to and manage the environment' (Massarella et al. 2021: 79). Such a shift requires moving away from approaches to transformation that O'Brien et al. (2013) label 'circular' (implementing new ideas within existing power structures) and towards those labelled 'axial' (fundamentally challenging the status quo).

A range of proposals to transform biodiversity conservation have been put forward, advocating for differing goals and means of transformation. One popular proposal, often termed 'half earth' or 'nature needs half', is to dramatically increase terrestrial and marine protected areas so that they cover at least half of the earth (Dinerstein et al. 2017; Locke 2014; Wilson 2016). The closely aligned '30 by 30' proposal, which advocates for 30% of land and sea to be in some form of protection by 2030 (Waldron et al. 2020), was endorsed as a global target at the 2021 IUCN World Conservation Congress and is the basis for target 3 of the Kunming-Montreal Global Biodiversity Framework, agreed at the 15th meeting of the Conference of Parties to the UN Convention on Biological Diversity (CBD 2022). Another popular proposal, often referred to as 'new conservation', aims to integrate conservation and human development concerns by conceptualising a 'post-wild' world that embraces technological innovation and market-based approaches to natural resource governance (Marris 2013; Marvier 2014).

These proposals have, however, been critiqued for not sufficiently addressing the underlying issues inherent to historical and contemporary conservation approaches that have contributed to injustices and may impede axial transformation. Critiques include a failure to sufficiently protect the rights of Indigenous Peoples and local communities affected by conservation (Kashwan et al. 2021; Schleicher et al. 2019; Krauss 2022); not adequately addressing the growing militarisation of conservation (Duffy et al. 2019) that reinforces rather than dismantles the problematic separation between people and nonhuman nature; and the continued promotion of conservation ideas that have their roots in colonial conservation practices, prioritise western science, and perpetuate top-down modes of governance (Domínguez and Luoma 2020; Kothari et al. 2019; Mbaria and Ogada 2016; Krauss 2021 and chapter five of this collection).

Convivial conservation has been proposed as a radical alternative to the half earth and new conservation proposals to address the aforementioned critiques and offer a socially just, democratic and inclusive form of biodiversity governance that aims for axial transformation (see chapter 2 of this collection for a more detailed overview of the convivial conservation proposal). Inspired by decolonial, youth, and Indigenous movements, convivial conservation aims to foreground social justice in conservation efforts, highlight the importance of attending to how global political and economic systems drive biodiversity destruction, and challenge the human-nature dichotomy prevalent in conservation efforts that aim to preserve an idealised 'wilderness' separated from humans (Büscher and Fletcher 2019; 2020). Convivial conservation calls for structural change in the current global economic model and the inequalities it creates - both among people and between humans and nonhumans (ibid.). Büscher and Fletcher (2020) link the convivial conservation concept with other complementary proposals for axial transformation in biodiversity governance, such as radical ecological democracy (Kothari 2014) and Territories of Life (ICCA Consortium 2021).

As explained further in chapter 2, the convivial conservation vision encompasses five elements of transformative action (Büscher and Fletcher 2019, 2020). First, it calls for a fundamental shift away from a focus on protected areas that separate humans and nonhumans, towards a focus on promoted areas, which encourage human frequentation and sustainable use. Second, it proposes a discursive shift away from needing to 'save nature' from people and towards recognising and celebrating human and nonhuman nature as integral elements of an overarching whole. Third, it advocates long-term engagement with biodiversity instead of short-term touristic voyeurism of wildlife in protected areas. Fourth, it questions the promotion of nature as spectacle and instead champions interactions with everyday nature. Fifth, it calls for a shift from the privatised expert technocracy that dominates conservation decision-making at international and national levels towards common democratic engagement and devolved governance that prioritises Indigenous and community groups. Translating these elements into practical measures, convivial conservation proposes: 1) conservation spaces that integrate rather than separate humans and other species; 2) direct democratic governance arrangements that challenge elite technocratic management; and 3) novel finance arrangements that redistribute existing wealth and resources.

However, aside from the initial proposition and theorisation by Büscher and Fletcher (2019; 2020; and chapter 2 of this collection) and engagement by some practitioners and scholars (Krauss 2021 and chapter 5 of this collection; DeVore, Hirsch, and Paulson 2019; Toncheva and Fletcher 2021; Collins et al. 2021; Dunlap 2020; Collins 2021), convivial conservation remains nascent in its conceptualisation and practical development. This edited collection has been put together as a means of critically engaging with and further developing the convivial conservation proposition. The collection brings together authors from diverse backgrounds with expertise in different contexts and disciplines, who draw on a wide range of case studies to contribute both empirical and conceptual reflections on the convivial conservation proposal. The collection is guided by two questions:

1) What are the potentials and pitfalls of convivial conservation as atransformative approach to conservation?

2) How can convivial conservation be developed and expanded both in theory and in practice?

Overview of the Edited Collection

The edited collection is split into four parts. Part I introduces the collection. In this first chapter, we offer some background on the collection's development and an overview of the rest of the book. We also present a discussion of some of the key author arguments and insights from this edited collection, towards a better understanding of the potentials and pitfalls of convivial conservation, and ideas about how it can be developed and expanded, from a range of different perspectives. We focus this synthesis on three critical issues that are highlighted across the contributions: 1) exploring how justice can be better conceptualised in convivial conservation in order to be transformative; 2) unpacking the concept and implementation of human-nonhuman coexistence; and 3) identifying and developing methodologies for investigating and facilitating transformative change in conservation research and practice. We argue that through further engagement with these critical issues, convivial conservation has the potential to contribute to transforming biodiversity conservation in the Anthropocene, and to avoid some of the pitfalls that proposals for transformative change commonly encounter.

In chapter 2, Büscher and Fletcher provide a synthesis of their convivial conservation vision, outlining the politics behind the proposal, and discussing some of the governance principles that they propose as central to the approach. This lays a foundation for the subsequent analytical chapters to critically engage with some of the elements of this initial convivial conservation proposal. Most of these contributions focus specifically on human-wildlife interactions, which is a central issue in debates about transforming biodiversity conservation in the Anthropocene more broadly (Lorimer 2015). We have organised the following chapters into three groups, based on the main emphasis of their analysis.

The first set of critical engagements in part II focus on growing calls to pluralise and decolonise conservation. Mathew Bukhi Mabele, Judith Krauss, and Wilhelm Kiwango begin by exploring the potential for 'going back to the roots' of conservation through *Ubuntu* and just conservation in Southern Africa. Christine Ampumuza then explores the lessons for convivial conservation offered by Batwa-gorilla relations in Bwindi Forest in Uganda. Judith Krauss analyses conviviality through a lens of decolonising conservation and explores pathways towards implementing a convivial Sustainable Development Goal (SDG) 15 focused on life on land. Paolo Bocci completes this section by highlighting the roles of both culture and agriculture in convivial conservation by analysing how 'resilience' is conceived and enacted in the Galapagos Islands.

Part III turns to the issue of human-wildlife interactions. The section begins with Massarella and Fiasco's analysis of 'coexistence' as an increasingly popular buzzword, asking whether it represents business as usual conservation or an opportunity for transformative change. Hanna Pettersson, Claire Quinn, George Holmes, and Steven Sait then explore how to better understand the conditions for human-wolf coexistence in North-Western Spain. Svetoslava Toncheva, Robert Fletcher, and Esther Turnhout continue this theme by unpacking a case of human-bear cohabitation in Bulgaria's Rodopi Mountains. This section is completed by Séverine van Bommel and Susan Boonman-Berson's argument for transforming convivial conservation through engaging more-than-human participation in research.

Part IV offers rich discussions on alternative governance and financing mechanisms through critical engagement with ideas proposed by Büscher and Fletcher in chapter 2, and exploration of new ways of configuring biodiversity conservation. The section begins with Fletcher and Büscher's proposal for conservation basic income (CBI) as a non-market alternative to market-based mechanisms common in mainstream conservation. Elaine (Lan Yin) Hsiao then explores how conviviality can be cultivated in disrupted socionatural landscapes through 'ecological peacebuilding' via a case study of Akagera National Park in Rwanda. Revati Pandya continues the exploration of alternative governance and financing mechanisms by unpacking how micro-politics influence prospects for convivial conservation around the Corbett Tiger Reserve in India. George Iordăchescu then analyses the potential for convivial conservation in Europe, advocating a move from wilderness protection to reclaiming the commons. The collection is then rounded off by Wilhelm Kiwango and Mathew Bukhi Mabele making a case for why convivial conservation needs complementing to be a viable alternative for conservation in the Global South.

Discussion of the Key Issues Raised by the Contributions

This section offers a synthesis of the contributions through exploration of three overarching themes emerging from the individual contributions. These themes can be identified across the three sections outlined above. We focus on three critical issues raised by the contributors, focused on: 1) exploring how justice can be better conceptualised in convivial conservation in order to be transformative; 2) unpacking the concept of human-nonhuman coexistence; and 3) identifying and developing methodologies for investigating and facilitating transformative change in conservation research and practice. Combined, analysis of these issues contributes to furthering discussions of the potential for convivial conservation to be a transformative approach to biodiversity conservation. Drawing on our three themes, we conclude by offering some recommendations for expanding the transformative potential of the convivial conservation approach.

Convivial Conservation and Transformative Justice

Justice is a contested term comprising several divergent dimensions (Svarstad and Benjaminsen 2020). When characterising different visions of transformative change in biodiversity conservation, Massarella et al. (2021) identify convivial conservation as a 'just transformation' approach. The goal of just transformation is to radically shift conservation research, policy, and practice in a way that pays particular attention to issues of power, addresses historical and contemporary injustices, and questions who is recognised and who gets to participate in knowledge production and decision-making (Temper et al. 2018; Martin et al. 2020; Álvarez and Coolsaet 2020; Mabele 2020). The concept of just transformation aligns with the idea of transformative justice, which is characterised by a shift away from affirmative action (e.g. making policy changes to increase representation of marginalised groups in decision-making) towards transformative action (e.g. questioning the power structures and assumptions that exclude these groups in the first place) (Fraser 2009; Temper 2019).

Although Büscher and Fletcher (2019; 2020; and chapter 2) situate justice as central to the convivial conservation proposal, they do not explicitly define it nor engage with different conceptualisations of justice and its role in transformative change. Several contributors to this collection address this gap by engaging explicitly with different notions of justice to further develop convivial conservation as a transformative approach. Contributors focus on epistemic, participatory and multi-species justice, and distributive justice, which broadly resonate with Schlosberg's (2004) idea of thinking about environmental justice in terms of three central 'pillars' of recognition, participation and distribution. We have thus organised our subsequent discussion around these concepts.

Epistemic Justice

Despite moves towards rights-based approaches and increased visibility of Indigenous peoples and local communities in discussions and discourses, conservation is still primarily based on, and driven by, the ideologies of Global North institutions, which routinely invoke western science to define global biodiversity crises, propose what they consider new and innovative solutions, and often exclude other forms of knowledge (Kothari 2021). This results in what is defined as epistemic injustice, whereby certain knowledge and worldviews are prioritised and dominant knowledge systems are imposed over others (Escobar 2010; Widenhorn 2013). Epistemic struggles are at the heart of social struggle, as well as struggles over 'the environment', and so transformative approaches to conservation must question hegemonic worldviews while making visible other ways of knowing, forms of politics, and modes of environmental governance (Icaza and Vázquez 2013; Temper and Del Bene 2016).

The intention of convivial conservation is to engage with the ways of knowing of Indigenous peoples and local communities living in biodiverse spaces, which often transcend the nature-culture dualism central to western epistemology and the fortress conservation approach (Büscher and Fletcher, chapter 2). However, as Kothari (2021) argues, many innovative, 'whole earth' approaches fall short of being truly transformative as they are still grounded in academic thought emerging from the Global North (see also Krauss, chapter 5). To facilitate just transformations, convivial conservation should therefore 'embrace the idea that a variety of knowledge configurations exist, going beyond those recognised by academia' (Álvarez and Coolsaet 2020: 63).

In her exploration of human-gorilla interactions at Bwindi Impenetrable National Park in south-western Uganda, Ampumuza (chapter 4) identifies a wide range of injustices perpetrated against the Indigenous Batwa people in the name of gorilla conservation. She argues that many of these injustices are rooted in western scientific knowledge, values and perspectives guiding conservation programmes, including the labelling of the knowledge of the Batwa people accrued over centuries as too unscientific. She also argues that convivial conservation proponents should be explicit about how to tackle epistemic injustice driven by the dominance of western-led conservation science. Similarly, through her study of human-wildlife conflict and coexistence in Akagera National Park in Rwanda, Hsiao (chapter 12) highlights how conservation approaches grounded in western scientific knowledge and practices reinforce both nature-culture dichotomies and the commodification of non-human life, which contribute to biodiversity loss and the erosion of traditional ecological knowledge.

Highlighting the continued influence of colonial legacies in conservation (Mbaria and Ogada 2016, Collins et al. 2021), Mabele et al. (chapter 3) argue for the need to be 'epistemically disobedient' (Mignolo 2011: 54). They challenge the dominant modes of problem framing in western science and the values and epistemologies of large conservation organisations by drawing on alternative philosophies that align with local values and ways of knowing the world. They discuss how embedding conservation in southern Africa in *Ubuntu* philosophy could act as a powerful tool for grounding justice issues—and conservation more broadly—in traditional ways of knowing, values, and notions of justice. Similarly, Krauss (chapter 5) highlights both the potential and limitations of Illich's conviviality (1973), and related ideas such as convivial conservation, to contribute to decolonising conservation by promoting grassroots, democratic decision-making, living within limits by the rich, and interdependencies between and within humanity and the environment. To be fully actualised as decolonial options, she argues, such ideas must avoid imposition from outside and incorporate intergenerational and marginalised viewpoints, particularly those disadvantaged by hierarchies of difference in terms of gender, race, age, status or (dis)ability. In chapter 6, Bocci makes a similar argument for conservation in the Galapagos Islands by showing how local farmers identify with the cultural philosophy of *arraigo* (belonging), which stands in stark contrast to the dominant framing of Galapagos as an inhospitable place that is visited only for tourism and research.

Putting epistemic justice at the heart of convivial conservation also includes learning from spaces in which people and large carnivores coexist, such as between humans and wolves in north-western Spain (Pettersson et al., chapter 8) and between humans and bears in the Rodopi Mountains of Bulgaria (Toncheva et al., chapter 9). It further involves learning from situations in which humans and animals have evolved together and have adopted informal institutional arrangements that enable coexistence (Ampumuza, chapter 4; van Bommel and Boonman-Berson, chapter 10; Toncheva et al., chapter 9). Convivial conservation can also learn from existing governance structures in spaces where social and ecological wellbeing are considered inseparable, and coexistence is driven by a desire for mutual care and justice, as in Territories of Life (Hsiao, chapter 12; Hsiao and Le Billon 2021), as well as from the experiences of implementing progressive laws such as the Recognition of Forest Rights Act (FRA) in India (Pandya, chapter 13).

In his study of the Crăciunel commons in Romania, Iordăchescu (chapter 14) argues for explicitly recognising and building on the approach to governance of local communities that combines sustainable use with conservation and rejects free-market logics and western framings of nature-culture relationships. He points out that it is also necessary to be open to the fact that conservation, as conceptualised and advocated by scientists or international organisations, may not always be the priority of Indigenous peoples and local communities. Bocci (chapter 6) and Massarella and Fiasco (chapter 7) further highlight the potential risk that alternative and potentially transformative ideas, such as *buen vivir* and *coexistence*, respectively, can become vehicles for reinforcing the status quo if not sufficiently pluralised and politicised.

Participatory and Multi-species Justice

Participatory justice, which is sometimes referred to as procedural justice, is concerned with meaningful involvement of different people in decision-making around a certain issue or mode of governance (He and Sikor 2015). Despite its transformative roots and increasing focus in conservation policy and practice, 'participation' has become another buzzword, with the focus often on affirmative techniques that do not meaningfully engage local people (Leal 2007). Convivial conservation instead advocates transformative approaches to participatory justice towards 'deeply participatory forms of engagement in which local actors are placed at centre stage' (Büscher and Fletcher 2019: 10). Its goal is to challenge the official narratives that present local communities as core problems for conservation and instead balance local people's active role in conservation decision-making with the awareness of wider political economic factors shaping their experiences. However, what this would look like in practice requires further elaboration, as this collection's contributors point out.

Bocci (chapter 6) advances the idea of democratic engagement by investigating the participation of local people living on the Galapagos Islands in conservation decision-making. He argues that making participation just, meaningful, and transformative requires continuous involvement of local people, re-framing of the relationship between humans and nonhumans, recognition of different worldviews and values, and a shift from focusing on individuals to focusing on overarching political contexts. He also highlights the heterogeneous nature of local people and the dangers of framing them as either victims or villains.

The issue of framing is also emphasised in the contributions by Hsiao (chapter 12), Ampumuza (chapter 4), and Kiwango and Mabele (chapter 15). In their work on human-bear interactions in the Rodopi Mountains in Bulgaria, Toncheva et al. (chapter 9) further highlight the need for participation to go beyond engagement in top-down initiatives, and instead facilitate design from the bottom up, in order to support human-wildlife coexistence. Pettersson et al. (chapter 8) echo this in relation to human-wolf coexistence in north-western Spain, challenging the continued focus on top-down initiatives and instead advocating for participatory approaches that build on local ecological knowledge. Similarly, Iordăchescu (chapter 14) emphasises the importance of building on local custodians' skills, knowledge and practices to enrich prospects for convivial conservation, while Mabele et al. (chapter 3) and Krauss (chapter 5) argue that decision-making must be devolved to local people to transform governance practices.

Several contributors address the issue of how convivial conservation might meaningfully address multi-species justice by incorporating nonhuman participation in the vision. Büscher and Fletcher (chapter 2) advocate a transcendence of human-nonhuman dichotomies that often drive conservation policy and practice. Their focus on justice in relation to nonhumans is linked explicitly to the ways in which capitalism alienates both humans and nonhumans, yet they assert the need to retain a privileged focus on human action and responsibility for an effective conservation politics. However, contributors to this collection encourage more consideration and incorporation of nonhuman perspectives and further engagement with the ontological, epistemological, and methodological implications of doing so. Whether in relation to wolves in Spain (Pettersson et al., chapter 8), mountain gorillas in Uganda (Ampumuza, chapter 4), or bears in Bulgaria (Toncheva et al., chapter 9), the contributions identify myriad ways that humans and animals continuously co-adapt their behaviour to coexist.

Based on their experiences of conducting research on and with animals in a range of countries and contexts, van Bommel and Boonman-Berson (chapter 10) challenge convivial conservation to be more systematic in the inclusion of nonhuman perspectives. Drawing on scholars like Bastian et al. (2016) and Haraway (2013), they argue that nonhumans must be treated as subjects (rather than objects) of conservation, and that human exceptionalism should therefore be challenged. Hsiao (chapter 12) argues for an emphasis on 'positive ecological peace', which targets underlying drivers of conflict such as the cultural violence of separating humans and nonhumans physically and conceptually, thus shifting from affirmative notions of participation to transformative ones.

Distributive Justice

Simply put, distributive justice focuses on the uneven distribution of conservation benefits and harms (Mabele 2020). Several propositions about how to address distributive justice put forward by Büscher and Fletcher (2019) are critically engaged with by contributors. In exploring the potential for advancing transformative conservation in Southern Africa, Mabele et al. (chapter 3) raise several questions related to the idea of 'promoted' conservation areas (Büscher and Fletcher 2020), particularly the legal and regulatory frameworks that would need to be applied. Mabele at al. ask who would own the land, what kinds of access and usage rights would be provided for local communities, how would a just distribution of costs and benefits be established, and how would disputes be settled about what is (not) permissible in 'promoted' areas? Pandya (chapter 13) raises a similar concern regarding land rights in her study of the Corbett Tiger Reserve in India by pointing out the diverse types of landholding statuses of communities living in the vicinity of the Reserve and how these form micropolitical environments that produce uneven distribution of conservation benefits across intersecting lines of gender, caste, and social class. There is thus scope for convivial conservation to engage more systematically with how it relates to women's lives, livelihoods and ways of knowing (Pandya, chapter 13, Ampumuza, chapter 4, Krauss, chapter 5).

In the convivial conservation proposal, Büscher and Fletcher (2020) identify the tourist industry as driving a number of conservation injustices, which is supported by several contributions to this collection. Bocci (chapter 6) highlights the embeddedness and dominance of tourism interests in conservation in the Galapagos Islands, often to the disadvantage of resident farmers who are more committed to landscape conservation. Pandya (chapter 13) discusses how the tourism market of Corbett Tiger Reserve has created tourism-based dependencies and differences in access to jobs and other economic opportunities for land-owning and landless households across class, caste and gender divisions.

In response to some of the challenges of the international tourism industry, Büscher and Fletcher (2020) advocate 'engaged visitation' as opposed to 'touristic voyeurism'. Kiwango and Mabele (chapter 15) argue that such a proposal might only be applicable to countries in the Global North. They explain that conservation in countries like Tanzania is driven by 'path dependencies' established during colonial times that are characterised by a reliance on international tourism, itself mainly grounded in nature-based attractions. Such attractions are, in turn, conserved through the protected area approach with all its challenges. They point out the significance of protected areas for Tanzania's foreign exchange earnings from international tourism and note that the revenues derived from short-term international tourists visiting protected areas to view charismatic megafauna without the presence of local communities is far higher than income earned from domestic tourists. The national government, conservation agencies, park management authorities, officials, and local communities rely on the international tourism revenue to fund national development projects and protect and expand wildlife conservation areas. These issues would therefore need to be addressed and transformed to make the idea of 'engaged visitation' a possibility in countries like Tanzania.

Toncheva et al. (chapter 9) describe a contrasting situation in the Rodopi Mountains in Bulgaria where a small, locally established tourism industry has emerged around the local brown bear population. They demonstrate how this wildlife tourism has developed organically and encourages visitor engagement in ways that benefit both local communities and brown bear conservation. In his study of the Crăciunel commons in Romania, Iordăchescu (chapter 14) also identifies the early stages of a locally-developed tourism industry around protected areas that is more just and inclusive because it is rooted in local priorities.

Alternative finance mechanisms are proposed as a component of convivial conservation to address conservation injustices. One such proposal, outlined by Fletcher and Büscher in chapter 11, is conservation basic income (CBI): a regular, unconditional payment to community members living in or near biodiversity-critical areas to facilitate their adoption of conservation-friendly livelihoods). Several contributors explore the potential to develop such mechanisms. While supporting the idea of alternative financing, Kiwango and Mabele (chapter 15) highlight the need to ensure that a mechanism such as CBI does not result in excessive economic valuation of wildlife and thereby contribute to perverse outcomes and further injustices. They argue instead for a 'community-based conservation insurance' scheme that subsidises farmers and herders for injustices caused by protected area conservation. This, they argue, would need to go hand in hand with decriminalisation of livestock herding and the recognition that households in rural communities routinely bear the costs of conservation interventions.

Ampumuza (chapter 4) also points out that while CBI may align with sharing principles held by Indigenous communities like the Batwa in Uganda, such mechanisms may risk further marginalisation by focusing too much on economic benefits and further positioning these communities as recipients. Hsiao (chapter 12) warns of the potential for financial mechanisms more broadly to contribute to further commodification of nonhumans. Iordăchescu (chapter 14) endorses the proposal for direct payments to members involved in managing commons but remains cautious about the long-term viability of external funding. Overall, the contributors point out that alternative finance mechanisms such as CBI are unlikely to result in transformative distributive justice if national and regional political economic contexts and local power relations are not taken into consideration (Hoang et al. 2019).

Büscher and Fletcher (2020) also advocate for historical reparations to compensate for past injustices caused by conservation interventions. This recommendation echoes other calls for reparations—via, inter alia, land tenure and access rights—to compensate Indigenous peoples and local communities for long histories of exclusion through protected area formation (Zurba et al. 2019). Büscher and Fletcher (2020) acknowledge that identifying who should receive reparations and how they should be distributed is a complex issue. As Ramutsindela and Shabangu (2018) show, processes of restitution are often extremely politicised and onerous for historically marginalised groups and do not automatically result in reparative justice for all members. Several contributors highlight these complexities while broadly endorsing the need to address historical reparations appropriate to the socio-political and cultural contexts. Hsiao (chapter 12) notes that historical reparations should not only address past actions of dispossession, but also the continuing impacts of cultural and slow violence in the present. Ampumuza (chapter 4) and Mabele et al. (chapter 3) also support the notion that reparations must address continued injustices perpetuated by the sustained focus on protected areas and exclusionary scientific approaches with colonial roots. Future generations and intergenerational dimensions of justice must also be accounted for (Krauss, chapter 5). Finally, Pandya (chapter 13) highlights the importance of attending to micro-politics as a prerequisite for such reparations.

Unpacking 'Coexistence' in Convivial Conservation

Human-wildlife coexistence is central to the convivial conservation vision and is reflected in the proposed elements of promoted areas and integrated landscapes, among others. Coexistence is considered to be a core element of transformative change in biodiversity conservation more broadly (Hazzah et al. 2019), yet the idea has been conceptualised in different ways. In their study of coexistence in theory and practice, Massarella and Fiasco (chapter 7) show that the term has become another conservation buzzword and is often used without in-depth consideration of its meaning. Massarella and Fiasco argue that although coexistence has the potential to be a transformative concept, it often manifests in practice as 'standardised packages' of apolitical tools. They therefore note, along with other contributors (Ampumuza, chapter 4; Pettersson et al., chapter 8; van Bommel and Boonman-Berson, chapter 10; Hsiao, chapter 12), that convivial conservation needs to further elaborate and flesh out the concept of coexistence.

Pettersson et al. (chapter 8) frame coexistence as a 'state in which people are able to live equitably and sustainably with wildlife, and where conservation efforts are carried out within the context of wider societal challenges'. Their ethnographic study finds that most clashes between people and wolves result from a mismatch between local values and those being imposed from the outside, as well as the unjust and unequal distribution of burdens and benefits in wolf conservation. They propose that centring local communities in knowledge production and management practices, which both recognise them as environmental stewards and compensate them accordingly, can contribute towards a re-framing of wolf conservation from species-based protection to the shared, justice-based 'living landscapes' which convivial conservation supports. Massarella and Fiasco (chapter 7) support this call to better link coexistence with justice and wider political economic and social contexts, identifying the potential contribution of convivial conservation to advance a concept of 'meaningful coexistence' that focuses on the broader relationships between humanity, capitalism and wildlife. However, van Bommel and Boonman-Berson (chapter 10) challenge the continued emphasis in convivial conservation on the human in human-wildlife coexistence by asking whether coexistence has any real meaning when it continues to separate humans and nonhumans.

Although coexistence may be the latest conservation buzzword, it is something that has been practised for centuries in many places throughout the world. Many authors have expressed concern that more traditional practices that facilitate coexistence may be lost or side-lined unless conscious effort is made to unpack and learn from the myriad socio-cultural, political, economic and historical factors that keep them alive (Mwamidi et al. 2012, de Silva and Srinivasan 2019). Pettersson et al. (chapter 8), Toncheva et al. (chapter 9), and van Bommel and Boonman-Berson (chapter 10) demonstrate how human-wildlife coexistence has developed organically over time in landscapes that have not been subject to a large degree of external intervention. Conversely, Kiwango and Mabele (chapter 15), and Ampumuza (chapter 4) show how decades of external intervention in the name of conservation has disrupted human-wildlife coexistence and devalued local coexistence practices and knowledge. Kiwango and Mabele (chapter 15), and Hsiao (chapter 12) also show how human migration caused by conflict and political-economic processes create new contexts for human-wildlife coexistence. Hsiao further demonstrates that place-based traditional ecological knowledge cannot always be assumed, and that conceptualisations of coexistence need to move past the idea of communities as homogenous entities that either coexist in whole or not at all. All contributors agree that coexistence is never a static state, nor is it always peaceful and free from conflict.

Transformative Methodologies and Convivial Conservation

The contributions to this collection emphasise that methodology is an important tool for facilitating transformative change

(Shrivastava et al. 2020). Despite convivial conservation's emphasis on incorporating insights from natural and social sciences (Büscher and Fletcher 2020; this collection), contributors to this collection maintain that precisely what this means in terms of methodology, epistemology, and ontology, both across different scholarly disciplines and in collaboration with diverse knowledge holders, requires further elaboration. Van Bommel and Boonman-Berson (chapter 10) assert that since research is performative, it is critically important that it does not reproduce and reinforce the nature-culture dichotomy that convivial conservation proposes to overcome. They identify the 'threshold concepts' of affect, embodiment, and multisensory communication as methods to better incorporate nonhuman actors into research processes. Ampumuza (chapter 4) and Mabele et al. (chapter 3) advocate developing research methodologies that draw on Indigenous and traditional philosophies, values, and ways of knowing. Multiple studies (Bocci, chapter 6; Hsiao, chapter 12; Kiwango and Mabele, chapter 15; Pandya, chapter 13; Toncheva et al., chapter 9; and van Bommel and Boonman-Berson, chapter 10) reinforce the importance of combining ethnography and extended engagement with 'situated knowledge' in different landscapes.

The contributors bring diverse analytic lenses to engage critically with and contribute to the convivial conservation vision and practice. Ampumuza (chapter 4), Kiwango and Mabele (chapter 15), and Mabele et al. (chapter 3) present convincing arguments for methodologies based on decolonial deconstruction (Tamale 2020, Murove 2012) of both conservation and research practice. Pandya (chapter 13) uses intersectional theory and feminist political ecology to frame a methodological approach for analysing the micro-politics of land ownership and livelihood opportunities for households living near wildlife reserves. Hsiao (chapter 12) demonstrates the value of a peace studies lens to convivial conservation thinking, while Toncheva et al. (chapter 9) show the complementarity between convivial conservation and a 'constitutionality' (bottom-up self-governance by community groups) approach (Haller 2020). Massarella and Fiasco (chapter 7) demonstrate how a science and technology studies (STS) lens can unpack processes of transformative change. Van Bommel and Boonman-Berson (chapter 10) show how a more-than-human theoretical lens enables collaborations across natural and social sciences to analyse intersubjectivity among non-human and human actors in conservation research. Pettersson et al. (chapter 8) advocate collaborative social and natural science approaches for developing integrative methodologies that focus on 'biocultural diversity', while Ampumuza (chapter 4), Iordăchescu (chapter 14), and Toncheva et al. (chapter 9) demonstrate the benefit of prioritising local knowledge and lived experiences in knowledge production.

Conclusions: Moving Convivial Conservation Forward in Theory and Practice

By drawing together the diverse contributions to this collection, across varied backgrounds, disciplines and areas of expertise, we can offer concrete suggestions for how to move convivial conservation forward in both theory and practice around the three themes of justice, coexistence, and transformative methodologies. In relation to justice, it is clear that further engagement with epistemic justice is needed (contributions by Ampumuza, Kiwango and Mabele, Krauss, and Mabele et al.) given convivial conservation's roots in the Global North (Krauss). Explicit engagement with how to address injustices perpetrated historically or currently in the name of western-based conservation science is needed, and care must be taken to ensure that convivial conservation does not become another top-down initiative that sidelines voices from the Global South (Kothari 2021). Engagement with epistemic justice in convivial conservation encourages iterative, bottom-up listening to build more integrated understandings of mutual care in living landscapes: by learning from existing practices of coexistence, governance structures and non-western ontologies, and from supporting grassroots movements as opposed to speaking on their behalf.

Epistemic justice closely links with both participatory and multi-species justice, and contributors highlight firstly the need for continuous participation and engagement of local people (Ampumuza, Bocci, Hsiao, Iordăchescu, Kiwango and Mabele, Mabele et al., Pettersson et al., Toncheva et al.). Participation must, however, be transformative as opposed to affirmative (Fraser 2009), focusing on challenging top-down structures of power and knowledge and instead building on local custodians' and stewards' skills. Diverse contributors equally emphasise the importance of addressing multi-species justice in convivial conservation, encouraging incorporation of nonhuman perspectives as well as engaging further with the ontological, epistemological and methodological implications of doing so (Ampumuza, van Bommel and Boonman-Berson, Hsiao, Pettersson et al., Toncheva et al.). In practice, this includes further engagement with threshold concepts linked to multi-species justice, such as valuing embodied knowing and other ways of knowing/communicating with nonhuman nature (Barrett et al. 2017).

In terms of distributive justice, contributors highlight a need for more elaboration on how to implement promoted areas in terms of rights, burdens and benefits (Mabele et al., Pandya). Although support for the idea of promoted areas is evident, it is clear that more consideration of the practicalities of the idea is needed. This would involve, among other things, micropolitical analysis of how costs and benefits are distributed across intersecting lines of gender, ethnicity, caste and social class. While contributors agree that alternative finance mechanisms such as a Conservation Basic Income could offer a much-needed alternative to neoliberal, market-based funding mechanisms, it is important for these mechanisms not to perpetuate excessive valuations of wildlife and injustices, reliance on external funding, and further commodification of wildlife (Ampumuza, Hsiao, Iordăchescu, Kiwango and Mabele). There is also broad concern with how to make alternative finance mechanisms for conservation viable outside of welfare states in the Global North.

We thus recommend that attempts to further advance alternative finance mechanisms as part of the convivial conservation approach are implemented in close consultation with partners in the Global South.

The convivial conservation proposals of shifting from touristic voyeurism to engaged visitation and historical reparations are also broadly supported by the contributors in this collection and the potential for both to facilitate transformative justice is highlighted. Challenges are, however, highlighted in relation to putting both of these ideas into practice in a way that is feasible and in a way that facilitates transformative justice. With respect to shifting from touristic voyeurism to engaged visitation, challenges link to a dependence in some Global South countries on foreign exchange earnings, vested interests prioritising tourists over farmer residents, and the power inherent in distributing economic opportunities through tourism (Bocci, Kiwango and Mabele, Pandya). Contributions in this volume also show that organically evolved wildlife tourism can in fact benefit local residents and conservation and so tourism should not be discounted completely in a convivial model of conservation (Iordăchescu, Toncheva et al.). Regarding historical reparations, it is clear that this must also be done in accordance with, and consideration of, local contexts and micro-politics and that it must not be assumed that its justice outcomes will match its intentions (Ramutsindela and Shabangu 2018).

One solid step that could be taken to facilitate transformative justice and address some of the potential epistemic participatory and distributive injustices highlighted in this collection is to engage meaningfully with alternative governance models grounded in local philosophies, such as *arraigo* (Bocci), *buen vivir* (Krauss) or *Ubuntu* (Mabele et al.). Much can be learnt from the myriad alternative ways of governing nature that do not rely on western scientific knowledge, that prioritise place-based and collaborative approaches, and that provide a basis for nonmarket, redistributive sources of locally controlled conservation funding (Kothari et al. 2019, Escobar 2018). Engagement with alternative philosophies will also support the reframing of Indigenous peoples and local communities as knowledge producers as opposed to just beneficiaries of conservation governance and funding schemes (Tauli-Corpuz 2010).

In relation to the idea of coexistence, contributors show that care must be taken to critically engage with terms and concepts that are at the heart of the convivial conservation proposition (Ampumuza, van Bommel and Boonman-Berson, Massarella and Fiasco, Hsiao, Iordăchescu, Pettersson et al.). Buzzwords such as coexistence often have their roots in transformative thinking but can lose their transformative potential easily (Chandhoke 2007) so there is a need for convivial conservation to better flesh out its interpretation of coexistence in theory and practice. This need links intimately with the previously-explained calls by contributors for bottom-up learning from existing practices of human-nonhuman coexistence. However, there is a distinct difference between contexts wherein human-wildlife practices have evolved organically without large-scale external intervention, and those where external intervention and political-economic processes disrupt local practices and knowledges. This reinforces our recommendation that convivial conservation proponents engage with some of the many different framings and practices of coexistence that can already be identified (de Silva and Srinivasan 2019, Dorresteijn et al. 2014, König et al. 2020, Hussain 2019) and situate this bottom-up learning within an understanding of wider relationships between humanity, capitalism and wildlife (Komi 2021). Two additional aspects of coexistence requiring further exploration in convivial conservation are how to move beyond an abiding focus on the 'human' in human-wildlife coexistence, and to explore the potentials for coexistence between humans given the social, political, economic and ecological factors encouraging both conviviality and conflict.

Diverse contributors emphasise the need for convivial conservation to further flesh out appropriate research methodologies (Ampumuza, Bocci, van Bommel and Boonman-Berson, Iordăchescu, Kiwango and Mabele, Pandya, Toncheva et al.). Building on justice and coexistence-related principles, this involves drawing respectfully on Indigenous and traditional values and ways of knowing. In terms of research methods, contributors support the use of ethnographic methods in pursuit of situated knowledge, including efforts to approach nonhumans in more equal term (Bastian et al. 2016). In line with discussions within this volume, we also recommend combining convivial conservation thinking with other diverse schools of thought (e.g., decolonial deconstruction, feminist political ecology, constitutionality, and science and technology studies). Pairing convivial conservation with such diverse approaches, including those that may at first not appear to present a wholly comfortable fit, can help enrich the discussion. Focusing on transformative methodologies also calls for integrated approaches that draw on natural and social-science approaches (Pooley, Bhatia, and Vasava 2021) and incorporate a range of local, Indigenous and non-western forms of knowledge (Zanotti et al. 2020).

In summary, the contributions to this collection show that the convivial conservation approach has the potential to radically transform existing approaches to biodiversity conservation, while also signalling some of the potential barriers that it will need to overcome to do so. It is important that convivial conservation stays open and continues to evolve in response to a plurality of ideas and perspectives. One of the common pitfalls of 'radical' proposals is the tendency to 'reinvent the wheel' when there are already myriad ideas, practices and initiatives grounded in the knowledge and experiences of different peoples, natures and spaces (Büscher and Fletcher 2020). By learning from such experiences of biocultural conviviality, and drawing on insights offered in this special section, convivial conservation may well have the potential to contribute to a just and (axially) transformative approach to biodiversity conservation in the Anthropocene. Learning across the dimensions of justice, coexistence and methodologies outlined in this overview will be vital in this process and we hope that diverse researchers, practitioners, and activists will continue to critically engage with convivial conservation going forward.

Chapter 2:

Towards Convivial Conservation*

By Bram Büscher and Robert Fletcher

Introduction

These days it is difficult to keep track of all the devastating conservation news that appears. Despite some holding to 'conservation optimism'[1], most of the scientific news about species, ecosystems and the climate is far from positive. The Living Planet Report 2018 states that 60% of all wild animals have disappeared since 1970 (WWF 2018) while other recent studies show that extinction rates are accelerating and that global biodiversity thresholds may soon surpass 'planetary boundaries' beyond which even more dramatic decline is inevitable (Meyer 2006; CBD 2010; Newbold et al. 2016; Watson et al. 2016; Tucker et al. 2018; IPBES 2019). At the same time, the myriad impacts of anthropogenic climate change continue to worsen, threatening to exceed this 'planetary boundary' as well (IPCC 2018). Witnessing this reality, some go so far as to pronounce it a sign of impending 'biological annihilation' (Ceballos et al. 2017).

All of this is tied up in growing assertions that we have now entered the 'Anthropocene', the alleged new phase of world history in which humans dominate the earth-system (Ogden et al. 2013). The Anthropocene idea is meant to indicate that we are living through socio-ecological transformations so fundamental that they – quite literally – change the very geological structure of our planet. It is not surprising, therefore, that this has led to heated debates in a conservation community already frustrated by the failure to halt spiralling biodiversity and extinction crises. These debates

* Originally published as: Büscher, B., and R. Fletcher. (2019). Towards convivial conservation. Conservation & Society 17(3): 283-296.

have inspired the rise of new radical proposals for revolutionising conservation, including 'new' conservation, 'half Earth' and others. These, in turn, have triggered major potential for (contemplating) radical change in conservation policy and practice.

In this essay we build on this potential and experimentation to outline a vision, a politics and a set of governance principles for the future of conservation, which we propose under the banner of 'convivial conservation'. Inspired by political ecology and real-world examples of saving nature differently, convivial conservation encourages transformative seeds to grow into a realistic and positive foundation for reconciling global conservation and development imperatives.[2] It proposes an explicitly political approach to conservation as one stream within a broader river of movements, struggles and ideas that seek to transcend the unsustainable status quo.

In the following, we spend little time developing an analysis of the Anthropocene conservation debates, broader movements and ideas that inform these. We do so already in a companion book (Büscher and Fletcher 2020). Instead, we focus on outlining the vision we offer in the book as well as some of the political and governance proposals that seek to operationalise this vision. The chapter is intended as an abridged and accessible companion to the book, while taking it further by presenting a sharper political intervention. It therefore lacks empirical foundation while schematising positions, debates and influences developed in detail in the book.

We begin by highlighting a new pressing issue that the Anthropocene conservation debates have yet to engage: the rise of authoritarian right-wing governments that have set their sights on conservationists and the environmental protection they advocate. We then briefly rehearse the Anthropocene debate and why this presents radical potential to confront this mounting threat. The remainder of the chapter builds on this to outline the elements of our convivial conservation proposal, concluding by reemphasising the need for a different conservation politics.

A New Moment in Conservation

While the myriad threats to biodiversity described above are bad news for conservation, we believe that this is not what we should be most worried about right now. Over the last years, we have seen increasingly authoritarian leaders like Trump, Duterte and Bolsonaro elected (and then deposed), driven by expanding right-wing, even (proto-)fascist agendas and networks. These developments are far more dangerous and worrying. Not because of the individuals themselves, but because of what they represent: a political economy increasingly becoming more intense, pressurised and erratic. We have referred to this earlier as the 'Trump moment'[3] in conservation, although after the 2018 Brazil elections we could add the 'Bolsonaro moment' as well. What this means is that Trump and Bolsonaro are not unfortunate 'accidents': they are an expression and outcome of the state of our political economy. They show that radical change is happening but that this is driven by a politics steeped in misogyny, violent anti-environmentalism, racism and market-fundamentalism that could reinforce institutional mechanisms and power (im)balances in favour of the status quo for many years to come.

So, what do mainstream conservation organisations call for to resist these increasingly extreme agendas? To resist the populist campaigns that supported Bolsonaro taking over the most biodiverse country on the planet and his brazen assertions to destroy the already troubled environmental, Indigenous and social movements within the country, along with the science that supports these (Magnusson et al. 2018)? The WWF flagship Living Planet report, released two days after Bolsonaro was elected, calls for a 'new global deal for nature and people' and urges 'decision-makers at every level' to 'make the right political, financial and consumer choices to achieve the vision that humanity and nature thrive in harmony on our only planet'. To operationalise this 'ambitious pathway', WWF, together with other organisations, will launch a new research initiative based around 'systems modelling' to help 'us determine the best integrated and collective solutions and to help understand the "trade-offs" we may need to accept to find the best path ahead' (WWF 2018: 8).

Other mainstream organisations advance similar strategies. Mark Tercek, CEO of the Nature Conservancy, reflecting on the 2016 US presidential elections and Brexit, admits that 'stronger political headwinds' are to be expected. Yet he still believes that 'we really can have it all—a future where people get the food, energy and economic growth they need without sacrificing nature'.[4] This is neoliberal consensus politics, driven often by moderate and centric political interests allied around the belief that contemporary capitalism can both be managed and rendered more sustainable and equitable (Fletcher 2014a). This politics is not new; it is deeply entrenched in conservation and sustainability communities more generally (Büscher 2013), although, as we will show, cracks have started to appear.

While we fully understand that conservation organisations wish to operate carefully politically, this supposedly 'middle-of-the-road' consensus rhetoric will not work against the forces now gathering and the extreme capitalist interests they represent and serve. Further models to develop more 'integrated and collective solutions' will not succeed where most proposed previously have failed. A 'new deal' wherein a generic 'us' or 'collective' can come together to understand 'trade-offs' sounds naïve at best in the current climate. The new authoritarian leaders and many other global elites (such as the Koch brothers) are clearly hell-bent to promote an agenda that is precisely the opposite. The mainstream response, therefore, and no matter how well-intentioned, increasingly appears as a technocratic politics of resignation. One that may consider itself pragmatic, practice-based and realistic, but that is out of touch with the political realities in which we live. We need another conservation vision and movement, one that takes seriously – and so positively confronts - the structural, violent and uneven socio-ecological pressures of our current economic system.

Conservation in the Anthropocene

In the last decade, triggered by the implications of the Anthropocene, a number of radical alternate approaches have emerged seeking to transform conservation policy and practice. The two most prominent are 'new' or 'Anthropocene' conservation and the neoprotectionist 'half earth' movement. These have caused quite a rift among conservationists and precipitated some of the bigger cracks in the neoliberal consensus noted earlier. According to new conservationists, the Anthropocene places an unprecedented burden on humans. Homo sapiens are seen to have changed global ecosystem functioning such that they now have to cultivate and manage the earth as one immense 'rambunctious garden' (Marris 2011). But this is not necessarily negative. Instead of mourning biodiversity loss due to anthropocenic change, new conservationists believe we should acknowledge and promote the new and potentially exciting possibilities that current global changes may bring (Pearce 2015; Thomas 2017; Schilthuizen 2018). Hence, what makes new conservation radical is that it aims to end conservation's long-standing infatuation with wilderness and ideas about 'pristine' nature as well as the conviction that these can be conserved as untouched protected spaces, away from humans. Nature and ecosystems always change, new conservationists argue. So why not embrace the 'new natures' that are currently evolving and use them to support human development?

Following its opening salvos in 2011 and 2012, new conservation provoked strong responses. Amongst these was a resurgence of 'neoprotectionism': a longstanding movement calling for a return to protected area expansion and enforcement. Unlike new conservationists, neoprotectionists do not believe that human-induced change is something (potentially) positive. To the contrary: they fear it will be the earth's undoing, precipitating the downfall of Homo sapiens and innumerable other species in the process (Wilson 2016). In the face of new conservation's bold acceptance of global human-centred conservation management, therefore, neoprotectionists have also upped their game. Instead of putting humans in charge, they want to put nature back in charge. Many even argue that at least half the entire planet – or even 60% (Mogg et al. 2019) – must be set-aside in a system of protected areas reserved for 'self-willed' nature. Only in this way, they assert, can an impending global ecological catastrophe be averted (Wuerthner et al. 2015). Instead of the radical mixing of people and nonhuman nature that new conservationists endorse, many resurgent neoprotectionists call for a separation between people and nature on an unprecedented global scale.

These two radical proposals present far-reaching challenges to what Brockington et al. (2008) term 'mainstream conservation'. This label encompasses a broad amalgam of different organisations, approaches and ideas. Yet, based on our long-standing research and a large literature, two key characteristics can be highlighted and generalised across this constellation for heuristic purposes. First, mainstream conservation remains grounded in efforts to dichotomise people and nature via promotion of protected areas, in conjunction with broader participatory, stakeholder-focused approaches, including community-based conservation models (Borgerhoff Mulder and Copollilo 2005; Corson et al. 2014). Second, mainstream conservation works within rather than beyond capitalism (Brockington and Duffy 2010; Cavanagh and Benjaminsen 2017). This has been true for a long time but has intensified during the neoliberal era (Igoe et al. 2010). The idea is that conserved nature can be turned into in situ 'natural capital' so that the creativity of the pursuit of profit can be linked to the protection of nature and the 'environmental services' it provides (Büscher et al. 2014). And although many conservationists may not see this trend as such, and may emphasise it is meant to appeal to rather than be like business, the effects in practice are the same: a deepening of the links between capitalism and conservation (Fletcher et al. 2019).

Clearly, whatever the Anthropocene means, there is widespread agreement that our current reality of global, human-induced ecosystemic and climatic change presents stark challenges for conservation. It is concern for this dynamic that has led to the radical proposals now on the table. For heuristic purposes, we present the different approaches along two main axes: from capitalist to post-capitalist positions on one axis; and from positions steeped in nature-people dichotomies to those that aim to go beyond these on the other. We realise that this typology is highly simplistic, starkly separating what is in reality a fluid spectrum of different approaches. But we find it useful to present things in this manner in order to clarify key issues of contention among different positions. Within this heuristic, then, we designate four main positions along these two axes: mainstream conservation, new conservation, neoprotectionism and, finally, what we call 'convivial conservation'. The resulting schematic is depicted in Table 1.

	Nature/culture dichotomies	Beyond N/C dichotomies
Capitalist	Mainstream conservation	New conservation
Beyond-capitalist	Neoprotectionism	Convivial conservation

Table 1. Four main positions on saving nature in the Anthropocene

Mainstream conservation, as we have argued, does not challenge the hegemonic, global capitalist order and is firmly embedded in myriad 'dualisms' wherein humans, and their society or culture, are seen as (epistemologically and ontologically) distinct from 'nature'. As mentioned, it is this latter element that new conservation targets and what makes it radical. *New conservation* portrays nature as an integrated element within a socio-natural 'rambunctious garden' to be managed by people. This management, in turn, can (and for some should) be ardently capitalist (Kareiva et al. 2012). Many key new conservationists are, for example, staunch supporters of 'natural capital' solutions to the environmental crisis (Kareiva et al. 2011; 2012). *Neoprotectionists* reject both of these elements. They are deeply and often deliberately committed to nature-people dichotomies, believing that separating people and nature is necessary to stave off a collapse of life-supporting ecosystems. At the same time, they have become increasingly critical of economic growth and consumerism (Wuerthner et al. 2014; Cafaro et al. 2017). In certain ways, with important exceptions, many neoprotectionists are thus rather critical of contemporary capitalism, either explicitly or implicitly.[5]

Our book (Büscher and Fletcher 2020) offers a detailed and nuanced discussion of the important differences among and within these various proposals, something we cannot do justice to in this paper. What we want to highlight here is that these two radical conservation approaches show that a conservation revolution might be brewing. Yet they cannot by themselves inspire a revolution, as neither truly addresses the integrated socio-ecological roots of the biodiversity crisis, nor do their politics adequately confront the reactionary political developments noted earlier. Having said this, however, it is crucial not to throw the baby out with the bathwater. There are important positive aspects in both radical proposals that should be nurtured and brought together into a more coherent alternative. While we reject new conservationists' contradictory support for capitalist conservation, we want to retain some of the imaginative energy they bring in striving to move beyond problematic dichotomies and to centralise the need to integrate nature and people by directly addressing inequality and poverty. At the same time, we largely agree with neoprotectionists' critiques of the capitalist growth/consumerist economy, but find this outweighed by their worrying proposals to separate people and nature, especially the nature-needs-half proposal, which would have massive negative social consequences if implemented (Büscher et al. 2017).

We therefore see these two positions as pointing towards the more fundamental transformation that is needed to allow conservation to effectively confront the mounting pressures of the Anthropocene. This is where *convivial conservation* enters. The crucial difference between mainstream conservation, the two radical alternatives now on the table, and our own convivial conservation proposal is that we explicitly start from a political ecology perspective steeped in a critique of capitalist political economy (Bryant 2015; Fletcher et al. 2015). This critique is built on a rejection of *both* nature-people dichotomies *and* a capitalist economic system demanding continual growth via intensified consumerism. This makes it the most radical of the four proposals. But also, the most coherent and realistic one. To put it simply: without directly addressing capitalism *and* its many engrained dichotomies and contradictions, we cannot tackle the conservation challenges before us or do so realistically within the current political climate. Convivial conservation is built on a politics of equity, structural change and environmental justice. It directly targets the extreme capitalist interests of the global elites, positively engages with but transcends technocratic beliefs of pragmatists and enthusiastically builds on the current upswell in many parts of global society that demand structural change.

Elements of a Vision

In the 1970s, Ivan Illich (1973) saw his revolutionary project as one of 'convivial reconstruction'; the transformation of society to focus on a frugal good life. The convivial reconstruction of conservation depends on and aids this broader project currently (and historically) pushed and supported by many post-colonial, Indigenous, emancipatory, youth, progressive and other movements, organisations and individuals around the world (Berberoglu 2018; Albó 2019). For this we need to allow ourselves to envision several major, positive transformations that might characterise postcapitalist convivial conservation. We propose five key elements of a convivial conservation vision.

From Protected to Promoted Areas

The default mode of conservation has commonly emphasised protecting nature from people, particularly through protected areas. Elaborate systems have been set up to govern who has access to (parts of) protected areas and how these (parts) ought to be used (see the IUCN classification system). This puts the focus on marking and emphasising the boundaries between human and nonhuman nature rather than celebrating the many inherent links between them (Sandbrook 2015; Fletcher 2017). Under convivial conservation, this would be reversed. The main goal of special conservation areas should not be to protect nature from humans but to promote nature for, to and by humans.[6] They should transition from protected to 'promoted areas', although not in capitalist terms (of marketing them as the basis of capital accumulation and hence exploitation via (eco)tourism or natural capital; see below). Rather, promoted areas are conceptualised as fundamentally encouraging places where people are considered welcome visitors, dwellers or travellers rather than temporary alien invaders upon a nonhuman landscape. This can only take place within an overall context focused not on exploitation or productivity but on conviviality: the building of long-lasting, engaging and open-ended relationships with nonhumans and ecologies.

This proposition includes an important discursive shift. 'Protected from' sounds negative[7], while promoted by and for is positive, and—significantly—democratic. As Purdy (2015) states, truly democratic politics are necessary when dealing with protected areas in the future. Some positive steps in this regard have been made, all around the world, including by the Indigenous and Community Conservation Areas (ICCA) coalition, the Forest Peoples Programme, and others.[8] But more is needed, especially given that some hard-won democratic experiments have recently been turned back in the fight against poaching and the broader militarisation of protected areas (Lunstrum 2014; Büscher and Ramutsindela 2016; Duffy et al. 2019). Important in this move is to continue to emphasise, with many neoprotectionists and (new) conservationists, all that is valuable in and about current protected areas (Dudley et al. 2018). This cannot be lost as the discussion progresses (Locke 2013); hence 'promotion' never means that every action is possible or desirable. The value of biodiversity requires promotion, too, especially vis-à-vis values linked to (unnecessary or excessive) extractive and destructive enterprise. But unlike neoprotectionists, we do not think this value will survive by positioning it against humanity and 'population growth', as it frequently is.[9] The deep value of nature, including its intrinsic or 'existence' value, only makes sense through and by its appreciation by humans. Hence, the only solution to protecting nature's value is to build an integrated (economic, social, political, ecological, cultural) value system that does not depend on (systemic) destruction of but on 'living with' nonhuman nature (Turnhout et al. 2013).

From Saving Nature to Celebrating Human and Nonhuman Nature

The next element follows logically: we must move away from the idea that conservation is about 'saving' only nonhuman nature. The main actors that humans save nonhuman natures from are other humans.[10] Yet since humans are part of a larger whole that contains nonhumans as well, we get into tricky territory when speaking about 'saving' nature from humans, reinforcing the very nature-society dichotomy we seek to dismantle. In fact, we have long suspected that something must be fundamentally wrong if we have to put boundaries between ourselves and nonhuman nature; this means, essentially, that we have to protect ourselves from ourselves. This contradiction can only be overcome by challenging the idea that conservation is ultimately and only about saving nonhuman nature.

We need to start instead by focusing on saving and celebrating both human and nonhuman nature equally. This may sound strange, even wrong, to many conservationists and political ecologists alike. Indeed, within the social sciences, there are strong 'turns' towards decentring the human and instead to put human and 'more-than-human' on an equal footing (e.g., Haraway 2008; Braidotti 2013). While we agree we need to take the 'more-than-human' much more seriously, this does not necessitate that human and 'more-than-human' must be given wholly equal standing. Following David Harvey (2000: 223), we need a 'broad agreement on how we are both individually and collectively going to construct and exercise our responsibilities to nature in general and towards our own human nature in particular'. Harvey, drawing on White, refers to this as 'learning to be distinctively ourselves in a world of others'.

Opening up the question of 'human nature' may be somewhat ambitious. But it is necessary, even if only briefly. As Sahlins (2008: 112) argued, the idea of human nature as competitive, self-interested and rational—the stereotypical 'homo economicus' underlying neoliberal forms of governance—is false (and now also challenged by '21st century economists'; Raworth 2017: 94). This reductionist idea of human nature has been responsible for creating needs, desires and actions that 'endanger our existence' and are certainly not convivial. Opening up the question of human nature, therefore, means asserting that there are 'various ways in which we can "be ourselves"' (Harvey 2000: 223); that we can construct needs, wants and actions differently, in line with sustainable conviviality. It also means, fundamentally, challenging the 'dangerous' processes of capitalist alienation that Harvey (2014) argues change and go against human nature. The point here is not that there is an essential human nature of any particular bent; rather, how subjectivity is expressed depends fundamentally on the social, political, economic and historical contexts that shape it. This means that if we want people to behave differently, towards each other and the rest of the world, we need to focus on changing these overarching contexts as well.

The fact that these points refer specifically to human nature does not mean they exclude nonhumans. A certain form of human exceptionalism can be(come) completely convivial. While a 'posthuman' perspective seeks to challenge human exceptionalism, an alternative perspective would assert that humans are in fact exceptional and unique; but that every other species and organism are, in their own way, special and unique as well. Decentring the human may therefore be best accomplished not by homogenising and levelling all forms of life but on the contrary by insisting on the unique nature possessed by each of these myriad forms. Convivial conservation allows for the celebration of this diversity while its 'saving' occurs in the context of recognising how differential needs, desires and actions of humans and nonhumans are always yet unevenly related to broader political economic trends and dynamics.

From Touristic Voyeurism to Engaged Visitation

As the way we promote and save nonhuman and human nature changes under convivial conservation, so must also the way we engage, see and experience nonhuman nature. At present, many of us primarily engage 'wild' nature, and especially parks, through commodified tourism experiences. But as copious research now demonstrates, tourism, as one of the largest capitalist industries in the world, is not usually the great saviour of nature it is often made out to be. On the contrary, it is both indirectly and often even directly responsible for the destruction of nature (e.g. Duffy 2002; Higgins-Desbiolles 2009; Fletcher 2011; Büscher and Fletcher 2017). But capitalist tourism is about more than just the destruction or conservation of nature. It is also a particular way of seeing and understanding nature, one that can be shorthanded as a type of voyeurism: peeking 'at' nature through commodified tours, spaces, sites and other experiences; often more aimed at ticking boxes (been there, done that, seen the 'big five', the Niagara falls, or what else) than at creating meaningful long-term engagement.

This is not to say that the latter does not exist. But one problem with a focus on 'conservation-funded-through-tourism' is that meaningful long-term engagement with nature seems to increasingly become an elite privilege rather than a democratic possibility. Visiting and/or owning 'pristine' nature is very often (and has long been) an elite activity, imbued with problematic racial, gender and class divisions (see Holmes 2012; Fletcher 2014b; Büscher 2016a). And even if capitalist tourism enables or leads to long-term deep engagement with species or ecosystems, this is too often used as escape from, not confrontation with or developing alternatives to the destructive dynamics of global capitalism (Bunn 2003).

Under convivial conservation, the emphasis will be on long-term *democratic* engagement rather than on short-term voyeuristic tourism or elite access and privilege. The details of this engagement are beyond this paper, but are inspired by the principles outlined by Shrivastava and Kothari (2012: chapters 9 and 10) and Cato (2013) based inter alia on bioregional economic development, sharing of state functions with civil society, new indicators of well-being, degrowth and a devolution of powers. Does that mean that short-term tours or trips will become impossible? We do not know. But it has become patently clear that we cannot afford to continue flying around the world in climate-changing airplanes in order to save nature through (eco)tourism. The alternative is to encourage long-term visitation focused on social and ecological justice (Higgins-Desbiolles 2009), preferably in relation to the natures close(r) to where we live.

From Spectacular to Everyday Environmentalisms

Capitalist conservation interactions with nature, including but not limited to tourism, are focused on what Igoe (2010; 2017) calls the spectacle of nature. Inspired by Guy Debord, the 'spectacle of nature' means that 'images become commodities alienated from the relationships that produced them and consumed in ignorance of the same' (Igoe 2010: 375). Conservation, in other words, is increasingly communicated and consumed through images of the very idealised, spectacular natures that are increasingly disappearing in reality.[11] These types of communication are often (necessarily) superficial, anti-political and devoid of context and despite many promises to the contrary, new media in practice often reinforce this dynamic (Büscher 2016b; Fletcher 2017). Under convivial conservation we must move away from the spectacle of nature and instead focus on 'everyday nature', in all its splendour and mundanity (Cronon 1996). Indeed, we argue that it is in mundanity rather than spectacle that we find the most meaningful engagement with the natures around us (Loftus 2012).

From Privatised Expert Technocracy to Common Democratic Engagement

The fifth element of our vision upholds that *all* people have to be able to (potentially) live with all nature. Hence, the way 'wild' nature is commonly managed, namely in a top-down fashion based on technocratic expert-opinions, is inherently alienating for most of us (which comes through in its most extreme form in Wilson's (2016: 192) vision of allowing most humans to only peer at the 'other' side of earth – nature's half – through micro-cameras). This, again, implies need for a much more democratic management of nature, focused on nature-as-commons and nature-in-context instead of nature-as-capital. This point is important for conservation generally, but perhaps especially in relation to the extinction crisis. As Heatherington (2012), Sodikoff (2012), Dawson (2016) and others argue, technoscience may save some species from extinction, but will not save them as part of a broader amalgam of 'living landscapes' that do long-term socio-ecological justice to humans and non-humans. 'Saving' species, they all emphasise, is meaningful only within broader social, cultural and environmental contexts.

A key issue here concerns the operationalisation of 'value'. Convivial conservation grounded in radical ecological democracy (Kothari 2014) would require that the value of natural 'resources' be determined locally rather than in abstract global (and increasingly algorithm-based, computerised) markets. This value would then need to be realised in ways that do not promote resources' commodification but rather provide autonomous funding streams that allow qualitative, multidimensional values to be preserved and promoted. Capitalism cannot mediate interests and values in a transition towards a more sustainable society (Massumi 2018). This is, fundamentally, because it prioritises one type of value above all others: 'value in motion', that is, 'capital'. By contrast, convivial conservation cannot and will not prioritise capital in making decisions about resource allocations, how to manage promoted areas, how to celebrate nature or how to organise engaged visitation.

So instead of asking how conservation can lead to more (necessarily monetised) 'value' in the future, we should start by asking how a (necessarily non-monetised) value is embedded in the here and now and in which contexts this value receives local and extra-local meaning. In short, we need to refocus from value in motion, or capital, to what we could call 'embedded value'. The latter's logic is not dependent on market-based commodity exchange whereby nature-to-be-protected has to provide 'services' to humans, but receives its worth from and through humans and nonhumans 'living with', understanding and appreciating each other (through cultural, artistic, experiential, affective or other non-commodified or –monetised forms). This requires, quite simply, that all conservation decisions are made not in terms of their contribution to capital and economic growth but in terms of value embedded in daily life and non-capitalist needs, wants and actions (Shrivastava and Kothari 2012).

ICCAs are a good example here. As Borrini-Feyerabend and Campese (2017: 13) explain, 'ICCAs embody many material and non-material values. Specific relationships and values should be identified by their custodian communities, not by outsiders', and may include: 'secured livelihood', ' social resilience', 'cultural identity', 'spiritual significance', 'pride and community spirit', 'sovereignty', 'links to community history', and; continuance' for the host community as the 'custodians of bio-cultural diversity' (idem). This, of course, is not to say that all is good and well with all ICCAs – as Borrini-Feyerabend and Campese (2017: 14) emphasise. But the challenges and political nature of ICCAs are recognised by the consortium, and this, together with their convivial vision, is crucial for moving conservation forward (Dudley et al. 2018).

From Natural Capital to Embedded Value(S)

These five elements of a convivial conservation vision enable what would still be a form of *conservation* but one very different from current practice, namely a use of parts of nature that is sustainable (i.e. not geared towards eternal quantitative growth and accumulation), whilst being part and parcel *of* nature. It would entail *living with* other aspects of nature in ways that balances human and nonhuman needs. Indeed, conservation itself would be integrated and (re)embedded within daily life and all other domains of policy and action rather than something we do mostly in protected areas or when donating to an NGO. Moreover, convivial conservation moves away from capital-inspired ways of 'rendering visible' the value of nature, and instead becomes a part of broader structures of democratically sharing the multidimensional wealth that nature embodies. As has been emphasised by non-Western, Indigenous and other communities and scholars for centuries already, the wealth of nature does not lie in how it enables the accumulation and privatisation of capital; it lies in the manifold ways in which it allows humans and nonhumans to live convivial lives (e.g. Berkes 2008; Singh 2015; Albó 2019). Sharing this wealth must therefore always trump its privatisation and subsequent accumulation.

How to do this will always be political, subject to interests, needs, histories and power dynamics. It will not lead to equilibrium, harmony and or perfect sharing, including in a postcapitalist world. But it will necessitate *better* sharing, certainly if human natures are growing accustomed to different systems of needs, wants and actions. In the process, we need to start 'seeing' nature differently. Nature, under conviviality, is always already visible. To 'render nature's values visible', as the capitalist TEEB (The Economics of Ecosystems and Biodiversity) project aims to do (MacDonald and Corson 2012), would thus be unthinkable. The importance of nature - the web of life, the basis of all life - should never have to be 'made' visible. Living with nature means that it is 'visible' by definition. 'Money' – the universal equivalent that is supposedly the tool to make nature 'visible' under capitalism – only renders nature visible on spreadsheets and through necessarily simplistic, technocratic decision-making models outside of relevant contexts (Sullivan 2018). This renders nature unidimensional – solely what it is worth 'to' humans-as-investors. It does not—cannot—facilitate the kind of lived relationship to *multidimensional* (human *and* nonhuman) natures that convivial conservation envisions.

But 'visible' is not the right word for conviviality, as we are focused here on the levels of *being* and *becoming* and their dialectical relationship. As humans are, so nature is – and vice versa. As humans become, so nature becomes – and vice versa. Living with nature, in many ways, is acute: it directly (ful)fills the senses – positively and negatively – and as such enables a continuous, direct and emergent feedback loop (we might call this metabolism!) 'between' humans and the rest of nature. Convivial conservation is therefore about different *uses, frames* and forms of *embeddedness* of multiple natures. It is about *not* setting nature apart but integrating the uses of (non-human) natures into social, cultural, and ecological contexts and systems (i.e., re-embedding). In each of the five elements of the vision, important practical steps can immediately be taken to bring convivial conservation into being. But before we get there, let us reflect on the process of transition itself.

From Here to There

So how do we get to convivial conservation? What, in other words, is our theory of change? We highlight three important elements: power, time and actors.

Dealing with Power

A central problematic for us concerns how to build resistance to the power of capitalism and its 'commodification of everything'. In much literature this issue seems to boil down to the question of whether effective action is about micro-politics or about 'taking (macro) power'. We argue that power is *both* structural and dispersed in micro-settings. Hence, we are not disputing that power is 'complex, scattered and productive' (Braidotti 2013: 26–27), but to leave it at that, which many poststructuralists do, is a fundamental mistake that plays in the hands of structural capitalist power itself. Zizek rightfully notes that a focus on an 'irreducible plurality of struggles' runs the risk of renouncing 'any real attempt to overcome the existing capitalist liberal regime' (Butler et al. 2000: 95).

In our writing, we have consistently argued for a co-constitutive understanding of structural power and the power of agency (see Fletcher and Büscher 2017; 2018). Hence dispersed forms of resistance matter, but these alone will not achieve our aims. The point is that these must be accompanied by more organised efforts to effect large-scale structural change so as not to be undermined by these same forces. Given the imperative to organise power across different levels of governance, this 'organised effort' must work through centralised structures, though not the contemporary capitalist state (Parenti 2013), and with power shared with and among civil society actors as well.[12]

Dealing With Time: A Two-Step Strategy of Change

Any act of change must—whatever else it is—be a political struggle and a strategy to deal with institutionalised forms of accumulated power across both material and discursive domains. Peck (2010) shows that this was actually a core component of neoliberals' own theory of change. As Milton Friedman famously proclaimed,

> Only a crisis – actual or perceived – produces real change. When that crisis occurs, the actions that are taken depend on the ideas that are lying around. That, I believe, is our basic function: to develop alternatives to existing policies, to keep them alive and available until the politically impossible becomes the politically inevitable. (2002: xiv)

The remarkable prescience of this statement implies that change requires both promotion of a coherent conceptual structure vis-à-vis the status quo and transformation in the underlying material structures able to create a new opening for this promotion.

This is no different in conservation. Despite neoprotectionists' occasional implicit assertions to the contrary, conservation is not somehow separate from the broader capitalist order but is an inherent part of it. This is why we believe a two-step strategy for dealing with change over time is most realistic, one that moves from (radical) reformism to systemic change away from capitalist modes of production, valuation, exchange and living. Hence, we are talking about a short(er) term and a medium to long(er) term strategy enacted at the *same time*. One part of the strategy must always be accompanied by the other, as each needs to lead to, and be inspired by, the other.

In the short term, we must do what we can to subvert the logic of capital in micro, mesa, and macro-political practice, through state, non-state and individual action simultaneously. In this we take inspiration from the community economies perspective pioneered by Gibson-Graham (2006), which points to the ways that postcapitalist practice can be effected in myriad forms within the overarching capitalist order.[13] In the medium to longer term, immediate actions must be accompanied by larger-scale efforts to conceptualise and build 'alternative economic spaces', based not on logics of capital and growth but of equality, radical ecological democracy and bioregional economics (Shrivastava and Kothari 2012; Cato 2013). Likewise, for conservation, the short-term actions described below always need to be inspired by and work towards the convivial conservation vision outlined above.

The actual outcomes of these interlinked strategies of change (for nature and conservation) depend on complex, contrived and contradictory processes that no one can foresee. Hence, this will require political expediency, shrewdness, organisation and persistence. But we do believe that this two-part strategy is the most realistic to start building an appropriate context for a productive future for global conservation.

Dealing with Actors

Within structures of power across space and time, different actors take different positions. These cannot be homogenised or generalised easily. And yet, it is important that we still do so for heuristic purposes. Following our conviction that conservation is but one element within a broader process of 'uneven geographical development', we need to acknowledge the variegated political positions of different actors within a fundamentally 'uneven' conservation landscape. This will allow us to *politically* account for the relation between local actors who live in/near conservation spaces or spaces of conservation interest, and the actors who in terms of their position in the global capitalist system live far from these, but put much pressure on them – and biodiversity *in toto*. After all, a major contradiction of conservation has long been that the focus of interventions is on local actors ('community based') because they have a *direct* link to certain species or ecosystems (Wells and McShane 2004). Conservation interventions focus much less often on extra-local actors responsible for adding to the general pressure on biodiversity. This demands redress.

To start doing so, distinguishing four different categories of global conservation actors is a useful starting point (see Figure 1)[14]. Actors within these four categories have differential (historical and contemporary) responsibilities and roles within and for conservation. Local residents who often live in or with biodiversity and who (still) depend on the land for subsistence, especially in tropical countries, comprise category 4: the lower rural classes. They are often (seen as) poor and have least contributed to global problems of biodiversity loss (historically and contemporarily). Yet they are most often targeted in conservation interventions and forced or 'incentivised' to change their livelihoods to meet biodiversity targets. Category 3 consists of the urban, semi-urban or semi-rural middle and lower classes throughout world, who do not depend directly on the land for subsistence and are mostly involved in global or local labour and consumer markets that they participate in but have little control over save for their consumption choices. Via this consumption they do heavily influence biodiversity in many places, but are often not part of or specifically targeted by conservation interventions, except as potential donors or the general 'public' for (political) legitimacy.

Next, we distinguish land-owning capitalist classes such as major capitalist farmers and/or landholders for agro-industry. They are often targeted by conservation, for example as partners in conservation efforts or as targets of (so-called) activist interventions or forms of resistance. In many places (e.g. Indonesia, Brazil, Central Africa) these classes are also part of violent frontiers of land conversion, and hence difficult to target and engage. Lastly, there are the global upper classes that are, politically, economically or otherwise, at the helm of the global capitalist system. Interestingly, these elites are often both urban and rural – owning multiple properties, including in rich residential areas in cities to be close to elite political-economic circles, but also with second, third or more properties in rural, semi-rural and biodiversity rich spaces, including large estates and private reserves (Holmes 2012).

Upper class elites are often recruited as funders or included on boards of conservation organisations, but rarely targeted as part of conservation initiatives aiming at behavioural or livelihood change, as they are often either seen as unreachable (they live behind walls, security systems, or simply remotely, etc) or as doing good for the environment through their philanthrocapitalism or other forms of conservation related charity (including through the privatisation of nature/parks, etc). Hence the upper classes play a strange double role as they are at the helm of the system that keeps the pressure on biodiversity intense and high, while considered either untouchable or even seen as championing conservation through their large donations to conservation causes, NGOs and more.

1. Upper classes	• Political, economic other elites, inherited wealth • At the helm of the global capitalist system • Multiple properties; including in wealthy urban neighbourhoods and (biodiverse) estates or areas
2. Land-owning capitalist classes	• Commercial farmers, large plantation or otherwise productive land owners • Responsible for/implicated in much land-use change, soil depletion, biodiversity loss, etc.
3. Middle and lower classes	• Urban, peri-urban, peri-rural working classes • Non-subsistence: dependent on wage labor, market-based commodity consumption
4. Lower rural classes	• Rural/forest communities, residents, dwellers • Partially or wholly dependent on subsistence activities • At the bottom of global capitalist system

Figure 1. Generic categorisation of classes important for conservation.

While empirical reality is much more complex than this figure can depict, its point is that convivial conservation should not aim only or even mostly at category 4 actors, as it tends to do at present. Rather, it should target actors according to their differential responsibilities and accountabilities in relation to both the direct and indirect impacts their actions have on biodiversity, as well as the relative power these actors possess within broader structures of capitalist accumulation. Paraphrasing Jason Moore (2016: 94), it is about identifying, targeting and 'shutting down the relations' that produce biodiversity loss.

In this way, we might reverse the model of 'polycentric' governance proposed by Ostrom and Cox (2010). In this standard model, governance is seen to start with local people and then must consider their embeddedness within overarching structures of governance with which they must contend to assert their space for self-governance. In our vision, by contrast, effective conservation governance would start by addressing actors in these superordinate levels in order to first target their actions, then work down towards the local people in direct contact with the biodiversity in question. In this way, the pressures exerted on local conservation initiatives can be proactively addressed at their source rather than merely retrospectively in relation to their impacts.

We should clarify that this governance model pertains only to how conservationists frame and confront threats to conservation, not to how decision-making regarding effective conservation should proceed. As previously stated, this latter must embody deeply democratic forms of engagement in which local actors are placed at centre stage. A comprehensive conservation politics, therefore, must simultaneously centre local people as key decision-makers in conservation planning and decentre them as the central targets of interventions aimed at behavioural change. This, we believe, is the only way to do democracy justice: to place the possibility for democratic arrangements in larger structures of power that strongly influence whether and how these succeed (or not) in practice. Phrased differently: merely focusing on local democracy without taking into account the power of 'outside' actors is naïve. The difficult tension between centring and decentring local people is therefore the right place to situate the politics of convivial conservation.

From The Long Term to the Short Term: Concrete Actions

Convivial conservation calls for consideration of new ways to transform mainstream forms of economic development as neoprotectionists contend, while at the same time transcending human-nature divides as promoted by new conservationists. What types of concrete, short-term actions befit this approach and might enable us to move closer to the broader vision outlined earlier? We propose several, along different registers and foci. These derive logically from the foregoing discussion but are anything but exhaustive (and indeed not intended to be).

Historic Reparations

Convivial conservation needs to start by doing justice to conservation's history, especially (neo)colonial and other dynamics of dispossession and displacement that long characterised protected area formation and are still ongoing today in many places. *Historic reparations*—mainly directed at category 4 actors—are thus in order, which we believe need to be focused on the relations between people and their land, the biodiversity conserved on or through this land and the benefits communities do or do not derive from these (Mollett and Kepe 2018). Importantly, these benefits, and the reparations, are material and non-material: acknowledgement of past (colonial) injustices and the (re)distribution of resources need to go hand-in-hand (Mbembe 2017: 182–183).

Ideally, reparations mean that local communities receive (access to) their land back or at the very least obtain co-ownership of or co-management responsibilities over it. We recognise that these are anything but straightforward issues, especially since the land, the dispossessed peoples and the contexts in which these functions have changed over time, and often drastically so (Koot and Büscher, 2019). Moreover, the value and needs of the biodiversity itself also need to be taken into account. These considerations can lead to myriad outcomes that must be worked out in context specific ways. Regardless of the contextual specificities, however, a concern with historical justice needs to pervade convivial conservation moving forward, with special attention for the ways that Indigenous and other (previously) marginalised peoples themselves lead and inspire different forms of resistance to the violence exercised in relation to the sixth extinction crisis (Mitchell 2020).

Conservation Basic Income (CBI)

Above and beyond historic reparations through repossession of land and resources we advocate a *'conservation basic income'* for communities living in or next to important conservation areas. We describe this proposal in much greater detail in another essay (chapter 11, this volume) but will briefly outline it here. A Conservation Basic Income (CBI) is a monetary payment to individual community members living in or around promoted areas that allows them to lead a (locally defined) decent life. We consider this the conservation equivalent of a 'basic income grant' that is the hallmark of the new 'politics of redistribution' within international development circles (Ferguson 2015).[15] This should be aimed at allowing people to (hopefully) sustain biodiversity-friendly livelihood pursuits without having to compete within a ruthless global marketplace in ways that undermine the sustainability to which these pursuits aim. CBI should be provided to communities by coalitions of resourceful conservation actors, especially (BI)NGOs, states and the private sector.

Clearly, there are major challenges in determining who should receive such a grant, but we believe the policy should be substantial and include both communities of place (residing close to the area) and communities of use (those making use of the area) that need it. Moreover, these payments are not meant to bribe or 'incentivise' communities away from their resources. They are meant to provide people with options for livelihoods that will always need to include use of and interaction with biodiversity and resources (ideally in a way similar to many ICCAs but certainly including a focus to care for biodiversity). This (financial) unconditionality linked (conceptually and practically) to care for biodiversity makes CBI fundamentally different than the payment for ecosystem services schemes already operating in many places (Fletcher and Büscher 2017; chapter 11, this volume). It should provide local people with more autonomy and options for democratic resource control vis-a-vis more powerful actors.

To enable these two actions, we suggest that conservation NGOs set up convivial conservation departments, which could replace or be merged with their current business or private sector liaison departments. This institutional innovation addresses two important issues: first, it enables a shift in stakeholders considered most important for conservation NGOs. These should be local people living in or around, or making use of, conservation areas, not wealthy companies as now often seems to be the case. Second, it enables a shift in the terms of engagement between corporations and conservation NGOs. Clearly, the policy of trying to 'engage business' on the latter's terms (by making nature profitable and turning it into natural capital) has failed; hence this relationship needs drastic rethinking.

Rethinking (Relations With) Corporations

Does this mean that conservation NGOs should no longer work with corporations? Not necessarily, but such engagement should proceed only under strict conditions. One of these is that conservation NGOs should only work with companies if the latter pledge that they understand the necessity of moving towards a different economic model beyond capitalist accumulation and GDP-based economic growth. Ideally, and for the longer term, this should be focused on degrowth (Kallis 2018), but for the short term this could be towards a circular or doughnut economy (Raworth 2017). If they are not willing to do so, then the NGO should not waste energy on 'engagement' as this would lead to a problematic position of dependency and allow for green washing. Rather, NGOs should spend their energy on building countervailing power from an independent position.

After all, major conservation BINGOs such as WWF, CI, TNC and many others often collude with actors in category 1, while targeting actors in category 3 merely for modest consumption changes and donations and directly targeting category 4 for livelihood restrictions - sometimes even to enable category 1 actors to buy nice biodiversity-rich properties. This is not just historically unjust but does little, in the end, to solve the problem. Hence conservationists' relations with corporations, and upper classes more generally, need to be drastically reconsidered.

We understand that this would inevitably exclude many large corporations that are not (yet) willing to consider the necessity for more radical change towards an alternative economic model. But even many corporations and their CEOs should and do realise that their future, as well as that of their children, depends on a healthy planet, which should provide ample reason to come on board with convivial conservation. We also realise that this means that many conservation NGOs, especially the large BINGOs, may lose out on currently essential sources of income. But if their main goal is maximum income instead of maximum (or even minimum!) benefit for nature *over the long term*, then clearly their priorities are distorted and not deserving of support. Foregoing such revenue will indeed be a hard choice, as less income would also mean a more limited ability to pay historic reparations and provide for CBI. But at least they become part of the solution again, rather than being part of the problem. And as a convivial conservation approach takes hold, new sources of funding would become available as states and IFIs refocus towards supporting CBI and other forms of redistributive remuneration (for example by radically reverting all current fossil fuel subsidies).

Convivial Conservation Coalition (CCC)

All this should lead to a different global coalition – not a natural capital coalition, but a Convivial Conservation Coalition (CCC) that focuses on the transition towards convivial conservation. The work of the CCC would focus on gaining power not to get money and a small seat at the table but rather to hold other powerful actors accountable for their actions while supporting and building countervailing power. This coalition can help local, place-based actors to defract attention away from only category 4 actors to include the others as well. This can be done, for instance, by mapping fine grained 'footprint chains' to identify the broader actors responsible for putting pressures on specific areas. An important example here is the Rainforest Action Network[16], which does exactly this, but also others like Greenpeace.

As more and more groups and organisations come on board, the coalition can become increasingly influential in shaping global conservation policy and consequently its materialisation within local spaces around the world. Yet convivial redirection can never be (just) top-down. It requires redirection in and rethinking concrete conservation spaces also. This, however, is part of the book but beyond the scope of this paper, which has focused more on the politics needed to start turning conservation into a force that can both resist contemporary authoritarian tendencies while imagining a more sustainable world.

Conclusion: Another Conservation Politics is Needed

The emergence of the Anthropocene has made the choices that conservation faces even more difficult than they already were. This, then, is the basic reality facing conservation: radical choices *have* to be made. The idea that we can incorporate all manners of different interests in finding a way forward (through 'integrated conservation and development projects', 'peace parks', or the like) or simply see 'what works' regardless of political context or commitment is over. Perhaps not (yet) in many policy circles or neoliberal, social democratic communities. But even these spheres are now, after Trump, Brexit and Bolsonaro, forced to consider that we can no longer ignore making radical *political* choices. This is not to say that we should not look for complementarities and things that unite. This remains vital. Yet we must always do so in the context of the broader systemic change that is needed, and full awareness that this is resisted violently by entrenched and institutionalised forms of power. To continue to try to please, accommodate or ignore these entrenched powers is a defeatist politics.

The alternative radical proposals now on the table go some way towards accepting and accomplishing elements of this. Driven by the credo 'desperate times call for desperate measures', they have led an increasing number of conservationists to propose radical changes to our society and economy to halt the current (socio)ecological crisis. But they do not get to the roots of the problems they address. New conservation points to the limits of a nature-culture dichotomy and the need to address poverty in cultivating effective conservation, while neoprotectionists point to the problematic promotion of capitalist conservation. At the same time, new conservationists fail to connect their critique of the nature-society dualism with a capitalism that perpetuates both the dualisms and poverty they wish to address, while neoprotectionists fail to explain how an autonomous nature could possibly be defended from this same capitalism that is grounded upon cannibalising nature in its quest for continual growth, nor how issues of poverty or social development could be addressed within their half-earth platform.

We thus hold that our convivial conservation alternative is more realistic for a simple reason: it is more logical and consistent with empirical reality than these other two radical alternatives. Following Wark (2015), we propose convivial conservation as a deliberate act of *alternative realism* that imagines conservation outside of the capitalist box. This we find a liberating exercise that allows for harnessing the anxieties triggered by the devastating implications of our contemporary crises in order to unleash positive energy and anti-catastrophic prospects. It also evokes time-honoured traditions of critical scholarship. If the point of critical scholarship is, ultimately, to change the world in which we live (Castree et al. 2010), then we need to make sure we actually respond to the world we live in. Current conservation politics does this half-heartedly. With the momentum on the side of increasingly authoritarian leaders and movements, this is a time to be astute and uncompromising in our response. Not by responding in kind. But by matching our politics to the challenges we face.

PART II

Pluralising and Decolonising Conservation

Chapter 3:

Going Back to the Roots: *Ubuntu* and Just Conservation in Southern Africa[*]

By Mathew Bukhi Mabele, Judith E. Krauss, and Wilhelm A. Kiwango

Introduction: Conservation in the Anthropocene

Worldwide, human activities are causing a precipitous decline in biodiversity and ecosystems (Brondizio et al. 2019), giving rise to growing discussions about how to 'save nature' in and beyond the current era of the Anthropocene, so-called to signify a period of large-scale and partly irreversible human-made changes to our environment (Hickel 2020). Systematic action to care for and save nature has thus never been this critical. However, many of the currently recommended strategies for conserving our environment are grounded in scientific philosophies premised on separating nature from human lives and livelihoods (Adams and Mulligan 2003; Salleh 2016; Domínguez and Luoma 2020), including through the concept of protected areas. While conservation thinking and practice varies across contexts (Adams 2003), conservation in southern Africa[1] has seen significant colonial influences, both historically and at present (Murombedzi 2003; Mbaria and Ogada 2016). As the US-inspired 'fortress conservation' (Brockington 2002) model, instituting strict separation between people and nature, inspired British hunters to create spaces and institutions dedicated to preserving fauna across the Empire, in sub-Saharan Africa, protected areas grew rapidly prior to 1960 to set aside land before colonial rulers lost power (Brockington et al. 2008). However, protected

---

[*] Originally published as: Mabele, M.B., Krauss, J.E., and W. Kiwango. (2022). Going Back to the Roots: Ubuntu and Just Conservation in Southern Africa. *Conservation and Society* 20(2): 92-102.

areas entail socio-ecological consequences for those who live close by, distributing fortune and misfortune among different stakeholders (Brockington and Wilkie 2015).

Consequently, alternative approaches prioritising socio-ecological justice seek to challenge the inequities produced and reproduced by the dominant modes of conservation. One example is the convivial conservation proposal (Büscher and Fletcher 2019; 2020), which among other measures seeks to replace protected areas with 'promoted areas' to create conservation strategies which promote nature for, to, and by humans rather than protecting it from humans. Especially in contexts with longstanding (neo-)colonial influences, facilitating social justice in conservation is predicated on careful decolonial and decolonising reflections to deconstruct colonial structures in thought and practice. Following Murove (2012) and Tamale (2020), we hereby use 'decolonial deconstruction' to represent an epistemic movement which exposes the 'darker side' of Eurocentric epistemologies and builds alternative epistemologies and philosophies. Therefore, inspired by 'decolonial options' (Tlostanova and Mignolo 2009; Mignolo and Escobar 2015)—i.e. focusing on problems created through the coloniality–modernity matrix of power and addressing them through de-colonial thinking—we identify conservation in southern Africa, and the socio-ecological injustices it has entailed, as such a problem. A 'decolonial option' for crafting context-fitting, decolonial conservation alternatives, in our view, is *Ubuntu*, a southern African philosophy rooted in notions of communitarianism, reconciliation, relationality, and interdependence (Ramose 2015; Nkondo 2007; Naicker 2011; Chemhuru 2019a).

Our paper thus asks: how does *Ubuntu* philosophy relate to radical ideas such as 'convivial conservation' in support of socio-ecologically just approaches in southern Africa? Specifically, how can *Ubuntu* help adapt convivial conservation's suggestion of promoted areas to the southern African context? With our work, we contribute to an emerging literature on decolonising conservation (e.g. Brockington et al. 2021; Collins et al. 2021), adding a specific focus on *Ubuntu* in light of the convivial conservation proposal to address conservation injustices in southern Africa. We see *Ubuntu* as a viable and necessary decolonial option for conservation in southern Africa, which can enrich convivial conservation's vision of facilitating socially just conservation. We thus contribute to the literature by bringing a specifically decolonial lens to the discussion on convivial conservation (cf. Krauss 2021).

To answer these research questions, our paper first reviews the history of conservation and particularly protected areas in southern Africa, emphasising the influences of colonial, and cognate, mind-sets. In a second step, we critically introduce the convivial conservation vision with an emphasis on the 'promoted areas' philosophy. After discussing the philosophical and practical tenets of *Ubuntu*, we reflect on the degree to which *Ubuntu* can help advance promoted areas and socio-ecological justice more generally. We argue that *Ubuntu* can help enrich convivial conservation proposals, particularly in southern Africa, by providing a long-established relational ethos of care between human beings and physical nature. By discouraging practices of individualistic and excessive extractions of nonhuman nature and embracing relationships between humans and nonhumans based on respect, solidarity, and collaboration, *Ubuntu* can foster decolonial conservation alternatives focused on socio-ecological justice.

A Short History of the 'Protected Areas' Philosophy in Southern Africa

Nature conservation through the creation of protected areas (PAs) has a complex history in southern Africa's ecosystems. At different periods, colonial authorities established PAs—as reserves, game-controlled areas, national parks, and private parks following the western model of conservation—to control and exploit revenues from hunting while evicting local populations (Neumann 1998; Kiwango et al. 2015; Noe 2019). The management and use of wildlife were thus firmly under the colonial governments. For example, in the then Tanganyika (now Tanzania), the Germans issued the first regulations for the use of wildlife for both the Europeans and the local communities in 1891 (Nelson et al. 2007). The creation of PAs was moulded after the 'Yellowstone National Park' model, which is grounded on a separation of nature from human lives and livelihoods (Adams and Mulligan 2003; Neumann 1998). This 'fortress conservation' model came to redefine land use in colonial territories through the strict separation of people from nature in the quest for leisure and consumptive utilisation (Brockington 2002; Brockington et al. 2008; Dressler et al. 2010). Mfune (2017) notes that the power of the PAs philosophy lies in the scientific narratives about human–environment interactions. The invention of biological sciences such as forestry in the late eighteenth century introduced what Scott (1998) describes as tunnel-vision knowledge forms: they brought into sharp focus limited understandings of complex realities to make careful measurements and calculations more viable. From 1900, the United Kingdom, with German support, began to apply the sciences in establishing uniform and standardised conservation policies and practices (Neumann 2002). For instance, several 'international' conservation conferences held in London recommended a system of national parks and set up convictions which criminalised traditional hunting practices, labelling them as savagery and threatening to flora and fauna. Colonial administrators thus recruited the sciences to rationalise nature, making it amenable to colonial states' exploitation, justifying separation between people and nature and cementing colonial ideas about nature (Adams and Mulligan 2003). The philosophy thus reproduced through colonial conservation a dualistic view of nature as distinct from people and society—seeing locals and their livelihoods as threats to ecosystems (Mfune 2017). As such, the colonial rule purported to bring order to the perceived chaos of the local communities, thereby disrupting traditional management systems (DeGeorges and Reilly 2008).

These colonially constructed worldviews shaped conservation and particularly PAs in the region, with significant social consequences.

Securing control over natural resources was key to the early formation of the colonial states in Africa (Neumann 1998; Scott 1998). Europeans colonised not only humans, but nature as well, in stark contrast to the African understanding of the inherent union between nature and society (Murombedzi 2003). The philosophy dismissed existing interactions between humans and ecologies. Rodgers et al. (2002) describe the pre-colonial freedom to convert and use resources for East Africans, with practices of conservation of scarce resources such as water springs and dry-season grazing through community sanctions. Resource control through the creation of PAs was important for the German Kaiser, and later, the British crown in colonial Tanganyika (Neumann 1998). The Selous Game Reserve was one of the first of its kind (Noe 2019). A complex set of rules was formulated to regulate resource access and use in both the forestry and wildlife sectors in the colony. Mirroring the London recommendations, all African settlement, cultivation, charcoal-burning, and grazing were outlawed in the newly created enclosures (Neumann 1998). For instance, the Maasai—predominantly livestock herders—were regularly evicted out of their interactions with surrounding ecosystems (e.g. the Serengeti, Mkomazi, Manyara, and Tarangire National Parks), blamed for competing with and excluding wildlife from water sources and good pastures (Brockington 2002). The separation of nature from humans subordinated Indigenous interests to commercial exploitation by the colonial settlers, as local people and their livelihoods were considered a hindrance to colonial economic interests (Maddox et al. 1996). In South Africa, DeGeorges and Reilly (2008) report that colonial rules excluded Africans from hunting because their methods were deemed 'un-sporting'. They introduced the Game Law Amendment of 1891, based on British Laws which banned Africans in South Africa, Malawi, Zambia, and Zimbabwe from their traditional hunting practices (DeGeorges and Reilly 2008; Murombedzi 2003). Such thinking disrupted local resource-use practices and notions of negotiated access to natural resources (Maddox et al. 1996), of communal property relations and customary land resources in African societies (Noe 2019). The use of European ecological sciences can be viewed as one of the outworking bureaucratic rationality dimensions used to secure their control on new colonies, marking the start of resource dispossession processes (Adams 2003).

In postcolonial African states, the colonial 'flavour' in conservation laws and practices is still visible (Wily and Mbaya 2001). This manifests in two ways. First, it is an independent state's mission to strengthen the political and economic authority needed to drive modernisation processes and control patronage resource networks (Nelson 2010). This happens through the rapid expansion of the PAs network. For example, currently, Tanzania has the largest PAs network, in which about 40% of the country is under some form of nature protection (Noe et al. 2017). In Zambia, PAs cover about 30% of the country's total land area, while national parks cover about 18% and Wildlife Management Areas (WMAs) cover a further 24% of the total land area in Botswana (Musumali et al. 2007). Attempts to initiate and implement the so-called 'community-based natural resource management' (CBNRM) approaches have all been modelled after the same problematic philosophy (Nelson et al. 2007; Kiwango et al. 2015; Mfune 2017). For instance, while it had been assumed that WMAs as a form of CBNRM would deliver both conservation and development goals, it is only conservation that seems to have gained, whereas development promises remain largely elusive. Kiwango et al. (2015) show that the creation of WMAs since 2003 in Tanzania has added about 3% to the total land area under protection. While the increased PAs networks have undoubtedly attracted more tourism investments, the local communities continue to bear the costs of conservation with a near-absence of promised development benefits (Noe et al. 2017; Kiwango et al. 2018).

The second way in which the colonial legacy is manifested is the creation of postcolonial conservation spaces which continue to produce conservation goals which neglect the intimate relationships between people and nature. The current resurgent forceful measures to apply the PAs philosophy, termed as 'militarised conservation' (Büscher and Ramutsindela 2015; Mabele 2017; Duffy et al. 2019) intensifies concerns over the colonial legacy in Africa's conservation spaces. Many of the current PAs follow the colonial-era forceful evictions of communities in the name of conservation and disease control. The evictions of the Maasai from Serengeti in 1959 is a case in point (Brockington 2002). In this case, militarised conservation refers to measures taken to respond to a conservation conflict (e.g. poaching of elephants, rhinos, and gorillas) which use more forceful and armed conservation measures and technologies originally meant for the military (Duffy et al. 2019). While it is often presented as a legitimate 'war' to save endangered species, Duffy (2014a) warns of the dangers as it may be used to enforce repressive and coercive policies, threatening social and environmental justice. What all this means is that there is a need for radical alternative conservation approaches grounded on decolonial and social-justice objectives. In the next section, we discuss one proposed approach called 'convivial conservation'.

Convivial Conservation and 'Promoted Areas': A Radical Alternative?

'Convivial conservation' has been suggested as a radical alternative to other dominant conservation ideas (Büscher and Fletcher 2019; 2020). Against a backdrop of other early twenty-first century paradigm-shifting proposals for conservation which are built on pre-existing market-based ideas (new conservation) or protection ideas (e.g. Half-Earth), convivial conservation sets itself apart by questioning some fundamental premises on which pre-existing conservation ideas have been built. It moves away from the market-based ideas perpetuated, amongst others, by the 'new conservation' proposals (Marvier et al. 2012), which propose embracing the private sector and its opportunities. Convivial conservation challenges the capitalist premise on which new conservation, akin to mainstream conservation[2], is built. Equally, it questions the human–nature dichotomy prevalent in both mainstream approaches and protectionist ideas, including the ever-higher proportions of the planet to be reserved 'for nature' (cf. Wuerthner et al. 2015; Wilson 2016). As such, convivial conservation seeks to go beyond both the capitalist premise of market-based approaches and the exclusion-based premise of strictly separating certain humans from nature. It sees both paradigms as, in different ways, promoting or countenancing an economic model which is built on capitalist, exponential growth, and as promoting or countenancing inequality-perpetuating ways of stressing divisions more than the many links between and among humans and nonhumans (Büscher and Fletcher 2019; 2020).

The convivial conservation vision encompasses several different elements (Büscher and Fletcher 2019; 2020). Firstly, it proposes shifting from PAs to promoted areas, which do not suggest that 'anything goes', but instead propose a more positive, democratic way of engaging with these spaces, which celebrates the many links between humans and nonhumans (Sandbrook 2015; Fletcher 2017). Secondly, it suggests moving from framing conservation as 'saving nature' to celebrating both human and nonhuman nature, thereby challenging the above-discussed human–nature dichotomy and the notion of saving only nonhuman nature. This approach would be replaced by celebrating diversity cognisant of differential needs and broader political-economic dynamics. Thirdly, convivial conservation highlights supporting engaged visitation over touristic voyeurism, shifting from short-term touristic, elite access towards long-term engagement (Fletcher et al. 2020). A fourth component challenges spectacular ways of engaging with nature, e.g. with an emphasis on charismatic megafauna, in favour of promoting everyday nature in all its splendour (Cronon 1996). A fifth component focuses on moving away from privatised expert technocracy towards common democratic engagement, emphasising that all humans should be able to live with all nature rather than having relationships mediated through top-down, technocratic knowledges, akin to visions proposed by the Territories and Areas Conserved by Indigenous Peoples and Local Communities (ICCAs) Consortium (Borrini-Feyerabend and Campese 2017).

Our study will focus on the first element, moving from PAs to promoted areas. The reason is threefold: firstly, PAs have played such a key role in shaping the socio-ecological geography of conservation in southern Africa, as discussed above. Secondly, given the role which PAs have played in distributing fortune and misfortune (Brockington and Wilkie 2015), they are an obvious starting point in any discussion on socially just conservation approaches. In combination, this means that PAs in this part of the world are a microcosm of various issues which those seeking to decolonise conservation have raised, ranging from producing and reproducing historical and colonial injustices to the role and recognition of whose knowledges and visions of conservation count (Adams and Mulligan 2003; Asiyanbi and Lund 2020; Domínguez and Luoma 2020; Sungusia et al. 2020; Krauss 2021).

Based on the aforementioned history of PAs in southern Africa, three points are particularly relevant in challenging PAs from the perspective of convivial conservation. Firstly, conservation institutions have been subject to accusations of imperialistic meddling and neo-colonialism based on examples of recreating patterns of exploitation by privileging elite access and trophy-hunting or using colonial imagery in marketing towards tourists (Brockington et al. 2008; Mbaria and Ogada 2016). In PAs, though they differ considerably in how much use is permitted and by whom across diverse categories (Dudley 2008), there are structural similarities with excluding subsistence use in favour of elite access. Secondly, as discussed above, PAs have been argued and demonstrated to have significant impacts on the livelihoods of adjacent communities (Brockington and Wilkie 2015; Oldekop et al. 2016), which can perpetuate dynamics of inequality. Finally, only specific types of knowledge and knowledge holders are incorporated into conservation and PA management, which can mean that resident populations or Indigenous knowledge holders are rendered invisible or ignored (Asiyanbi and Lund 2020; Rubis and Theriault 2020). All these dynamics, we argue, merit questioning as part of any radical alternative and decolonial options.

The suggestion of promoted areas, based on Büscher and Fletcher (2019; 2020), differs from PAs in several key respects relevant to the decolonisation and deconstruction of the dominant conservation philosophy. Very explicitly, they are not about protecting nature from certain people, which emphasises boundaries between human and nonhuman nature despite the many links which connect them (Sandbrook 2015; Fletcher 2017). Rather, promoted conservation areas are to 'promote nature for, to and by humans' (Büscher and Fletcher 2019: 286; 2020: 92) without relying on revenue from tourism and elite access, welcoming people as visitors, dwellers, or travellers, and not temporary invaders. As Büscher and Fletcher (2019) acknowledge, this is predicated on a wider context geared towards conviviality, instead of exploitation or productivity. They propose emphasising all that is valuable in and about current PAs, without permitting all behaviour and actions. However, the key difference is not positioning nature against humanity and population growth, but instead building an integrated value system which does not depend on destroying, but on 'living with' nonhuman nature. This system would equally be predicated on continuous debate around what activities are permissible, of which would go against sustainable democratic development (Büscher and Fletcher 2020).

To develop radical alternatives, there is much about Büscher and Fletcher's (2019; 2020) vision of promoted areas which compares favourably to PAs. Regarding the first above-described criticism of PAs, promoted areas would not continue the colonial tradition of excluding residents in favour of elite access or legitimising the extractive behaviours which have placed people in the privileged position to gain such access. Linking to the second point of reproducing inequalities, the explicitly democratic setup instead could give voice to local residents in the continuous debates about what is and is not permissible in promoted areas. The idea of promoting all which is valuable equally has the potential to give stronger voice to locally based value systems, including *Ubuntu*, prioritising more relational, equitable ways of linking human and nonhuman natures. Thus, as the vision takes strong interest in the interconnectedness of human beings with nature, it essentially supports the potential of *Ubuntu* in reinvigorating African environmentalism (Chemhuru 2019b), as further explored in the next section.

However, more work remains to be done to flesh out the details which can make or break the ability of promoted areas to offer radical, more equitable alternatives. A first, crucial observation concerning Büscher and Fletcher's (2019; 2020) idea of promoted areas is that very important details on the 'how', 'who', or 'what' remain murky. Who would be driving and determining the modalities of this transition from protected to promoted areas? Who would own land or use rights going forward? How would disputes be resolved if there were disagreements on what is, or is not, permissible in a 'promoted area'? In keeping with both Illich's ideas of conviviality (1973) and Elinor Ostrom et al.'s work on common-pool resources (1999), such decision-making would need to be devolved to local levels, which is predicated on robust rules and genuine democratic devolution, neither of which are givens. It is unclear how in the detail such dialogue- and democracy-based structures would work in terms of promoting and protecting the interests of more vulnerable community members based on gender, income, or (dis)ability, never mind intergenerational interests. Moreover, the proposal does not offer definitive answers on how promoted areas are, or are not, different from existing community conservation projects, and how they have incorporated vital insights around power dynamics or risks of elite capture (e.g. Noe and Kangalawe 2015; Zafra-Calvo and Moreno-Peñaranda 2017). More fundamentally, why would this shift be desirable for the majority of current PAs, since it means moving away from a key unique selling point they had hitherto championed? If they did shift, how would promoted areas overcome historical injustices perpetrated in the name of conservation, possibly on the same land? The convivial conservation idea of historic reparations, i.e. material and non-material compensation for past inequities, is a viable starting point. However, Büscher and Fletcher (2020) themselves acknowledge the need for context-specific solutions, which require solid methodology and the implementation of broad-based, participatory engagement with the needs of all to identify and overcome decades or centuries of injustice with multidimensional and inclusive solutions.

Another key point is the role of Indigenous knowledges in shaping promoted areas. The idea of continuous, inclusive debates as the basis of determining permissible behaviours and positive outcomes for 'promoted areas' is predicated on the involvement of local voices. However, precisely how local knowledges would be incorporated in shaping and managing promoted areas remains unclear. In the minefield of local, communal, state, and private land rights and interests, how can convivial conservation elevate local and traditional knowledges to a status in which they can challenge the make-up, logics, and policies of such promoted areas over and against all competing logics? Incorporating local knowledges systematically may be the most reliable defence against promoted areas, or convivial conservation for that matter, becoming yet another monolithic mega-idea which is unable to be responsive to, cognisant of, and adaptive for the differential local needs and histories which Büscher and Fletcher (2019; 2020) recognise. How can this be ensured? Finally, what if traditional, local knowledges would reject all external ideas given external imposition's bleak histories, instead choosing a completely different set of rules? On all these counts, we believe that *Ubuntu*-based notions could be helpful to adapt convivial conservation to southern African contexts and address the queries we raise above, as we further flesh out below.

Ubuntu as a 'Decolonial Option'

Ubuntu is a philosophy and a way of life associated with many African societies. Ewuoso and Hall (2019) refer to *Ubuntu* philosophy as African ethics. Linguistically, the word *Ubuntu* originates from the Nguni cultures—Zulu, Xhosa, and Ndebele— in South Africa and Zimbabwe (Le Grange 2019), although Gwaravanda (2019) notes that *Ubuntu*-related values can be used to represent environmental thinking from related cultures[3] in Mozambique, Zambia, Malawi, Namibia, Botswana, Lesotho, and Swaziland. It is a particular ethic of care for other human beings as well as the physical world (Waghid and Smeyers 2011; Ewuoso and Hall 2019).

In this paper, we see *Ubuntu* as an ethic of care predicated on the practices of mutuality and sharing between humans and nonhumans. Thus, we conceptualise the idea of promoting nature for, to, and by humans rather than protecting it from humans, following such an ethic. So, with mutual caring and sharing, Indigenous human beings benefit from nature through appropriate ways of relating and interacting with the nonhumans, as under *Ubuntu*, a person's needs are met in relations to others' needs. That is, in the *Ubuntu* ethic, there is no conception of anthropocentricism, as humans and nonhumans are moral counterparts. The ethic articulates the human interconnectedness and dignity which an individual has towards other beings (Waghid and Smeyers 2011), as expressed by the popular maxim 'A person is a Person through others' (Terblanché-Greeff 2019: 97). It suggests that a community is a triad composed of the living, the living-dead (ancestors), and the yet-to-be born. This depicts life as wholeness, as life extends to the environment and past and future generations (Terblanché-Greeff 2019). 'Other beings' and 'others' here include all other entities which are not human beings, giving *Ubuntu* its distinctive respect for life of humans and nonhumans (Mawere 2012).

So, *Ubuntu* represents Indigenous ethics for salient behaviours and ways of thinking about the relationality between a person and other persons and nonhuman beings. It has recently been used as a moral foundation for societal reconciliation from the resource injustices which black Africans suffer since the colonial and apartheid South Africa (Molefe and Magam 2020). Communion, relationality, and reconciliation thus make up core elements of the *Ubuntu* philosophy, advocating communal relationships and political implications which allow individuals 'to experience their lives as bound up with the good of their communities, as opposed to liberal politics that is mainly concerned with securing conditions for individuals to lead autonomous lives' (Nkondo 2007: 91). In that sense, *Ubuntu* focuses on concerns for the equal and just distribution of resources between and amongst societies (Etieyibo 2017). It is such African ethics that makes *Ubuntu* 'less individualistic and anti-egoistic…and…more communal than Western ethics' (Ewuoso and Hall 2019: 97). These *Ubuntu* ethics may not be necessarily unique to African societies, but they certainly were not imported from other continents (Ewuoso and Hall 2019).

Some scholars thus conceptualise *Ubuntu* as an alternative knowledge framework which contrasts with current Western ways of thinking and knowing about human interactions with nature in southern Africa (e.g. Nkondo 2007; Mawere 2012; Ramose 2015; Chibvongodze 2016; Molefe 2019). For these scholars, *Ubuntu* brings an African discursive lens in the generation and justification of knowledge as well as the rationality of beliefs and ethics in both conservation and development (Tavernaro-Haidarian 2018; Chemhuru 2019a; Terblanché-Greeff 2019). With *Ubuntu*, 'knowledge is generated and justified through communal discourse and through the cultivation of relations with others' (Tavernaro-Haidarian 2018: 230). *Ubuntu* articulates what Tavernaro-Haidarian (2018) calls a 'deliberative epistemology', which contrasts the individualistic and competitive Western ethics, closely linked to capitalist economies and their destruction of ecosystems (Terblanché-Greeff 2019). In contrast to Cartesian epistemology, *Ubuntu* values communality, caring, and respect for others

(Tavernaro-Haidarian 2018). Under *Ubuntu*, a person's humanness thrives on incessant interactions with other entities, humans, and nature (Ramose, 2015). Nature has then a moral status as it sets the teleological dimension of existence, making humans and nonhumans moral counterparts (Chibvongodze 2016; Chemhuru 2019b). These values suggest an ethic of sufficiency, whereby one's needs are met in relation to others' needs (Terblanché-Greeff 2019). They particularly gel well with convivial conservation and its element of promoted area as a form of 'living well with' both humans and the physical world.

Against the aforementioned history of the coloniality of conservation knowledge and practice, some African scholars conceive *Ubuntu* as a tool for transformation in the context of formerly 'colonised' southern Africa (e.g. Murove 2012; Chilisa 2017; Naude 2019; Tamale 2020). This thinking aligns with the movement for the decoloniality of knowledge. Decoloniality involves disengaging, disrupting, and delinking from legacies of western patriarchal knowledge philosophies and their legacies of socio-political injustices and epistemic domination (Mignolo 2011; Tamale 2020). Simply put, decoloniality 'means decolonial options confronting and delinking from coloniality, or the colonial matrix of power' (Mignolo 2011: xxvii). Within this broader movement, we consider *Ubuntu* a decolonial option for advancing projects of epistemic decolonisation in southern African conservation—convivial conservation being one such project in our case. This parallels with Naude's (2019) argument for *Ubuntu* as an example of how to decolonise Western knowledge foundations. For Naude (2019), *Ubuntu* represents the strongest form of de- and re-contextualisation and decentring of the coloniality of knowledge in Africa. Within this perspective, decentring colonial perspectives to re-initiate social justice thus becomes an important decoloniality goal.

The ethic of *Ubuntu* becomes an antithesis of dehumanising conditions which the coloniality of knowledge brings in different facets of African day-to-day lives (Murove 2012; Tamale 2020), including conservation (e.g. Chibvongodze 2016). As knowledge coloniality produces social inequities and disrupts the moral fabric of African life (Mignolo 2011; Murove 2012), *Ubuntu*'s task is to reinvigorate African notions of social justice (Letseka 2014; Chilisa 2017; Tamale 2020). One such dehumanising condition is the above-discussed PAs philosophy, whereby colonial state conservation dehumanised local people through 'enclosures' of nature away from human lives and livelihoods (Nelson 2010). In relation to this process, as a decolonial option and tool to deconstruct knowledge coloniality, *Ubuntu* brings possibilities for a 'new humanity', as entrenched colonial structures which dehumanise people are epistemically dismantled and disobeyed (Mignolo 2011; Tamale 2020). As a project of decolonisation, *Ubuntu* thus brings back African traditional ethics of justice and fairness. It does so by informing the indigenisation of knowledge production systems. Museka and Madondo (2012) see *Ubuntu* as a tool to indigenise environmental pedagogy for creating the culture-specific ecological education ingrained in African ethics. Chilisa (2017) points out that ecological sciences are one of the systems which need indigenisation. There are ongoing efforts: for instance, the South African Ministry of Education has replaced the old colonial/apartheid Eurocentric science curricula with inclusive curricula which exemplify *Ubuntu* values such as humanness, communalism, interdependence, equity, social justice, and moral responsibility (Ogunniyi 2020). As there is no *Ubuntu* without fair communal justice (Letseka 2014), such indigenisation of sciences and curricula represents a decolonial attempt to deconstruct and re-contextualise knowledge and practices which inform and address ecological problems, respectively.

The discourse *Ubuntu* has not, however, gone without challenges. Gwaravanda (2019) questions the generalised conceptions of *Ubuntu* across diverse African cultures and communities, arguing that *Ubuntu* represents the cultural standpoints of the Nguni cultures and not of the societies in East, West, and Central Africa. Instead, as Ewuoso and Hall (2019) put it, *Ubuntu* represents a philosophical construction which 'unifies a wide array of the moral judgments and practices found among many black Africans spanning a large geographical area in sub-Saharan Africa, and over a broad time period' (Ewuoso and Hall 2019: 96). The spirit of *Ubuntu* thus lives on across African societies. Tamale (2020) shares her experience regarding how rural folks from Egypt to South Africa and Senegal to Ethiopia exhibit *Ubuntu* in their unfettered hospitality and generosity towards her, a total stranger. For Tamale, *Ubuntu* is by no means a romanticism for the long-gone African past. Nonetheless, there are still concerns about whether *Ubuntu* can provide an escape from epistemic coloniality when languages expressing *Ubuntu*, publication and dissemination outlets, and interpretative categories are borrowed from the West (Naude 2019). This is a fair criticism. However, as Tamale (2020: 22) asserts, what is important with the discourse around *Ubuntu* as a decolonial option is 'to sharpen our consciousness about Western coloniality', while being aware that 'it is impossible to reject everything Western *in toto*', but still demanding the redistribution of the control of knowledge, institutions, and authorities. The goal for redistribution links *Ubuntu* with other Indigenous epistemes such as *Swaraj* in India and *Buen vivir* in South America as decolonial projects of deconstructing capitalist development for social justice (Kothari et al. 2019). Afro-descendant groups in South America are invoking *Ubuntu* to gain a more nuanced understanding of *Buen vivir* (Le Grange 2019).

So, *Ubuntu* has the potential to foster a celebration of both human and nonhuman natures. Its operationalisation in the spirit of promoted areas may be currently lacking, but its principles such as relationality, communitarianism, solidarity, and mutuality are relevant for changing the PAs approach. Moreover, lessons on how it could be operationalised can be drawn from several initiatives. For example, Mawere (2012) shows how the Shona people in Norumedzo communal area, south-eastern Zimbabwe, are using *Ubuntu* in conserving thicket forest (*Jiri*) rich in edible stink bugs (*Encosternum delegorguei*) locally known as *Harurwa*, and loquats locally known as *Mazhanje*. Both locals and strangers are advised through the area's

Chief, surrounding Chiefs, and the Police Chief not to tamper with *Jiri*. When the *Harurwa* and *Mazhanje* season comes, the area's Chief pays tribute to both the Police Chief and surrounding Chiefs, exhibiting practices of sharing and mutuality. The mutual sharing fosters a sense of resource ownership and care even for outsiders. Reinvigorating such ethics requires wider 'epistemological rupture', a moment of destroying old ways and forming 'new modes of knowing that create new conditions of possibility for seeing, understanding, and thinking' (West 2016: 7). This is happening with changes of education curricula which present nature as having no other reasons to exist except serving human interests (Museka and Madondo 2012). The vision is to tame science to promote human virtues and social justice within societies (Ogunniyi 2020). The mission is thus about harnessing benefits of ethics which are within Indigenous people's existential realities, grounding them in *Ubuntu* to evoke the eco-friendly Indigenous traditions and environmental consciousness and stewardship which is written in people's hearts (Museka and Madondo 2012).

Discussion and Conclusion

We have argued that for southern Africa, the proposed convivial conservation revolution is best fitted with decolonising conservation science, policies, and practices in order not to impose another external set of ideas around conservation, but incorporate the deconstruction of the hegemonic philosophy. We explored the potential of *Ubuntu* as a decolonial option (Tlostanova and Mignolo 2009; Mignolo 2011) to facilitate a decolonial reimagining of conservation in southern Africa through its ethos of relationality and communality. We have used the ethos of communion, justice, and relationality enshrined in *Ubuntu* to discern the ethics of coloniality in conservation philosophies in southern Africa. Colonisation and coloniality have left traces in the policies and practices of conservation in southern Africa to this day, resulting in diverse socio-ecological injustices both past and present[4]. As possibly their most prominent example, we have focused on the protected areas which practice the strict exclusion of local residents to the benefit of wealthy far-away visitors. At the same time, we have used *Ubuntu* to question and query the radical proposals of convivial conservation, including promoted areas, as potential vectors of decolonial deconstruction and harmonious human/nonhuman coexistence in southern Africa. We show below how our thoughts on *Ubuntu* could help promote decolonial, equity-focused conservation, and we address the questions raised about convivial conservation's and promoted areas' applicability to southern Africa.

Such decolonial deconstruction is in the first instance premised on decolonising epistemologies and knowledges by delinking from the colonial matrix of power. As the science underlying protected areas continues to be rooted in Western ontologies and epistemologies, often without ways for local or traditional knowledges to contribute or be taken seriously (Asiyanbi and Lund 2020; Rubis and Theriault 2020), decolonial thinking becomes synonymous with 'being epistemically disobedient' (Mignolo 2011: 54). *Ubuntu* thus becomes an epistemology of transformation (cf. Tlostanova and Mignolo 2009). It facilitates delinking from the Western ontologies and epistemologies not in the sense of abandoning them, but in inventing decolonial visions, horizons, and discourses for a postcapitalist future (cf. Mignolo 2011). *Ubuntu* becomes a tool for channelling epistemic disobedience with regard to how hegemonic conservation science and practice define human–environmental interactions. There are some limitations to *Ubuntu* as discussed above. However, we have highlighted where and how Ubuntu diverges from the tools of hegemonic conservation science and practice, and leveraged its grounded, relational insights as vectors of decolonial action specifically regarding protected areas and the alternative proposed by convivial conservation—promoted areas.

We see an *Ubuntu* ethos thus as a powerful tool to promote local, Indigenous knowledges and ontologies in establishing and managing promoted areas beyond traditional conservation science.

Ubuntu carries a wider African communitarian approach (Tavernaro-Haidarian 2018). This aligns with one of the goals of decoloniality, which is to have social organisations centred on what Mignolo (2011: 52) asserts as the 'Indigenous notions of the communal' which points toward a non-capitalist horizon of society, which is 'the overall horizon of decolonial options' (p. 311). Highlighting the relational and communal responsibility between human and nonhuman natures as the starting and end point of all knowledge, *Ubuntu* can thus help shape and animate promoted areas' idea of celebrating all life—human and nonhuman, charismatic, and non-charismatic—through an ethos of relationality. Besides, the relatedness between the humans and nonhumans suggests an interconnectedness between the two entities, attesting that the principle of separating humans from the nonhumans was never an African moral ethic. The interdependence between humans and nonhumans allies with what convivial conservation represents in the terms of conviviality, i.e. 'the building of long-lasting, engaging and open-ended relationships with nonhumans and ecologies' (Büscher and Fletcher 2019: 286). For adapting convivial conservation to southern African contexts, *Ubuntu* would thus offer a viable avenue to integrate Indigenous knowledges into promoted areas and convivial conservation more generally, addressing one of our above-explained concerns by avoiding external imposition and promoting local knowledges, needs, and histories (cf. also Krauss 2021).

What is more, *Ubuntu* can therefore help overcome the separation between humans and nonhumans rooted in the coloniality–modernity nexus precisely because of its relational ethos. The schism between human and nonhuman nature which emanates through strict protected areas from an abiding Western human–nature dualism (Salleh 2016) negates the moral accountability of an individual to other humans and nonhumans on which *Ubuntu* is premised (Murove 2012). Building on Murove's (201) insights, we further argue that the colonial-rooted scientific philosophies premised on separating nature from human lives and livelihoods are grounded on distorted assumptions and understandings of human beings in African contexts. The efficacy of *Ubuntu* lies in relational rationality, i.e. the understanding of a human being as a relational being shaped with ethics of sufficiency, communitarianism, solidarity, and interdependence. This challenges the Eurocentric, individualistic, and self-interested understanding of a human being which tragically dominates the science behind the PAs philosophy. Protected areas as a philosophy of modernity in environmental conservation was thus a contradistinction of African traditionalism in human–nature relations. Precolonial modes of human–nonhuman relations were seen as a traditionalist way of organising the world, to be replaced by modernity through the systematic separation of nature from human lives and livelihoods, including by way of protected areas. The idea was that, as Mignolo (2011: 3) puts it, 'there is no modernity without coloniality'. The colonial experience of conservation in southern Africa is both centred on the promise of modernity and also is a tangible manifestation of modernity's repercussions for human lives and livelihoods, particularly in the light of the socio-ecological inequities it continues to produce.

Ubuntu defines individuals through their relations to other humans and nonhuman others, challenging any Cartesian nature–human dualisms which are at the root of the strict exclusion of local residents from PAs. Instead, *Ubuntu*'s interconnectedness and mutual respect negates a need for exclusion for the purposes of safeguarding protection, instead supporting promoted areas' overcoming of human–nature separations through a sense of mutual responsibility rooted in relational self-identities. Equally, *Ubuntu*'s relational ethic of care could help address our concerns about how to flesh out vital details of convivial conservation in regard to owning land and use rights and shifting decision-making power to the local level: the *Ubuntu* philosophy could help organise effective dialogues to manage governance, resolve disputes and conflicts, and protect the interests of vulnerable community members based on gender, income, (dis)ability, and intergenerationality.

Finally, *Ubuntu* significantly adds to the promoted areas proposal by providing a moral justification for choosing sufficiency as a purposeful economic strategy. Contrary to some objections that *Ubuntu* may be reinvigorating an ideal romanticised African past, it is rather a continuous, relational lived experience 'espoused as a contradistinction to *laissez faire* capitalism and economic liberalism which undergird the oppressive status quo' (Tamale 2020: 232). This quote highlights *Ubuntu*'s potential also for overcoming the socio-ecological injustices resulting from unbridled economic growth and extractivism given the emphasis on safeguarding the well-being of all, including those previously at the receiving end of socio-ecological injustices engineered by PAs often for touristic benefits. In *Ubuntu*, economic relations are not defined by endless accumulation of wealth, rather following the principle of sufficiency in society and in natural resources and the environment, as the prerequisite to social equality (Murove 2012; Ramose 2015). In the *Ubuntu* ethic, the principle of sufficiency thus guides an individual's accumulation and consumption of wealth (Murove 2012). Since promoted areas, as does convivial conservation as a whole, propose moving towards an ethos of economic sufficiency instead of extractive, capitalist logics, *Ubuntu* and its strong respect for other beings and all of nonhuman nature can help justify morally and ethically shifting away from infinite wealth accumulation for the benefit of people and planet. This sufficiency ethos would thus address our queries about how and why protected areas, and the wider economic system, would move away from profit orientation towards more relational understandings of value, a shift on which convivial conservation is predicated. While this would require a reorganisation of society and economy more generally, we focus here only on the benefits which this ethos of sufficiency would entail for conservation in southern Africa.

Convivial conservation overall could thus benefit from *Ubuntu* in terms of promoting relational ideas, ontologies, and philosophies from southern Africa, through the ethics of caring and mutual respect for humans and nonhumans, and the concomitant moral justification for choosing economic sufficiency. Following postcolonial African scholars, Murove (2012) argues that any decolonial deconstruction project in African societies has to be based on the ethic of *Ubuntu*. As Chivaura (2006) asserts, sustainable approaches to endogenous conservation and human development cannot be attained by using imposed non-African notions. We therefore agree with Murove's position in the sense that convivial conservation as a project of deconstruction of the thinking and action around human–environmental interactions has to be grounded in the movement for decoloniality of knowledge. For the above-stated reasons, *Ubuntu* is a viable decolonial option for conservation in southern Africa which can enrich convivial conservation's promoted areas' proposal to the benefit of all. We welcome further research which empirically tests our theoretical discussion by building *Ubuntu*-informed promoted areas in southern Africa. A second avenue for further research could review how our suggested adaptations of convivial conservation link with other local contexts with distinct histories and needs across the globe. Finally, we would welcome a systematic discussion of how our proposals on adapting convivial conservation relate to broader global attempts at decolonising conservation.

Chapter 4:

Living with gorillas? Lessons from Batwa-gorillas' convivial relations at Bwindi forest, Uganda[*]

By Christine Ampumuza

Introduction: Conservation Dynamics and the 'New' Challenge

For a long time now, conservation of biological diversity has been dominated by fortress and community conservation models. The fortress conservation model operates through fines, fences and militarisation of boundaries to ensure strict separation between human and non-human natures (Brockington 2002; Duffy 2014a). Over time, this model proved to be counter-productive, prompting attempts to make changes to the model. The changes included enlisting communities into conservation through the Community-based Conservation (CBC) model (Kothari et al. 2013); as well as attaching a financial value to nature through market-based conservation mechanisms (Bishop and Pagiola 2012). However, as Büscher (2016b) argues, such changes still reinforce the original ideals of fortress conservation and have failed to curb the deteriorating environmental situation. Moreover, some conservationists continue to emphasise the need to allocate half of the earth to biodiversity (Locke 2013; Kopnina et al. 2018). These calls illuminate the fact that conservation practice is not ready to let go of the fortress model for at least some time in the future. For example, in the 'half earth' proposal, (Wilson 2016) makes apparent the traditional thinking that 'nature' needs to be protected by some humans from other humans by sealing off networks of protected areas void of humans. Although the need to protect biodiversity is justified, Büscher et al. (2017: 408) have analysed this proposal and

---

[*] Originally published as: Ampumuza, C. (2022). Living with gorillas? Lessons from Batwa-Gorillas' convivial relations at Bwindi Forest, Uganda. Conservation & Society 20(2): 69-78.

found it to be, 'Infeasible, and will have dangerous and counter-effective consequences if implemented. The only logical conclusion of the Half-Earth proposal would be injustice on a large scale without effectively addressing the actual roots of the ecological crisis'.

The persistence of this fortress thinking also continues to marginalise Indigenous peoples' knowledge, capabilities, and long-term contributions to the survival of species (Montgomery et al 2020). Yet various scholars have demonstrated that through their long-standing interactions with their environment, Indigenous tribes made important discoveries and have specialised knowledge of the animal and plant species they live(d) with. Examples of these scholarly works include Pitman's (1935) accounts of the daily interactions between Indigenous Batwa and gorillas of Bwindi, Uganda, and Amir's (2019) exposition on local peoples' knowledge on gorillas and how this knowledge was marginalised by western scientists. Away from gorillas, Kistler et al. (2018) makes the role of Indigenous people apparent in the evolution of maize, and Kajobe (2007) reveals how Indigenous Batwa's taxonomy of stingless bees aided the study of the nesting biology of these bees. The body of literature on Traditional Ecological Knowledge (TEK) emphasises that, 'local traditional knowledge [...] rooted in an intimate and long-time involvement in local ecosystems, can be a crucial tool and source of knowledge for long-term sustainability and immediate resource conservation' (Menzies and Butler 2006: 1).

Although TEK has been recognised for more than two decades (Menzies and Butler 2006), the persistence and prominence of fortress thinking and the renewed emphasis on separating humans from non-humans points to a problem in TEK scholarship. The problem, Gómez-Baggethun and Reyes-García (2013) argue, is that TEK has predominantly focused on documenting, and lamenting the loss of TEK among Indigenous peoples and communities. As a result of the increased recognition of how traditional knowledge has been marginalised, some scholars have argued for a need to decolonise science and suggested some methodologies that reclaim the position of Indigenous people's knowledge (see Smith 1999; Cannon 2019). Büscher and Fletcher (2019: 286) have proposed the idea of convivial conservation—'the building of long-lasting, engaging and open-ended relationships with non-humans and ecologies'—to address the flaws of mainstream conservation. In their proposal, Büscher and Fletcher (2019) outline the five major elements of convivial conservation as: 1) moving from protected to promoted areas; 2) from saving nature to celebrating human and non-human nature; 3) from touristic voyeurism to engaged visitation; 4) from spectacular to everyday environmentalisms; and 5) from privatised expert technocracy to common democratic engagement. Importantly, convivial conservation emphasises historic reparations, including paying a Conservation Basic Income to affected local communities, as one of the ways to address the injustices that characterise mainstream conservation. It appears that this proposal echoes Indigenous peoples' arguments about the nature of being—inseparability and co-becoming of human and non-human worlds (see Suchet-Pearson et al. 2013). In other words, although the term was coined recently by Büscher and Fletcher, Indigenous people like the Batwa in Uganda have always practised convivial conservation through their long-standing open-ended interactions with nature.

The convivial conservation proposal aligns with the increasing evidence that 'nature' is neither pure, timeless nor static, but rather vibrant and inhabits everywhere (Lorimer 2015). Various species have exhibited adaptability to multiple and even different spaces. Notable examples are Asian elephants that seemed to have adapted to disturbed primary forests as well as the seasons of shifting cultivation known as chena cultivation (Lorimer 2010). Likewise, Hurn (2015) explains that Chacma baboons *Papio ursinus* of the South Africa's Cape Peninsula have been able to 'adapt to increased urbanisation through, amongst other techniques, the exploitation of non-traditional foodstuffs appropriated from their human neighbours' (Hurn 2015: 152). Ampumuza and Driessen (2021) reveal that mountain gorillas in Bwindi have adapted to cultivated fields and the presence of various groups of people with their gadgets such as tourists, and scientists among others. In his account of the lively biogeographers of the Asian elephants *Elephas maximus*, Lorimer (2010), notes the move by the Sri Lankan Department of Wildlife Conservation to open up to conviviality by testing the possibility of 'temporal resource partitioning'. This conviviality involves time-sharing between the elephants and chena cultivators, 'whereby elephants only graze outside of national parks during the fallow season for shifting cultivators' (Lorimer 2010: 500). This particular example of conviviality provides insights on how convivial conservation may already be working in practice.

Scholarly work on time sharing, resource partitioning, and other strategies such as respectful avoidance (Fletcher et al. 2020), common-sensing (Boonman-Berson et al. 2016) or learning to read the communication cues of non-humans (Hinchliffe and Whatmore 2006); seem to imply a possibility of coexistence. I take this coexistence to be premised on an ontology of interconnectedness of the human and non-human worlds. This way of being in intricate connectedness with nature is similar to what I discern in Indigenous ontologies (Suchet-Pearson et al. 2013) and therefore a point of intersection to be explored further. The Sri Lanka example provides evidence that governments can indeed make deliberate moves towards adopting context-specific conviviality informed by histories of the human and non-human relations. By accentuating meaningful long-term engagement and connectedness beyond or even without financial attachment, the conviviality model of conservation resonates with the aforementioned emphasis on traditional human and non-human relations. This makes convivial conservation an attractive proposal capable of reclaiming the place for traditional ecological knowledge in conserving biodiversity. This is so because the propositions put forward in the convivial conservation proposal seek redress of the historical exclusion of Indigenous communities— and therefore their ecological knowledges.

Unfortunately, the ontological roots of western conservation and the knowledge production processes that institutionalised this version of conservation are not given due attention in convivial conservation. Krauss (2021) explains other gaps in Büscher and Fletcher's (2019; 2020) proposal such as not explaining how the proposal builds on experiences with community-based and Indigenous conservation efforts in diverse contexts, lack of clarity on the practicalities of implementing the proposed elements, and failure to problematise gender issues: in sum, it is important for convivial conservation to continuously learn from Indigenous Peoples and local knowledges in diverse contexts and avoid external imposition by safeguarding that especially marginalised voices and knowledges are heard (Krauss 2021). Indeed, in order to create the radical transformation promised by convivial conservation (Massarella et al. 2021), I argue that it is important to problematise the foundations of conservation itself. Although both Ivan Illich's conviviality and convivial conservation proposals are rooted in the Global North (Krauss 2021), the idea comes through as a 'new' way of doing conservation, and a solution to the challenges of mainstream conservation. There is a question whether convivial conservation is sufficiently different from the way mainstream conservation was birthed to solve the problem of biodiversity loss. Because, as Kothari (2021) notes, Global North conservationists need to listen to the voices of the global South conservationists, especially the Indigenous people.

Therefore, I argue that taking interest in understanding multiple ontologies—varied ways of being—and knowledge production processes can ensure that convivial conservation actualises its transformative and decolonising potential. In a review of Büscher and Fletcher (2020)'s recent book, *The conservation revolution: Radical ideas for saving nature beyond the Anthropocene*, Dunlap (2020: 3) notes that paying more attention to the connection and affinity of convivial conservation to 'Indigenous horticultural practices, forest gardening and permaculture will advance its praxis'.

In this chapter, I advance this argument by applying it to the Batwa of Bwindi's Indigenous knowledges on living with gorillas. I do this by using insights from decolonisation literature, and stories told by the Batwa of Bwindi, to highlight the various ways in which convivial conservation can be advanced by taking into account multiple ontologies and knowledges from Indigenous and other conservations.

The following sections of the paper are arranged as follows: first, I explain the analytical concepts that guided my research. Next, I provide an overview of conservation practices at Bwindi, followed by a description of the methods used for this study. Thereafter, I use the stories told by the Batwa and other studies on Indigenous knowledges and practices to explore the ways in which Batwa's conservation knowledge and historical relations with gorillas could advance convivial conservation at Bwindi, and enrich convivial conservation more broadly.

Multiple Ontologies and Ontological Discord

Conservation practice has undergone several waves of change in line with paradigmatic and policy shifts, and global events such as colonialism, scientific advancements, and social movements (Ahebwa 2012). Various conservation practices and subsequent changes have been largely informed by particular views about nature and society. The main view by western scientists was that of a pristine nature, enshrined in the concept of wilderness (Adams 2013). This nature, therefore, had to be protected from humans, especially the Indigenous peoples whose lifestyles were perceived to be destructive, giving rise to protectionism model of conservation (Otto et al. 2013). Over time, the focus on nature has changed with the rising critique of the nature-society divide and silence about the injustices and structures underlying protectionism (Adams 2005; Martin et al. 2015). This critique is best illustrated by the literature known as political ecology—a field that has also undergone changes since its inception in the 1970s (Escobar 2010). While political ecology used to pay attention to power and broader conceptualisations of nature (Escobar describes this as PE1), and 'PE2' focused on engaging with epistemological debates, Escobar (2010) traces a new wave of critique (PE3), that pays more attention to issues of ontology.

I use the term ontology to mean the nature of reality and way of being (Woolgar and Lezaun 2015). I position myself in the body of literature that considers researching ontology as a way of problematising the assumption of a singular ordered world (Woolgar and Lezaun 2013). The turn to ontology is traceable in other fields such as medicine (Cussins 1996; Mol 2002), tourism studies (van der Duim et al. 2013), and natural resource management (Suchet-Pearson et al. 2013). A notable, and perhaps transformative, argument in these works is that; 'reality does not precede the mundane practices in which we interact with it, but is rather shaped within these practices' (Mol 1999: 75). This stance posits that reality is multiple, which has been illustrated using various examples such as the human body in medicine (Mol 2002), and gorilla tourism (van der Duim et al 2014) among others. Law (2015) uses the multiplicity argument to challenge the western/North-centric world-view of a single container world:

> one-world metaphysics are catastrophic in North–South encounters(...) They turn other worlds into the mere beliefs of people who are more or less like you and me – and correspondingly more or less (probably more) mistaken. They insist, in the end, that there is a universe and that we are all inside it, one way or another(...). On the contrary, (...) we do not live in a single container universe, but partially participate in multiple realities or a fractiverse. (Law 2015: 134)

Mol's (2002; 1999) and Law's (2015) multiplicity arguments imply that different realities coexist alongside each other. Among these are the Indigenous ontologies (Suchet-Pearson et al. 2013) alongside Western/Northern ontologies (Law 2015) The above quote from Law (2015) describes the western/northern ontologies characterised by singularity, separation and control. Suchet-Pearson et al. (2013: 196) explain that an Indigenous ontology—which is also multiple—can be best understood as an ontology of co-becoming where humans and non-human worlds share in and are all responsible for the continuous becoming of the world. Such a world replaces the language of separation, human-centeredness and control with the language of mutuality, connectedness, of becoming-together, diversely, respectfully and carefully in the world. Since convivial conservation also emphasises connectedness, understanding how Indigenous knowledge relates to convivial conservation is important. Such an understanding cannot only enrich both Indigenous knowledge and convivial conservation but also ease the current impasse in mainstream conservation. This impasse is defined by continued loss of biodiversity despite the numerous interventions (Büscher et al. 2017). I argue that ontological discord—the lack of harmony between Indigenous and other ontologies—is at the root of this impasse.

In this paper, I dwell on the disharmony between contemporary/ expert conservationist and Indigenous people on the nature of reality. Contrary to what most conservation planners commonly assert, I argue that this is a significant conservation problem at Bwindi, not the growing population, nor the need for alternative livelihood options to be provided for by market-based interventions. Rather, any intervention to address this core problem would start from the understanding of and explore the human and non-human connectedness that incessantly makes Bwindi and the world in general. This idea informed my empirical observations of the ways through which the Batwa's historical relations with gorillas could inform a foundation for all attempts to adopt a convivial conservation model at Bwindi. Before I proceed to the methods that inform this research, I first present a brief overview of conservation practices at Bwindi to set the context for the sections that follow.

Overview of Conservation Practices at Bwindi

Bwindi Impenetrable National Park is located in Southwestern Uganda, East Africa. The forest was first protected in 1932 as a forest reserve before becoming the Bwindi Impenetrable National Park in 1991 (Butynski and Kalina 1993). The Batwa, who were former hunter-gatherers, lived with other species at Bwindi for many years before European explorers and mainly the western scientists perceived them and their lifestyle as a threat to other non-human species. Now, the Batwa live in villages near the forest boundaries. They always emphasise the deep connectedness of humans, animals, and plants to the extent that they describe gorillas as relatives who stayed in the forest (Ampumuza et al. 2020).

As noted by Ampumuza et al. (2020), the declaration of Bwindi as a national park marked the start of the process to detach humans from non-human nature as all human activities, settlement, and access to the forest were halted. These changes in human and non-human relations sparked local communities' struggles to reinstate their access and traditional relationship with the forest. In their attempts to do so, 5% of the forest was burnt in 1992 (Mujuni et al. 2003) and park staff were denied communal services such as buying foodstuffs from the community (Ahebwa 2012). To address community concerns, Integrated Conservation and Development Projects (ICDPs) were introduced at Bwindi to implement a CBC approach (Blomley 2003; Mujuni et al. 2003).

ICDPs included restricted access to harvest ecologically determined quantities of selected species of plants for medicinal and livelihood use under the Multiple Use Zone (MUZ) intervention (Blomley 2003). In addition, gorilla tourism with a revenue sharing scheme (20% of park entrance fees reimbursed to a pool from which community livelihood projects are funded) was introduced (Ahebwa et al. 2012; van der Duim et al. 2014). In spite of these attempts to address the community concerns, Baker et al. (2012) note that enclosing Bwindi Forest as a park and ICDPs still play a critical role in the conflicts around Bwindi. This is because even the seemingly community responsive interventions are premised on a protectionist philosophy of controlling access, maintaining the boundaries, and designing all interventions, while the key decisions such as how much or what species to harvest, or not harvest, are taken by 'expert' scientists. Important to note is that these scientists are usually physically, emotionally, and spiritually detached from the forest. It is of little wonder that 'despite over 25 years of ICD at Bwindi, people still harvest resources illegally from the park' (Baker and Brinckerhoff 2015: 8). This is because, in my view, conservation 'experts' are still locked into the protectionist mode in which all interventions, community based and otherwise, focus on compensating communities with alternative livelihoods, and sources of income, rather than addressing communities' long-standing connectedness to all forms of nature where they dwell. Moreover, all the conservation models at Bwindi are predominantly informed by a particular mode of knowing championed by western scientists such as Fossey (1974) and Butynski (1984) that completely write out the knowledge and experiences of the local natives, especially the Batwa who have had historical relations with the gorillas.

From the overview above, it is clear that the bottom line to the conservation impasse at Bwindi is a discord between 'expert' conservationists' and communities' beliefs about the nature of being/ontology. Such discord is discernible in the assumption that Indigenous people are not conservationists and the underlying belief by conservationists that communities are threats to biodiversity. Such beliefs led, and continue to lead, to biased conclusions evident in descriptions such as 'Bwindi has become an island of forest in a sea of rural farmers and pit sawyers. There have been a number of encroachments along the boundary and in many places there is no transition zone between park and pasture' (UNEP-WCMC 2011 57). Other conclusions based on these biased views about communities continue to dominate debates on Mountain Gorilla *beringei beringei* conservation. Such debates argue for restricting encounters or space sharing between humans and gorillas (Butynski 1984; Seiler and

Robbins 2016). Moreover, communities, especially the Batwa, who have historically shared the forest with gorillas and other animals view non-human nature as an inseparable inherent part of humans. They feel strongly attached and a part of not only the fauna, but also the entire Bwindi environment (Ampumuza et al. 2020).

Methods: Storytelling

For this chapter, I used storytelling as a method of collecting data on the Batwa's past experiences living with gorillas. Stories not only provide vivid depiction of events, but also enable the researcher to observe emotional/non-verbal cues as stories are being told (Rooney et al. 2016). Both, the content and the ensuing emotions, provide rich information for social research. Storytelling as a qualitative tool for data collection works well in research around communities with rich oral traditions because stories clearly bring out the relational ways of being (Palacios et al. 2015).

The results of this chapter are drawn from a total of five personal stories told by Batwa (3) about their interactions with the gorillas, and scientists (2) whose ecological studies at Bwindi were guided by Batwa. There are not many surviving Batwa who grew up in the forest. I focused on the elderly Batwa (2 males and 1 female) who lived in the forest for at least 11 years before their eviction, and treated each as a separate case because they lived in different parts of the forest. I held multiple storytelling sessions with each individual in different places including at a fire place, in their homes, aboard a vehicle to and from Bwindi, and after meetings with Non-Governmental Organizations' (NGO) project staff.

Information obtained from these stories was triangulated with ethnographic village stays conducted in five different villages ranging from three weeks to one month, and unstructured interviews with two scientists who have worked with the same Batwa on research and other projects for more than ten years. This information was further supplemented with a review of literature about the Batwa and their life in the forest. In order to analyse the stories, I analysed the content of the stories for key emerging themes.

Tracing Conviviality in Stories of Historical Batwa-Gorilla Relations

The inseparability of human and non-human nature was central to all stories narrated by the Batwa. The connectedness is so engrained in their lives that it permeated through all their talks whereby they continuously referred to other non-human entities and the forest land as 'part of us'. They often mentioned that 'we are not complete without all these things' because of the long-term interactions.

Because of the connectedness mentioned above, the Batwa's ways of knowing the behaviour of gorillas and other non-humans was, and still is through sensory cues, experiential and spiritual sensibilities, and not by means of objectively observable variables. The Batwa particularly reminisced about how they progressively learned to read the imprints left by the gorillas, and to pay attention to their spiritual prompts to guide their movements and activities in the forest. They learned from what could be considered negative experiences. For example, one of the Batwa elders, who has guided several researchers in Bwindi, explained that while still living with the forest and other inhabitants, his relative was killed by a stressed gorilla because the animals had not yet learned when to avoid close encounters. He explained that

> gorillas are spiritual beings that is why an encounter with gorillas on my way to hunting signalled that I should not proceed. But there were also instances where we accidentally bumped into a solitary or group of gorillas. Those were the main causes of attacks, and in defence killing the gorilla before he killed you was the option. It still feels sad to think that I did that but to be honest, it happened. Over time we learned to pay attention to many non-verbal signs to guide our interaction with other members in the forest. For example, on our way to hunting, we looked out for cues such as scents, consistency of faecal matter, footprints, trails, leftover foods and vocalizations.

We interpreted watery stool as a sign of fearful flee from danger. In such cases we would take a different route to avoid attacks from an already frightened individual. (Batwa male elder, September 2019)

This excerpt illuminates the need for continuous learning of the ways though which our non-human counterparts communicate as an important aspect of conviviality (Boonman-Berson et al. 2016). Such a kind of openness to learning also implies allowing our affective faculties to be connected with those of our fellow dwellers on earth. The Batwa stories further demonstrated this devotion to connectedness as expressed in the following extract:

with time, we learned that gorilla's negative emotions (expressed through charging, attacking and biting) were partly a result of stress from high temperatures, and food scarcity. This is because we realised that attacks were common during the dry and hot months. Of course, life was stressful for us as well during those times. (Batwa female elder, June 2019)

Further to this, stories from researchers indicated that Batwa deployed these experiences or modes of knowing during fieldwork. For example, one of the researchers narrated:

On one of our field days, my other research assistants suggested that we go back to the forest to follow the gorillas and observe their afternoon behaviour. It was during those very dry and hot months and the sun was scorching hot. My Mutwa [singular for Batwa] research assistant warned us; the sun is too hot and you want to follow the gorilla? They will certainly attack and bite you! (Scientist, August 2019)

The warning in the above excerpt demonstrates the sensibility of the field assistant to the connectedness of the weather, gorilla's bodily processes, and the field exercise. In other stories of encounters with bees, elephants, chimpanzees, as well as people from other tribes, Batwa often explained that they paid attention to past experiences, scents, vocalisation, faecal matter, leftover foods, and most importantly listened to their 'spirits' in order to adapt to the changing moods, and experiences of their co-inhabitants of Bwindi forest.

It is important to note that these relations have not been erased by several decades of physical separation. In fact, all my research participants were surprised when I asked about their views on the restoration of human and non-human relations. They wondered if there was a time when the two were ever separated because to them 'physical separation by boundaries never separates the inner connection, unless if you are talking about restoring the physical interaction' (Female elder 2, August, 2021). This belief was justified by narrating several instances revealing the more-than-physical connectedness between the Batwa and non-human co-inhabitants of Bwindi forest. They disclosed that most of the relations with other nature transcend physicality since particular individuals had, and still have special revelations, powers and abilities to speak with nature.

Two particular situations stand out: first, while on a walk through the forest, one of my colleagues probed further about the possibilities of taking us to worship at the sacred tree that the guide had mentioned. Our guide informed us that he was not eligible or gifted to step in that particular section of the forest. He added that even if the eligible person was with us, we still could not be taken because it is forbidden. Further to that, our guide revealed that even mentioning the name, or pointing to the direction of that spot in the forest had serious consequences on one's body. In another story, a female Mutwa shared an example when she called up obukyere (a type of amphibian) from the stream on their way to collect seeds from the forest, and another when she talked to an agitated gorilla to save her non-Batwa colleagues from the attack. She clarified that on both instances, she did not use vocalisation as it is with those who habituate gorillas. At the stream, she simply informed obukyere that she had longed to see them, and they immediately gathered at the spot where she was. She collected and thanked them for giving her the energy and released them back into the stream. For the gorilla, she simply pleaded for forgiveness and the Silverback went away. She explained that this is all possible even after several years of physical separation because their connection with nature starts even before someone is born as the mother introduces the growing foetus to her outside environment. This idea was corroborated by a male participant who shortened our conversation in order to perform a ritual in a nearby community forest for his pregnant wife.

Although these connections still exist despite the physical separation, the Batwa still suffer the consequences of the separation evident in the stories of their current life outside the forest. Some of them indicated that their supernatural instincts to go and visit the forest, or particular hot springs for healing, meditation, revive their energies or simply get immersed in nature are constrained because these reasons do not make sense to the conservationists. They are only allowed to collect the stipulated materials at a time approved by the park managers. In their narration of the current situation, all participants challenged the view that they pose risks to the gorillas. To them, this view can only be validated by reflecting on whether biodiversity, including gorillas, existed at the time 'intruders' first visited Bwindi.

Finally, the Batwa view western conservation as 'detached and profit-driven,' which is the opposite of their reality of conservation. They expressed strong convictions that non-human nature of Bwindi misses them too, that is why they respond at any opportunity of their physical interaction with the forest such as the call to participate in projects such as the Bwindi Batwa Forest Experience. To them conservation is not about protecting species, but rather a change of who should be in the forest (tourists, rangers, researchers) and who should not (local communities). They further acknowledged that it would be very difficult for them to regain unlimited physical interaction with the gorillas because the forest was turned into a 'garden' for government and partners to harvest money. Yet to them, the intrinsic value of the feeling and communion brought by physically interacting with other nature is invaluable as one of them concluded that:

> government tries to bring projects under revenue sharing scheme and some benefit from them but most of us are left out. But what they do not understand is that no amount of money can give me the feeling I get as I sit in the hot spring and interact with all the trees, herbs, insects and other animals. In our beliefs, nature is not bought or paid for. We shared our resources, even when we first interacted with abairu settlers; we did not ask for money, we simply shared forest products and they too shared with us their farm products. The same can still be done. We know that the government cannot let go of the tourism money, but let them share the forest with us. They should remain in charge of tourism, but allow us unrestricted physical interaction with the forest. (Female elder, August 2021)

The facial expressions of this particular participant as she narrated the feeling of interacting with the hot spring and the surrounding environment is incomparable to worth anything in this world. I could feel the nostalgia in her voice, with eyes closed facing upwards and her hands spread out, while tears uncontrollably rolled down her cheeks. All these observations motivated me to explore the ways in which convivial conservation can radically transform the western view of conservation by capturing these views of reality.

Discussion: Advancing Conviviality in the Context of Bwindi

In this chapter, I started by delineating the core conservation problem at Bwindi as ontological discord—the disharmony between 'expert' conservationists' and the Indigenous Batwa's knowledge of reality. I argued that the Batwa practised convivial conservation, although they did not label it as such. Additionally, I noted that Krauss's (2021) analysis highlights several gaps in the proposed convivial conservation model, including insufficient attention to knowledge production processes, and practical ways of implementing the proposals. However, I argue that there is need to take a step back and problematise the roots—ontologies—that produced and sustain mainstream conservation, as a starting point to realising convivial conservation. To do so, I use Batwa's stories of practical convivial conservation with a view of advancing convivial conservation by challenging the ontology and knowledges that produced western conservation in various ways.

First, attempts to decolonise conservation or provide alternative conservation models need to pay attention to ontology. This is important because, as Mol (2002: 7) argues, ontologies 'inform and are informed by' the objects we deal with such as bodies, systems and technologies, and in this case, nature, threats to nature and conservation models. So far, I have noted that whereas northern ontologies purify nature and view humans as threats to this nature, the stories told by the Batwa, like other Indigenous ontologies, indicate a different reality. The stories indicated that their mundane practices of gathering, hunting, worship, bathing in hot springs, and treatment of ailments among others weaved into deeper, inner and more than physical relations. And, through these relations, the Batwa, the forest and all other nature co-constituted each other. In fact, the female elder's story of her 'conversation' with gorillas and 'obukyere', especially the fact that these non-humans responded or acted according to her verbal utterances, attests to the persistence of relations even after decades of physical separation. These stories provide insights into the practical ways through which the shift from spectacular to everyday environmentalism proposed by convivial conservation can be planned by taking into account the multiple ontologies already highlighted by Law (2015), Suchet-Pearson et al. (2013), Pitman (1935) and Amir (2019) so that not a single ontology is considered at the expense of another. This is not far-fetched because Mabele, Krauss and Kiwango (2022) demonstrate that the convivial conservation proposal to move from the concept of protected areas to promoted areas resonates with the *Ubuntu* philosophy.

Additionally, the philosophy is also seen in practice through human and non-human relations of care and co-becoming. The revival of these relations and intersections point to the possibilities of overcoming the pitfalls brought about by ontologies that emphasise separation in western conservation.

Second, ontologies define the mode of knowledge production. Convivial conservation's focus on re-initiating human and non-human ways of co-becoming suggests a shift in the mode of knowledge production for inhabiting with nature. This shift relates to the argument for historic reparations for the damages caused in the process of implementing both mainstream and the 'new' market-based conservation. While Büscher and Fletcher's (2019; 2020) argument for historic reparations focuses on people and their land, Smith (1999), Amir (2019) as well as Mbaria and Ogada (2016) point out that colonisation not only parcelled up people's land but also their knowledge and minds. Hence, if convivial conservation wishes to be a decolonial approach, it should begin by broadening the scope of reparations to address the colonization of local knowledge and focus attention on decolonizing conservation knowledge production. As my analysis of the stories of the Batwa reveals, the western construct of nature and conservation was the starting point of dispossession, militarisation and all other injustices they have experienced since the establishment of the Bwindi Impenetrable Park. The ecologists demeaned local ways of life, knowledge, and accounts of human-wildlife interactions, dismissing them as unscientific, and excluded them from their publications (Amir 2019).

Unfortunately, as Smith (1999) observes, such trends are traceable to date regardless of whether or not the Indigenous peoples are located in the South or have become scholars in the North. For example, one can feel Spivak's (cited in Smith 1999) frustration by the consolidated opposition to Indigenous knowledge in the academy, and how scholars from the North do not want to listen or take seriously the contributions of scholars from the South. But what exactly does decolonising conservation knowledge practically entail? Cannon (2019) argues that decolonising requires non-Indigenous scientists to deliberately step back and let Indigenous peoples take the lead. Such a step will be rooted in a realisation and understanding that the knowledge held by Indigenous people is not inferior or less scientific than western science/knowledge (Cannon 2019). Smith (1999: 98) argues that this paradigm shift will be a deliberate 'long-term process involving the bureaucratic, cultural, linguistic and psychological divesting of colonial power'.

However, as the Batwa stories reveal, and as Büscher and Fletcher (2019) have observed, going back to the original state of affairs is not feasible. Instead, the task of realising the idea of convivial conservation requires scholars and practitioners to reinstate and incorporate Indigenous peoples' realities into research and resultant publications. Particular attention should be paid to the knowledges that arise from more-than-physical interactions and observations during fieldwork. As the Batwa stories show, it is these ways of open-mindedness—to learn from, to be affected by and affect our fellow dwellers on earth (human and non-human)—that mark the starting point of convivial living. Therefore, even our methods and final outputs of these methods should adjust to these sensibilities. In short, this means multiplying realities by drawing from various claims: scientific, Indigenous and any other that may arise depending on the context (see, for example, Tsai et al. 2016). Practically, there should be an increase in publications from scholars from the South, either singly or jointly with their counterparts on the North, and acceptance of such as science too. Therefore, by restoring Indigenous and Southern peoples' ontologies and knowledges, convivial conservation scholarship can productively contribute to this aspect of reparations.

Finally, in addition to the call for historic reparations, Büscher and Fletcher (2019, 2020) suggest a Conservation Basic Income for people living in or near in conservation areas. My reading of their explanation is that there is a category of people who have accumulated wealth from exploiting resources at the expense of the less or not-wealthy category, and the first should share it with the latter. This idea is somewhat akin to the sharing principle held by the Batwa, but differs in a sense that the Batwa-sharing transcends material stuff to values, physical and other spaces as well as values. Moreover, as highlighted in the stories told by the Batwa, financial sharing arrangements at Bwindi take the form of a revenue-sharing scheme that is riddled with complications in its implementation and exacerbated by corruption (see also Ahebwa, et al. 2012; Franks and Twinamatsiko 2017). The income argument is theoretically a good idea; however, it also places the communities in a recipient position and risks reproducing marginalising effects. As much as these communities are economically disadvantaged, they are greatly endowed with social, cultural, spiritual and intellectual wealth that is only hampered by the restrictions of 'western conservation' ideals (Ampumuza et al. 2020). Therefore, although the sharing of income is a good idea, it should be expanded to include sharing of powers and control of the sites that define the communities involved.

Conclusion

This chapter has used insights from stories of Batwa's historic convivial relations with non-human nature at Bwindi to explore ways through which convivial conservation can be advanced. I explained that the foundations of 'western conservation' and its related challenges lie in disregarding and omitting other ontologies and knowledges about conserving biodiversity (see also Adams 2005). Although the first western explorers, ecologists and later colonialists witnessed the said conservation practices, they dismissed them as barbaric, superstitious, or inferior. Subsequently their publications on the reality of nature and guidelines to conserve that particular reality of nature did not acknowledge other realities of what constitutes nature. I have also argued that most of the propositions put forward by convivial conservation resonate with Batwa and other Indigenous ways of relating with non-human nature. However, convivial conservation should explicitly problematise the ontologies that inform and are informed by mainstream conservation and also ensure that the concept's rooting in Global North academia does not further marginalise other ways of knowing. The scope of historic reparations should go beyond land to include knowledges, and while the idea of a Conservation Basic Income may seem a good welfare idea, it is likely to jeopardise the objective of convivial conservation by placing local communities in a subservient position. If convivial conservation is to be realised, then its scholars and advocates should take a step back and allow communities to co-create knowledge with their human and non-human counterparts via affective means as illustrated by the Batwa's ways of knowing nature.

Chapter 5:

Decolonising, Conviviality and Convivial conservation: Towards a Convivial SDG 15, Life on Land?*

By Judith E. Krauss

Introduction

> The only solution to the environmental crisis is the shared insight of people that they would be happier if they could work together and care for each other.
> Ivan Illich (1973: 50)

In their article 'Towards convivial conservation' (2019, also chapter 2 of this collection) and book *The Conservation Revolution* (2020), Büscher and Fletcher propose a transformative vision for conservation which partly builds on Ivan Illich's 1973 *Tools for Conviviality*. Conviviality, as developed by Illich and other scholars in Cuernavaca, Mexico, proposes a society founded on justice and freedom in responsible interdependence, implemented through participatory, democratic decision-making. A convivial society is also founded upon knowledge and tools not serving individualized profit and industrialized production, but the common good, while limiting resource consumption for the rich. This unified vision and related principles have recently inspired increasing debate (e.g. Caillé et al. 2011; Alphandéry et al. 2020). The still-evolving ideas of 'convivial conservation' aim to move beyond recent proposals around 'new conservation' and its market-based antecedents, and the countervailing, vociferous support for exclusion- or restriction-based ideas. Büscher and Fletcher's vision (2019; 2020) instead champions

---

* Originally published as: Krauss, J.E. (2021). Decolonizing, conviviality and convivial Conservation: Towards a convivial SDG 15, Life on Land? Journal of Political Ecology 28(1).

co-existence, biodiversity and justice, and challenges broader drivers of environmental degradation rooted in the primacy of economic growth.

At the same time, there has been intensifying debate about decolonizing policy, practices and research around conservation, the environment and political ecology, calling for conservation ideas and approaches to acknowledge, address and move beyond abiding unequal dynamics rooted in colonial pasts and perpetuated through socio-ecological injustices to the present (Asiyanbi 2019; Domínguez and Luoma 2020; Kasaona 2020; Lang 2018; Mbaria and Ogada 2016; Ogada 2017; 2019; Schulz 2017; Survival International 2018; Sultana 2021; Zanotti et al. 2020). Illich's conviviality is either at the root of, or contributing to, diverse discussions of transformative change away from dominance by industrialist paradigms from the Global North (Caillé et al. 2011; Alphandéry et al. 2020), while convivial conservation is also increasingly debated as a radical, transformative option for biodiversity conservation that prioritizes justice (cf. Massarella et al. 2021; and others in this collection).[1]

Consequently, this chapter asks: what role could conviviality play in envisioning alternative, decolonizing conservation ideas? To what extent can the ideas of conviviality and convivial conservation, with roots in the Global North, serve as decolonial options (Mignolo & Escobar 2015; Tlostanova and Mignolo 2009)? Can they highlight issues which have arisen as a result of the coloniality-modernity matrix of power, and use decolonial thinking and writing to address them? This is an important question because there is a need to assess how these convivial ideas enable moving beyond top-down conservation paradigms, policies and practices which are rooted in colonial, racialized understandings of human and nonhuman nature and their interrelations, and which perpetuate social and ecological injustices. The chapter's original contribution is thus analyzing conviviality and convivial conservation through a decolonizing lens. It argues that Illich's conviviality and related ideas have much to offer in envisioning alternative, decolonizing conservation ideas as a unified philosophy: one that promotes grassroots, democratic decision-making, living within limits by the rich, and emphasizing interdependencies between and within humanity and the environment. However, to be fully decolonial options, they need to avoid imposition and must adequately incorporate intergenerational and marginalized viewpoints to address hierarchies of difference across dimensions such as race, gender, age, status or (dis)ability. After a discussion of positionality and research design, this chapter starts by making a brief case for decolonizing conservation. It will introduce Illich's and related understandings of conviviality before summarizing Büscher and Fletcher's (2019; 2020) proposals for convivial conservation. It will then situate both proposals' strengths and challenges through a decolonizing lens. A final section outlines how these considerations could be applied to reforming the Sustainable Development Goal (SDG) 15 (UN 2015) dedicated to conserving biodiversity and ecosystems.

Positionality and Research Design

I am adding my voice to a growing chorus questioning how we got here, and how conservation can change (e.g., Adeyeye et al. 2019; Kasaona 2020; Mbaria and Ogada 2016; Rodríguez et al. 2007). My considerations come from the position that natural resource conservation is vital given high rates of biodiversity loss (Diaz et al. 2019), while acknowledging that conservation, and indeed any manifestations of decolonial, decolonizing or convivial conservation will not take the same form everywhere. Western-centric logics continue to dominate the ways nature is understood, and these have widespread ramifications for policy and practice. It is important to question them (Adams and Mulligan 2003).

I must acknowledge my own positionality as a white person working for a British university writing about conservation. I am aware of some key risks inherent in this chapter, including jumping on the decolonizing bandwagon (Moosavi 2020), and the wider danger of contributions by white scholars (including Illich, Büscher and Fletcher) receiving more attention than those of scholars and knowledge-holders of color. My aim is to reflect the sentiment expressed so aptly by an Aboriginal activist group in Queensland in 1975: 'If you have come to help me, you are wasting your time. If you have come because your liberation is bound up with mine, then let us work together' (often ascribed to Lilla Watson alone, but attributed to the collective by her; Toporek 2013: 21). Consequently, I have striven to avoid a neo-colonial, recolonizing or appropriating position, by drawing on and giving due credit to diverse authorship and scholarship beyond Northerncentrism (Moosavi 2020), building on several years of learning from and engaging with decolonizing and decolonial debates (cf. acknowledgements and other co-authored work, e.g. Collins et al. 2021, and Mabele et al., chapter 3, this volume).

The case-study of SDG 15 in relation to convivial conservation is appropriate for several reasons. Firstly, the SDGs were meant to be different, after the Millennium Development Goals were formulated by a 'small group of rich countries' without input by the global community or from civil-society organizations (Sen and Mukherjee 2014: 189). The SDGs were originally proposed by government representatives from Colombia and Guatemala, explicitly aimed to go beyond previously agreed language (Chasek and Wagner 2016), and sought to leave no one behind (UN 2015: 1). However, it has been shown that the SDGs do not fundamentally challenge existing global power asymmetries (Gupta and Vegelin 2016) and can contravene decolonial intentions (Hope 2022; Krauss et al. 2022). The SDGs' relevance for conservation policy is their importance as a global governance paradigm influencing practice and monitoring of progress towards development goals. I focus on the detail of SDG 15, the SDG dedicated to terrestrial conservation and ecosystems, illustrating its problems and how we could move beyond it (Maldonado-Torres 2007). I situate recent interest in conviviality and convivial conservation with regards to broader decolonizing conservation efforts, while providing concrete suggestions for how to distil conviviality and decolonizing principles into a framework that shapes the present and future of conservation in SDG 15.[2]

A Brief Case for Decolonizing Conservation

To discuss conviviality and convivial conservation through a decolonizing lens, it is important to highlight why 'decolonizing conservation' is increasingly debated. It is vital to first clarify what is meant by decolonizing. Fanon (2002) describes with great force of language the abiding, systematic, all-encompassing violence perpetrated by colonialism. Across all spheres of life, including education, livelihoods and infrastructure, colonialism created debasing and inhumane hierarchies of difference solely based on skin color, to distinguish between colonizers and the *damnés*, literally the damned (Fanon 2002). This has produced abiding patterns of coloniality and power which affect all human relations, including labor and knowledge production (Maldonado-Torres 2007). These block genuine mutual learning among equals (Quijano 2007). Building on Fanon (2000), Tuck and Yang have argued that decolonization is not a metaphor (2012): efforts to diversify curricula in Northern universities cannot be conflated with the violence of settler colonialism and the need to restore land to Indigenous peoples. While it is unclear to what degree Tuck and Yang's (2012) equation of decolonization with repatriating Indigenous land and life is specific to settler colonialism, their reminder of the long-lived pain inflicted by colonialism and colonization is important. Collins's insightful concept of 'colonial residue' (2019) highlights colonization and coloniality manifest in people and societal structures, shaping the ownership and the fate of land and resources, and the structures influencing and implementing these decisions. Collins's work on Guyana and Suriname, profoundly shaped by colonial relations, questions what 'decolonizing' could return to. Here, Maldonado-Torres's (2016) distinction is relevant between specific historical periods of colonialism and colonization, and the abiding power dynamics resulting from colonial-and-cognate mindsets ('coloniality'). In his understanding, decolonial work encompasses efforts to rehumanize the world and break 'hierarchies of difference that dehumanize subjects and communities and that destroy nature' (2016: 10).

In this spirit, this chapter uses 'decolonizing' and 'decolonial' interchangeably. Both encompass efforts to break down hierarchies of difference constructed in colonial times, and that persist to this day through racialized power dynamics and perpetuation of socio-ecological injustices. Decolonizing conservation is used as a way to attain the breaking down of colonial structures called for by Maldonado-Torres, while addressing the matrices of power which underlie and result from them. This dual understanding will ensure a focus on the principles and processes of decolonization, rather than seeking to identify any non-colonial point of return. The emphasis on the residues left by colonization and colonial ways of thinking does facilitate attention to decolonial options (Mignolo and Escobar 2015; Tlostanova and Mignolo 2009): this means using decolonial thinking and writing to identify and address ongoing injustices which are rooted in the past, and linked to land and resources.

Ideas of conservation rooted in colonial, racialized understandings of human and nonhuman nature perpetuate and exacerbate social and environmental injustices for those living or working with conservation in the Global South. Conservation combines diverse movements and world views (Adams 2003; Chua et al. 2020; Sandbrook et al. 2019). However, some problematic ideas conceived in the Global North have proved pervasive: for instance, romanticized ideals of untouched, 'wild' nature, which were formulated in opposition to the Industrial Revolution, were transferred to the Global South[3] (Adams and Mulligan 2003; Plumwood 2003). They are intricately linked to a dualist separation of humans and nature (Salleh 2016), equally conceived in the Global North. Among the stricter protected areas, these ideas have consequences for local peoples whose livelihoods can be altered or eliminated by being separated from resources for the sake of preserving 'wild' nature. These dynamics can lead to land in the Global South, and the aspirations of people who live on it, being regarded as less important than imposed conservation ideals (Asiyanbi and Lund 2020; Kasaona 2020). This entangled web of European-derived ideas entails significant social, economic and ecological consequences for those living and working with conservation, yet biases around race or gender often go unacknowledged (Adams and Mulligan 2003, Duffy et al. 2019; Mbaria and Ogada 2016). These and other examples are not only problematic in and of themselves for the contexts and peoples involved. Hall's (1992) crucial insight is that the ways that ideas are represented *limit* other ways of constructing these notions: this means that Eurocentric ontologies, epistemologies, and policy formulations dominate and displace alternative framings which could prioritize Indigenous, decolonial, and justice-focused logics.

Unjust ideas are inextricably linked with knowledge and knowledge production, which are fundamentally imbricated with power (Noxolo 2017). They start with structures in need of decolonizing in higher education and in pedagogy (e.g. Bhambra et al. 2018; Langdon 2013; Mbembe 2016; Santos 2018). Scholars from the Global South have long emphasized the importance of local leadership in setting conservation agendas (e.g. Kothari 2021; Rodríguez et al. 2007). An open letter with over 230 signatories critiqued the recent debate around 'new conservation' and countervailing protection support, arguing it was formulated by a narrow group of mostly male conservationists from the Global North. Instead, they called for a more-inclusive vision, granting equal roles to women and scientists and practitioners of diverse ethnicities and cultures (Tallis, Lubchenco et al. 2014). The types of knowledge recognized and legitimated tend to diminish local expertise, and even participatory forest management predominantly builds on formal, scientific knowledge provided by professional foresters (Sungusia et al. 2020). Conscious, equitable efforts to acknowledge and empower knowledges and knowledge holders beyond a Western canon are vital in any efforts to decolonize conservation (Agrawal 1995; Chilisa 2017; Shackeroff and Campbell 2007; Zanotti et al. 2020). Indigenous knowledges and labor, central to many conservation and conservation research projects, are characterized by complex, alternating processes of erasure, performance and 'survivance'[4]: stark power asymmetries with conservation actors require careful negotiations with prevailing knowledge systems (Rubis and Theriault 2019).

Introducing Conviviality

In 1973, in his influential book *Tools for Conviviality*, Ivan Illich formulated an explicit vision of a convivial society, i.e., one built on 'individual freedom realized in personal interdependence' (1973: 12). Alongside survival and the control of work as key conditions for conviviality, Illich names justice, which is commonly 'debased to mean the equal distribution of institutional wares' (1973: 12), but in fact needs to be both distributive and participatory (1973: 38). Rather than equality being in the possession of industrial goods, justice to Illich emphasizes participation in decision-making and creating new images of the future that are not contingent on another person's enforced labor, learning or consumption.

Conviviality, which Illich sees explicitly as the opposite of industrial productivity, is 'autonomous and creative intercourse among persons, and the persons with their environment' (1973: 12). The only limit on freedom is to guarantee another's equal freedoms. It is important to note, however, that freedom for Illich is not understood as maximally free markets in the sense of *laissez-faire*-economics, but as freedom in responsible interdependence. His thinking rejects 'tools' (understood as all instruments and mechanisms of material and consultative production) being hijacked by elites and experts to reinforce hierarchies and decision-making by the few (cf. Deriu 2014; Garcia 2009). Instead, Illich emphasizes the significance of broad-based participatory processes: for safeguarding individuals' access to communal tools, and for reaching social agreements. In short, conviviality is a passionate appeal not to cede control of society to the few, but to encourage the many to reach agreements that enhance individual freedom cognizant of interdependencies between people, but also with the environment and planetary limits (Barkin 2019). To Illich, this convivial vision was not only a line of thinking, but a vocation (Atasay and Bourassa 2013). It incorporated inclusive, broad-based decision-making, justice considering all human and environmental interdependencies, and curtailed resource consumption by the rich. This strength of conviction may account for why his ideas inspire scholars to this day, to build transformative visions (e.g. Caillé et al. 2011, Alphandéry et al. 2020).

Following study in Austria and the Vatican, and his work as a priest with Puerto Ricans in North America, Illich expressed sharp criticism of the institutionalization of religion. He saw the roots of Western modernization and industrialization as interlinked (Mert 2015). Illich's book, *Tools for Conviviality* (1973), resulted particularly from conversations at the research center in Cuernavaca, Mexico, which he helped establish. Illich's thoughts are fundamentally radical in terms of questioning commonly accepted pillars of the world's systems, such as compulsory education or industrialized lifestyles (Zaid 2011). This predilection for doubting the bigger picture is reflected and rooted in Illich's vocal criticism of the Western-centric Roman-Catholic church, and his critique of modernization as manifest in the developmentalist paradigm of the Truman years, the export of which to Latin America he saw as disastrous (Hornedo 2002; Olvera and Márquez, n.d.).

Since the heyday of his writing in the 1970s, Illich's work has inspired many. Illich's thoughts on deschooling society (1971) have sparked debate among education scholars for decades (e.g. Gintis 1972; Narodowski and Botta 2017) and, in combination with his ideas on conviviality, raise questions about knowledge being made freely available online (Hart 2001; Jandrić 2014). Computer pioneers such as Lee Felsenstein were inspired by Illich to make computers available and accessible to ordinary people rather than just to the technological elite (Isaacson 2014); arguably, open-source software is the embodiment of convivial tools (Janaszek 2010). Equally, for scholars of bioethics (Garcia 2009) and degrowth (Espejo 2011), conviviality resonates in terms of recognizing human, social and environmental interdependencies and limits. Caillé et al.'s dialogues on the convivial society which is to come (2011) was further developed into the *Convivialist manifesto: Declaration of interdependence*, which was signed by French-speaking authors from over ten countries. In recognizing interdependence among humans and with the environment, it formulates four principles: common humanity, common sociality, legitimate individuation, and creative opposition (Alphandéry et al. 2013; Convivialist International 2020). This has since been developed into a second, more internationally oriented convivialist manifesto which adds as a fifth principle common naturality and recognizing humans' interdependence with, and responsibility for, nonhuman nature. It imagines, and aims to inspire concrete steps towards, a post-neoliberal future in light of youth mobilization, accelerating climate change and the erosion of humanist ideals (Alphandéry et al. 2020; Convivialist International 2020).

Some thinkers discuss conviviality without reference to Illich. Bauman's (2013) *modus covivendi*, i.e. negotiating living with people of divergent mindsets, has some parallels, but no explicit reference. Hinchliffe and Whatmore (2006) side with more posthumanist understandings of conviviality (e.g. Castree and Nash 2004), citing Illich's perceived (more implicit than explicit) focus on the environment as a reason to look beyond his work. Instead, they develop a 'politics of conviviality' to negotiate the messiness of living together with more-than-humans in urban spaces (2006), which is another source of inspiration for Büscher and Fletcher (2019; 2020). However, my focus is Illich's conviviality: the reasons are his thinking's abiding transdisciplinary relevance (cf. e.g. Caillé et al. 2011), its popularity as a value-based and ethics-based tool (Hidalgo-Capitán and Cubillo-Guevara 2017), its rejection of excessive consumption of the rich. Illich's work is thus unique as a unified philosophy promoting participation and justice, living within limits by the rich, and interdependence, compared with other versions of conviviality, while showing some intellectual parallels with decolonization.

Different authors have traced the links between Illich's thinking and two much-discussed philosophies in the decolonial space: *buen vivir* (Giarracca 2010; Cortez n.d.) and *Ubuntu* (Inman 1999; Shizha 2016). Albó (2011) illustrates that the Aymara notion of *suma qamaña* or *vivir bien/buen vivir*, means to live, dwell, rest and care for others in a good, generous manner. A second, important pillar is living well with nature, Mother Earth or *Pacha Mama*. In combination, the two mandate that the world should not revolve around economic growth, but around human growth, and that humans should accept a strong sense of reciprocity with and be a harmonious part of *Pacha Mama* (Albó 2011). This is while recognizing that economic, political and social power structures are significant barriers to the implementation of these principles. The idea of *suma qamaña* is thus embedded within intense convivial reciprocity between people and nature, going far beyond material connections. This extends equally to the notion of just resource extraction limits, and the prioritization of ethical values over economic values (Giarracca 2010), both of which parallel Illich. Equally, there are parallels between conviviality and *Ubuntu*, which Chemhuru (2019b) defines as a philosophy from southern Africa that, unlike much Western thought, starts with communities and their interconnectedness rather than the individual. '*Umuntu Ngumuntu Ngabantu*', derived from the Nguni people— Xhosa, Ndebele and Zulu (Le Grange 2019)—is understood to be its quintessence, meaning a person is a person through another person (Naicker 2011: 458). A person is understood through the triad between those who have passed, those who are alive, and those who are yet to come (Terblanché-Greeff 2019). This ethic of care extends beyond humans towards the physical and natural world (Chibvongodze 2016; Ewuoso and Hall 2019), which constitutes a key parallel to Illich's conviviality (Inman 1999). Scholars including Naicker (2011) and Terblanché-Greeff (2019) emphasize that *Ubuntu*, given its inclusive, interdependent premise, is well-suited to capture and promote the voices of under-heard communities in global discussions around environmental change. This parallels Illich's emphasis on giving a voice to all, including the least heard. Illich's understanding of conviviality thus converges with *buen vivir* and *Ubuntu* on resource consumption limits for the rich, as well as principles of joint, participatory decision-making as part of a commitment to responsible, just interdependence with humans and the environment.

What makes Illich's conviviality attractive as a decolonial option for conservation, and enriching to existing decolonizing debates, is tapping into an existing, unified approach that incorporates several crucial elements as integral, equal parts of cohabitation. Firstly, it emphasizes the conviviality of humans with their environment as a form of freedom in responsible interdependence. For conviviality to succeed, prior agreement on this concept of mutual, interconnected responsibility between and within people and the environment is crucial. Convivial approaches do not equate to 'anything goes', which would violate the notion of mutual responsibility on which *Ubuntu* and Illich converge. Secondly, it involves challenging the excesses of industrial production and resource extraction by the rich, akin to *buen vivir*, to rein in industrial growth as well as to challenge the schism between those who have too much and those who don't have enough. Thirdly, Illich's conviviality makes equity compulsory, rather than optional, emphasizing that living together well is predicated on distributive and participatory justice. Finally, it promotes the type of grassroots decision-making and consultation that has long been championed for marginalized people, but rarely implemented in conservation schemes (Kiwango and Mabele, chapter 15 of this collection; Adeyeye et al. 2019). The unified commitment to limit resource consumption and promote justice and inclusive democracy are all integral pillars of Illich's thinking in a way that is absent from much dominant conservation thinking (Krauss 2022), inspiring alternative ideas.

Introducing Convivial Conservation

Over the past decade, 'new conservation' has been advocated to save nature, especially by Kareiva, *et al.* (e.g. Marvier et al. 2012). They argue that in an era of perhaps unstoppable large-scale anthropogenic change, embracing the opportunities it creates, such through as corporate partnerships, is the model to promote much-needed biodiversity conservation. This approach, which arguably builds on prior market-based conservation ideas, was met with resistance by a countervailing movement favoring instead a renewed commitment to protecting nature by excluding people from it and restricting use (e.g. Wuerthner et al. 2015). Convivial conservation, building partly on Illich's conviviality, aspires to move beyond both these paradigms and their antecedents, but is also a response to the bigger political-economic picture, in which certain political imaginaries increasingly favor anti-environmentalist, nationalist and arguably anti-grassroots stances.

Büscher and Fletcher (2019; 2020), in the first element of the convivial conservation vision, propose moving from protected to *promoted areas*, which are 'fundamentally encouraging places where people are considered welcome visitors, dwellers or travelers' (2020: 92). This chimes with the second proposal, shifting from saving nature to celebrating human and nonhuman nature, discarding the idea that certain humans should save nonhuman nature from certain other humans who need to be excluded from it, and instead championing both human and nonhuman nature as special and unique in recognition of their diverse needs and interdependencies. A third aspect concerns shifting from touristic voyeurism to engaged visitation, proposing that seeing 'wild' nature should not be a short-term elite privilege but a long-term democratic engagement based on the principles of socio-ecological justice and degrowth. A fourth aspect emphasizes the importance of overcoming 'spectacular' nature and commodified images in favor of everyday environmentalisms (cf. Cronon 1996, on what nature to aspire to). A final suggestion concerns moving away from privatized expert technocracy to common democratic engagement, and from monetized value to a non-monetized 'embedded value' through humans and nonhumans living together, much in the spirit of 'areas conserved by Indigenous peoples and local communities' (ICCAs; Borrini-Feyerabend and Campese 2017).

To their credit, Büscher and Fletcher (2019; 2020) also develop their vision into proposals for concrete actions. These encompass:

- historic reparations, i.e. compensating marginalized communities for past injustice perpetrated in the name of conservation;

- a conservation basic income for community members in or around protected areas to lead a locally defined decent life;

- rethinking (relations with) corporations, given the need for a different economic model prioritizing extraction limits and eventually degrowth;

- a global 'convivial conservation coalition' promoting just conservation.

Finally, Büscher and Fletcher's (2019; 2020) theory of change entails, firstly, thinking about power as both structural and dispersed, while advocating for a co-constitutive understanding of structural power and the power of agency in organizing resistance to effect structural change at all levels. A second aspect of their theory of change are actors, and they categorize differential historical and contemporary responsibilities within conservation into four classes, to emphasize the role of extralocal actors in putting pressure on biodiversity. These are the upper classes (i.e. global elites), land-owning capitalist classes, middle and lower classes, and lower rural classes. The third aspect, time, involves short-term and longer-term steps to attain the convivial conservation vision. Somewhat akin to Illich's conviviality, what could make convivial conservation attractive as a decolonial option in conservation is the critical stance towards the status quo given historical inequities, a commitment to justice through participatory, democratic decision-making and challenging the human-nature separation, while making an effort to offer concrete alternative suggestions. Although it is important to stress that these ideas are still evolving, the following section will query in more detail how these positive proposals link to conviviality and broader decolonizing principles.

Conviviality and Convivial Conservation as Decolonial Options?

Table 1 (below) is a summary of key convergences and divergences between Illich's notion of conviviality, and Büscher and Fletcher's convivial conservation (2019; 2020). I use this as a precursor to discussing some problematic points and omissions across both approaches.

	Illich's conviviality	Büscher & Fletcher's convivial conservation
Parallel: Radical aspirations	• Challenge tenets of society: industrialized production, elite decision-making in favor of justice, participation • Freedom = creative, autonomous intercourse for people and nature	• Challenges Western-inspired dualistic separation of people and nature • Celebrates human/nonhuman nature; appreciative interdependence • Challenges the Capitalocene, i.e. capitalism-driven large-scale changes to nature and Earth that result from the 'age of capitalism'
Parallel: Participatory decision-making	• Skepticism towards elite-owned, non-participatory decision-making • Tools (= all knowledge/all governing mechanisms) need to serve the common good • But: how to identify and address hierarchies within communities (cf. below)?	• Move away from governance by top-down, expert opinions • Shift from protected to promoted areas (protected areas can be unjust) • Engaged visitation • Does not mean 'anything goes' • Support for conservation areas governed by Indigenous and community groups (ICCA), but: how to learn from reported challenges in community-based conservation linked to genuine participation? How to identify and address hierarchies within communities?
Parallel: Messiness & conflict	• Conflict: not competition for scarce resources, but can create new freedoms and avenues through negotiated, convivial disagreement	• Living together can get messy (cf. Paulson 2001; Hinchliffe and Whatmore 2006)
Divergence: Living within bounds	• The rich must live within bounds • 'Significant benefits for the poor demand a reduction of the resources used by the rich, while significant benefits for the rich make murderous demands on the resources of the poor' (1973: 68) • How to move away from conservation paradigms shaped by Illich's 'the rich'? How to avoid the murderous demands on the resources of the poor from past approaches? [including both i) market-based conservation approaches: payment for ecosystem services/REDD+, Lund et al. 2017; Börner et al. 2017; and ii) restriction-based approaches: human-wildlife conflict or crop-raiding around strict nature reserves/protected areas (Tumusiime and Vedeld 2012; Brockington and Wilkie 2015; Domínguez and Luoma 2020)]	• Could have been more explicit, but supports degrowth and a call for consideration of deeper, international drivers of environmental degradation • Could differentiate more how and which humans, in terms of their racialized, gendered and power-laden differences and asymmetries, drive the large-scale changes to nature subsumed as the Anthropocene (Collins 2021)

Divergence (?): Austerity/Creative playfulness	• Austerity according to Aristotle's and St. Thomas Aquinas's understandings of conviviality as disciplined, creative playfulness	• Celebrating rather than saving nature (similar to creative playfulness) • Describes Illich as transforming society to focus on a frugal good life, though Illich does not exclude all enjoyments, but only whatever distracts from/destroys personal relatedness (1973: xxiv); Illich also recognizes ecological limits not as self-constraint (unlike the German title of *Tools for Conviviality*), but as liberating, by eliminating unnecessary distractions like excessive consumerism • Similar outcome, not the same wording
Divergence: Concrete suggestions for conviviality	• Illich's understanding leaves room for ambiguity and uncertainty, both in definition (Deriu 2014) and in implementation • This is probably deliberate, given passionate support for participatory processes, but also complicates translation into practice	• Concrete actions proposed for convivial conservation vision, but could be more specific: 1) historic reparations, 2) conservation basic income (both empowering under-heard voices, redistributing resources, though equitability of redistribution?) 3) new relations with corporations 4) convivial conservation coalition: positive, to incorporate diverse organizations

Table 1. Summarizing parallels and divergences between Illich's (1973) conviviality and Büscher and Fletcher's (2019, 2020) convivial conservation. Source: Author.

A recurring theme across these convergences and divergences is that neither approach to conviviality provides full details on how these positive ideas are to be implemented, in ways that further decolonial thought and challenge and overcome hierarchies of difference. On the one hand, the lack of detail somewhat alleviates the risk of these suggestions, which have roots in the Global North, being imposed without allowing for the necessary, locally driven decision-making which both convivialities advocate and which is in keeping with the decolonial objection to universal solutions (Connell 2007). On the other hand, this lack of definitive answers could also hamper practical implementation of these ideas at all scales as effective, inclusive decolonial options. For instance, there is a considerable literature detailing the successes and challenges of community-based conservation schemes in involving and empowering local residents. Büscher and Fletcher (2019: 2020) do not discuss in much detail how diverse efforts in the community-based conservation space have proved instructive for designing and implementing their vision, outside of expressing their support for conservation areas governed by Indigenous and community groups. In particular, it is vital to know more about how they aim to address reported challenges surrounding community-based conservation including formalization potentially causing local residents to lose access and rights (Hajjar et al. 2021), areas being hampered by imperfect devolution of capacities and funding (Kiwango and Mabele, chapter 15; Tran et al. 2020), or struggles with elite capture or abiding state control (Noe and Kangalawe 2015). Fundamentally, challenging power asymmetries is premised on acknowledging hierarchies at all levels, including within communities and households, with care needed not to idolize 'community' ideas (Agrawal and Gibson 1999; Brockington et al. 2008). Further elaboration is necessary because Illich, Büscher and Fletcher, are limited in terms of explicitly emphasizing and highlighting ways to address these hierarchies within communities and households.

Similar uncertainties remain around the specificities of

mechanisms to implement Büscher and Fletcher's (2019; 2020) historic reparations, which they acknowledge address difficult issues and must be resolved in context-specific ways. They discuss communities receiving their land back, but again without detailing how unequal power dynamics within communities would be accounted for in this redistribution, or how the interests of future generations would be considered. Finally, while both convivialities acknowledge conflict and messiness in living together, further details remain to be developed on mechanisms to mitigate and manage human-human and human-nonhuman conflict in an equitable, convivial spirit that is cognizant of historical-political contexts. While the convivialist manifesto (Alphandéry et al. 2013) lists 'managed conflict' as one of its four core principles (Humbert 2017), this would also need to be operationalized both between humans and between humans and wildlife in ways that take account of environments that are often fraught with violence and oppression (Lorimer 2010; Duffy 2014b).

Beyond these convergences and divergences, there are problematic points in Illich's conviviality which Büscher and Fletcher's (2019) work either replicates or arguably neglects to address sufficiently. Zaid (2011), referencing the Kantian put-down that some people see things very clearly once they have been told where to look, argues that Illich's extraordinary perspicacity was in 'knowing which way to look.' While that assertion is generally true, some peculiar blind spots exist which are present in spirit, but not in explicit wording in both forms of conviviality: the first is gender. While Illich's later work (e.g. 1981; 1982) very explicitly draws attention to women's often hidden and underappreciated contributions to society, *Tools for Conviviality* is silent on the role women play, although Illich's support of participatory processes implicitly recognizes their expertise and voice. Büscher and Fletcher's (2019; 2020) work, equally, does not problematize gender, though their participatory stance parallels Illich's in spirit. Considering gender in local conservation to facilitate equitable participation of women especially, requires explicit attention and well-designed processes cognizant of factors including access criteria, and distribution of costs and benefits from participation and joint management (Agarwal 1997; Meinzen-Dick and Zwarteveen 2001; Mukadasi and Nabalegwa 2007; Sundberg 2004). In light of decolonial calls to challenge the modern-colonial capitalist system of gender relations (Lugones 2010; 2020), this lack of explicit engagement with gender is a problematic blind spot if power asymmetries are to be challenged through participation, including within communities and households (for convivial conservation, this is addressed by both Ampumuza, chapter 4 of this collection, and Pandya, chapter 13).

Indigenous knowledges are more implicit than explicit in both elaborations of convivialities. As discussed above, knowledge production is imbricated in power dynamics (Noxolo 2017), and challenging Eurocentric ways of viewing, measuring and naming the world is vital for decolonization (Freire 1987; Madianou 2019; Quijano 2000; Tuhiwai Smith 2012). Although Illich does not mention Indigenous knowledge production explicitly, his conviviality is committed to facilitating participatory knowledge access and production across all disciplines, and rejects producing knowledge only for the elite and for supporting industrialization and development. Similarly, there is limited discussion of knowledge production, and specifically the role that Indigenous and non-Western knowledges play in convivial conservation. Büscher and Fletcher's proposals (2019; 2020) privilege Indigenous voices particularly in areas governed by Indigenous and conservation groups, while the fifth element of the convivial conservation vision explicitly draws on Indigenous knowledge in developing local and extra-local embedded value, rather than Northern monetized value. While these perspectives are present in spirit, they merit highlighting as points to develop more explicitly from a decolonizing viewpoint.

One final silence of both convivial perspectives is intergenerational justice, rendered all the more important by rapidly advancing climate change and biodiversity loss. Given that future generations do not have a seat at the table, how can their freedoms and dependence on present-day behaviors factor into decolonial and participatory decision-making processes? This issue is addressed by *Ubuntu* where past, present and future generations are seen as interdependent. How can this be achieved, especially in the – often Global Southern – areas likely to be most affected by environmental degradation? Ironically, the oft-criticized 1987 Brundtland report delivering the best-known definition of sustainable development, highlighted the importance of meeting the needs of the present without jeopardizing future generations' ability to do the same (WCED 1987). While Illich is entirely silent on the matter, Büscher and Fletcher (2019: 2020) express their solidarity with youth, post-colonial, Indigenous and emancipatory movements. However, in Büscher and Fletcher's (2020) theory of change, time is conceptualized as a function of change; there are no explicit considerations of how the proposed convivial conservation suggestions will benefit future generations. In fact, there is a more explicit consideration of the past, through reparations for conservation injustices, than of the future (Büscher and Fletcher 2020: 103-104), although the objective of changing the economic paradigm and humanity's relation to nature is to improve the socio-environmental context long-term.

In sum, in order for convivial ideas to be fully actualized in conservation as decolonial options, some key lessons emerge. Conviviality and convivial conservation crucially converge on the importance of radical change, the involvement of participatory decision-making privileging under-heard voices, and the messiness of living together, requiring equitable resolutions. Conviviality's emphasis on the rich not making murderous demands on the resources of the poor is a pertinent reminder of one *buen-vivir-*linked motivation for decolonizing conservation. The implications of this idea, also in light of historical contributions to anthropogenic environmental change by the Global North (Collins 2021), merit fleshing out more fully within convivial conservation proposals. Among the most notable silences in both convivialities are the lack of explicit attention to gender, Indigenous knowledge, and intergenerational justice, all of which are important vectors according to decolonial thinking. While convivial conservation usefully takes steps to propose concrete actions, further work remains to be done in applying both convivialities to local contexts, as the details and specificities of such decision-making or research processes co-determine the degrees to which they are able to address and overcome hierarchies of difference along lines of race, gender, age, status or (dis)ability. Crucial challenges thus remain around co-developing convivial, locally suitable participation mechanisms which privilege under-heard voices and avoid reinforcing power inequalities, while upholding Illich's ideas of agreed, reciprocal responsibility for shared resources as Büscher and Fletcher themselves emphasize (2020). All these laudable objectives will require genuinely convivial, inclusive implementation processes that avoid external imposition and replicating local or global power asymmetries (Kothari 2021).

Towards a Convivial SDG 15?

For people seeking to develop convivial and decolonizing alternatives for conservation, SDG 15, *Life on land*, is a prominent challenge. International paradigms including world heritage sites (Noe 2019) can institutionalize prioritizations of what is to be 'saved' and how, which can entail significant implications for conservation policy and practice locally. As an agreed global governance framework, the SDGs exemplify Hall's (1992) crucial point that 'framings' can frustrate other ways of constructing topics. To challenge their predecessors, the Millennium Development Goals which were formulated by rich countries (Sen and Mukherjee 2014), the SDGs were developed based on governmental support and input from civil-society organizations (Ibrahim 2018), though making contributions to them was complex (Long 2018). Nevertheless, questions have been raised about whether the SDGs still replicate hegemonic, dominant notions privileging the privileged, e.g. by prioritizing the interests of agribusiness (Spann 2017), advancing a highly contested variant of neoliberal, capitalist development (Weber 2017), and functioning as anti-politics (Hope 2020) e.g. in undermining decolonial territorial agendas through a strengthened consensus between powerful actors (Hope 2022). Building on an analysis of the ideas of conservation present in SDG 15 (Krauss 2022), I will critique SDG 15 (brief summary in Table 2) from convivial (conservation) and decolonial viewpoints, and formulate some alternative suggestions , as a contribution to on-going review processes around the SDGs.

Firstly, from the viewpoint of conviviality, SDG 15 does not implement Illich's aspiration to live within means, particularly for the rich. There is very little in SDG 15 or indeed the SDGs more generally that engages with any kind of limits, never mind specific limits for the already rich in terms of Illich's fundamental dichotomy (Lim et al. 2018; Krauss et al. 2022). In Illich's conviviality proposal, sharing resources equitably is vital. A convivial principle would therefore be respecting ecological limits globally, beyond specific hotspots, while safeguarding equitable distribution of resources between currently privileged and non-privileged. This would equally align with decolonial thinking, particularly with *Ubuntu*'s respect for unborn generations contributing the vital intergenerational-justice dimension. In keeping with *qamaña* (Albó 2011) and *Ubuntu* (Naicker 2011), responsibility for other people would go hand in hand with responsibility for the planet, far beyond the protected areas and biodiversity hotspots on which many SDG 15 indicators focus.

From the perspective of convivial conservation, SDG 15 does not sufficiently promote rights and decision-making of residents, rural peoples and the disenfranchised. The Convention on Biological Diversity's 2011-20 Aichi strategic targets for biodiversity contain a target, Target 11, which explicitly references the needs of women, Indigenous Peoples and local communities and the poor and vulnerable. Despite the Indigenous Peoples' Major Group calling for awareness of Indigenous rights and disaggregation of indicators and data for Indigenous peoples (2015), there is no such commitment in

SDG 15, not even an explicit connection to the—in itself limited—reference to participatory governance in SDG 16.7. Not making an explicit commitment in SDG 15—either overall or for protected areas—to bolstering all types of under-heard communities, including women, ignores the relevance of institutions, for example protected areas, in distributing fortune and misfortune (Brockington and Wilkie, 2015). Consequently, Büscher and Fletcher (2019) propose democratic decision-making arrangements wherever possible, which would equally align well with conviviality and decolonizing.

SDG 15: Protect, restore and promote sustainable use of terrestrial ecosystems, sustainably manage forests, combat desertification, and halt and reverse land degradation and halt biodiversity loss
15.1 By 2020, ensure the conservation, restoration and sustainable use of terrestrial and inland freshwater ecosystems and their services, in particular forests, wetlands, mountains and drylands, in line with obligations under international agreements
15.2 By 2020, promote the implementation of sustainable management of all types of forests, halt deforestation, restore degraded forests and substantially increase afforestation and reforestation globally
15.3 By 2030, combat desertification, restore degraded land and soil, including land affected by desertification, drought and floods, and strive to achieve a land degradation-neutral world
15.4 By 2030, ensure the conservation of mountain ecosystems, including their biodiversity, in order to enhance their capacity to provide benefits that are essential for sustainable development
15.5 Take urgent and significant action to reduce the degradation of natural habitats, halt the loss of biodiversity and, by 2020, protect and prevent the extinction of threatened species
15.6 Promote fair and equitable sharing of the benefits arising from the utilization of genetic resources and promote appropriate access to such resources, as internationally agreed
15.7 Take urgent action to end poaching and trafficking of protected species of flora and fauna and address both demand and supply of illegal wildlife products
15.8 By 2020, introduce measures to prevent the introduction and significantly reduce the impact of invasive alien species on land and water ecosystems and control or eradicate the priority species
15.9 By 2020, integrate ecosystem and biodiversity values into national and local planning, development processes, poverty reduction strategies and accounts
15.a Mobilize and significantly increase financial resources from all sources to conserve and sustainably use biodiversity and ecosystems
15.b Mobilize significant resources from all sources and at all levels to finance sustainable forest management and provide adequate incentives to developing countries to advance such management, including for conservation and reforestation
15.c Enhance global support for efforts to combat poaching and trafficking of protected species, including by increasing the capacity of local communities to pursue sustainable livelihood opportunities

Table 2: SDG 15 and targets. (UN, 2015, pp. 15–16)

From a decolonizing viewpoint, another key shortcoming in SDG 15 is perpetuating conservation trajectories which have produced racialized socio-ecological injustices and power asymmetries. SDG 15 relies variously on protected areas, i.e. risking the replication of problematic dynamics of restriction and exclusion (SDG 15.1, 15.2, 15.4), which arguably furthers the suggestion that as long as natural resources can be protected from certain humans, all shall be well. That is a colonial conservation model. At the very least, incorporating social-equity indicators into SDG 15's conservation management should have been vital (cf. e.g. Zafra-Calvo et al. 2017).

A flaw in SDG 15 on which both convivialities and decolonizing converge is that it lacks recognition of interdependencies between and within humans and the environment. There is a general issue with 'siloing' in the SDGs, which identify 17 separate goals without much consideration of interlinkages or trade-offs between them (Pradhan et al. 2017). This recurs with SDG 15's overall goal, which delineates different resources: 'Protect, restore and promote sustainable use of terrestrial ecosystems, sustainably manage forests, combat desertification, and halt and reverse land degradation and halt biodiversity loss' (UN 2018). Similarly, SDG 15's twelve targets and their indicators fail to acknowledge links with other SDGs, for example around poverty (SDG 1) or economic growth (SDG 8) – despite conservation having frequently occurring and substantive implications for nearby communities. As none of the Goals can be addressed in isolation, a convivial and decolonizing alternative would need to recognize systematically the many interconnections between resources and SDG themes, so as to reflect and capture the many interdependencies between the social, economic and environmental aspects of conservation (cf. Toomey 2020).

Conclusion

This chapter has explored what role conviviality could play in envisioning alternative, decolonizing conservation ideas. After some considerations on positionality and research design, I made a brief case for decolonizing conservation in light of the socio-ecological injustices which racialized understandings of human and nonhuman nature and their interrelations entailed, through colonization and through continued colonialities of power and knowledge.

In a second step, I looked at the work of Ivan Illich on conviviality and related iterations of the concept, juxtaposing it with Büscher and Fletcher's (2019: 2020) convivial conservation approach. There are parallels, divergences and omissions, and the suitability of both concepts as decolonial options were explored. Finally, SDG 15 was examined from both convivial and decolonizing viewpoints, emphasizing shortcomings around a firm commitment by the Global North to live within bounds (conviviality), participatory decision-making privileging under-heard voices (convivial conservation), and a risk of perpetuating unjust trajectories through a reliance on protection and exclusion (decoloniality).

The chapter has argued and demonstrated that Illich's conviviality and related ideas promote a unified philosophy that has much to offer. Both convivialities discussed in this chapter emphasize the grassroots perspective, democratic decision-making, constraining resource use by the affluent, and interdependencies between and within people and the environment. Both approaches converge, crucially, on the need for radical transformations of the status quo, the importance of participatory decision-making privileging under-heard voices, and the messiness of living together, requiring equitable solutions. Conviviality is insistent that the rich must make far less demands on the resources of the poor, in light of their historical contributions to anthropogenic environmental change (Collins 2021). This needs greater attention in convivial conservation proposals. To be actualized fully as decolonial options, both forms of conviviality need to address gender differences, Indigenous knowledges, and intergenerational justice much better. While convivial conservation makes concrete suggestions for change, further work remains to be done in applying both convivialities to local contexts. Addressing and overcoming hierarchies of difference along axes of race, gender, age, status or (dis)ability needs greater specificity. These laudable objectives will require genuinely convivial, inclusive implementation, avoiding the replication of local or global power asymmetries (Kothari 2021).

Chapter 6:

'Rooting' Beyond 'Resilience': The Case For Culture And Agriculture In Convivial[*]

By Paolo Bocci

Introduction: The Promise of Resilience

On June 13, 2013, Ecuadorian President Rafael Correa landed on Santa Cruz Island, in the Galápagos, for a reunion *del gabinete itinerante* (of the itinerant cabinet). Here, the Ministry of Agriculture and the director of the Galápagos National Park presented future projects of conservation and development in the highlands, involving both, park rangers and farmers. These projects signalled a remarkable shift in the official management of the islands that had been in the making during the previous three years. As the latest Management Plan (Plan de Manejo, referred to as the MP hereafter) of the Galápagos National Park, which had just been completed, spelled out, conservation on the islands would extend beyond the protected areas and consider both protected and human areas as integrated. It did so, 'for the first time ever in the history of the Galápagos,' by framing the archipelago as a complex socio-ecological system (SES) and by centring conservation around 'resilience' (Parque Nacional Galápagos 2014: 15). Under this plan, conservation would thus become 'more' than traditional conservation, aligning itself with the goal of multispecies flourishing that the 2008 Ecuadorian constitution famously set with the proclamation of *buen vivir* (good life).

According to the MP, 'resilience' would account for the capacity of the whole archipelago to both maintain its biodiversity and ensure sustainability by offering 'an integrative and inclusive

---

[*] Originally published as: Bocci, P. (2022). 'Rooting,' for change: The role of culture beyond resilience and adaptation. Conservation & Society 20(2): 103-112.

management' (Parque Nacional Galápagos 2014: 23). Promising a participatory approach, the concept of resilience in SESs has gained popularity in conservation worldwide during the past decades, as conservation practitioners and scientists have searched for new methods to address the steep rise of global biodiversity loss and connect it to the well-being of local, often marginalised, communities (Berkes et al. 2000; Fischer et al. 2009). In contrast with conservation's early preoccupation with maintaining or restoring a static nature, resilience considers anthropogenic disturbance as inevitable and focuses on how a plurality of actors, such as ecologists but also local residents, can ensure that the entire ecosystem continues its functions.

A plan for establishing *buen vivir* and resilience in one of the world's most famous protected areas, the Galápagos National Park, seems to converge with the 'convivial conservation' concept. Proposed as 'a vision, a politics, and a set of governance principles for the future of conservation', 'convivial conservation' wants, among other goals, to move past old but persisting dichotomies between 'humans' (in fact, local residents) and nature and to strengthen forms of democratic politics in conservation (Büscher and Fletcher 2019: 284). On the Galápagos as elsewhere, the resilient SES approach promises to do just that: to set at once a more pragmatic goal for conservation (as opposed to restoration of pristine places) and to become a tool for more inclusive participation (Graham and Cruz 2007; Parque Nacional Galápagos 2014). Both, the resilient SES framework and convivial conservation proposal, point to local participation as a critical tool to address the persisting challenges of conservation today, which, despite single positive outcomes, has not been able to reverse the global trends of biodiversity loss, habitat destruction, and climate change (Ceballos et al. 2015; Pörtner et al. 2021).

Despite this apparent convergence of goals, and while acknowledging the positive aspects of this approach, this chapter argues that the conceptualisation of 'the human factor' in resilient

SESs often limits local participation to compliance to existing plans of conservation. In so doing, 'participation' under a resilience approach ignores the potential that a more nuanced understanding of humans' relation to non-human nature poses for rethinking conservation as a whole—and not just for imparting cosmetic tweaks to the system that gesture towards equity. Convivial conservation, on the other hand, calls for addressing assumptions and practices of both protectionist and market approaches, which are both at play on the Galápagos. Both of them grappling with the exacerbation of biodiversity loss, one renews protectionist claims to separate more land from humans (Wilson 2016), the other by seeking alliances within the neo-liberal economy, whereby a fraction of the wealth accumulated at the expense of nature (be it through industry or tourism) funds conservation projects (Kareiva 2014). Yet, if convivial conservation wants to deliver on its promise of radical change then it needs to more explicitly address how it proposes to define participation in terms that are clearly distinct from the one of resilience.

In this chapter, I engage with the question of participation by looking at the management of the highlands of the Galápagos' four inhabited islands, where farmers live alongside the park's protected areas. As the Ecuadorian government meeting in 2013 announced, the new objective of resilient SESs [is to] set in motion several new projects that bridged the divide between rural and protected highlands, promising win-win solutions for farmers and ecosystem conservation. However, these first experiments largely enrolled locals only as participants in already established conservation projects, while continuing to treat farmers primarily as actors who pose a danger of ecological degradation. Although these plans defined local residents as 'allies of conservation,' the approach often resulted in farmers participating in multiple, time-consuming meetings where such projects were presented, and in donating uncompensated labour for the execution of such projects. All the while, farmers had little to no involvement in the design of such projects, and conservation agencies showed little to no interest in understanding locals' role in conservation beyond the one of willing participants in the resilience framework.

While I focus on farmers' marginalisation under the thinking approach of resilience systems, I argue that they are not just victims of conservation but also actors who are already practising a scalable alternative to the current management of the Galápagos islands. Drawing on over a decade of ethnographic research, I show how farmers on the islands care for cultivated crops and native vegetation, the soil, and the highlands as a whole. Farmers have cultivated a deep sense of attachment to the islands, which I theorise as 'rooting'. This form of connectedness challenges the foundational assumption informing both conservation and tourism: that the islands are only a place to visit. These cultural and agricultural elements of their life in the highlands contains practical and historically informed indications of co-living on the islands. Rather than focusing on the usual questions of 'why' or 'how much' locals participate, then, this chapter reframes local participation around practices and beliefs of mutual obligation and care.

The following sections provide a theoretical discussion of participation in conservation in general and especially within an SES approach, followed by its conceptual and practical application in the Galápagos. After a discussion of my methodology, the last two sections of the chapter show how farmers have sought to engage in conservation by aiming at a shared, composite well-being beyond the park's confines. The concluding section spells out how the convivial conservation concept can draw on these grounded experiences to articulate a qualitatively different role for local communities that is based on a social-justice rather than either a protectionist or market-based conservation agenda.

The Missing Piece in Participation and Resilience: Politics

Today, practitioners and researchers alike consider participation as a key tenet of conservation. Participation now consistently figures as a tool in conservation management from the local to the international scale, and it is applied not just in protected areas but also in sites devoted to payment for ecosystem services (PES) and other market-based conservation projects. While definitions and typologies of 'participation' abound, participation often refers to forms of involvement in conservation projects by local residents that empower them, as well as a key factor in the success and durability of such projects. While scholarly critiques of exclusionary conservation and its colonial matrix date back to the seventies, participatory conservation gained worldwide popularity under the banner of community-based conservation (CBC) in the nineties, following the 1992 Convention on Biological Diversity (Berkes 2004; Ghimire and Pimbert 2013).

CBC projects largely accelerated the decades-long transition from a protectionist stance toward a more participatory (including resilience-based) one, although in constant tension with old and new protectionist proposals. Protectionism derived from ecological theories in the early twentieth century that conceived change within an ecosystem as desired only when functional to the establishment of an optimal 'natural' (without human) state. This approach has traditionally promoted the identification of patterns of anthropogenic change, the protection of individual species, and the separation of swaths of land or sea from human activities (Wilshusen et al. 2002; Goldman 2003).

Conversely, since the 1970s, the ecological concept of resilience has promoted a human-in-nature conservation paradigm. Unlike older ecological theories, resilience embraces disturbance and uncertainty as constitutive properties of, respectively, ecosystems and ecological theories—the latter falling under the umbrella of the 'new ecology'. This approach has led to a burgeoning field of analyses and policy interventions in ecology and beyond: as policy framework, resilience has a strong footing in areas as diverse as development, disaster response, finance, and security (Walker and Cooper 2011). In conservation, resilience has promoted many positive changes. Aside from its emancipation from early equilibrium theories in ecology and strict protectionist approaches in conservation, resilience has also allowed to move past the rigid determination of carrying capacity or maximum sustained yield (MSY). Lastly, resilience has also enabled meaningful collaborations with Indigenous communities, although some interventions have been more successful than others in avoiding the reification or instrumentalisation of their environmental knowledge (Cote and Nightingale 2012).

To strengthen the resilience of an SES means, among other goals, to promote diversity and redundancy, and to broaden participation (Biggs et al. 2015). Normative claims about the positive outcomes of participatory conservation have accumulated over the decades; however, so has the frustration about lack of systematisation of this approach. By instituting multiscalar and continuous feedback loops, the SES framework has offered a more rigorous approach to the application of participation. Social scientists, however, have raised issues about how a resilient approach defines participation (Walker and Cooper 2011; Cote and Nightingale 2012). While SES studies treat the natural system as in flux and complex, they often understand society as a static entity, insofar as they neglect issues of power or offer functional explanation of human agency. This approach runs the risk of narrowing local participation to the aggregate role of stakeholders, or to rarefying it to the category of individual choice, in disregard of institutional arrangements as well as power dynamics. As a concept that developed independently from critical work in political ecology, geography, and anthropology, resilience is now widely adopted by market-based approaches in conservation (Fletcher et al. 2016). The latter, market-based conservation approach, invokes participation as a means for reaching 'consensus solutions' on technocratic, 'pragmatic' measures that often avoid interrogating the political context within which conservation operates.

Resilience and sustainability are both conceived as properties of a system that ensure the 'delivery of ecosystem services' rather than socio-ecological justice (Folke et al. 2016). Resilience, in particular, overlaps with the language of disaster capitalism when it treats crises as 'windows of opportunity' (Cumming and Allen 2017), ignoring the disproportional harm on marginalised communities and the exacerbation of inequalities resulting from 'slow' or fast-paced environmental crises. A similar case happens with participation: in a scenario, for example, of unequal access to natural resources within a society, encouraging 'more' participation without addressing the skewed access to those resources can led to an entrenchment of inequalities rather than their alleviation (O'Brien 2012). On the Galápagos, early attempts to formally include residents have similarly resulted in the disproportionate influence of powerful constituents, such as tourism representatives, who avoided restrictive measures for themselves while shifting attention (and restrictions) to other segments of the population with significantly less political clout such as local fishers (Lu et al. 2013; Barragan-Paladines and Chuenpagdee 2017). Resilience's supposed qualities of adaptation, uncertainty, and openness in fact operate within the same assumptions about conservation, impervious to the mounting critiques of its shortfalls by political ecologists, anthropologists, and geographers (Nelson et al. 2007; Walker and Cooper 2011; Cons 2018).

Resilience also recasts the role of agriculture within conservation. Conservation programmes have long considered farmers as a threat, earlier largely because of anti-local sentiments, and today animated by concerns about the devastating ecological effects of agribusiness (Welch et al. 2013; Soutullo et al. 2020). Focusing on resilience, models such as agroecology and eco-agriculture promise to increase plant diversity and perennial plant cover, to improve trophic interaction at multiple scales, and ultimately to strengthen local and regional biodiversity. These proposals, thus, argue for a mutually beneficial relationship between agriculture and conservation. On the one hand agriculture would benefit from the ecosystem services generated in the region it is located, such as water availability, soil retention, pollinators, and natural buffers to climatic extremes. On the other, conservation would be able to expand its scope of influence beyond protected areas, which the very socio-ecological system framework recognises as a flaw (Wezel et al. 2016; Liere at all. 2017). However, while offering viable alternatives to agribusiness, policies following these approaches have seldom moved beyond metrics such as desired environmental outcomes and productivity (agricultural output) to measure of their efficacy. Even when they contemplate 'non-commodity outputs' in an attempt to situate agricultural practices within local cultures, such metrics still maintain a dichotomous relationship between people and nature (Kremen and Miles 2012; Gliessman 2021).

These and other critiques of how environmental governance involves locals (including REDD+ programmes and prior informed consent), however, should not result in the repudiation of local participation as a whole. A similar backlash against local participation resulted after mounting critiques of CBC programmes in the 1990s; the backlash led to the rise of bio-regional and landscape approaches that, by design, were less concerned with incorporating local dwellers in their plans (Peterson et al. 2010). Today, as protected areas continue to expand, mostly in the global south and neo-protectionist claims gain more force (Brockington and Duffy 2011; Massarella et al. 2018), critiques of participation in resilient SESs conservation must not further weaken involvement of local communities.

Convivial conservation advances an integrative, 'whole earth' approach that promotes territories and their human inhabitants, rather than pitting one against each other (Büscher and Fletcher 2020). To that end, Büscher and Fletcher (2020: 164) propose a shift from protected to promoted areas: 'places where people are considered welcomed visitors, dwellers or travellers rather than temporary alien invaders upon a non-human landscape'. 'Promoted areas' want to rethink the connections between human and non-human away from the pervasive logic among conservation biologists and practitioners of conflict and competition. Yet, as convivial conservation wants to contribute to a decolonial agenda, who should inform this new conservation agenda: local dwellers or 'welcomed visitors' (Kothari 2021)? Second, at what level and how can locals contribute to conservation? Below, I advance the concept of 'rootedness' (*arraigo*) to reflect on the significance of farmers' care for the islands. Rather than mere compliance to already set conservation programmes, 'rootedness' allows us to appreciate locals' participation for its potential to shape a new understanding of coexistence and conservation on the islands.

Methods

This chapter draws primarily on dialogues I have sustained with over 80 farmers of the four inhabited islands during my fieldwork stints, amounting to more than two years, between 2008 and 2018. Recently, in response to the COVID pandemic, I have continued my dialogue with a dozen of farmers over phone conversations. During my stay on the islands, I conducted over 200 open-ended interviews and a dozen focus-group workshops with farmers. Moreover, I engaged in participant observation with farmers, state agronomists, biologists and ecologists, and park rangers. I regularly participated in the monthly meetings of the four farmers associations in Santa Cruz and, when possible, of those in San Cristobal and Isabela. In addition, I interviewed the three directors (during the time-frame of my overall fieldwork) of the provincial Ministry of Agriculture and Fishery (MAGAP) and over a dozen of the state agronomists working on agriculture in the islands. I also interviewed National Research Institute of Agriculture and Fishery (INIEP) agronomists and soil scientists as they conducted research on the islands and participated in their field trips. In Quito, I conducted follow-up interviews with the same INIEP researchers and, at the headquarter of MAGAP, I interviewed state agronomists and the assistant to the Minister. For over four months in 2013, I participated in the daily work and *salidas de campo* (field trips) of MAGAP agronomists. In 2013 and 2018, for a total of six months, I collaborated with the MAGAP directors on ongoing projects to strengthen agroecology in the archipelago. I produced and presented two reports evaluating the two plans for islands' *buen vivir* and green practices in agriculture.

To understand the political and economic context of conservation and agriculture, I conducted repeated interviews with members of other associations (fisherfolks, artisans), the director of Institute for The Popular and Solidarity Economy (IEPS) of the Galápagos, representatives of the state bank (Banco del Fomento), the two directors and other officials of the Government Council (Consejo de Gobierno, the highest governmental institution on the islands), and mayors and representative of the three coastal town of Puerto Ayora, Puerto Villamil, and Puerto Baquerizo Moreno, as well as the representative of four parishes on these three islands. Further, I conducted multiple interviews with the director and other members of Invasive Species Fund (FEI), the Galápagos National Park (PNG), Charles Darwin Foundation (CDF). Additionally, I participated in over 40 field trips with CDF scientists and park rangers, as well with members of Conservation International (CI), Island Conservation (IC), and local conservation organisations. Lastly, I interviewed international state and private donors in visit on the islands.

The long-term commitment in my research has allowed for collaboration within and beyond the scope of my work. In this spirit, I taught English to their children, worked with farmers on their land, and, more broadly, tried to help when possible, whether by calculating their sales, thinking together about distribution, or talking on their behalf to tourist agencies and cruises in order to find new markets. My participation in their daily lives avoided the informant fatigue that, on the Galápagos, arises in response to, and compromises, both research and conservation projects. Crucially, this methodology permitted me to appreciate the cultural and political relevance of their practices and beliefs in enacting a form of convivial conservation, which is the contribution of this chapter.

From Threats to Allies: The Evolution of Local Participation in Conservation

The Galápagos have long conjured the image of a pristine place inhospitable to humans. This archipelago, composed of thirteen large islands and over one hundred rocks 1,000 km west of mainland Ecuador, evolved for millions of years without human presence until the sixteenth century. It was not until 1832 that the nascent state of Ecuador established permanent settlements on the Galápagos—a short period indeed in the islands' geological history. The reasons for this image of a pristine place, however, are far from biogeographical alone. The islands are the mythical birthplace of Darwin's revolutionary theory of evolution, that motivated sustained conservation efforts from the US and Europe that framed the islands as a pristine place. While producing this image of the archipelago, conservationists perceived local residents primarily as encroaching on this pristine space. Infused with classist and racist assumptions about people in developing countries and especially the Latinos, foreign naturalists indicated in several reports that local presence threatened not only biodiversity, but also what the islands promised to offer to science and tourism (Hennessy 2018; Bocci 2019b). While hostile to certain forms of human presence, however, conservation in fact encouraged and depended on other humans: tourists and scientists. In the following years, almost 97% of the islands became protected areas, where no (local) human could go, while at the same time the islands began to open to international tourism.

The quality of 'pristine' that conservation advocates attached to the islands, then, did not set the goal of producing a space without people, but rather one with few local residents.[1] Given its dependence on tourist money, state conservation has largely understudied the ecological consequences of international tourism to the islands. This conservation paradigm led to considering local in-migration as a prime threat to the islands' ecological integrity. Expressing concerns about rising human pressure on fragile ecosystems, resource overexploitation, and the spread of invasive species, a 1998 Special

Law for the Galápagos strictly regulated residency on the islands. The Law contemplated a temporary work visa for mainland Ecuadorians, but only on a renewable one-year basis. Permanent residency is limited to those who had lived on the islands for three years prior to the Law, along with their spouses and children. However, the Law did not address the booming number of tourists on the islands, which has quadrupled in the past 15 years (Walsh et al. 2018). More broadly, conservation reforms have evaded discussions about international tourism as a driver of local in-migration from mainland Ecuador even in the past two decades. The law proved, unsurprisingly, ineffective at improving conservation. In 2007, the Ecuadorian state and, soon after, UNESCO declared the islands 'at risk' and a World Heritage Site 'in danger' (Sevilla 2007; UNESCO 2007). More protectionist interventions followed as a result, with further biocontrol measures and additional restrictions on fishing and in-migration (Lu et al. 2013). Although UNESCO pointed to the issue of tourism too, no cap on the total number of visitors was placed during the following years. Satisfied with the protectionist measures targeting locals, UNESCO withdrew the Galápagos from the list of 'in danger' heritage sites in 2010 (Sanchez 2010).

These declarations of crisis nevertheless led to the park's proposal of systems thinking in conservation. Led by a pool of local and international conservation scientists, this proposal advocated moving away from a unique focus on the Galápagos' protected areas and analysing the non-linear, multiscalar feedback loops between humans and ecosystems in the whole archipelago. In so doing, it promised to get to the causes of land change, and not simply to register their effects (González et al. 2008). Furthermore, in contrast to a static understanding of ecology, the proposal drew on the key concept of resilience in SES to plan conservation measures around the goal of maintaining ecosystem functions. The 2014 management plan (PM) of Parque Nacional Galápagos states that this integrative ecosystem functions approach has informed ten years of conservation activities. The PM acknowledges that it is the first official conservation document which addresses 'the islands as a whole' (Parque Nacional Galápagos 2014: 21). Breaking with over four decades of tradition that excluded local residents, the 2014 PM used SES methodology as the sole management tool of the islands, claiming that 'a rational and harmonious co-presence [of humans and protected areas]' is possible. Given tourism's close reliance on the well-being of the ecosystems, the plan argued that the choice between conservation and development was false. Rather, this relationship was mutual, in that development relies on conservation, and vice versa: 'there is no conservation without development, nor development without conservation' (*'no hay conservación posible sin desarollo, ni desarrollo sin conservación'* (Parque Nacional Galápagos 2014: 23).

The PM's framing of development and conservation as a mutual relationship followed national directives to centre the economy around the well-being of people and environment: the concept of *buen vivir*. On a provincial level, however, the park's claims to radically reconfigure conservation and development around *buen vivir* continued to promote conventional protectionist measures, albeit under a new conceptual framework. In other words, if the PM's conservation paradigm was new, conservation assumptions and goals were not. The plan's inclusion of human areas was articulated by placing the responsibility for conservation outcomes on local residents. The PM claimed that as a complex socio-ecological system, the Galápagos' ecosystems would provide services to the benefit of society, and therefore people should 'recognise that the resilience capacity of marine and island ecosystems has limits that must not be exceeded' (Calvopiña et al. 2013: 15). Resilience, then, included residents in the calculus of conservation, but framed them as a problem, because 'many of the direct and indirect drivers of change [in the protected areas] originate in the populated zones' (Calvopiña et al. 2013: 6). Rather than politics, the problem was considered to stem from individual behaviours:

> the current dominance of the [unsustainable] model is
> determined, to a large degree, by the choice of local residents

who select short-term economic growth pattern in which there are few limits to the use of ecosystem services and most of the subsequent benefits are invested in obtaining consumer and material goods. (González et al. 2008: 13)

The emphasis on individuals over structural conditions fit within national plans. *Buen vivir* positioned citizens not only as the goal of politics (that is, in providing them a dignified and fulfilling life), but also as its main actors. However, the government codified a strict definition of citizenship based on people's adherence to *buen vivir*, thus marginalising and even excluding those who did not comply. Similarly, the PM involved Galápagos residents but limited their role to participating in conservation plans, with the assumption that conservation most challenging task was going to regulate local residents' behaviour. As a result, under the goal of promoting participatory processes, the Plan listed the activities of 'environmental communication, participation, education, and interpretation', all forms of unilaterally imparting knowledge rather than establishing a dialogue (Parque Nacional Galápagos 2014: 17).

The PM's emphasis on resilience allowed for the important call to move conservation's focus away from single species to ecosystem variables such as land use, nutrient and water distribution, soil properties, and species abundance. The traditional singular attention to charismatic species has proven effective in attracting money for research and conservation (Santander et al. 2009), but it runs the risks of losing sight of slow but in the long term 'irreversible changes in the system' (González et al. 2008: 13). The section below, on conservation in the highlands, shows how resilience theory continued the assumptions of tourism as a source of funding for conservation and of locals as actors to be educated (and contained).

Implementing Resilience in the Highlands

On the four main inhabited islands, the highlands are divided between rural and protected areas. However, the highlands share climate, soil properties, and the presence of invasive species across the landscape. Compared to the coastal plains, temperature in the highlands is significantly lower, with precipitation an average of three times higher (Trueman and d'Ozouville 2010). Rainwater and humidity are responsible for making the highlands the most diverse land ecosystems of the Galápagos. This climate also ensured the survival of settlers, who largely depended on agriculture and cattle ranching in the highlands for well over a century before the advent of tourism. From the nineteenth to the mid-twentieth century, state-sponsored colonisation through agriculture was responsible for the increased population on the islands. Today, humid soils are a crucial condition for the spread of invasive species like *Psidium guayava*, *Rubus niveus*, and *Cedrela odorata* that have propagated in fallow or minimally managed farmland and then crossed over to the park Ecologists consider invasive species as the single biggest threat to the Galápagos' biodiversity (Atkinson et al. 2012).

With the newly stated goal of strengthening the resilience of the highlands as a single SES, the park began to encourage interventions that addressed unwanted ecological change across the human/protected areas divide. In response, the 2014 provincial plan of MAGAP argued for investing in agriculture in the Galápagos on the basis that it can be an effective form of controlling invasive plants (Guzmán and Poma 2013). Rural highlands are, in fact, mostly abandoned, as a result of decades-long politics catered to tourism and conservation (SIGTIERRAS 2014). Despite unprecedented, decades-long efforts at eliminating these species, the park had succeeded in eradicating only those invasive plant species with relatively slower propagation, or those whose presence in the archipelago was still limited at the time of the eradication campaign (Atkinson et al. 2012). Stronger agriculture, MAGAP asserted, would result in more cultivated land, and thus less open terrain, for invasive plants to spread. Furthermore, it claimed that a higher local production would decrease the volume of imported food, one of the main vectors of new pathogens and invasive species on the islands.

Once it framed farmers as allies in conservation, MAGAP launched projects to develop organic agriculture to limit the use of chemical pesticides and fertilizers (cf. also Robinson et al. 2018). Similarly, the park enrolled farmers in projects for invasive species control in areas on both sides of the park's perimeter. While the conservation goals were clear, these projects stressed the win-win outcomes for both the environment and farmers. For instance, 'improving the quality of production and producing safe and nutritious food using eco-friendly methods', the MAGAP asserted, would 'ensure the health of farmers, consumers, and the environment' (Guzmán and Poma 2013: 27).

My ethnographic research with farmers instead showed that these projects were, first, time-consuming and often even required farmers' uncompensated labour. A project for ecological restoration and support to agriculture, for example, asked farmers to 'donate' vegetable saplings they had germinated, to grow them without the support of fertilizers and pesticides (even organic ones), and to conduct weekly measurements of their growth. All this served to test a new water-saving technology for plants, although the experiment ran right before the rainy season. Second, when measures tackled shared issues among farmers and conservationists such as invasive species, these interventions rarely constituted 'help' to farmers. The integrated plan to control *Rubus niveus*, for example, enrolled a few farmers in a project to clear this invasive plant species along the border of their farms and the park. The farm areas contiguous to the park, of high elevation, the furthest removed from roads and irrigation infrastructure, and often on steep inclines, were the areas where farmers least needed help with *Rubus niveus*, if they needed it at all. Finally, some of these projects continued the narrative of farmers as ecological threats, while diverting attention from larger causes or even manifestations of the same issue. For instance, in 2017 the provincial MAGAP organised a clean-up campaign of plastic from farms. This campaign drew attention to the few plastic bags and empty plastic bottles on the farms, while leaving unremarked the enormous issue of ocean plastic and microplastic (affecting both the protected and human areas) within the confines of academic research by CDF scientists.

Although the projects set important goals to protect biodiversity and strengthen the resilience of rural and protected highlands, they have neither addressed farmers' needs nor the underlying drivers of ecological change: the rising influx of people and goods sustained by ever growing tourism. Instead, the preoccupation with in-migration dominates both conservation and agriculture policies of the highlands, leaving farmers with little support and not fulfilling any of the stated goals of integrated socio-ecological management. Farmers, for example, have faced rising challenges during the past two decades as the workforce has dwindled due to restrictions on local in-migration and competition from higher-paying jobs in tourism. Further, climate change has increased erratic seasonality and thus exacerbated the issue of water scarcity, another key concern for agriculture (Echeverria 2020). Although they invoke food security and strong agriculture, the park's and MAGAP's plans have only marginally addressed the issue of water, and have ignored altogether the long-standing requests of seasonal workers and more robust state support.

Meaningful state support to farmers would disturb a key tenet in local conservation because it ostensibly drives in-migration. This approach rests on a false equivalency, assuming that if agriculture in the past caused in-migration from the mainland, then limiting agriculture today would have a similar effect albeit in reverse. However, the limited support for agriculture today has not led to the desired result of curbing in-migration, which continues to be driven by tourism. As a result, farmers have been forced to abandon cultivation on their lands, with negative ecological repercussions for the highlands and increased economic insecurity due to higher reliance on tourism. Although promoters of the resilient SES framework for the Galápagos promised to move past the geographical scope of protected areas and to address the causes of systemic change as a whole, the policy approach and the conservation measures around invasive species and in-migration in the highlands failed because they continued to regard farmers as responsible for in-migration and other ecological crises (Laso 2020). Consequently, the park entrance fee, a considerable source of revenue for conservation and public services on the islands, continues to allocate no funds to agriculture today (Congreso Nacional 1998).

Beyond Participation

My analysis of conservation in the highlands shows how not only the legacy of the old protectionist paradigm but also the participation under the new regime of resilient SESs limit the possibility for rethinking conservation on the Galápagos. It is as though resilience, the capacity of a system to absorb a shock while retaining its functions and structure, becomes a property not of the Galápagos but of its conservation paradigm, which has maintained its 'identity' despite the ongoing challenges and crises. Confronted with a plethora of challenges during the past three decades, protectionist conservation has demonstrated extraordinary resilience by continually innovating itself while steering clear of questioning tourism as its fundamental tenets (Grenier 2007). In the name of resilience, the park has put forth ambitious societal goals, such as 'the identification of the most appropriate tourism model for Galápagos', which is considered 'a top priority of research and planning for the next few years' (González 2008: 12), or the strengthening of an *cultura isleña* (island lifestyle) in consonance with the archipelago's fragile ecosystems. These important declarations, however, lack any substantive indication of how to achieve these goals. The SES framework, with its promise to synthetise all fluxes and actors into one single paradigm, risks being more grandiose than useful. After all, a systemic approach might not be the right tool to change the very entrenched system and interests of conventional conservation.

My long-term fieldwork and engagement with farmers reveal an alternative path that farmers propose for conservation on the islands.

The very issues of lifestyle, geographical opening, and reliance on tourism are the ones that farmers contest daily in their practices and values. Counter to a society largely dependent on touristic consumption, quick visits, and the image of deserted islands, farmers establish long-term ties with the islands, which I refer to as *arraigo*. Obviously, farmers are not a homogenous category. Aside from differences in gender, age, time on the islands, and province of origin in the mainland Ecuador, farmers on the Galápagos enjoy (or suffer from) different legal status, ranging from undocumented to permanent residents. This has profound consequences on their access to land, capital, market, and state assistance (as well as health, education, and mobility). Further, in the context of scarce labour, limited access to land, water scarcity, and competition with import produce, some farmers also take other jobs as taxi drivers, carpenters, and fishers. The goal of this chapter, however, is not to discuss these differences, but to present several scalable lessons that emerge from within the diversity of farmers' life on the islands.

First, this culture of *arraigo* stems from the fact that farmers situate their dwelling on the Galápagos within a much longer temporal frame than that of a tourist economy (Bocci 2017). This history has produced cultural values and attitudes towards the islands that grew out of a difficult life in isolation and with limited resources. Memories of subsistence agriculture during early colonisation inform an understanding of the fragility of the ecosystems and the human communities that have directly depended on them. Farmers who belong to families with generations on the islands, which sometime span almost 100 years, invoke this past as they practice a careful use of resources (such as water), which conservation now nominally proclaims under the goal of sustainability. This history also shapes these farmers' awareness of the limits to living on the coast and the scepticism around a tourist economy based there. With a modicum of water, fertile soil, and shade, the highlands were, until five decades ago, the only place for survival. On the other hand, living on the coast, aside from minimal subsistence fishing (of lobsters, crabs, and the endemic mollusc canchalagua), was long inhabitable (Ospina 2001).

Second, most farmers establish ties with the islands through their commitment to feeding the local community. Amidst a changing climate, tenuous state support, the influx of imported food, and an insufficient labour force, farmers voice pride in growing food and sustaining the local community. Against the rhetoric of farmers as anti-environmentalists and thus not a desirable presence, farmers vindicate their essential role in the society. Farmers feel a sense of responsibility not only for the community's well-being, but also for the thriving highlands. Their nomenclature of desirable versus undesirable species sometimes diverges with the park's restoration agenda, which is based on native versus alien status. More often, however, their actions converge around targeting invasive species, which spread on cultivated and protected areas alike. Some farmers also keep native plants on their properties for ecological reasons, such as providing habitat to certain birds, or maintaining microclimatic conditions of air and soil humidity. Their reasons are also aesthetic and cultural, more broadly, as farmers protect endangered native plants 'as an inspiration as how to survive in a place like this', as a farmer once put it to me. Other farmers lament how people from the coast buy land in the highlands to build hotels or bed and breakfasts. Unfamiliar with, or even uninterested in, the highlands' ecology, these new owners indiscriminately cut down all trees—young, invasive ones as well as old, endangered ones—even though they might not have the money to build for years, if ever. These farmers, in contrast, see themselves as part of the highlands, not only because their livelihood, but also due to the affect and care that emerge from daily connections to other species and the landscape. A farmer who also owns a house in the coastal town told me that she can stay there only for a couple of days maximum, as she soon 'feels the need to check on the animals [in her farm], but she also miss[es] the woods too much' (pers. comm. 2018).

Third, during my decade of research, farmers have repeatedly affirmed the highlands' (and agriculture's) unique capacity to ensure survival in the times of local or the global crisis, such as the oil spills in 2001 and 2019, the 2009 global financial crisis, all resulting in significant reduction in tourism and extreme hardships for the local community. In response to the ongoing COVID-19 pandemic, the province shut itself for tourists from mid-March in 2020 until the end of June 2020, and tourism continued to be at historic low for the rest of 2020. To my informants, the lock-down engendered considerable losses as the demand for produce and meat plummeted. One of my friends lost all of her 100 pigs to starvation, since the restaurants that gave her food scraps for the pigs (in exchange for the meat at reduced price) had all closed. However, despite the financial and health concerns, enduring lock-down in *fincas* (farms) in the highlands was bearable, as farmers could feed themselves and move about their farms. Many farmers told me that being immersed in a landscape teeming with life gave them a welcome respite from the local news, unlike what residents in the coast experienced while stuck in small apartments. 'The air is different here', a friend told me as we talked on the phone, referring to both the local air devoid of virus but also a less gloomy atmosphere (pers. comm. 2020). Although I had heard the argument before, COVID has only fortified the importance that farmers place on self-sufficiency by establishing long-term, mutual connections with the islands, rather than solely relying on outside tourist money.

Fourth, rather than passively waiting for top-down instructions on how to participate in the highlands, farmers are already deliberate actors in the landscape. And, in the context of ongoing climate and socio-ecological change, they act with flexibility and inventiveness. Sometimes farmers generate new solutions to long-standing, although worsening, problems. For example, during a recent severe drought that lasted for seven months, a farmer cut wild plantain trees at the base of their trunks and planted them next to dying orange trees. Rich in minerals and water, these trunks alone helped his orchard survive. In other cases, farmers recover past strategies that are almost forgotten: when the pasture had dried out during another harsh dry season, a farmer remembered and applied his grandfather's solution—cutting and crushing banana leaves for livestock, helping cows endure the food shortage. In other cases, farmers repurpose existing farming techniques to suit new needs. For instance, scions of *porotillo* tree (of the Erythrina family) grow without help if planted on the ground. Farmers on the Galápagos have long used them to delimit farms. Now, farmers with exiguous capital, often undocumented, use them in their lots to sustain crops with heavy fruits, such as tomatoes and green calabash, as a cheaper alternative to wires and sticks. Lastly, contrary to the image of powerless farmers trafficking in nostalgia, farmers have actively challenged their marginalisation and affirmed the values I discuss here. During the last decades, they organised through state cooperatives to increase their political relevance, although these efforts were stymied by red tape and the overarching unfavourable political disposition towards agriculture on the islands. More recently, farmers have formed networks of peer support, establishing seed banks and opportunities to share their knowledge about navigating ecological and social challenges alike.

Conclusion:
Arraigo and Its Importance for Convivial Conservation

After decades of exclusion from conservation planning, and with the majority of the population working in extractive industries (tourism and fishery), society on the Galápagos has long been regarded as lacking a rooted sense of place and of not having a unifying culture (Ospina 2003). To the contrary, by voicing their pride in feeding a local community, farmers produce not only a new sense of belonging to the islands, but also of a community itself. Agriculture, then, can be a vehicle for culture (Bocci 2019a). Farmers' practices can practically orient the whole society away from fast growth and the premise of no culture towards values of *arraigo* and long-term commitment.

Farmers think of the Galápagos as a place to live and relate to, and not to consume with short visits. Protectionist conservation, in both its old and new form as resilient SES has instead treated the archipelagos' inhospitable conditions as characteristics to preserve, although this model has opened the doors to mass tourism. Farmers curb the spread of present weeds and slow the introduction of new ones. As farmers tend to the crops, engage in mundane observation (unlike the tourists' search for the spectacular), and care for the landscape, they effectively articulate a convivial conservation paradigm for the islands as a whole. They have not only revealed the problems with current conservation approaches, but also showed a way out: their reclamation of infested terrain works not only as a metaphor, but as an actual guide to improve the ecological conditions and biodiversity on the he islands. They have also shown how tourism is no less an invasive process than the alien species targeted by conservation agencies and scientists. This vision might sound foreign and even blasphemous on the Galápagos, as a sign of the advancement of the human frontier on a natural sanctuary. However, it draws on a history that is a century older than conservation on the islands, one that offers indications of how to reconfigure the islands after tourist conservation.

Convivial conservation must affirm the cultural and political valence of local participation beyond resilience, towards building a viable alternative to the SES paradigm. This paradigm shift cannot be that of resilient SESs, which I described above as hindering systemic change rather than promoting it. Convivial conservation needs to more explicitly attune to local actors already enacting alternatives to protectionist conservation. On the Galápagos, this attunement would help us position farmers under a new light: not as 'polluters' that conservation must turn into allies, but as actors that have formed a sense of belonging to the islands, which is necessary to moving away from organising the islands as a tourist facility. This proposal rejects the apolitical (in fact neoliberal) posture that places responsibility on the individual. SESs, specifically, promise a holistic understanding of all factors but fall short of including political and also epistemic factors (what knowledge is privileged). Here, instead,

I have discussed farmers not for their individual choices, but rather as historical, cultural, and social forces that are carving out socio-ecological relations in dissonance with the current nexus of tourism and conservation. The emphasis on a more profound, qualitatively different role of locals in conservation and environmental issues at large is essential to convivial conservation's goal to transitioning conservation away from a northern, protectionist agenda towards one that that is local and driven by a social-justice agenda.

PART III

Rethinking Human-Wildlife Interactions

Chapter 7:

Human-Wildlife Coexistence: Business as Usual Conservation or an Opportunity for Transformative Change?[*]

By Kate Massarella and Valentina Fiasco

Introduction

Since the early 2000s, the concept of coexistence has become central to wildlife governance discourses, as well as wider biodiversity conservation discourses. Coexistence is the focus of myriad academic inquiries (e.g. Pudyatmoko et al. 2018; Pooley et al. 2021; Frank et al. 2019; Madden 2004; Carter and Linnell 2016), and is a central theme of conferences and events, including Jane Goodall Institute ConservAction week 2019 (https://jgisconference2019.peatix.com) and Human Dimensions of Wildlife conferences (https://sites. warnercnr.colostate.edu/pathways/history/). It is explicit in many NGO missions, including Defenders of Wildlife who aim to 'foster transformation in both human attitudes and how wildlife and people interact, from conflict to coexistence' (Defenders of Wildlife 2021). We thus identify coexistence as a 'buzzword' – a popular term that signifies a desired shift in the understanding and management of an environmental issue, becoming instrumental in the policy-making arena (Cornwall and Brock 2005; Bock 2012).

In the context of human-wildlife interactions (HWI), coexistence signifies a shift away from the focus on human-wildlife conflict (HWC) that has long been a central part of conservationists' work (Hazzah et al. 2019; Frank 2016). It is argued that a focus on conflict limits the possibilities for meaningful change in how HWI are

---

[*] Originally published as: Fiasco, V., and K. Massarella. (2022). Human-wildlife coexistence: Business as usual conservation or an opportunity for transformative change? Conservation and Society 20(2): 167-178.

perceived and managed, due to a number of factors. First, HWC has negative connotations and implies incompatibility of human and wildlife interests (Pooley et al. 2017). Second, a focus on conflict reflects a simplistic framing using Western analytical categories that belie the complexity of HWI (Goldman et al. 2010). Finally, a focus on conflict obscures the fact that much 'human-wildlife' conflict is actually 'human-human' conflict between people with diverging values, interests and priorities (Peterson et al. 2010; Glikman et al. 2019). Shifting emphasis onto coexistence is an opportunity for 'radical innovation' to 'shake up the conservation agenda' (Hazzah et al. 2019: 360).

Despite the growing popularity of coexistence, few attempts have been made to define the term (Pooley et al. 2021). The definitions of Frank (2016: 2), who defines coexistence as 'when the interests of humans and wildlife are both satisfied, or when a compromise is negotiated', and Carter and Linnell (2016: 575), who define coexistence as a 'dynamic but sustainable state in which humans and large carnivores co-adapt to living in shared landscapes' remain the most widely referenced. Yet, as our analysis shows, these popular definitions do not reflect the diverse meanings and uses of coexistence. Notable studies have started to unpack coexistence in more detail (e.g. Pooley et al. 2021; Frank et al. 2019; Lute et al. 2018). The focus is largely on coexistence as an ideal outcome at the local level, emphasising behavioural, emotional and psychological factors (known as the 'human dimensions') and a better understanding of place-based social-ecological systems. However, critical investigation into coexistence as a signifier—a political object through which 'crucial contests over meaning' happen (Rear and Jones 2013a: 376)—is lacking, and it is this gap that this chapter addresses.

Our critical exploration of coexistence is particularly timely as the term is increasingly being used within diverse proposals for transformative change in biodiversity conservation, developed to address the accelerating loss of global biodiversity (Massarella et al. 2021). These proposals call for a paradigm shift in how humans perceive and manage our relationship with non-human nature (Lorimer 2015; Srinivasan 2019), how conservationists perceive and relate to people who live in and close to areas of high biodiversity (Mbaria and Ogada 2016; Hazzah et al. 2019), and in the political economic structures that perpetuate crises (Otero and Nielsen 2017; Büscher and Fletcher 2019). Differing concepts of coexistence, including 'peaceful coexistence' (Bekoff 2015) and 'sustainable coexistence' (Otero and Nielsen 2017; Pudyatmoko et al. 2018) are central to many of these transformative proposals.

Coexistence is also a central theme in convivial conservation; the transformative proposal with which this book engages. Convivial conservation is a 'vision, a politics and a set of governance principles' that responds to pressing issues facing biodiversity and its conservation, including global political economic structures, the rise of authoritarianism and growing social and ecological violence (Büscher and Fletcher 2019: 283). Convivial conservation calls for transformative change in global political economic structures and more consideration of environmental justice (Büscher and Fletcher 2019; 2020). The goal is to move towards a system that better enables 'meaningful coexistence' between humans and non-humans, as opposed to the 'shallow commodified encounter[s]' that are driven by, among other things, an over-emphasis on tourism and other market-based conservation approaches (Fletcher et al. 2020: 207). However, like many of the transformative proposals that use the term, the convivial conservation proposal is yet to define what it means by coexistence.

We address these knowledge gaps by asking how coexistence is being framed and how it is translated into practice, and what function(s) the term is fulfilling. We also ask what the implications of these findings are for transformative change in biodiversity conservation, and what the role of convivial conservation could be in bringing about the desired paradigm shift associated with coexistence. We draw on critical scholarship of buzzwords, along with science and technology studies (STS) concepts including boundary objects, signifiers, idea translation and standardised packages to analyse interviews, webinars, online resources and documents, and unpack how human-wildlife coexistence is manifesting in discourse and practice among academics and practitioners. We then discuss the implications of these findings for transformative change and convivial conservation. Studying buzzwords enables exploration of which actors dominate discussions, so that contested meanings, ideological differences and power structures can be highlighted (Cornwall 2007). We contribute to the understanding of buzzwords, as well as transformations to sustainability scholarship, by highlighting the importance of buzzwords in the process of transformative change and theorising how these words can both catalyse and block change. We also contribute to the development of convivial conservation, identifying how it can help realise the transformative potential of coexistence.

Exploring Buzzwords in the Context of Transformative Change

This research is grounded in the sub-field of political ecology that critically engages with environmental discourse. Discourse is defined as 'an ensemble of ideas, concepts and categories through which meaning is given to social and physical phenomena, and which is produced and reproduced through an identifiable set of practices' (Hajer and Versteeg 2005: 175). Discourse analysis is based on the understanding that although issues such as climate change and biodiversity loss are real, the way they are framed—that is the assumptions, interpretations, methods, values used to understand and communicate them—is socially constructed (Leach et al. 2010). Framings matter since they discursively establish what the problem is, who is responsible and who has the legitimacy and authority to solve it, ultimately determining courses of action that privilege some actors and disadvantage others (Hajer 1995). Discursive struggles over meaning are therefore common, particularly in the case of biodiversity conservation (Büscher and Whande 2007).

Individual words—especially those classified as buzzwords—are important units of discourse analysis. Buzzwords are political objects that reflect broader trends in environmental understanding and management (Cairns and Krzywoszynska 2016), reflecting a host of meanings, images and storylines, and playing an important role in framing policy solutions (Cornwall and Brock 2005). Buzzwords can motivate people and mobilise resources by signifying that 'they have now got the story right and are really going to make a difference' (Cornwall and Brock 2005: 1043). Examples of buzzwords that have been studied discursively include 'participation' (Leal 2007), 'sustainability' (Brown 2016; Scoones 2007) and 'good governance' (Mkandawire 2007; Büscher and Mutimukuru 2007). Studies find that buzzwords become powerful by being ambiguous in meaning while signifying an agreed-on normative goal (Cairns and Krzywoszynska 2016) and that their often-radical roots quickly become diluted or lost altogether (Mkandawire 2007; Chandhoke 2007). It is thus important to study buzzwords: how they develop, how they travel and how they influence practice, as well as to ask what functions buzzwords *as words* fulfil (Cornwall and Brock 2005).

We draw on some core concepts from STS and political theory in our exploration. The first is the concept of signifiers, which are units of language that represent (or signify) concepts and ideas (Laclau and Mouffe 1985). Conceptualising words or phrases as signifiers positions them as political objects that are used as 'an attempt by the agents of a discourse to subtly transform or renegotiate meanings of the term as it concurrently used by agents of another, competing discourse' (Rear and Jones 2013a: 375). The (somewhat subconscious) aim is to establish what is known as a 'hegemonic signifier' whereby the dominant meaning, or framing, becomes so powerful that it has reached the status of common sense (Rear and Jones 2013b; Laclau and Mouffe 1985). Through this process, certain 'facts' about the world we live in become 'stabilised' (Latour 1987; Fujimura 2010). 'Wilderness' can be described as a hegemonic signifier, as despite its contested meaning, one framing (that of North American conservationists) dominates

(Cronon 1996). Establishment of a hegemonic signifier can have a wide range of implications, not least in relation to justice, as their apparent universality conceals struggles over ideology and contested meanings, leaving unquestioned injustices caused by actions done in their name (Cornwall 2007; Rist 2007).

Other signifiers, such as 'biodiversity' (Gustafsson 2013) and 'global citizenship' (Moraes 2014) are described as 'floating', as they float between different epistemic communities, adopting multiple meanings depending on the worldviews, values and priorities of each community (Farkas and Schou 2018). The goal thus becomes stabilisation of the meaning of floating signifiers and the associated environmental policy and practice (Rear and Jones 2013a, Cornwall 2007). Other signifiers, such as 'sustainability' (Brown 2016) and 'resilience' (Weichselgartner and Kelman 2015), are described as 'empty', as they become emptied of meaning and instead become tools for justifying multiple goals and limiting contention (Moraes 2014; MacKillop 2018). Empty and floating signifiers often function as 'boundary objects' that facilitate action by being 'both adaptable to different viewpoints and robust enough to maintain identity across them' (Star and Griesemer 1989: 387). Boundary objects, such as 'sustainability' and 'conservation corridors', are easy to translate, enabling cooperation across disciplines and between science and policy (Goldman 2009; Scoones 2007).

STS inquiry also focuses on the travel of signifiers, challenging what was historically framed as processes of diffusion, meaning concepts do not change as they spread and are just accepted or rejected by different actors, and instead identifying processes of translation, whereby concepts are modified as they come into contact with different actors (Latour 1984). Buzzwords often begin as signifiers of radical change but as they travel, they become modified and lose their transformative potential, translated in a way that maintains the status quo (Chandhoke 2007; Mkandawire 2007; Brown 2016). In fact, the strong ideological connotations buzzwords often evoke can be used to legitimise and re-energise existing policies and interventions (Büscher and Mutimukuru 2007). This process of idea translation continues as buzzwords become material reality through policies and interventions. The ambiguity and flexibility of boundary objects can be combined with—or translated into—'standardised packages' of methods, approaches and tools (Fujimura 2010), such as modelling, wildlife ecology and wildlife corridors (Goldman 2009). This results in boundary objects being 'fluid in meaning' yet 'solid in their presentation' (Goldman 2009: 338), becoming translated into technical fixes that simplify and depoliticise complexity (Scoones 2007; Li 2007).

Critical scholars exploring transformations to sustainability have found that what is labelled as transformative change is often shallow and does not reflect radical shifts (Blythe et al. 2018; O'Brien et al. 2013), with 'transformation' itself considered a buzzword. We therefore posit that by unpacking the term coexistence in relation to buzzwords, signifiers, boundary objects, processes of translation and standardised packages, we provide important insights into contemporary debates on the processes of, and barriers to, the transformations to sustainability that convivial conservation—and others—call for. Our analysis supports understanding of key issues identified in the study of transformative change (Blythe et al. 2018), including how and why radical ideas lose their transformative edge through processes of translation (Mkandawire 2007), and why concepts with transformative potential may not translate into practice (Corson et al. 2020).

Materials and Methods

We focused our analysis of framings and practices of 'conservation professionals': academics, practitioners and activists. It is these groups who are currently most active in defining and using the coexistence buzzword (although as we will discuss further, the actual practice of coexisting with wildlife is far from new), and the perspectives of these professionals influence broader HWI policies (Lute et al. 2018). Data was collected by the second author between June and September 2020, using three main sources: literature (academic papers, books and NGO documents), webinars and videos, and semi-structured interviews. A qualitative, inductive approach to data collection was taken with all three data sources collected simultaneously. A combination of purposive and snowball sampling was used (Blackstone 2012). Both authors are familiar with the HWI discussion so started by purposively identifying key academics and practitioners for interview, representing a wide range of approaches to HWI and different country contexts, as well as core texts and NGOs (see Table 1).

Additional data sources were identified using the snowball method, asking participants to recommend other texts, webinars, conferences and interviewees. Literature and online sources were identified by doing google searches using key search terms *Human-wildlife coexistence*; *Human-wildlife conflict + coexistence*; *human-carnivore conflict + coexistence*; *human-carnivore coexistence*; *coexistence*; and *human-wildlife coexistence + cohabitation*. Analysis focuses on content published between 2014 and 2021 to capture the most recent coexistence discourse at the time of data analysis. Data was collected and analysed until 'data saturation' was reached (Fusch and Ness 2015). Data collection was both enhanced and restricted by COVID-19. The focus on online content meant that there was more access to more conferences and seminars, but the challenges people faced reduced availability of interview participants. We note that not all countries/ contexts are represented and that the perspectives collected are from 'professionals' only and do not reflect the full picture of coexistence in discourse and practice. However, this 'professional' perspective gives a good idea of how the coexistence concept is influencing international and some national activity on HWI.

Method	Data collection	Regions represented
Semi-structured interviews (24)	Academic-practitioners (4); practitioners (8); academics (10); academic-activists (2)	South/Central America (3); North America (6); South Asia (4); East/ Southern Africa (5); Europe/UK (6)
Online Content	NGO/non-profit/foundation materials (12 organisations) Lectures/seminar (7*) Online conferences (6*)	South/Central America (9); North America (8); East/Southern Africa (5); East/South Asia (5); Europe/ UK (3)

Table 1: Data collected.

Multiple cases and presenters

All interviews and video materials were transcribed and organised using ATLAS.ti software. Data analysis began inductively (Blaikie 2007), guided by key elements of discourse analysis summarised in section two. Key features were identified and compared across data to find patterns. Features included problem definitions, common assumptions, proposed solutions, practices of blame, contrasts and consistencies (Mogashoa 2014), and received wisdom: long-established assumptions often based on simplistic interpretation of information that drive certain framings and storylines (Leach and Mearns 1998).

The Discourse and Practice of Coexistence
The Hopeful Mission of Coexistence

Like all buzzwords, coexistence signifies current thinking and trends in environmental management (Cairns and Krzywoszynska 2016), in this case related to HWI. Traditionally dominated by conservationists grounded in natural sciences, understanding and reducing conflict was central to wildlife management practice, led by the rationale that much killing of wildlife was a direct result of damage to human property. The emphasis was on protected area (PA) formation to reduce human-wildlife competition (Amaja et al. 2016). However more recently, and in part due to the rising influence of the 'human dimensions' field of conservation social science, the discourse of HWI has shifted. This shift includes moving from an emphasis on PAs to conservation both within and outside of PAs (Dorresteijn et al. 2014; Western et al. 2019; Hartel et al. 2019). The concept of coexistence has become a signifier for this shift:

> I think coexistence has to have some element of co-occurrence... if animals only live in sort of the proverbial Zoo of Yellowstone where they're killed as soon as they leave Park boundaries or something, you'd be hard pressed to make the case, at least in my mind, that that would be called coexistence. (interview, academic – social ecology – and practitioner, USA)

A desire to shift from negative framings of wildlife management that HWC signifies, towards more positive discussions of what 'better futures look like' (interview, academic–environmental historian, USA) is identified. Coexistence signifies a 'move away from this constant focus on what we think is wrong to also looking at what we think is right' (interview, academic–social science–and activist, India), focusing instead on 'all the neutral to positive interactions people have daily with wildlife' (interview, academic–natural sciences/human dimensions–and practitioner, Canada). Coexistence thus signifies an opportunity for imagining a 'different way of living' (interview, academic–political ecology, UK), offering an alternative 'human philosophy' for conservation (interview, academic–social ecology–and practitioner, USA). This positive outlook is reflected in the use of coexistence within the discourse of the 'conservation optimism' movement that strives to 'build a world in which nature and people can coexist' (https://conservationoptimism.org/).

The idea of coexistence often signifies the importance of Indigenous Peoples and local communities and acknowledges the role of 'the knowledge, the abilities and histories of communities' in facilitating coexistence (interview, academic–social science–and activist, India). Concerns that the traditional knowledge and cultural practices enabling coexistence might be lost over time due to broader socio-economic changes are also reflected in academic papers (e.g. Mwamidi et al. 2012; de Silva and Srinivasan 2019), interviews and webinars on coexistence:

> In Kenya... local Maasai communities have lived with their livestock alongside wildlife... maintaining a landscape of exceptional biological and cultural diversity. This coexistence is enabled primarily by the increasingly threatened communal and semi-nomadic form of local land use, which encourages mobility to ensure survival. (recorded lecture: Western, 2019)

The 'hopeful mission' of coexistence reflects three core characteristics of buzzwords. First, they have a strong, shared normative goal (Cairns and Krzywoszynska 2016; Cornwall 2007). Second, they signify a desire, and potential, for radical change, at least in the early stages of their use (Chandhoke 2007; Mkandawire 2007). Third, and closely linked to the previous points, buzzwords signify that academics, policy-makers and practitioners have finally landed on an idea that will bring about much-desired transformative change (Cornwall and Brock 2005). This shared vision enables coexistence to function as a boundary object by combining a normative goal with an adaptive flexibility that enables use across multiple epistemic communities (Scoones 2007; Goldman 2009). We now unpack some of the ways in which different epistemic communities frame and use coexistence, first highlighting the two most dominant framings (sections 4.2 and 4.3) before discussing an alternative approach (section 4.4).

Coexistence as Co-adaptation

The academic field known as human dimensions of wildlife has been instrumental in establishing coexistence as a buzzword, developing a particular framing that we loosely call 'coexistence as co-adaptation'. Although nuanced across organisations and individuals, common characteristics of this framing can be identified. The burgeoning academic field draws on psychology and behavioural studies to understand how humans and wildlife can 'co-adapt' and better tolerate one another (e.g. Amit and Jacobson 2017; Dietsch et al. 2019, Ceauşu et al. 2019; König et al. 2020). Academics working in this field understand humans and non-humans as existing in complex socio-ecological systems that are context-specific, dynamic and influenced by myriad factors (Lischka et al. 2018). Different scales of governance and their interaction with local values and behaviours are also explored (e.g. König et al. 2020; Glikman et al. 2019).

A focus only on conflict or on achieving a situation where all species live in harmony is framed as counterproductive, with coexistence instead conceptualised as a process of co-adaptation between humans and wildlife towards tolerance (König et al. 2020) or 'sustainable coexistence' (Pudyatmoko et al. 2018). A core concept is the 'conflict-to-coexistence continuum': a framework used by conservation social scientists to describe HWI, to 'shed light on coexistence and tolerance, rather than only conflict', and to be used as an analytical tool to investigate the 'reasons behind negative to positive attitudes/behaviours toward wildlife' (Frank 2016: 741).

Several practitioners and organisations also draw on this framing of coexistence. For example, the Sri Lankan NGO Trunks & Leaves aims to facilitate 'peaceful coexistence of people and elephants' by promoting community well-being, supporting livelihoods, and understanding factors influencing human behaviour towards elephants (https://trunksnleaves.org/). Their approach reflects the importance of involving local communities in conservation and ensuring that they benefit from interventions, which is highlighted by both academics and practitioners:

> A key principle of course should be [a] community-based approach... there is almost no other way we can get acceptance or stewardship. (interview, academic–social science, UK)

The EU platform on coexistence between people and large carnivores also focuses on community engagement, using expressions like 'exchanging knowledge' and 'working together in an open-ended, constructive and mutually respectful way' (https://ec.europa.eu/environment/nature/conservation/species/carnivores/coexistence_platform.htm).

However, ideas about coexistence developed in the academic sphere go through a process of idea translation (Latour 1984) as they are adopted by practitioner organisations. In some instances, academic emphasis on tolerance shifts to an ideal of 'positive' or 'peaceful' interactions, with coexistence described as:

> The sharing of time and space (between) wildlife and humans, in a way that the negative impacts are lowered, and the positive impacts are maximised. (interview, practitioner – conservation biologist, Costa Rica)

Rather than emphasising co-adaptation, the focus of many human-wildlife management interventions is on behaviour change, particularly through education programmes:

> We try to promote tolerance for coexisting with these animals, by education… The idea is to make people understand that these animals live in our backyards, and we need to change our behaviour at times so that they can survive. (interview, academic – environmental science – and practitioner, Canada).

Instead of focusing on the multiple actors at different scales that are part of socio-ecological systems thinking, the emphasis in practice largely remains on the local level and the values and behaviour of people living close to wildlife. Education programmes are assumed to be needed because 'people have not had any educational training about how to safely live with elephants' (recorded lecture: Von Hagen, 2020) and other animals. Academics and practitioners also advocate for financial support in the form of compensation schemes for predated livestock. For example, the Big Life Foundation has created a predator compensation fund to offset part of the financial burden from local livestock owners and 'reduce the motivation for retaliatory killings' (https://biglife.org/what-we-do/human-wildlife-conflict-mitigation/predator-compensation).

The practice of coexistence mirrors community-based conservation approaches in advocating for the inclusion of local communities in the design, implementation, and evaluation of conflict mitigation strategies and conservation interventions. This typically means involving local communities in research or in the development of alternative livelihoods, such as ecotourism initiatives and green labels for local produce. Integrated Conservation and Development Projects (ICDPs) are used to minimize the economic impacts of HWC on local livelihoods with the goal of increasing the tolerance of people towards wildlife. An example of this is the 'human-elephant co-existence for livelihood protection' initiative founded by the World Bank's Global Wildlife Program in Sri Lanka, which aims to generate a 'wildlife-based economy to ensure the benefits from wildlife outweigh the costs associated with living among them' (https://blogs.worldbank.org/voices/corridors-coexistence-reducing-human-wildlife-conflict).

Our analysis of coexistence as co-adaptation shows that although the discourse indicates a potential paradigm shift for HWI management, in practice it currently manifests in 'standardised packages' of long-standing tools, technologies and approaches to conservation (Fujimura 2010; Goldman 2009), including education, financial incentives and ecotourism. This is a common pattern in international conservation and development, as complex ideas are simplified and 'rendered technical' (Li 2007). One of the reasons for this translation, we posit, is that coexistence is largely framed within Western ways of knowing (for example by quantifying attitudes and behaviours) that align with the values and objectives of conservationists. This framing is amenable to practice but does not challenge the status quo. We continue to follow this trend as we look at a second dominant framing of coexistence.

Coexistence as Conflict Mitigation

The idea of coexistence has also been adopted by people and organisations working within the natural sciences, including wildlife ecologists and organisations like Defenders of Wildlife, Wildlife Conservation Society (WCS) and WildEarth Guardians. Here, the idea of coexistence is translated through an ecology research lens. Framed using community and landscape ecology notions, HWI is often described in terms of spatial overlaps. Just as 'coexistence theory' in community ecology offers a functional perspective on how multiple competing species coexist (Chapron and López-Bao 2016), the natural science-based framing of coexistence focuses on competition between people and wildlife:

> In an area of northern Botswana roughly the size of Yellowstone National Park, 15,000 elephants compete with 15,000 people for

access to water, food, and land. (http://www.ecoexistproject.org/challenge/area/)

Concerns about an increasing human population and habitat loss are identified (Chartier et al. 2011), with an emphasis on gaining specialised knowledge of the behaviour and ecology of wildlife to control HWI and keep people and wildlife in their designated spaces (Chapron and López-Bao 2016). This focus on spatial overlap manifests in concepts such as 'connectivity conservation' (Keeley et al. 2019) and 'landscapes of coexistence' (Rio-Maior et al. 2019). In practice, these concepts translate into a need for more wildlife dispersal areas and corridors (e.g. Othman et al. 2019) in order to bolster the existing 'network of ecologically representative, effectively managed, and financially viable protected areas' (https://www.wwf-congobasin.org/what_we_do/sustainable_protected_areas/). Thus, although coexistence is linked to broader ideas of land sharing, it is used by some academics and practitioners to advocate for further land sparing, sometimes justifying the relocation of people living close to PAs and corridors:

In partnership with other stakeholders, like UN-Habitat, [the park] helps place the community in proper areas like a settlement surrogate… We are using this opportunity to free wildlife corridors. (interview, practitioner – wildlife manager, Mozambique)

The idea of coexistence is also translated into education campaigns to 'communicate what is conservation, what are the benefits of conservation' (interview, wildlife manager and practitioner, Mozambique) to local communities, along with the implementation of conflict mitigation tools like electric fences and predator-proof livestock enclosures:

What is coexistence? Simply put, it's helping people share the landscape with wildlife using innovative tools to reduce the

conflicts that people have with wildlife in their natural habitats.
(promotional video: Defenders of Wildlife, 2019)

The discourse and practice of 'coexistence as conflict mitigation' is framed as being a small-scale, place-based issue in the context of a specific region or PA. The emphasis is on solving HWC in these spaces quickly, rather than investigating and addressing political-economic processes and broader social issues. The more transformative parts of the coexistence framing identified in section 4.1 become lost, as the idea is translated into more standardised packages of conservation thinking and practice. Moreover, it appears that coexistence is being used to legitimise long-standing approaches to conservation that separate people and wildlife (Jeanrenaud 2002), which can lead to widespread injustices (West, Igoe, and Brockington 2006).

Returning to the Roots of Coexistence

In the previous two sections, we have unpacked some of the dominant ways that coexistence is, as an emerging buzzword, being used in wildlife management discourse and practice. Coexistence is largely conceptualised at the global scale within Western institutions and translated into standardised packages of tools. This contradicts the broader understanding of coexistence as something that has been historically practised by Indigenous Peoples and local communities across the world (Mwamidi et al. 2012), which we have already touched upon. Some activists and academics are therefore challenging the Western conceptualisation of coexistence, instead arguing for a framing that is grounded in Indigenous and local community worldviews, values and practices:

[Coexistence] needs to recognise that it is not humans and nature, but human beings as part of nature... the whole notion of interdependence and this is where other worldviews, whether it's *Ubuntu* from Southern Africa or *Buen Vivir* or Sumaq kawsay from Latin America or Kyosei in Japan, become important.

Academics working closely with Indigenous Peoples and local communities, grounded in disciplines like anthropology, political ecology and environmental justice, show how many Indigenous Peoples and local communities do not see themselves as being in competition with wildlife but rather see coexistence as deeply rooted in their culture and identity (e.g. Kolipaka 2018). Human societies are perceived as being part of evolving social relationships with the natural world. For example, in his study of human-snow leopard interactions in Pakistan, Hussain (2019) shows how the complex and reciprocal relationship between livestock keepers and snow leopards maintains rather than threatens the animal's population. This contradicts the current coexistence practices outlined in the previous two sections, where coexistence is still often envisioned as the resolution of conflicts that need to be managed through outsider intervention. Academics and practitioners taking this alternative approach to coexistence thus challenge the conflict to coexistence continuum, with conflict instead considered part of coexistence:

> Coexistence can happen both through conflict and cooperation, or collaboration, they are both part of coexistence. (interview, academic – political ecology, Netherlands)

Another important element of this framing is the desire to re-politicise wildlife management, countering the depoliticising effects of the tools and incentives that are so far manifesting as coexistence practice. Human wildlife interactions and conflicts are framed as a product of historical and contemporary political-economic processes and societal change, including colonialism and neoliberal capitalism, that have changed relationships between people and wildlife (de Silva and Srinivasan 2019; Hussain 2019). This political framing is central to the convivial conservation proposition, which calls to address 'the structural, violent and uneven socio-ecological pressures' that underly conservation conflicts (Büscher and Fletcher 2019:

284). The idea of 'meaningful coexistence' put forward by convivial conservation proponents aims to conceptualise coexistence as much bigger than just local HWI, encouraging tourists to consider sustainable and socially just ways of interacting with biodiverse landscapes (Fletcher et al. 2020).

Another common thread among academics and activists advocating this approach is environmental justice. This incorporates a strong critique of Western-dominated knowledge production around human-wildlife interactions and management that conceptually separates people and nature (TallBear 2011). Instead, coexistence reflects the fact that people 'feel like [they] are a part of nature and not so much disconnected from it' (interview, academic–social science, Uganda). Rights-based conservation practices that are focused on land-ownership, community-led decision making, participatory research and the appreciation of traditional coexistence practices also reflect this framing.

However, although we have identified these conceptual threads within our data, they are not always framed as 'coexistence' explicitly. Similarly, the word coexistence is not being taken up and used as a buzzword to the extent it is in the more dominant approaches (see the previous two sections). This could be because for some Indigenous Peoples and local communities, coexistence is a 'self-evident' notion (interview, academic–anthropology–and activist, Switzerland) and not something that needs to be managed by outsiders. In this sense, coexistence can be seen to be signifying a shift in Western thinking, rather than reflecting genuine engagement with lived experiences of HWI (Hussain 2019). As such, practitioners and organisations that take the general approach outlined in this section, including Survival International (https://www.survivalinternational.org/) and the Indigenous and Community Conserved Areas (ICCA) Consortium (https://iccaconsortium.org/), seem cautious about the use of the term coexistence.

Nevertheless, it seems that the idea of coexistence is being reclaimed by organisations like Kalpavriksh, and other critical social scientists and activists focusing on HWI. They frame coexistence as an alternative to an exclusionary approach to conservation, highlighting how traditional local livelihoods and human settlements are not necessarily detrimental to conservation. They propose that Indigenous Peoples and local communities have a key role in the safeguarding of wildlife and habitats, and that conservation could benefit by not only including people, but also protecting and incorporating traditional practices of coexistence. They argue that an understanding of local knowledge, culture and perspectives that have allowed coexistence to occur is to be prioritised over interventions that risk disturbing local equilibriums (webinar: Rai 2021).

Coexistence, it seems, is being reclaimed by activists, as well as by some academics and practitioners, in a way that aligns with its progressive roots. We thus identify coexistence as a floating signifier: one that takes on different, competing meanings across epistemic communities (Farkas and Schou 2018). This, as we will elaborate on more in section five, presents an opportunity for change, as the term (unlike 'sustainability' and other buzzwords) is yet to be emptied of meaning or stabilised (Rear and Jones 2013b). Interviewees from different epistemic communities noted the changing nature of coexistence and many expressed an openness to its evolution. In some cases, the use of coexistence encouraged critical reflection on the practice of 'importing recipes' (interview, practitioner–conservation biologist, Costa Rica). However, some academics and activists remain cautious and argue that interventions taking an alternative approach to coexistence can still become translated into standardised packages. For example, Goldman, De Pinho, and Perry (2013) argue that innovative initiatives, such as Lion Guardians in Kenya (http://lionguardians.org/), are still driven by an assumed need for external intervention and a reliance on standardised packages of conflict mitigation tools.

Coexistence, Transformative Change And Convivial Conservation
Through our analysis of coexistence in discourse and practice, we

have conceptualised the term as a buzzword and boundary object. Coexistence reflects current thinking in HWI and signifies a shared normative goal, while being ambiguous enough to be easily adopted by a wide range of epistemic communities across academia and conservation practice (Goldman 2009; Cairns and Krzywoszynska 2016; Star and Griesemer 1989). The normative goal of coexistence reflects a general shift in thinking in HWI and reflects the progressive and radical character of other buzzwords (Chandhoke 2007; Mkandawire 2007). Yet the idea of coexistence is ever-changing, translated through the worldviews, values and perspectives of different epistemic communities (Latour 1984). Several different framings of coexistence have thus emerged and our analysis of three of these framings shows that coexistence is far from a fixed—or hegemonic—term. It can instead be conceptualised as a floating signifier (Laclau and Mouffe 1985). Our analysis has several implications for transformative change in HWI management, and biodiversity conservation more broadly. We now consider these implications before reflecting on what this means for convivial conservation.

The Opportunities and Risks of 'Coexistence'

We posit that the evolving nature of coexistence provides potential opportunities for HWI theory, policy and practice. Although some suggest that floating signifiers have less credibility than empty or hegemonic signifiers (e.g. MacKillop 2018), we argue that the non-fixed status of coexistence provides an opportunity for transformative change (Rear and Jones 2013b; Brown 2016). Coexistence still signifies an intention and desire for radical change in the way in which HWI are managed, reflecting assumptions that people and wildlife can share landscapes (Boonman-Berson et al. 2016), that broader systems, processes and structures influence HWI (Pooley et al. 2017), and that the knowledge and practices of Indigenous Peoples and local communities must be prioritised (Mwamidi et al. 2012). The fact that some activist organisations, NGOs and academics (including those theorising convivial conservation) are trying to maintain the transformative roots of coexistence provides an opportunity. As a boundary object, coexistence is also a meaningful concept for diverse epistemic communities, from ecologists to anthropologists, and between academia and practice. As such, it can provide a useful tool for the increased interdisciplinary engagement needed to tackle the challenges of biodiversity loss (Pooley et al. 2017).

However, as coexistence becomes used more widely, it is losing its transformative potential and largely manifests in practice as 'standardised packages' of long-standing tools, technologies and approaches (Fujimura 2010; Goldman 2009). Coexistence therefore risks becoming a positive-sounding label for business-as-usual HWI management, following the pattern of other buzzwords by losing its transformative edge as it is translated and stabilised through existing narratives, structures and processes (Blythe et al. 2018; Leal 2007; Mkandawire 2007). Boundary objects favour conceptual stabilisation because that enables diverse approaches to be considered part of a unified approach to conservation (Wyborn 2015), and in the case of coexistence, this stabilisation is likely to favour one of the two dominant framings identified in our analysis. Transformative elements of coexistence, including Indigenous and local knowledge and practices, broader political-economic factors and environmental justice, run the risk of being lost as the term becomes depoliticised or 'rendered technical' (Li 2007). There is also the risk that an uncritical acceptance of the term coexistence, and the signified shift away from wilderness ideology, means that hybrid management approaches 'come without awareness of what was wrong with the wilderness approach in the first place' (Hussain 2019: 154).

Another limiting factor is the way in which coexistence knowledge is being generated and used. Although coexistence unites epistemic communities, wildlife and people are still largely studied separately by different disciplines and from opposing paradigms (Pooley et al. 2017). As such, the human-nature dichotomy that is at odds with the concept of coexistence remains. Western science dominates coexistence thinking, developing 'knowledge products' that can be used in intervention design (Mosse 2004). Received wisdom, such as a perceived need to educate and change the behaviour of local communities remains largely unquestioned (Leach and Mearns 1998). Transformative approaches to coexistence that reflect the ways Indigenous Peoples and local communities know and value nature are side-lined, reducing the resonance of the term among these communities (Weeratunge et al. 2000). The concept of coexistence thus risks further legitimising the neo-colonial dynamics of some wildlife management, resulting in unjust modes of intervention (Howitt and Suchet-Pearson 2006; Büscher and Mutimukuru 2007).

Coexistence and Convivial Conservation

The convivial conservation vision is built on the premise that transformative change in biodiversity conservation is imperative and that the roots of this radical change can only be realised via processes of politicisation and pluralisation (Massarella et al. 2021). The focus on politicisation and pluralisation is highlighted as the basis for just transformations to sustainability more broadly (Martin et al. 2020; Blythe et al. 2018). Our analysis of coexistence supports and builds on this focus by identifying politicisation and pluralisation as key tools in the discursive battle to facilitate the term's transformative potential in the context of HWI management. Through our analysis, we identify two potential roles for convivial conservation. First, and in relation to pluralisation, convivial conservation should look to the work already being done by progressive organisations like Kalpavriksh and the ICCA Consortium, as well as academics and activists predominately based in the Global South, and act as an ally in their struggle to foreground the experiences, knowledge and voices of Indigenous Peoples and local communities. Convivial conservation originated from academics in the Global North and so care must be taken to not become another top-down initiative that side-lines voices from the Global South (Kothari 2021). The focus instead should be on using both research and the channels of influence awarded to Global North academics to amplify the many different approaches being taken to coexistence by Indigenous Peoples and local communities.

The second potential role relates to politicisation and this, we argue, is where convivial conservation can make the biggest impact on coexistence discourse and practice. In HWI (and broader biodiversity) research there is a notable omission of insights into the impact of political economy (Fletcher and Toncheva 2021). This is despite academics, activists and progressive organisations highlighting the continued influence of factors such as colonialism and neoliberal capitalism on HWI (see https://www.radicalecologicaldemocracy.org/). As our analysis shows, coexistence is largely depoliticised during the process of translation, manifesting as standardised packages of tools and incentives that fail to address deeper social, political and economic drivers of HWC. Alongside academics like de Silva and Srinivasan (2019), Hussain (2019) and Margulies and Karanth (2018), proponents of convivial conservation can investigate the links between HWI and political economy in order to support a transformative shift in focus away from a sole focus on the attitudes and behaviour of local communities and the needs and behaviour of wildlife. The global research project associated with convivial conservation (https://conviva-research.com), which comprised of academics from the Global North and Global South, contributed to this goal (Massarella et al. 2021).

We also suggest further development of the concept of 'meaningful coexistence' put forward by Fletcher et al. (2020). This signifies a need to shift the attention of conservation onto the impact that broader political-economic processes (such as multi-national business, global consumption habits and international tourism) have on HWI. Meaningful coexistence could also incorporate the shift from protected to 'promoted' areas advocated by convivial conservation, which re-frames biodiversity-rich areas as 'places where people are considered welcome visitors, dwellers or travellers rather than temporary alien invaders upon a nonhuman landscape' (Büscher and Fletcher 2020: 164). Developing this idea of meaningful coexistence could provide an important tool in the pursuit of transformative change in HWI, so that coexistence does not become another one of conservation's empty signifiers.

Chapter 8:

'They Belong Here': Understanding the conditions of human-wolf coexistence in north-western Spain[*]

By Hanna L. Pettersson, Claire H. Quinn, George Holmes, and Steven M. Sait

Introduction

In Europe, the ongoing trends of rural abandonment (Cimatti et al. 2021), shifting wildlife value orientations (Bruskotter et al. 2017) and increasingly supportive conservation legislation (Cretois et al. 2019), have enabled large carnivore populations to increase in number and recover historic ranges (Chapron et al. 2014). Since protected areas are too few and too small to make up viable habitats (Boitani and Linnell 2015), and because culling is limited by the European Habitat Directive, there are few practical and legal means of preventing large carnivores from expanding into agricultural landscapes. This generates questions about how humans and carnivores could share these spaces in ways that enable mutual flourishing. An increasing number of institutions endorse a coexistence model for European carnivore conservation (López-Bao et al. 2017; Cretois et al. 2019), in which carnivores are integrated within humanised landscapes and protected throughout their range. This model constitutes significant challenges to protecting carnivores, mitigating negative impacts on local communities, and addressing disagreements about conservation management (Mech 2017).

Human perceptions and behaviour often determine carnivore abundance in shared landscapes (Llaneza et al. 2011; Mech 2017). For the coexistence model to work, communities need to be able

* Originally published as: Pettersson, H.L., C.H. Quinn, G. Holmes, and S. Sait. (2022). 'They belong here': Understanding the conditions of human-wolf coexistence in North-Western Spain. Conservation & Society 20(2): 113-123.

to adapt to (returning) carnivores and be resilient to the higher degree of unpredictability that is inherent in integrated conservation spaces (Carter and Linnell 2016). It requires human tolerance of co-habitation on a scale that has not existed in recent memory (Boitani and Linnell 2015). However, the state of knowledge of what underpins such adaptive capacities and tolerant attitudes is insufficient (Lozano et al. 2019; Pooley et al. 2021). While decades of research through a conflict lens have yielded substantial knowledge of factors that lead to dysfunctional relationships with wildlife (Redpath et al. 2013; Adams, 2015), little is known about what fosters and perpetuates resilient coexistence (Carter and Linnell 2016). Current interventions are still largely focused on addressing carnivore impacts and intolerant behaviours of a particular social group, often failing to consider underlying issues and motivations (Pooley et al. 2017). This may cause biased representations of human-carnivore interactions, since positive and neutral relationships often exist alongside dysfunctional ones, on both local and national scales (Peterson et al. 2010; Fernández-Gil et al. 2016). In order to advance the debate, we need in-depth studies of the prerequisites of coexistence, and the opportunities and challenges encountered by human and non-human inhabitants in shared spaces.

This research explored the factors underpinning successful coexistence in Sanabria-La Carballeda (S-LC), which has one of the highest densities of wolves in Europe. Applying a coexistence lens, we analysed the main socio-ecological conditions of this region's uninterrupted and relatively harmonious relationship with wolves. This conceptual approach included exploring the influence of broader political-economic trends, both informal and institutional, power dynamics and justice concerns on this relationship. Specifically, the research sought to explore: 1) how coexistence in S-LC has been perpetuated through time; 2) what coexistence in S-LC has meant for wildlife and people; and 3) the main trajectories of change that may influence coexistence in the future. We also explored the possible implications for integrated conservation areas and approaches elsewhere.

The chapter consists of three parts: the first explores our conceptual approach to human-wildlife coexistence; the second explores coexistence within S-LC; and the third discusses the implications and possible outcomes of the research.

Conceptual Context

Our conceptual approach is underpinned by recent scholarship on coexistence, biocultural diversity, and convivial conservation.

In recent years, coexistence has gained prominence within the field of human-wildlife interactions (König et al. 2020; Pooley et al. 2021). This focus complements, and partly replaces, the previous focus on human-wildlife conflicts that has been widely critiqued for its tendency to reinforce a human-nature dichotomy, ignore the underlying social elements of disputes, and over-emphasise top-down legal and technical solutions (Peterson et al. 2010; Pooley et al. 2017; Lozano et al. 2019). Within this research, resilient coexistence is understood as a series of conditions that create 'a dynamic but sustainable *state* [italicized by author] in which humans and large carnivores co-adapt to living in shared landscapes where human interactions with carnivores are governed by effective institutions that ensure long-term carnivore population persistence, social legitimacy, and tolerable levels of risk' (Carter and Linnell 2016: 575).

This state does not imply a complete absence of conflicts and trade-offs; although the extent of negative interactions that are deemed acceptable, and for which party (people or carnivores), is still being debated. According to Chapron and López-Bao (2016), coexistence with carnivores is the case so long as they persist in self-sustaining populations, implying that it is primarily about achieving species protection. In line with Pooley et al. (2020), we perceive a difference between protecting biodiversity and promoting coexistence. We favour a conceptualisation of coexistence as a state in which people are able to live equitably and sustainably with wildlife, and where conservation efforts are carried out within the context of wider societal challenges (Redpath et al. 2017; Linnell and Cretois 2018). This is more consistent with current conservation agendas, certainly in Europe, which aim to protect and restore both wild spaces and certain (agri)cultural landscapes (Pretty et al. 2010). The conceptualisation is also more conducive to participatory approaches, which have greater potential to generate local stewardship for nature and wildlife than 'command and control' approaches (Bennett et al. 2017).

Mainstreaming this coexistence model is hampered by current sectoral governance and disciplinary silos within academia (Hartel et al. 2019). There is a lack of collaboration between stakeholders whose primary aim is the conservation of certain (often charismatic) species, and those focused on the conservation of landscapes and cultural heritage, yielding separate and sometimes incompatible solutions (Torralba et al. 2018; Fagerholm et al. 2020). The concept of biocultural diversity reconciles these strands. It describes the interactions between people and nature at a given time in a given place, and the cultural and natural aspects arising from these links. Within Europe, where the spheres throughout history have become indivisibly interlaced, pursuing nature conservation separately from its cultural contexts could in many locations be counterproductive (Pretty et al. 2010; Bridgewater and Rotherham 2019).

Convivial conservation, advocated by Büscher and Fletcher (2019: 289), offers a new and more holistic conservation paradigm. This vision departs from nature-culture dualism and proposes 'not setting nature apart but integrating the uses of (non-human) natures into social, cultural, and ecological contexts and systems (i.e., re-embedding)'. Since the erosion of cultural and biological diversity is often caused by the same drivers, such as climate change, over-exploitation and homogenisation of landscapes (Henle et al. 2008; Pretty et al. 2010), an integrated approach is necessary to address these underlying challenges. Convivial conservation also engages with people's relationship to their land and past conservation practices, such as (neo)colonial dynamics and dispossession, that are vital to make historical reparations and address injustices within current conservation policy (Büscher and Fletcher 2019).

Coexistence and conflict are thus parts of a constellation of possible human-wildlife interactions and relationships. Both must be understood by examining economic, cultural, political and power dynamics; the agency of humans and non-humans; as well as the social and ecological legacies of past interactions (Redpath et al. 2013; Pooley et al. 2017). The novel contribution of a shift from conflict to a coexistence lens comes from the way it draws attention to conditions and dynamics that could allow both humans and animals to flourish in the context of broader systemic change, rather than merely reducing conflict in a particular place.

Case Study Presentation: Wolves and Villages in Spain

We explore coexistence through a case study of human-wolf interactions in Spain[1]. Wolves are widely recognised as one of the most complex coexistence challenges in the northern hemisphere, particularly for agricultural communities (Kuijper et al. 2019). It is a highly adaptive apex predator prone to seeking out anthropogenic food sources, and it is considered a flagship species in most European cultures. Exploring what fosters coexistence with such a polemic species could, therefore, inform work with other expanding and/or controversial species.

Due to their continuous presence in Spain, traditional methods of preventing wolf attacks on livestock have been maintained in some places, such as shepherding and the keeping of livestock guardian dogs (LGDs) (Álvares et al. 2011). During the past 40 years, the Iberian wolf (*Canis lupus signatus*) has recovered and expanded significantly, from 200-500 at its lowest point in the 1970s to currently more than 2,000 today, making it the largest wolf population in western Europe (Blanco and Cortés, 2009; JCyL 2018). The intersection of its large wolf population, the great number of priority habitats, and the persistence of shepherding cultures make Spain highly relevant for the study of coexistence.

The study focussed on a selection of municipalities within the administrative region of S-LC in the Zamora province. It was selected for its exceptional wolf density, stable at approximately 7-10 individuals/100 sq. km since the 1980s; its preserved preventative methods; and its public acclaim as a wolf-watching destination (Vicente et al. 2000; JCyL 2018; Martínez 2019). The area is dominated by a low mountain range (800-1,200 m above msl), which contains the 67,000 ha regional hunting reserve Sierra de la Culebra and the 23,000 ha adjacent Lake Sanabria Natural Park. Both areas were established in the 1970s and have been included within the Natura 2000 network since the 1990s (see Figure 1).

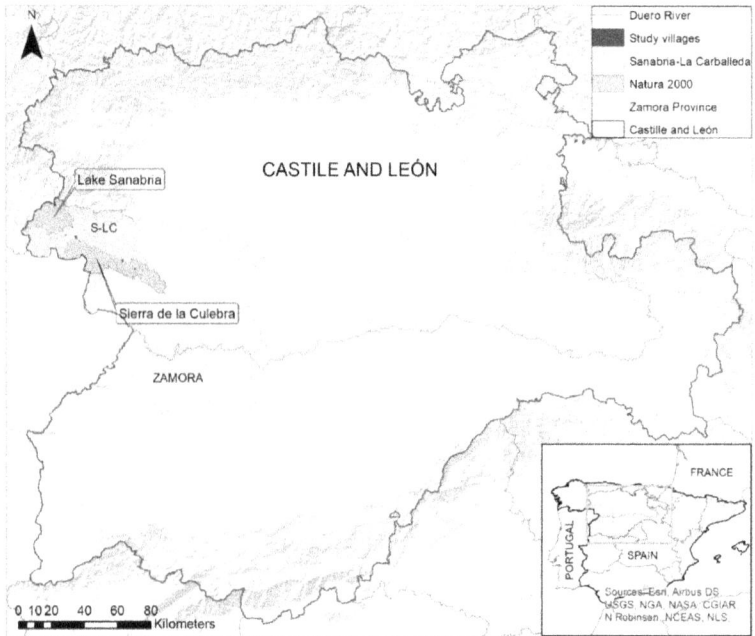

Figure 1. Map of Sanabria-La Carballeda (S-LC), located within the autonomous community of Castile and León. The villages within or adjacent to where informants were located are marked in brown. North of the Duero River, the wolf is included in Annex V of the Habitat Directive (managed as game species), while to the south it is protected in Annex IV

The study villages have been characterised by subsistence agriculture, but the sector has decreased significantly over the past 50 years. The Spanish transition towards democracy (1977–1982) and entry into the EU (1984) increased social mobility in the S-LC region. Its marginal soils and harsh climate rendered most farms uncompetitive in a globalised agricultural market, leading to a rural exodus that particularly decimated its shepherd community (Fernández Gónzalez 2013). In 2018, its population density was less than 5 inhabitants/sq. km and several villages had been completely abandoned (Martínez 2019). The remaining shepherds (sheep and goats) and farmers (cattle) graze their livestock on perennial meadows and in mixed forests and scrub, of which the majority is municipal property (Fernández Gónzalez 2013; Blanco 2017).

With the farming sector in decline (making up 7.28% of provincial GDP in 2017) (SEPE 2018) and the industrial sector practically non-existent, Zamora is dependent on its service sector. Over the past 30 years, this sector has been enhanced by a growing tourism industry (3.65% of the provincial GDP in 2017) (SEPE 2018), which in S-LC to a significant extent is driven by an interest in the wolf. High wolf density and the favourable topography of La Culebra, with intermingled hills and open spaces that facilitate observation, have made the area emblematic for wolf-watching, in Spain as well as internationally (Martínez 2019).

Data Collection and Analysis Methods

The case study was conducted through an experience-based assessment of community conditions, which elicits the knowledge of community members to survey factors and processes related to adaptive capacity and resilience (Smit and Wandel 2006). The approach is well suited for the appraisal of the complex systems within which human-carnivore interactions are embedded. Primary sources consisted of observation data and key informant interviews. Secondary data consisted of management plans, newspaper articles and documentaries on the topics of human-wolf interactions, depopulation and rural abandonment in Spain (see SI 1 and SI 2).

The lead researcher undertook site-based fieldwork from January 2020 to May 2020, which was approved by the Research Ethics Committee at the University of Leeds (AREA 19-018). In order to gain a broad perspective of coexistence in the area, we focused on villages with the presence of tourism, wolves and traditional agriculture. Participant and non-participant observation was continuous and included meetings and events, wolf-watching activities and accompanying farmers and wildlife managers during their daily tasks, which was recorded in a fieldwork diary. Within or connected to the communities, we identified and selected interviewees who were deemed particularly affected by the presence of wolves, or who were involved in species or area management (see SI 1). In total, 33 semi-structured interviews were carried out in Spanish, tape-recorded and subsequently transcribed. Questions were centred on rural issues and trends, perspectives on human-wildlife interactions and aspirations for the future. Questions about wolves, unless brought up by the interviewees, were asked at the end in order to understand their primary concerns.

We did not presume to deduce coexistence conditions or their determinants a priori but used a grounded theory-type approach (in line with Mabon et al. 2020), which allows interpretative flexibility during data collection and analysis. We processed primary and secondary data through thematic coding using the NVivo software. A crude coding structure was established according to the research questions, which was expanded through an iterative process with themes that emerged from the data. This inductive approach allowed the data codebook and structure of the results to stem from conditions and trajectories deemed important by the informants themselves (see SI 3). The findings were then contextualised through the concepts outlined above to empirically support and expand current scholarship on coexistence.

The sample size and scope of the research were limited by time and spatial constraints, and to some degree by language and cultural barriers. Follow-up and comparative studies from other coexistence areas would add nuance to the idiosyncrasies of S-LC and its implications for efforts to achieve coexistence elsewhere.

Findings

We begin by describing the socio-ecological context of human-wolf interactions in S-LC; followed by an elaboration of four main coexistence conditions that emerged from the data and the associated trajectories of change that may impact these conditions. The final section contextualises the results and discusses the wider implications of using a coexistence lens to study and govern human-wildlife interactions.

The Trajectory of Human-Wolf Coexistence in S-LC

Similar to other locations in Europe and North America (Bruskotter et al. 2017), people in S-LC have within their lifetime observed the wolf pass from being defined as a pest, both legally and in the public discourse, to an animal that is widely revered and commodified as a tourist attraction. When the countryside of S-LC was still extensively populated and farmed, people's primary defence against wolf attacks consisted of human presence (many small flocks of sheep demanded constant vigilance from shepherds) and various methods of killing wolves (traps, snares, poison and shooting). However, according to interviewees, the persecution was intermittent and retaliatory rather than a government-organised scheme as in other parts of the country. This contributed to S-LC becoming one of the last wolf bastions in Spain, albeit with declining numbers (Vicente et al. 2000). The trend was reversed in 1970 when the wolf's national status was changed from 'vermin' to 'game', which regulated the time, number and the approved methods with which wolves could be hunted (Blanco and Cortés, 2009).

Around the same time, Sierra de la Culebra was declared a hunting reserve. The declaration encompassed new policies of forest and wildlife management, including the reintroduction of red deer

(*Cervus elaphus*), which had become extinct in the early-1900s. The species boomed thanks to favourable habitat conditions, making La Culebra renowned for some of the highest densities and highest quality of trophies (indicated by antler size) in the country (Vicente et al. 2000). This type of big game hunting has traditionally been dominated by the upper class and political elites, while local hunters were limited to small game such as foxes, grouse and hares. According to administrative staff, these hunting practices converted the reserve into a haven for wolves and ungulates, from where populations expanded into the surrounding region.

While wolf and deer numbers increased, human inhabitants continued to decline. Various informants perceived it as a deliberate scheme by governing institutions, in which they were being 'educated to leave'. The processes of depopulation eroded social cohesion and the communal management of local commons, leaving increasingly isolated farmers to fight what they perceived as a losing battle to maintain traditional landscapes and cultures:

> If it continues along this road, it will disappear. Another thing would be if they [the administration] notice what is happening and start incentivising pastoral farming. But it would have to be an enormous jump, because if there is no generational turnover right now, […] the new people who come won't know anything about the land. Because people traditionally take over from someone or have someone who can show them. But if this disappears… Who will come to the village to set up farming when this is all virgin land? (Shepherd, 2020)

Coexistence Conditions

A triangulation of academic publications, observation and informant interviews elucidated four main conditions of wolf persistence in the area:

Favourable habitat

The ecological conditions for the wolf in S-LC have improved since the 1970s, when the habitat for wildlife was severely fragmented (Vicente et al. 2000). A common perception among informants was that wolves in those times survived by predating on livestock. The forest cover has since increased dramatically (both native and planted), and so too wild prey populations (red deer, roe deer, wild boar) (San Miguel et al. 2016). To some extent, this has facilitated a spatial separation of human and wolf activities. For example, informants often credited the booming ungulate populations for decreased livestock losses to wolves over the last decades.

However, the expanding forest cover and rising prey populations were also major causes for concern among local informants. S-LC's farmers must nowadays dedicate a significant proportion of their resources to addressing scrub encroachment on their private and on common lands. They indicated that maintaining these pastures open is essential to prevent wolf attacks, since LGDs can more easily survey the flocks, and since wolves have less shelter to mount their ambush. In addition to scrub, deer and boar are decreasing agricultural yields, damaging vegetable gardens, causing traffic accidents and increasing the prevalence of zoonotic diseases. Interestingly, our observations indicated that local communities were often more exasperated by deer than by wolves. 'It would be better for me if they [the hunters/administration] came here and killed 600 deer, and didn't kill any wolves. […] There are grounds that I had reserved for the cows, and when I get there the deer have already gotten to it' (Farmer, 2020).

From a historic perspective, the social and ecological transitions in S-LC have been drastic, rendering the systems practised for millennia nearly obsolete within the span of half a century. When discussing the landscape for wolves and shepherds in the future, several shepherds wryly remarked that wolves will clearly be 'the winners'. A local wolf expert emphasised that the disappearance of shepherds could be detrimental to wolf conservation in the long term, since the buffer zones between human communities and natural areas, traditionally maintained by shepherds, would be decimated. This could increase the risk of negative interactions in the villages, as wildlife would quite literally be 'on people's doorstep'. In addition to eroding local knowledge and customs, landscape homogenisation also threatens certain species associated with meadows and pastures, including within Natura 2000 areas (Fuentes et al. 2011). Wildfires have also increased dramatically over the last few decades, partly due to the growing expanse of flammable scrub (JCyL 2014).

Sustained coping mechanisms

The tangible impacts of wolves in S-LC are primarily experienced by rural communities, particularly livestock owners. Among this group, versions of the sentiment 'we have always lived with them' were frequently expressed, and we found a general acceptance of wolves as part of the local system, whether cherished or disliked. The various coping mechanisms that have resulted from the convergent evolution of wolves and shepherding have been passed down from generation to generation. Sheep and goats are enclosed at night, accompanied by a shepherd during the daytime, and kept with numerous LGDs. While the efficacy of LGDs to defend cattle was more contested, we found that many cattle farmers kept them regardless, and there was an informal system for matching spare LGD puppies to those who needed them. The number of dogs among our informants ranged from four to 21. For instance, a pack of 18 LGDs had effectively prevented attacks on a flock of 1,400 sheep for as long as the shepherd had been active. However, the viability of LGDs is undermined by national legislation that fails to recognise them as working animals. The law dictates that they should be kept on a leash, and the owners risk prosecution if LGDs attack people or pets. Preventative measures also constitute a significant economic burden and are highly labour intensive, which respondents considered to be one of the main reasons for younger generations' disinclination to engage in traditional farming.

Irrespective of these issues, there was a broad consensus among locals and civil servants that the measures were effective at limiting wolf attacks in their area. While farmers still lost livestock (in 2017 there were 344 damage claims in the province of Zamora) (JCyL 2018), attacks were mostly opportunistic on animals that were left behind or strayed from the flock (locals called them *'oveja del lobo'*, meaning the wolf's sheep). Events in which multiple livestock were killed at the same time were said to be rare.

When locals were asked about their main concerns, the wolf was usually listed after issues such as low agricultural profitability, depopulation, deregulation of social services, lack of infrastructure, low generational turnover, and an inefficient governance system. The relatively low level of antipathy against wolves was reflected in media coverage, where few of the articles about wolf-related grievances within Spain originated from the study area. Instead, as shown by Delibes-Mateos (2020), such articles disproportionally originate from the southern part of the province, where wolves have recently returned. While the cultural legacy of S-LC contained a wealth of frightening stories about wolves (corresponding with those described by Álvares et al. 2011), the present sentiments among locals were dominated by indifference or delight. Fear, apart from concern on behalf of livestock and pets, was largely absent. In one instance, the lead researcher observed an event in which a wolf became trapped in a villager's chicken coop while attempting a raid. It later escaped, and the commotion was described in the local newspaper in terms of a 'delighted' villager and a 'poor, sick little wolf' who 'regained freedom' during the night. When asked how he thought wolves should be governed, a shepherd (in 2020) replied: 'Instead of letting them spread, that they lived always in the same area. Here for example, in this area. [...] Here it is possible to live with the wolf, but there are areas where it won't be possible'.

These examples illustrate a generalised tolerance and coping capacity of S-LC's communities, which has evolved over generations. It supports earlier findings from a similar region (Llaneza et al. 2012), which highlighted the importance of long periods of cohabitation to establish harmonious human-wolf relationships. This ability to live and produce alongside or despite wolves is gaining repute as proof that coexistence is possible. A growing number of documentaries, newspaper articles, and campaigns have centred on a group of S-LC shepherds and farmers considered emblematic for their preventative measures, such as the keeping of LGDs. Additionally, we identified a widespread pride among locals of this expertise of the area's shepherds (see SI 2). However, current agricultural policies in Spain are incentivising cattle over sheep and intensive agriculture over traditional pastoral systems (San Miguel et al. 2016). Cattle require less protection from wolves since they are larger and more easily fenced, and are consequently becoming increasingly dominant in the sector, while sheep and shepherds are declining. Cattle raising provides more time for farmers to diversify their income, which they perceived as essential in a sector where, after decades of unfavourable market conditions, the economic margins are very narrow. However, the transition to cattle is an emerging coexistence challenge due to the vulnerability of young calves. Their growing numbers in combination with decreased vigilance have now become the main source of wolf attacks and associated disputes in S-LC (JCyL 2018).

Managing wolves as game and compensating damages

In the northern half of Castile and León (see Figure 1), the wolf is listed in Annex V of the Habitat Directive and managed as a game species. A range of stakeholders cited this partial protection as essential for coexistence in general, particularly in S-LC. The consistently high density of wolves in the last decades was considered a proof of concept, often contrasted with the poor conservation status of wolves in areas where they are strictly protected by Annex IV. This includes Andalusia, where wolves are now believed to be extinct; and Portugal, where poaching is a significant issue (although there is limited evidence that legal hunting decreases poaching, see Blanco 2017). While wolves still die of unnatural causes in S-LC, it is in low numbers. In 2017, the official figure was 34, mainly from traffic accidents (JCyL 2018). In contrast with complete protection, the regular hunting of wolves gave many locals a sense that they were 'under control', something they considered essential for all wildlife in order to prevent overpopulation and disease. The 2019-2022 hunting plan in Zamora province approved the hunting of 29 specimens per season from its estimated 30 wolf packs, of which the majority are to be hunted in La Culebra (JCyL 2019). For both wolves and deer, the hunting fees are substantial. The wolf permits in La Culebra are auctioned with a starting bid of EUR 3,600 (plus an additional EUR 2,500 in fees and 21% tax) (JCyL 2020). The income from hunting (around EUR 120,000 per year in recent years, according to the reserve administration) is divided proportionally among the 12 municipalities which own 70% of its area amongst themselves. Various locals cited the importance of this income for the maintenance of municipal infrastructure and other necessities.

As part of the management plan, the regional government is also responsible for compensating for direct damage from wolves to livestock within hunting reserves. Outside of the reserves, shepherds and farmers are compensated only if they have specific insurance, for which the deductible is covered by the government in case of attacks. In either case, there was wide consensus that submission and payment of claims were incredibly cumbersome and slow. Claims are only granted if attacks can be proven, which is often impossible since carrion-consuming species are abundant in the area.

> Yes, I have insurance. But it doesn't make much sense, what it costs me in fees means that it doesn't compensate for the cost of the livestock if it gets killed. […] First I have to find it. And how am I then to prove to the Junta [the regional government] that it was the wolf who killed my foal? They will tell me 'bad luck, amigo'. […] They won't pay you. And if they do it won't be what it is worth, it will be nothing. (Cattle and horse farmer, 2020)

> But what is certain is that to the south of the river Duero, because it [the wolf] is a protected species there, damages are

paid out faster. [...] But because the wolf to the north of the river Duero is a game species, it is possible to hunt it, well, I don't know, for some reason the payments are delayed. And people become angry with all the rights in the world. (Civil servant, 2020)

According to official statistics, the numbers of registered and compensated damages north of the Duero river have declined in recent years, particularly for sheep, while remaining stable for cattle (JCyL 2018). However, our findings indicate that due to the ineffective bureaucracy, many farmers abstain from reporting anything but major losses, resulting in an official underestimation of damages.

Notwithstanding its historic role in saving the species, wolf hunting is today a deeply polemic topic in Spain, and we perceived growing support for the strict protection of wolves. This was evident in the media and campaigns from informal groups, political parties, and NGOs. In S-LC, this view was enhanced by the growing importance of wolf tourism. Views diverged within and between stakeholder groups about the role of hunting in sustaining coexistence in the future, and whether it could be compatible with wolf tourism. Uncertainty over the impact of culling on pack structure, and its efficacy in preventing livestock damages (see Eklund et al. 2017), contributes to this division, noticeable in how certain facts from scientific papers and reports were cherry-picked to support particular standpoints. Further exacerbating the situation is a lack of transparency in how and why decisions regarding wolves are made by the authorities. We found a systemic distrust of politicians and the authorities, on all levels, throughout the studied communities. The regional government has been prosecuted on various occasions for insufficient scientific grounds justifying their hunting quotas, leading to temporary hunting bans, the most recent in 2019 (Blanco 2017; Camazón 2020). Simultaneously, hunters perceived increasing social pressure and aggression from animal-rights groups, which they believed was partially to blame for the low generational turnover within the hunting sector. There is now mounting pressure to harmonize wolf management in Spain by declaring it strictly protected throughout the country (MITECO 2020). Thus, the future of hunting in S-LC, and its broader implications for wolves, is uncertain.

Tourism

In recent decades, the ability to commodify the wolf has become an important justification for coexistence. The year 2015 saw the inauguration of Iberian Wolf Centre in Sanabria, a 21 ha interpretation centre, and a part of a socio-economic revitalisation project linked to the regional Wolf Conservation and Management Plan (https://centrodellobo.es/). The centre, with its two packs of captive-bred wolves, has cemented the status of the S-LC as the 'Land of the Wolf.' Wolf imagery is readily displayed throughout the area, on touristic information material and on various paraphernalia sold in village shops. There are 12 wolf-watching businesses that completely or partly base their operations in La Culebra, four with local offices, and an estimated 3,100 visits in 2017 (Martínez 2019; Lora Bavo and Villar Lama 2020). According to a study from La Culebra in 2012, wolf tourists represented almost half of the overnight stays in rural accommodations (Blanco 2017). Tourism in S-LC is otherwise limited to the summer months. Wolf observation, a year-round activity, has therefore become important to somewhat mitigate this seasonality. The economic impact of the sector was widely acknowledged, and a majority of the interviewed mayors saw tourism in general, and wolf watching in particular, as essential to ensure a future for their municipality.

Concomitant with the growing demand for nature tourism across Europe, the sector in Spain will likely keep expanding and attracting tourists to rural areas where bears, lynx and wolves may be observed (MAPAMA 2017). The increasing volume is a challenge for local and regional administrations. They do not receive any direct income from tourism (there are no park fees), but are responsible for providing and maintaining infrastructure, regulating businesses and preventing the negative impact on wildlife. Growth notwithstanding, wolf tourism still represents a small percentage of the local economy, and one that is dependent on outside patronage rather than the communities' own production. As became evident during the COVID-19 pandemic (which broke out during the fieldwork period, halting all tourism activities), the industry is fickle and prone to sudden changes in demand. Wolf tourism is also unfeasible in most areas outside of the hunting reserve, and Spain in general, since topography, forests and other factors make wolf-watching difficult and unpredictable.

Fostering Coexistence and Conviviality—What Can S-LC Teach Us?

In order to understand coexistence in S-LC, we return to the elements outlined by Carter and Linnell 2016.: social legitimacy, tolerable levels of risk, mutual adaptation, carnivore population persistence, and effective institutions.

What characterises coexistence in S-LC was not an absence of disputes. Some locals dislike and find wolves problematic, and a minority react accordingly (for instance by publicly voicing anti-wolf opinions). Nevertheless, for the most part, wolves are considered a legitimate element of S-LC's fauna. While opinions diverged about acceptable population size and impact, we did not encounter anyone who advocated for the extinction of wolves, or who would not tolerate some level of wolf-related inconvenience, which is consistent with earlier findings from the region (Martínez 2019). It contrasts findings from elsewhere in Europe and North America where wolves are perceived as the main concern of rural inhabitants, and where tolerance to wolves decreased with proximity to the nearest wolf habitat (Blanco 2017; Bruskotter et al. 2017). The relatively high tolerance of S-LC's inhabitants, and their ingenuity to protect their livestock, have been important for the recovery of wolves across the Iberian Peninsula, since the area has constituted a buffer zone from which wolves could reclaim territory. People's tolerance is likely a product of the uninterrupted process of adaptation to sharing space. People who decide to live and produce in S-LC are aware of the wolf as a local idiosyncrasy and can readily learn about efficient coping mechanisms from senior shepherds. Similar findings were made in Albania, where locals attributed the relatively few wolf attacks on livestock to inexperience or poor shepherding (Trajce 2017). Since wolves are expanding across Europe (Cimatti et al. 2021), these examples of convivial practices and attitudes, and the embodied knowledge of these stakeholders, are crucial to informing conservation policy in the coming decades (Carter and Linnell 2016). That deer seem more contested and troublesome than wolves in S-LC supports theories that (re)introduced species tend to generate more disputes than those with permanent presence (Linnell and Cretois 2018). However, we encourage further exploration to ascertain how widespread this perception is in S-LC. The importance of habit to the legitimacy of a species is a challenge to conservation. It could mean that the return of many large-bodied mammals will be accompanied by long periods of turbulence and dispute before more convivial relationships can be established. It raises the question of how the process of legitimising and becoming accustomed to these species can be accelerated, including the development of efficient and locally appropriate coping mechanisms.

Our findings align with Von Essen and Allen's (2018), in that rural inhabitants usually recognise that modernisation is unavoidable and tolerate associated changes, as long as they are gradual and can be unified with major elements of the prior status quo. We thus contend that effective institutions, capable of working across scales and connecting social and ecological issues, are essential in fostering and perpetuating people's willingness and ability to coexist with wildlife. They must address the disparity in living conditions between urban and rural people, perpetuated by unequal access to social services, subsidies that incentivise quantity over socio-environmental indicators, and the decoupling of consumers from producers (as detailed by Leal Filho et al. 2016; Navarro and López-

Bao, 2018). In S-LC, informants agreed that it was not the wolves themselves that were the problem, but how they and their rural surroundings were governed. Farmers and villagers considered the administration to be ignorant of their reality, unresponsive to their needs, and felt excluded from decision-making processes. This sentiment was exacerbated by the poor performance of damage compensations schemes, mirroring earlier findings of the inherent problems with ex-post payment schemes (see Nyhus 2016). The disinclination within both Spanish and European policy to support functional coexistence relationships exacerbated the vulnerability of communities such as S-LC to surrounding challenges. It also undermined habitat protection and public accessibility within Natura 2000 areas through increasing scrub encroachment, wildfires, and crumbling infrastructure (Fuentes et al. 2011). Ineffective governance is thereby neglecting the very conditions that have fostered conviviality in S-LC by perpetuating low generational turnover, depopulation and urban-rural polarisation. As shown elsewhere, wolves can easily become symbols for such issues, particularly when locals feel disempowered (Peterson et al. 2010; Madden and McQuinn 2014).

The situation in S-LC reflects a policy reality that remains biased towards conflict rather than incentivising and enhancing coexistence, for example, by legally and economically supporting guardian dogs and initiatives that stimulate markets for local produce. Another example of this phenomenon can be observed in Idaho, which recently passed a law that calls for the killing 90% of the state's wolves, with the stated rationale to appease angry hunters and farmers (Oppie 2021). Analysing the situation through a coexistence lens could have elucidated alternative relationships and pathways. One example is Lava Lake Farm[2], which raises free-roaming lamb in an area with wolves and other large carnivores, with minimal losses.

Given burgeoning global restoration agendas (e.g., 'UN decade on ecosystem restoration'[3]), there is an increasing urgency to explore and build on existing ways of leading convivial lives with 'problematic' species such as the wolf. If areas that are emblematic of wolf coexistence are overlooked and their traditions and cultures rendered obsolete, it may reinforce the image of the wolf as 'the beast of waste and desolation'[4] and further intimidate areas that are expecting their return.

Governing for Sustainable Coexistence

Our study supports earlier findings that large carnivore conservation cannot be decoupled from other aspects of rural policy, and that coexistence measures should be mainstreamed within wider rural development programmes (Linnell and Cretois 2018). Present disputes in a system may indicate where to direct efforts and serve as a catalyst for positive change (Madden and McQuinn 2014). Our data indicate that most disputes in S-LC spring from the unequal distribution of responsibilities and benefits of wolf conservation. Local communities, particularly farmers and shepherds, face the practicalities of coexistence, while a different set of stakeholders (e.g. hunters, tourists and wolf-related businesses), who often live elsewhere, are the predominant beneficiaries. Although farmers and shepherds indirectly benefited from increased economic turnover and service provision associated with hunting and tourism, they received no direct benefits that could alleviate their precarious economic status or the increased workload required to prevent wolf attacks. As a local shepherd put it in 2020: 'The ones of us who live in wolf territory have significantly less quality of life than those who don't. So you will always lose, always. [...] Even if you are economically compensated for all the costs you have from the wolf, even then you will lose'.

This illustrates a generalised conundrum within conservation; that that actors who are directly dependent on and living with natural resources tend to be the most negatively affected by wildlife, least enriched by species protection, and most targeted by interventions that strive to change behaviours and livelihoods to meet biodiversity targets (Büscher and Fletcher 2019; Jordan et al. 2020). If left unaddressed, this disparity will keep undermining coexistence and the perceived legitimacy of conservation policy. The negotiation of the European Green New Deal and the revised Common Agricultural Policy offers a window to adjust funding mechanisms according to more just and environmentally sustainable principles. The mechanisms (that have been reviewed elsewhere, see Marsden et al. 2016; Navarro and López-Bao 2018) must be flexible in order to address idiosyncratic local needs—which could range from the provision of infrastructure (barns, fences, producer-consumer networks), services (scrub removal, communal shepherding schemes) or support with bureaucratic and legal issues (land rights and application procedures). One approach that has been successfully applied to identify these needs and which builds on local embodied knowledge is Participatory Action Research, which is based on intimate collaboration between researchers and communities (Milich et al. 2020). Local participation in the establishment of conservation priorities, which was accomplished by a regional mediation initiative within our study area[5], could counter authoritarian and alienating policies and improve local stewardship of wildlife (Redpath et al. 2017; Büscher and Fletcher 2019).

The effects of such policy interventions may result in a shift away from damage payments, due to their long-term economic unviability, particularly as carnivores keep expanding, and failure to incentivise good practice (Nyhus 2016). An alternative may be ex-ante payments for those residing in a carnivore area, similar to the support to farmers in certain marginal areas. One such scheme for large carnivores has been rolled out with some promising results in Sweden (see Persson et al. 2015). Another interesting proposition is a Conservation Basic Income, combining the social benefits of Universal Basic Income with the focus on environmental protection of the Payment for Ecosystem Services' programme (Fletcher and Büscher 2020). However, many questions remain for both of these schemes before they can be applied on a larger scale, for instance concerning the delineation of territory, funding, and legitimacy. These queries notwithstanding, we believe these schemes could contribute to a more hopeful and equitable conservation policy by incentivising convivial practices and ensuring that areas with functioning coexistence prosper in the long term.

Population Management of a Flagship Species

The peculiar status of S-LC as a destination for both observing and hunting wolves created an interesting dynamic and gave rise to incongruent views about the area's past and future coexistence conditions. It is illustrative of a global trend in which increasingly mutualist animal ethics clash with local, often more utilitarian views of wildlife (such as trophy hunting), and the practicalities of wildlife management in marginal(ised) landscapes (Bruskotter et al. 2017; Pooley et al. 2017). Given the flagship status of large carnivores and the reoccurring lawsuits by NGOs and civil society, it seems unlikely that S-LC's approach, based on culling and recreational hunting as a means of control, would be accepted on a larger scale (Blanco 2017). A complete ban on lethal control seems equally unfeasible, since the nature of coexistence means that the dynamics that would regulate wolf populations in a completely 'natural' system are significantly altered. As noted by Mech 2017., wolves can and will adapt to almost any type of habitat as long as there are viable sources of food, whether anthropogenic or wild. Since wolves have high reproductive potential, they will continue to expand their ranges in the absence of threats, increasing the pressure on domestic livestock and moving closer to suburbs and cities. In policy advice for the European AGRI Committee 2018., it is therefore acknowledged that some level of lethal control will always be needed, and Boitani and Linnell (2015: 67) further note that in Europe, 'human influence on all trophic levels is pervasive, legitimate, necessary and often even desirable'.

However, even an inherently pragmatic position on control, for instance, only targeting individual animals that cause damage, is likely to be controversial. Decisions about where and when wolves should be culled, legally hunted, or protected will require transparent and participatory approaches in order to successfully balance the goals of carnivore conservation with the goals of preserving rural culture, population and production in marginal areas (Linnell and Cretois 2018).

Conclusion

Studying the histories and conditions of human-wildlife relationships helps us identify where and when different animals are perceived to belong or be out of place (Pooley et al. 2017). In this research, we have illustrated that the use of a coexistence lens to study human-wildlife interactions is instrumental to identify areas from which to seek knowledge and inspiration on how to promote convivial conservation. In the case of S-LC, we found a clear manifestation of functioning coexistence, but also threats to the stability of this state. Our work with impacted communities indicated that boosting sustainable farming practices could ensure both wolf conservation and the preservation of local cultures, thereby enhancing the area's reputation as a successful coexistence model.

Where the conflict lens has repeatedly produced the same apolitical and technical solutions (i.e., preventative measures, efforts to change attitudes and compensation payments), our approach based on promoting 'bright spots' and biocultural diversity can help bridge disciplinary silos and accelerate transformative changes in conservation policy (Pretty et al. 2010; Bennett et al. 2015). A shift in policy orientation, from reducing conservation conflict to enhancing coexistence, would mean dedicating more resources to addressing underlying socio-ecological issues and promoting resilience of convivial lifestyles and behaviours, embracing the plurality of ways in which they can be manifested. This aligns with Büscher and Fletcher's (2019: 288) principles that conservation should go beyond preserving only non-human nature, and that it should be conducted within the 'broader amalgam of "living landscapes" that do long-term socio-ecological justice to humans and non-humans'. By ensuring dignity, inclusivity and supporting communities to develop with global transitions, it is possible to preserve Europe's vibrant and entangled biocultural diversity, while shifting towards more harmonious human-nature interactions. There are undoubtedly more positive examples which we could build on—we just need to look for them.

Chapter 9:

Convivial Conservation from the Bottom Up: Human-Bear Cohabitation in the Rodopi Mountains of Bulgaria[*]

By Svetoslava Toncheva, Robert Fletcher, and Esther Turnhout

Introduction

This chapter presents a case study of human-bear interaction in the Rodopi mountains of Bulgaria, which we argue represents an unusual instance of relatively successful cohabitation characterized by locally developed strategies for living together with bears. Bears have an ambiguous position here in terms of conservation: while they are formally protected by Bulgarian and overarching European legislation, many live outside of strict protected areas (PAs) and therefore occupy overlapping space with people. The specific context of postsocialism (Drondel 2016) has necessitated largely bottom-up initiatives rather than imposition of approaches formulated by external conservationists, as in the majority of conservation cases globally (Fletcher 2012). Consequently, the case can be characterized as a form of 'constitutionality' emphasizing 'local agency and creativity in the construction of novel institutions to deal with environmental issues' (Haller et al. 2016, 69). This dynamic is illustrated in particular by strong reliance on local ecological knowledge (LEK) and use of ecotourism as a key conservation strategy, which unlike in many other cases where the activity is introduced by outsiders (Fletcher 2009), here it is understood by locals as their own initiative. The present study thus contributes to a growing body of research exploring the potential for convivial

---

[*] Originally published as: Toncheva, S., R. Fletcher, and E. Turnhout. (2022). Convivial conservation from the bottom up: Human-bear cohabitation in the Rodopi Mountains of Bulgaria. Conservation & Society 20(2): 124-135.

conservation to facilitate human-wildlife coexistence in the Anthropocene by investigating a case of bottom-up constitutionality wherein people and animals have adjusted to living together in a context of limited state oversight.

The study also contributes to research concerning human-wildlife conflict and coexistence. Large predators are commonly seen as a major challenge for conservation due to such factors as damage to domestic animals and crops and direct threats posed to human life (Treves and Karanth 2003). Yet preservation of such predators is also commonly a central conservation objective due to their status as keystone species, attributed with regulating other species' population density and hence producing trophic cascade effects (Van Valkenburgh and Wayne 2010). The majority of research concerning how to facilitate large predator conservation has until recently focused on human-carnivore conflicts and their potential prevention, rather on understanding mechanisms facilitating successful coexistence (Frank et al. 2019; Hodgson et al. 2020).

In conservation practice, addressing human-wildlife conflict usually occurs within PAs by wildlife agencies that work to prevent conflicts (Treves and Karanth 2003) or through reliance on externally-funded compensation schemes (Dickman et al. 2011). However, research concerning alternative ways to manage or prevent conflicts where people and nature coexist outside of formal protected areas has been less apparent. Frank and Glikman assert that '[f]uture research should showcase coexistence and tolerance' to highlight 'positive attitudes/behaviour and explore factors (i.e. values, culture and location of residence) that foster positive psychological dispositions and coexistence towards wildlife' (2019: 14). The present study responds to this call by exploring a case in which local residents have learned to coexist with bears within an overlapping space. The factors responsible for this situation are relevant for understanding how to encourage human-wildlife coexistence more broadly. While the role and perspective of the wildlife in question is of course important in explaining such dynamics (Boonman-

Berson et al 2019; Ampumuza and Driessen 2021), addressing this is beyond the scope of this paper and hence has been explored in a complementary one (Toncheva and Fletcher 2022). In the following analysis we therefore focus on the humans' approach to negotiating interactions with bears.

We begin by situating our analysis within growing discussion of the potential of convivial conservation to foster human-wildlife coexistence through broader socio-economic transformation (Büscher and Fletcher 2019; 2020). We highlight our contribution to this discussion in exploring underexamined processes of bottom-up convivial programming through synthesis with a constitutionality perspective. We then explain the methods used in this study. Following this, we describe the particular context of our case within postsocialist Bulgaria. We then outline and analyze the various strategies that contribute to human-bear cohabitation in this context. We finish by highlighting the implications of our study for investigating and facilitating similar processes of what Haller and colleagues (2020) elsewhere term 'convivial constitutionality'.

Towards Convivial Constitutionality

Discussion of convivial conservation arose in response to growing debate around assertions that we have entered a new geological epoch—the Anthropocene—in which human action and institutions increasingly dominate the planet (Lorimer 2015). For some, this assertion has evoked a sense of urgency to strengthen conservation efforts through enforcement and expansion of protected areas (Wuerthner et al. 2015; Wilson 2016) or via market-based instruments (Kareiva et al. 2012). Others, however, have used it to rethink the very category of nature and specifically to question the dichotomy between culture and nature central to the global conservation movement historically (Brockington et al. 2008; Lorimer 2015). Overcoming this dichotomy implies accepting the fundamental entanglement of humans and nonhumans and thus understanding 'natural' areas as the consequence of co-production by both (Haraway

2016; Lorimer 2015). The notion of conviviality takes this perspective in training critical reflection on how humans and nonhumans can live well together and cohabit overlapping spaces (Hinchliffe 2007; Turnhout et al. 2013; Büscher and Fletcher 2019; 2020).

Building on such discussions, as well as Ivan Illich's (1973) exploration of conviviality as a project of societal reconstruction more broadly, Büscher and Fletcher (2019, 2020) propose convivial conservation as a strategy to transcend both strict protectionism and market engagement. This proposal resolves into three main principles: developing 1) conservation spaces that integrate rather than separate humans and other species; 2) direct democratic governance arrangements that challenge elite technocratic management; and 3) novel finance arrangements that seek not to commodify conserved resources but instead redistribute existing wealth and resources.

Thus far, the convivial conservation proposal has primarily been promoted for global policy discussions and adoption by international organizations (Büscher and Fletcher 2020). While the approach explicitly acknowledges cases embodying aspects of the approach in diverse local initiatives (ibid, 149), cases of this sort have not been systematically analyzed in relation to the core principles previously outlined. And while micro-level human-nonhuman interactions have been previously explored from the perspective of conviviality more generally (Hinchcliffe et al. 2005; Hinchcliffe 2007), these studies have largely neglected attention to the wider political dynamics within which such interactions are embedded. In response, Haller and colleagues (2016) advance the concept of constitutionality to emphasize 'community members' views on participation, the strategies they employ in negotiating such initiatives, and the extent to which they can develop a related sense of ownership in the institution-building process for common pool resource (CPR) management' (p. 68). They argue that successful constitutionality commonly encompasses several preconditions including an: '(a) emic perception of need of new institutions,

(b) participatory processes addressing power asymmetries, (c) preexisting institutions, (d) outside catalysing agents (fair platform), (e) recognition of local knowledge, and (f) higher-level state recognition' (ibid., 80). Combining a constitutionality perspective with the convivial conservation principles previously outlined offers a novel and productive lens through which to explore community-led initiatives in terms of their potential to enact forms of 'convivial constitutionality'. While Haller et al. (2020) propose this in introducing the composite concept, they do not elaborate on how the two frameworks can be brought together in a synthetic analysis as we do herein. Within this synthesis, Haller and colleague's (2016) elements of constitutionality can be cross-referenced with Büscher and Fletcher's (2020) principles of convivial conservation. The integrated framework can then be used to assess the relative success or challenges faced by efforts to cultivate conviviality in human-nonhuman relations at the local level by evaluating such efforts in terms of criteria for just and effective conservation and for bottom-up commons governance simultaneously.

A central element of the convivial conservation proposal is promotion of human-wildlife coexistence (Büscher and Fletcher 2020; see also Turnhout et al. 2013). Coexistence, or cohabitation, has been promoted more widely within conservation discussions to shift focus away from a historical focus on human-wildlife *conflict* (Frank et al. 2019). Cohabitation presumes that humans and wildlife can peacefully share a common space (Hinchliffe 2007). The term also challenges *management* as a problematic category legitimizing human control over other species (Boonman-Berson et al. 2016). In discussions of human-wildlife conflict, for instance, two main solutions to conflict management are offered: 1) modification of animals' behavior (often by radical measures, such as killing); and 2) prevention of activities that overlap in space (e.g. by fences, zoning, relocation, etc.) (Treves and Karanth 2003; Hodgson et al. 2020). The emphasis is thus frequently on management of animals rather than management of people, who are often a (if not *the*) major factor in such conflicts (Margulies and Karanth 2018; Frank et al. 2019). Moreover, such approaches rely on establishing problematic boundaries between humans and other species. To move beyond such approaches thus requires a new 'politics of conviviality' emphasizing practices of mutual adjustment and learning to live together (Turnhout et al. 2013; Boonman-Berson et al. 2016; Büscher and Fletcher 2020).

To do so effectively entails acknowledging 'the roles of culture and values in human–wildlife coexistence' (Pooley et al. 2017: 514; see also Dickman et al. 2013). A large body of research has documented so-called local or traditional ecological knowledge (LEK or TEK) and its role in shaping the interactions between people and nonhumans, often opposing this to modern expert or scientific knowledge (Berkes 2008; Berkes et al. 2000). Defined as a 'cumulative body of knowledge, practice, and belief that pertains to the relationship of living beings' (Anadón et al. 2009), to describe a form of 'situated knowledge' that is 'simultaneously local and global' (Nygren 1999: 268), LEK emphasizes the existence of a locally developed system of knowledge supporting the management of human-nature relations differing from the technocratic scientific approach dominating conventional conservation efforts (Nygren 1999). As previously noted, LEK is also integral to a constitutionality approach (Haller et al. 2016).

An important aspect of LEK in our case concerns its role within the development of ecotourism as a key support for bear conservation. Ecotourism has been widely advocated as a strategy for sustainable development integrating biodiversity conservation (Weaver and Lawton 2007; Honey 2008). Consequently, much scholarly attention has sought to evaluate ecotourism's effectiveness as a conservation tool (Stronza 2007; Honey 2008) and has highlighted various problems commonly encountered in this effort (Mowforth and Munt 2016). Ecotourism promotion is frequently grounded in the premise that economic benefits will encourage local people 'to protect what they receive value from' (Honey 2008:

162). Yet multiple cases demonstrate how ecotourism often results, on the contrary, in imposing western ideas and representations or functioning as a tool for political control (see e.g. Duffy 2002; West and Carrier 2004; Honey 2008; Fletcher 2009).

In particular, the promised economic benefits of ecotourism involvement have been described as representative of a sustainable development discourse that reframes lively nature as a passive environment containing valuable capital to be sustained (Escobar 1996). This commodification of nature, or 'construction of nature as service provider' (Sullivan 2009: 23), is thereby often introduced via ecotourism into local populations' lifeworlds (Fletcher 2009). Such commodification can drain landscapes of their local socio-cultural significance, replacing this with universal monetary value and further disconnecting people from nonhumans (West and Carrier 2004; West 2006; Hutchins 2007).

Despite such critiques, recent attention focused on the examination of the sociocultural context within which ecotourism develops demonstrates how in a number of cases people transform and resist 'novel cultural influence' in ways that allow them to maintain some control over their engagement in the activity (Fletcher 2009: 281). Hence, the extent to which ecotourism transforms local behavior and perspectives in unwanted ways 'remains unclear' (ibid., 281). Our case study interrogates this important yet under-researched process, exploring how ecotourism development has proceeded in this context, and how it has engaged specifically with the lifeworlds of local people.

Materials and Methods

The study is based on four months of ethnographic research conducted between June and September 2018 by the first author (Toncheva) in the village of Yagodina (Figure 1). During this time Toncheva conducted 30 semi-structured and semi-directive interviews. Informants were selected via snowball and purposive sampling that sought to include different groups of relevant stakeholders: hunters, ecotourism guides, employees in tourism, pensioners and children[i], among others. Some of the interviews were tape-recorded, while others, following the wishes of informants, were documented in a field diary. In the case of local ecological knowledge, the interview data were complemented by administration of 16 questionnaires each containing 72 questions assessing LEK concerning brown bear's ecological and cultural salience to another set of respondents. These questionnaires were not intended to pursue representative sampling of the total population for statistical analysis but merely to complement in-depth interviews with comparative qualitative material collected from a broader range of local residents.

In addition, Toncheva conducted participant observation throughout the research period, including the accompanying of two bear watching trips by British tourists for two full weeks and participation in a bullet casting ritual (more on this below). As tourists were not the primary subject of research, participation in tourism trips was used to observe how ecotourism is performed and organized, what knowledge is used in its delivery and how tourists enter the human-bear cohabitation space, as well as to observe the behaviour of the bears at the bear-watching hide. This experience also enabled learning how to recognize signs of bear activity (prints, flipped around stones, communication trees, etc.) and better understanding bear behavior due to the multiple lectures delivered by the guide (which were also tape-recorded) during the trip.

Analysis of all this material is grounded in Toncheva's long-term observations of the village, having been employed as a mountain guide there for more than a decade. Consequently, some conclusions, such as the consistent absence of significant human-bear conflicts, are based on patterns observed during a much longer time than the formal research period. This makes Toncheva something of an insider or native researcher in the field site. While this positionality carries the benefit of long-term knowledge and experience concerning the dynamics under investigation as well rapport with local residents affording access to backstage spaces, it also presents the potential to overlook significant issues due precisely to this familiarity and the biases it might introduce into data collection and analysis (Bernard 2011). To guard against this danger, all observations and interpretations have been extensively discussed and debated among the three authors prior to presentation herein.

Postsocialist Conservation

Bulgaria is a leading country in Europe in terms of biodiversity protection but is rarely addressed in the existing conservation literature. Occupying only 2.5% of EU territory, the country supports about 70% of protected bird species and around 40% of PAs (Natura 2000). Yet the country faces numerous threats to biodiversity due to lack of enforcement, corruption, the existence of a grey economy, and disregard of legislation (including European legislation).

Bulgaria has undergone a long period of transition after the collapse of the socialist regime—the period of so-called postsocialism (Creed 1995; Drondel 2016)—and it is still struggling to find its way within the common European cultural and economic space. It has faced serious challenges applying European environmental regulations, provoking negative reports from the European Commission claiming that the country has not fulfilled the definition of Natura 2000 protected territories nor clearly introduced measures to protect habitats and endangered species. Indeed, recent assessments conclude that policy measures in relation to about 50% of protected species are insufficient[2]. Given both inadequate application of environmental legislation and plans for its enforcement, building still takes place within Natura 2000 zones. Such issues present serious threats to biodiversity and, together with non-regulated development (and often a lack of state presence), constitute serious challenges for Bulgarian conservation. At the same time, this relative absence of government-directed conservation has afforded the emergence of local arrangements, particularly in rural spaces like the one documented in this chapter, to govern how humans interact with wildlife.

Bears have become an important focus of national conservation efforts, having been granted protected status by the state since 1993 (Red List of Bulgaria) and later through European legislation after the country's accession to the EU. Although bears' protected status requires their habitats to be included under Natura 2000 protection, many remain outside formal protected areas. Such is the case in the Rodopi mountains, a region with one of the highest bear populations but where, due to various economic interests, no national parks have been established; there are only small, fragmented areas designated as nature reserves. This makes it the region with the most intense human-bear interactions (Дуцов и др. 2012). The total Bulgarian bear population is currently believed to be 600–800, with the population in Rodopi between 206 and 334 (on the basis of collected genetic samples from hairs and scat; Frosch et al. 2014). This number is lower than the carrying capacity calculated by a habitat suitability model developed by Zlatanova (2010), according to which the region could accommodate 430-540 bears (with a potential population of 1000-2000 for Bulgaria as a whole). Suitable habitat in Rodopi is considered the largest and most important in the country, which, given the lack of PAs and the numerous mountain villages there, has led to inevitable human-bear encounters encompassing various conflicts and other interactions.

Yagodina is located in the heart of Rodopi (see Figure 1). During the socialist period, the village experienced land collectivization combined with state planned agriculture and animal breeding, leading to economic development encompassing various employment opportunities (including three active factories, large levels of animal breeding—around six thousand sheep—production of dairy products, timber, etc.). After the socialist collapse, the population faced severe problems: land fragmentation provoking ownership conflicts, lack of financial recourses for cultivation, social transformations related to urban outmigration, privatization (and in fact abandonment) of existing enterprises and, as a result, scarcity of employment opportunities. The long transition did not improve but actually worsened the area's situation with the population facing a lack of state or foreign investment and hence were left to develop alternative livelihood strategies in the context of available natural resources. Logically, one of these avenues was tourism, given the village's location in the high mountains proximate to two famous gorges (Buynovsko and Trigrad) and caves (Yagodina and Devil's Throat) as well as the well-preserved nature with extremely high biodiversity.

Figure 1. Map of the study area: the village of Yagodina

Yagodina is surrounded by forest, all of which has been officially state-owned and managed since socialist times. Yagodina's forest is excellent habitat for brown bears whose numbers, according to the local population, have increased significantly in recent years. This increase is seen to have been facilitated by the agricultural decline experienced during the last 30 years (under postsocialism), during which huge amounts of previously cultivated land has been abandoned. This has led to an unplanned rewilding (Lorimer et al. 2015) wherein now one can see forests where, according to local people, 'we used to grow wheat before'. Population decline due to outmigration in search of employment and removal of the border fence between Bulgaria and Greece (which is, according to many, 'where most bears came from') also contribute to the area's bear population increase.

A further reason for this increase is that bears have been granted a protected status. Exceptions are problematic bears that can be shot after the granting of a special permit from the Ministry of Environment and Food, following investigations and proof that the animals have actually caused economic or physical damage. Measures against bear poaching are considered so strict, by some respondents, that 'it is easier to kill a man and get away with it than to kill a bear'. Still, the fine for illegal hunting is not so high, even by local standards (up to 5000 lv. or 2500 euro), especially considering the prices for bear products on the black market.

A final factor contributing to the high bear population is the extremely high endemic biodiversity in the surrounding forest. The great variety of species provides an abundance of food for bears, such as wild berries (strawberries, raspberries, cornelian cherries, bilberries, etc.), various roots and grasses, ants, and so forth. This contributes to the lack of conflict and successful cohabitation while also causing various interactions since local livelihoods also comprise forest activities to gather wild foods. Due to this natural abundance, the bears rarely approach Yagodina and have not caused any property damage, while most encounters occur in the forest around livelihood activities or hobbies: hunting, gathering of plants (mushrooms, herbs, berries), hiking/walking, fishing, agriculture (hay collecting, harvesting) or around the nearby caves.

Stories told by the elderly population suggest that there have always been bears around; people between 70 and 90 years old remember encounters that occurred during their parents' lifespan. Still, assertions by local inhabitants that bears' number is much higher now suggests that the animals' previous presence was not so obvious under socialism, due to the villages' economic development and the more stringent restrictions over human mobility (due to border control) occurring then, as well as the fact that bears did not enjoy protected status and were allowed to be hunted and killed.

According to local hunters, who are most familiar with the bears around Yagodina, the latter now number about 10–13 just in areas around the village. As many people believe so many bears were never present before, this forces both humans and bears to adapt to a new situation in which both species must adapt to live together.

A Landscape of Tolerance

As the bears are recognized as fellow inhabitants of the shared space by local residents, they are an important and often discussed topic. The village of Yagodina is relatively small (less than 500 people) and largely homogenous. This means that everybody knows one another and that the village square functions as a center for exchange of news. Bear issues are therefore discussed while drinking coffee in the morning or over a *rakia*[3] in the local bar in the evenings. While not everyone has seen a bear themselves, bears are therefore part of the local lifeworld: we never encountered a villager who had not heard of a story of human-bear encounter even if they had not had a personal one. Most encounters are occasional meetings by chance, occurring predominantly to local hunters or people involved in other forest activities. However, bears have been seen even by people just driving on the road or visiting nearby caves.

Bears are large predators that mainly provoke fear, even for some inexperienced hunters during close unexpected encounters. At the same time, the local population's attitude towards bears is predominantly positive, in part because encounters are rare and because bears are only considered dangerous when they are threatened or when human and bear territories cross. A higher risk is attributed to certain categories of bears: females with cubs and *stuvnitsi* (aggressive bears which are more carnivorous). Still, cohabitation is determined by the attitude of both species who attempt to avoid one another and do not enter conflict situations. Respondents described various methods that could potentially diminish encounters: making a noise, avoiding areas known as bear habitats, as well as some traditional practices such as invoking prayers or spells (a practice that is, however, rarely used nowadays).

In traditional Bulgarian culture, the village or the inhabited space is considered the known, cultivated space as opposed to the forests and fields beyond (Георгиева 1993). Despite ongoing processes of modernization, Yagodina's high altitude and relative isolation contribute to preservation of certain traditional cultural patterns. Fieldwork data thus evidences that a common division of space between our (here, in the village) and that *out there* (the forest, the habitat of the bear) still exists. Within this division, the bears' core habitats can also be considered intimate space which should not be entered by others (humans). This idea is supported by informants' claims that bears should not be disturbed in their territories and, likewise, that they should not enter the space inhabited by humans (the village).

As previously mentioned, the majority of human-bear interactions occur in what we refer to as *cohabitation space* beyond the village: the nearby forests, meadows, rivers and agricultural lands wherein people and bears interact and which are permanently occupied by both species. People are aware of the bears' presence in these shared spaces because they are able to read the various signs bears leave behind (Hinchliffe et al. 2005; Boonman-Berson et al. 2016). Overturned stones are considered evidence of a bear's presence as people are aware that bears feed on the ants found underneath. Another aspect of the landscape associated with bears are the numerous rock holes and caves, which hunters identify as winter hibernation sites. Bear prints and scat, their most obvious markers, are also often encountered.

Some respondents assert that bears don't usually come close to the village. However, this boundary is occasionally crossed, since some villagers have observed signs of bear presence at the outskirts of the village or near their fields and sheep farms. Prints have also been seen near roads, around a newly built hotel which lies a little outside the village and near beehives.

The bears in the area are not managed in the sense that this term is commonly used by conservationists, as people do not act to deliberately produce a certain kind of behavior or fear in bears. Nor do people actively try to prevent bears from entering human spaces; the occasional boundary crossing that does take place is not considered a threat. Non-invasion of each species' core space by the other is surely a major reason for the lack of conflicts in the area. The cohabitation space, on the other hand, is the shared territory that has thus far been peacefully inhabited by both humans and bears. This peaceful coexistence is reflected in the positive attitude of those interviewed when discussing whether humans and bears are able to share the same space or whether bears should instead be separated in PAs. The majority of people claim that co-existence is indeed possible, providing various justifications including the following:

> Bears should be free, in protected territories they would feel like in a prison.

> I am against these reserved areas, here is better (for the bears). If we all care, not disturb them in their natural habitat they would live better.

In sum, the majority of people claim that humans and bears can cohabitate peacefully. We therefore characterize this as a *landscape of tolerance* for both humans and bears.

Local Ecological Knowledge Concerning Bears

Villagers express a sense of pride that bears can be seen around the village. Bears are considered symbols of power and bravery as well as of the Rodopi mountains as a whole. Bears' character is described as calm and shy, but they are also considered able to remember things for a long time and can be therefore resentful. These beliefs can be related to traditional images of the bear in Bulgarian folklore. The idea that the bears remember for a long time, for instance, is part of these beliefs and has been narrated in folklore tales.

One of these describes a man who rescued a bear's cub, after which the mother, out of gratitude, brought him some gifts. While talking to the bear the man mentioned that her breath smelt badly, after which the bear asked him to hit her on the head with an axe, which he eventually did. Sometime later they met again in the forest and the man asked the bear if they could renew their friendship. The bear showed him the healed wound and told him that she had already forgotten about it but, on the contrary, never forgot his offensive words about her breath[4].

Bears are traditionally considered symbols of power whose attacks are feared, thus various protective practices exist to provide safety and security. Even a saint is attributed the function of lord of the bears — Sveti Andrey[5] (St. Andrew) — on whose feast (30 November) bears used to be honored and were part of ritual practices. According to folklore, bears' favorite food is corn, which used to be given to the bears on St. Andrew's feast. As these beliefs are, however, associated with Christianity, it is questionable whether we could relate this to the corn villagers leave for the bears as Yagodina is traditionally a Muslim community. However, many traditions are shared by both Christians and Muslims, so in regions traditionally inhabited by bears this is possibly the case. According to these beliefs, by giving cooked corn to the bear, people can divert it from damaging people's crops and livestock. Interestingly, the same function is attributed to the corn left at the bear hide by hunters.

An element of the local Muslim tradition is the *muska* — an amulet prepared by the imam that contains prayers with a protective function. Although it still exists in the area, not many people still use it. However, some people refer to special words (in Turkish) that people used to tell the bear during encounters and that forced the bear to walk away. As one man stated, 'I know from my grandfather, some time ago someone met a bear and told her something in Turkish - bear, go your way I will go mine. And the bear left'.

Some also refer to prayers told before one walks into the forest, which were very likely prayers specially used as protection from bears. Another informant explained, for instance, 'Once people used to say some words before they left for somewhere: I hope that today nothing will happen to me, to be lucky and not meet any animals—bears, snakes, wolves'.

A vital element of local folklore are traditional practices aimed at reducing post-traumatic stress after a bear encounter. The most popular of these still practiced today, and mentioned by literally all respondents, is *casting of a bullet*. This is a type of healing magic in Bulgarian folk medicine (Гоев 1981) aimed at treatment of fear. It is practiced only by women while the competence is passed from individual to individual and normally from generation to generation. It can be performed for various reasons but is mainly aimed at healing stress from traumatic experience. In relation to bear encounters, the need for treatment was explained by one man as follows: 'XX had seen a bear and couldn't sleep, the bear was large and stood up, at one o'clock at night (this happened). He was in the car and drove back, and then the bear ran away'.

The healing practice should preferably be performed in the morning (soon after the sunrise) at days beginning with S (C in Cyrillic) which are Wednesday and Saturday (in English). This reason for this was unknown (many traditional practices cannot be explained by practitioners who generally claim that this is just how it has always been done). The patient should undergo the casting procedure three times and therefore bring therefore bullets that have been shot (into a tree) and collected. Something should be paid to the healer for the spell to work.

A further cultural practice that still exists but is infrequent nowadays (though mentioned a few times during interviews) is incandescence. The same healer could perform this as bullet casting. To undertake the procedure, the one who encountered a bear must collect various elements such as hair, wood, leaves, etc. from the place where the encounter occurred. These materials are then mixed with sugar and garlic and burned at a crossroad. The patient should then walk around the fire three times while being 'hit with a curling tong', as the healer explained. The whole procedure is accompanied with spells.

Ecotourism in Yagodina

A large number of Yagodina residents admit that the village is still inhabited today largely due to the development of tourism in the last 10–15 years as an alternative to previously existing employment opportunities. Tourism seemed a logical alternative in the context of postsocialism due to the region's natural assets: the nearby caves and gorges, which have become widely known in the last two decades and have transformed the region into one of the country's most popular tourist destinations. Tourism growth was supported by construction of a viewing platform in 2007 over the Buynovsko gorge just above Yagodina, named Eagle's Eye for its stunning views. This platform attracts thousands of visitors, both Bulgarian and foreign, every summer, when the single lane road along the gorge becomes crowded. This type of tourism can be classified as conventional (Mowforth and Munt 2016) as it lacks an ecological purpose. However, this is the largest employment niche for locals. Respondents estimate the number of villagers involved in tourism as high as 90% and view tourism as an essential livelihood that literally keeps the village alive.

As an alternative to, and in parallel with, this conventional tourism, ecotourism centred on hiking has also been established during the last decade. The main actor in this is a British tour operator working with foreign partners (British, Dutch, American, etc.) who brings foreign clients into the region for different itineraries. This tourism is represented to clients as responsible, sustainable[6] and as beneficial for the environment. Respondents considered this tourism beneficial in providing employment opportunities and bringing some investments in the region. In particular, it has directly resulted in foreign tourists occupying the village hotels, visiting the caves, buying and using local products, and so forth.

A specific form of tourism recently developed within this ecotourism niche (by the same tour operator) comprises excursions to encounter bears. Inclusion of brown bears in tourism in Yagodina began with construction of a special place for bear observation: a bear hide. Building the hide is considered a local initiative directly connected with a group of local hunters. This group comprises around 30 members and is organized in a manner typical hunting parties in Bulgaria. Thus, it has a chairman and members (legal hunters) who are responsible, among other duties, for management and preservation of the wild game in the adjacent hunting area, which is state property and under the jurisdiction of the National Forestry. Among the common activities group members undertake are consultations and decision-making regarding maintenance and feeding of the wild game, growing crops for this purpose, establishment of shelters and, of course, hunting together. Hunting follows established state regulations which designate particular periods during which it is allowed as well as the amount of game which can be hunted without threatening its overall population.

While some disagreement regarding the bear hide's funding and the role of the local tourist union exists, people agree that it was built by the hunters on the 'example of similar observation places' nearby. The building is half dug into the ground and blends into the surroundings with its grass roof and green color. A rounded metal barrel, functioning as a feeder (Figure 2), was placed about 50 meters away, illuminated by a solar-powered lamp resembling the moon's natural light. The lamp is gradually turned on at night during observations, reducing the risk that the bears are disturbed. The hide is located 30 minutes' drive from the village, and tourists are driven to it along forestry tracks by the hunters, who also work as guides. The three locals employed as guides in this activity are experienced hunters who also accompany tourists during the observation and provide information about the bears' behavior.

Figure 2. The feeder containing corn at the bear hide. Source: Svetoslava Toncheva

This obvious monopolization of bear tourism by hunters does not seem to be questioned by the majority of other locals either. This shows that the group of the hunters has, albeit unofficially, been granted the role of managers of bear-related activities as falling within the group's overarching responsibilities. It is also due to the fact that the activity does not appear particularly beneficial; some of the guides claimed that they could benefit much more if involved in other forms of tourism such as driving tourists to the Eagle's Eye viewing platform.

The British tour operator also plays a major role in bear tourism via organization of specialized tours centered around the bears. Interestingly, this tour operator not only guides bear trips but is also an ecologist performing research on bears, as founder of a nongovernmental organization aimed at bear conservation and preservation of the Rodopi Mountains' rural heritage[7]. He presents a slightly different perspective on establishment of the bear hide:

There were camera traps (of the hunters) to observe what animals are around…what they didn't expect was that the bears started coming. They told me that and this idea came…to put up a hide…it would be interesting for the visitors and also bring economic benefits.

After the bear hide was built, the tour operator organized specialized trips in cooperation with the hunters, aimed at tourists interested in biodiversity and bear conservation in particular. The role of the local guides in these is that with respect to Bulgarian tourists interested to visit the bear hide: to drive the tourists to the site and provide information. The specialized trips, however, are full day activities and are organized with the promise to not only see brown bears (Figure 3) but also to learn more about their ecology and behavior. The tour operator explained:

These trips have been specifically designed to be educational and not simply the standard bear watching holidays offered by other companies in Europe. A major focus of the holidays is to educate participants about the ecology and behaviour of bears, as well as conservation issues connected with the protection of both the bears and bear habitats. The holidays are thus additionally contributing to bear conservation by hopefully inspiring participants on the trip to become more knowledgeable advocates for bear conservation worldwide.

The trip's name—the Realm of the Brown Bear[8]—reflects this multipurpose character. It has thus far brought around five groups of foreign tourists per season, each staying in the village for a week and visiting the bear hide daily. This results in around 25 trips to the hide per season which the tour operator declares in advance, meaning that the bear hide is reserved for his groups for this period of the year. These trips bring more economic benefits for the local population than other occasional visitors to the hide who rarely stay overnight.

Figure 3. Bears feeding at the bear hide. Source: Svetoslava Toncheva

One of the primary objectives of ecotourism, as previously discussed, is its function as an economic incentive for conservation. Local people are aware that the foreign groups undertaking bear tourism stay in their village for a week specifically because of the bears. This suggests that they realize an economic benefit from their coexistence with the bears, since tourists don't just occupy the village hotels and guest houses but also eat village food and purchase local products (honeys, jams, mushrooms, herbs, souvenirs and handicrafts) and services. Fieldwork data supports this conclusion.

As documented several times in the research, the local population acknowledges the role of the bears in tourism and the latter's contribution. The general evaluation of bear ecotourism is thus very positive despite not benefiting everyone equally or to a significant extent. Yet the fact that bear tourism brings more direct benefits to some than others is seen as potential source of conflicts. As one women not involved in bear tourism explained, 'This is always difficult, people involved with the bear hide benefit, they make money, others could be jealous'.

The dimensions of this income, however, help to explain why there are few significant conflicts around this type of tourism thus far. The hunting union is the main beneficiary of bear ecotourism yet estimate it as 'not particularly beneficial'. According to hunters, revenues generally cover the costs of the bears' food (a few thousand kilograms of corn per year), vehicles' fuel, the guides' time and a small amount to support their union. Still, the local bear hide is described as 'the most developed' in the region with people being sent there from other places. Due to this tourism, the hunting union is able to support its various activities: the provision of food for game animals at the feeders, the planting of oat fields that keep the game in the region, social gatherings, and so forth.

As currently no bear inflicted damage has occurred, bear tourism functions, particularly for the hunters, as a direct incentive to maintain the bear population. Hunters' paradoxical role as bear conservationists seems beneficial for the bears since hunters are also the bears' main threat (bears are still illegally hunted in some regions of Bulgaria despite legislation and EU compensation schemes). As one hunter and bear guide admitted, 'So far they [the bears] have a good role, that's why we don't chase them away'.

Most economic benefits come from foreign tourists, who are not only seen as more interested in wildlife, but also wealthier than Bulgarians, and therefore able to afford the higher fees for visiting the bear hide. Therefore, the majority of participants in bear tourism remain foreign, predominantly Western Europeans.

An important factor that contributes to the present sustainable level of bear tourism is that it is not the main tourism in the area but rather a small addition to it. The low levels of bear tourism are seen by some as presenting potential for further development, while others, mainly hunters, claim that they deliberately don't advertise it and prefer to limit its extent. This is understandable considering their motivation to maintain populations of other animals for hunting (as evidenced by camera traps, the bear hide is still used by other wild animals such as wild boar, deer, etc.). Low levels of bear tourism are also beneficial for the bear population and the region's ecological integrity. As the bear guide and ecologist explained, if there are too many or too frequent tourists visiting the bear hide, there is a danger that environmental disturbance will increase above a sustainable threshold, and that this will negatively impact the bears and other wildlife in the vicinity.

Development of bear tourism, as already mentioned, is thus seen as 100% a local initiative. This means that either the foreign tour operator's role is not fully acknowledged or the fact that the company has been present in the village for more than a decade means that it is no longer considered external. Moreover, the aforementioned tour operator brings groups for the bulk of the tourist season and hence leaves little space for other operators to enter the region. Unlike in many cases where ecotourism projects impose certain outside views on the local population (West 2006; Fletcher 2014b), therefore, in the present case we find local people occupying a central role in the activity or in equal partnership with nominal outsiders.

Discussion

The research results and the long-term observations of human-bear relations in Yagodina demonstrate how humans and bears have established particular cohabitation practices as result of their interactions in overlapping space. The lack of concrete management strategies imposed from the outside has given people and bears freedom to establish their own mechanisms for negotiating interactions. This bottom-up approach allows such mechanisms to develop in the context of local realities and lifeworlds rather than via external ideas concerning how conservation should function. Lack of state conservation frameworks and control imposed from above has led in this case to the establishment of practices of adaptation and learning to live together, rather than substantial modification of behavior by either species. Development of these cohabitation mechanisms and the fact that they are thus far fairly functional affords characterization of this as a landscape of tolerance.

Important factors explaining this situation identified in this analysis include the following:

First, local perceptions are characterized by a non-dichotomous division between nature and culture, within which only the immediate village space is separated into a human-centric category. Cohabitation and the sharing of common space is thus seen as a natural living condition for both people and bears.

Second, tolerance results from efforts by people to understand the bears, their behavior and needs, thus granting the animals their necessary space rather than viewing bears solely with fear or aggression. 'Looking through the eyes' of the bears seems, therefore, an essential precondition for successful cohabitation. Our discussion of LEK concerning bears shows that they occupy a significant place in local people's lifeworlds. The general knowledge of bears, in this relation, is shared by all inhabitants who can read (Hinchcliffe et al. 2005; Boonman-Berson et al. 2016) the bears' signs and understand the animals as permanent inhabitants of the shared space, interactions within which are a natural occurrence. Particular elements of LEK comprising traditional folklore (now mostly disappearing) also promote positive images of the bears as symbols of fertility and power. The most functional element of this folklore seems to be the protective and stress releasing practices, especially the casting of a bullet. This shows the functionality of LEK for the human-bear cohabitation by mitigating possible negative effects after an encounter with a bear and, in this way, maintaining balance within the system of relationships.

Third, ecotourism established around the bears has, in this particular case, proven beneficial for their conservation. This is due to several factors. One is tourism's maintenance at low levels, thus minimizing its local sociocultural and ecological impacts. Additionally, bear tourism is considered by local people their own initiative and not imposed from outside. The role of the main tour operator, while foreign, is not considered an external intervention but rather a partnership and contribution to the village's main current livelihood strategy. For this reason, local people remain managers of their own resources and influential actors in the tourism process. Still, bears' management is attributed to a particular group, namely the hunters. Our research demonstrates that their role in establishing the bear hide and managing bear tourism is generally not questioned by the population who consider this type of ecotourism beneficial, even if only a few people receive direct income from it. Bear tourism functions, therefore, as an economic and conservation incentive in particular for the hunters by supporting their activities and their positive attitude towards the bears, rendering them, paradoxically, the main bear conservationists.

Bear tourism is, moreover, thus far compatible with human-bear cohabitation due to the manner in which it is organized: by a researcher and ecologist in a noninvasive way, with respect for specifics of the bears' behavior and needs. The fact that it is kept at low levels by all actors, albeit for different reasons – by the tour operator in consideration of the bear population and by hunters with the aim to preserve other wildlife for hunting – is also beneficial for the bears by preventing impacts that could disturb the region's ecological integrity.

Further, the limited income ecotourism generates doesn't ensure large economic benefits and is, consequently, not a strong source of conflicts, being only a small addition to the mainstream tourism that is the community's dominant livelihood strategy. This non-reliance on market expansion (Büscher and Fletcher 2020) not only limits possible conflicts but also prevents the further commodification of nature and the animals' disconnection from local cultural values and meanings (West 2006; Hutchins 2007).

Moreover, in contrast to copious research documenting how ecotourism promotion can transform local lifeworlds, due to unintended factors (the language barrier and the role of the tour operator) no such negative effects are observed in this case. This contributes to maintenance of boundaries between the local lifeworld and the outside world, preserving the specifics of local human-nature relations in the face of global integration. In addition, the importance of bears for tourism functions as *symbolic capital* providing a sense of pride for the local population that bears are part of their lifeworlds and landscape.

Conclusion

Our analysis demonstrates aspects of all three central principles of convivial conservation (Büscher and Fletcher 2020): integrated spaces in which people and wildlife comingle; localized and (relatively) democratic forms of governance; and non (or at least little) commodified forms of income generation. Additionally, in demonstrating how these principles have been implemented locally in the absence of significant direct intervention by either state agents or international conservationists and how these have shaped institutions with a clear sense of local ownership, the case also appears to exemplify various of the preconditions Haller et al. (2016) outline as requisite to successful constitutionality.

First, the case clearly presents an 'emic perception of need' for effective collective action with respect to human-bear coexistence. Second, it also exhibits a largely 'participatory process' comprising a majority of local residents to develop such action, although whether this process indeed effectively addresses power asymmetries within the community remains in question.

Third, the case seems to exhibit 'preexisting institutions' for managing human-bear relations, mostly entailing division of space between the different species' core zones of occupation as well as guidelines concerning how to negotiate human-bear interaction. Of course, this conclusion must be tempered by acknowledging various limitations in our analysis of the case. In particular, our study remains limited to the period during which direct participation occurred and hence remains merely a snapshot of the longer historical trajectory within which recorded dynamics are embedded. While the study is able to document how local practices and forms of knowledge are expressed and function at this particular point in time, therefore, it is not able to analyze how they have changed and developed leading up to this point. Hence, the extent to which these dynamics can be considered durable *institutions* in the sense that CPR researchers tend to understand this term remains questionable.

Fourth, the case demonstrates the presence of 'outside catalysing agents' contributing to governance practices, particularly with respect to the foreign tour operator helping to stimulate ecotourism development in support of bear conservation. The case also most definitely entails strong 'recognition of local knowledge' as the basis for cohabitation practices.

With respect to Haller et al.'s (2016) fifth and final precondition— 'higher-level state recognition' of local practices—the situation is ambivalent. On the one hand, it is clear that relatively peaceful coexistence between people and bears is underpinned by state ownership of the land within which the two species meet as well as formal regulation (both state and EU) protecting bears within this space. On the other hand, beyond this neither state forces nor other powerful outside actors (e.g. large conservation NGOs) are actively present in the local context, hence local actors remain largely autonomous in the execution of cohabitation strategies. In this sense, the case can be seen to exemplify dynamics of *subsidiarity* as per Ostrom and Cox's (2010) ideal multi-tier model of natural resource governance in which most immediate decision-making is left to local-level actors in relation to which state agents exert a largely background supportive role.

In conclusion, the analysis suggests that the relative absence of significant human-wildlife conflict in this case is due in large part to the fact that human-bear relations embody most elements of the convivial constitutionality framework we have introduced to analyze it. In developing the analysis, the study has therefore also demonstrated the potential for the framework to guide investigations of cases of human-wildlife conflict and coexistence more broadly. It can be used to assess both those aspects of the framework that are functioning effectively within a given case and of those that necessitate more focused attention and cultivation. We therefore invite other researchers to explore to what extent such this same framework can prove productive in their own contexts of study in working to foster conditions for convivial cohabitation more widely.

Chapter 10:

Transforming Convivial Conservation: Towards More-Than-Human Participation in Research[*]

By Séverine van Bommel and Susan Boonman-Berson

Introduction

'How do you know that the sheep are happy?' one of my colleagues asked. 'Maybe you are just creating zombie sheep'. I, the first author, was discussing with some colleagues about a research programme on Livestock Guardian Dogs in Australia and their role in mediating the coexistence of livestock producers and wild dogs (including dingoes). We were discussing whether Livestock Guardian Dogs are more effective in preventing predation by dingoes and wild dogs than the lethal control methods (baiting, killing, or trapping) predominantly used in Australia. I mentioned that producers were claiming that their stock had become calmer, and easier to handle, and that the general well-being of their stock had improved after the introduction of the Livestock Guardian Dogs due to a dramatic reduction in predation. I recounted how the researchers were interested in investigating the 'landscapes of fear' (Laundre et al. 2010) that the Livestock Guardian Dogs were creating for wild dogs and, in doing so, creating 'landscapes of happiness' for the sheep.

'Convivial conservation' as defined by Büscher and Fletcher (2019: 283), offers a 'post-capitalist approach to conservation and promotes radical equity, structural transformation, and environmental justice...to create a more equal and sustainable world'. Although Lorimer (2010) does not invoke such a concept, he describes the idea of convivial biogeographies in the context of elephant conservation

[*] Originally published as: van Bommel, S., and S. Boonman-Berson. (2022). Transforming convivial conservation: Towards more-than-human participation in research. Conservation & Society 20(2): 136-145.

by highlighting the recognition of non-human subjectivities.[1] The etymology of conviviality indicates that 'con' translates as 'together' and 'viviality' translates as 'to live'. Drawing on these etymologies of conviviality, we argue that conviviality, or living together, implies much more than the 'coexistence' of different 'stakeholders' in spatial proximity. The concept of convivial conservation, if it is to be truly transformative, needs to fundamentally engage with the question of intersubjectivity of humans and all non-domesticated non-human beings that have been targeted by mainstream conservation as 'nature' or 'wildlife'. In addition, to contribute to convivial conservation's claim to be more consistent with empirical reality (Büscher and Fletcher 2019: 293), requires a deeper understanding of the various forms of mutual understanding between humans and non-humans. From our perspective, applying the principles of conviviality to conservation should include more-than-human participation in research.

Although the opening example of guardian dogs pushes the boundaries of animal sciences, it does not engage with intersubjectivity. Researchers were still representing what they interpreted as landscapes of happiness for the sheep or landscapes of fear for the wild dogs. The sheep and wild dogs did not directly communicate these sentiments to researchers. It is difficult to envisage methods that enable inter-subjective communication so that non-human beings 'speak' for themselves. We are familiar with methods that allow for voices and knowledges of marginalised actors to be included in the research process thereby addressing structural inequalities in knowledge production and use—which is an important ingredient of convivial world-making (Donati 2019; Staddon 2021). However, while we focus on giving voice to the marginalised human groups, it remains unclear how to respond to the increasing calls in literature to include more-than-human participants as co-investigators in research (see Lorimer 2011). Despite the growing recognition and theoretical arguments for including the inter-subjectivities of more-than-human participants in conservation research, it remains a methodological challenge in practice.

In this chapter, we focus on how researchers are engaging with non-human others through multi-species work in nature conservation. We identify some ways in which they are dealing with the methodological challenges of including the inter-subjectivities of non-human others. We provide a brief review of the literature on more-than-human participation in research and examine some threshold concepts and methodologies used by researchers. We also present some boxed examples of personal research experiences of inter-subjective engagement with non-human others. We conclude with a reflection on how engaging the inter-subjectivities of more-than-humans in conservation research might contribute to a truly transformational conviviality in conservation practice.

Intersubjectivity in Conservation Research and Practice

Convivial conservation, as proposed by Büscher and Fletcher (2019), stresses the importance of celebrating the many inherent links between humans and non-humans, the need to build long-lasting, engaging, and open-ended relationships between them, as well as a change in thinking toward 'living with' non-humans. It is argued that current conservation concepts and practices do not sufficiently recognise and engage with structural inequalities that are caused by our capitalist economic system. Drawing on insights from political ecology, Büscher and Fletcher (2019) argue that a transformation of the system is needed to achieve structural change and conviviality. However, if we unpack the meaning of conviviality a bit more, then we see that in convivial conservation 'the corresponding conservation values are predominantly instrumental, along with the human values of equity and environmental justice' (Berkes 2021: 14). In other words, convivial conservation talks about conviviality primarily in terms of human values and interests rather than human and non-human inter-subjectivities and thereby misses addressing non-humans more prominently as 'stakeholders' or participants in the co-production of conviviality. In addition to that, although convivial conservation recognises and engages with the interactions between human stakeholders and the 'more-than-human' environment, non-human counterparts are often not seen as being able to 'speak for themselves' (Van Dooren and Rose 2016; West et al. 2020). If included at all, the voice of non-human beings is represented by natural scientists who tend to 'speak for' them (e.g., plants and animals) and abiotic/physical elements (e.g., rivers or mountains). From the point of view of inter-subjectivity as the basis for conviviality, this 'speaking for' need to be practised with care, otherwise it becomes problematic. Particularly if conviviality implies a sense of mutual engagement and interaction that is based on dignity and respect then foregrounding human inter-subjectivities without including more-than-human subjectivities (Haraway 2008), simply reproduces human exceptionalism and makes it difficult, if not impossible, to recognise that human life and relations are intrinsically interdependent with more-than-human lives (Laidlaw and Beer 2018). If the concept of convivial conservation seeks to transform conventional mentalities and approaches in conservation, then it needs to fully engage with a wide range of non-human inter-subjectivities in both research and practice. It needs to develop and include a richer recognition of agency, embeddedness, and an expansive sense of situated knowledges of more-than-human beings.

Calls for more-than-human participation are not a wildly outrageous new fad. Many scholars have argued for more-than-human participation and deliberation in relation to environmental concerns over the past decades. Dryzek (1995; 2008), for example, has suggested broadening the Habermasian idea of communicative action to include 'deliberating with non-human' and has argued for 'openness to non-human signals' in social-environmental interactions (cited in Driessen 2014). Scholars like Lorimer (2011) argue for a more 'symmetrical' approach in fieldwork, reading, and writing which addresses the uneven power relations between humans and more-than-humans in conservation research. Locke and Buckingham (2016) address the need for new, more interwoven, ways of multidisciplinary collaborations to be able to grasp the complex human and non-human dynamics. Van Dooren and Rose (2016) point to the idea of storytelling, which includes attentive listening and responding to non-humans, as a way to engage with these human and non-human dynamics. Researchers such as Bastian et al. (2016) argue that the Anthropocene calls for reconsidering the anthropocentrism in current research methodologies. Others note that one of the most important drivers of the socio-environmental crisis we are facing today is the ongoing, western mode of separating human and non-humans (Barrett et al. 2017; Abram 2010). Rose (2015: 130) observes that if we want to rethink the way in which humans and non-humans live together then it is the responsibility of humans to acknowledge the 'needs, desires and interests' of our more-than-human counterparts in research. Hence the call to develop research methodologies as transformational tools that help (re)connect with more-than-humans (Kirksey and Helmreich 2010; Madden 2014; Buller 2015; Bastian et al. 2016).

More-Than-Human Participation in Research

Non-human approaches to research represent a new 'turn' that starts from the assumption that 'we cannot adequately understand humanity in isolation from non-human species implicated in human life' (Locke and Munster: 2015: 1). The underlying philosophical idea is that we can only understand what it means to be 'human' if we contrast it with something that is 'non-human'. Therefore, the category of 'people' is co-produced with the category of 'non-people'. This means that humans and non-humans are interdependent upon each other, and they have a rich history of co-evolving and co-becoming.

In traditional multi- or inter-disciplinary research teams, there is a division of tasks, in which natural scientists investigate and report on the more-than-human aspects of non-human life and world while social scientists primarily focus their attention on interpretations, values and meanings of non-human life for humans and their social contexts. More-than-human participation in research challenges this 'nature–culture' divide that maintains rigid disciplinary boundaries in science. It also challenges the ways that Science and Technology Studies (STS) scholars have been studying natural scientists and the way that natural sciences enact more-than-human life encompassing animals, plants, and the environment. These type of STS approaches often miss how non-humans participate in the construction of reality themselves instead of simply being brought into being through enactment and performative practices of people (Swanson 2017).

Over the past few decades, several interdisciplinary researchers have sought to include humans and non-humans more symmetrically in nature conservation. Zooanthropologists and ethologists that study animal sentience and well-being have challenged the predominant assumption that sense-making and meaning are solely human domains of experience and that animals only respond based on primitive instincts (Aerts et al. 2016; Marchesini 2016). Karen Strier (1993), for example, asked why anthropologists did not consider themselves primatologists given that animals—like humans—have meaning-making capabilities and inhabit rich social lifeworlds (Despret and Buchanan 2016; De Waal 2016).

These theoretical debates and empirical studies contributed to the emergence of multi-species ethnography as a field that problematises the assumption of sole human intentionality and agency and tries to rethink human-animal relations in terms of mutuality. It seeks to understand how humans and non-humans together engage in sense-making to co-create the world in interaction (Lulka 2009). Candea's (2010; 2013) work with meerkats showed how humans and non-humans become attuned to each other through interactions during research. This process of attunement enabled Candea to understand and describe their behaviour even though the meerkats did not 'speak' in their own voices. O'Mahony et al.'s (2018) work with wolves also looks at the process of attunement, although their fieldwork did not involve direct encounters with wolves. Attunement was mediated by technology and other artefacts which enabled interaction and co-construction of lived experience and produced 'translocated empathy'.

Other researchers have gone a step further and investigated how the landscape, human and non-human relationships are co-constituted in interaction. Barua (2014), for example, argues for a 'dwelt political ecology' approach which recognises that landscapes are produced by people and animals dwelling and interacting with each other. Boonman-Berson et al.'s (2016) research with bears shows that cohabitation in wildlife management requires assigning a central role to human-wild animal-landscape interactions. Their work demonstrates the shift in power relationships between humans and non-human beings in nature conservation when their interactions are examined alongside more-than-human biophysical elements. Bastian et al. (2016) observe that more-than-human participatory research reveals how humans and the diversity of more-than-humans are 'intertwined in shared worlds' and 'both involved in the production of these worlds'. Although it is not possible to attribute shared goals and meanings in such conservation settings, the everyday practices and interactions do lead to co-constructed landscape outcomes (Mancini and Lehtonen 2018).

Threshold Concepts: Affect, Embodiment, and Multisensory Communication

Although many researchers acknowledge that non-humans are active in shaping conservation research processes (Lorimer 2008), the practicalities of 'how' to do research with non-humans are often not addressed. 'It is relatively easy to say that we need to take non-humans more seriously, but it is quite difficult to know what knowledge practices we might use to ask about non-human practices' (Swanson 2017: 85). Based on a review of publications that consciously attempt to engage with the non-humans in conservation research, we identify three 'threshold concepts' that include the voices of non-human participants: 1) affect, 2) embodiment, and 3) multi-sensory communication.

The idea of 'threshold concepts' was introduced by Meyer and Land (2006) as concepts that 'identify particularly troublesome, transformative, irreversible and integrative ideas central to a discipline or field of study' (Barrett et al. 2016: 132). Threshold concepts can transform deep, and often unconscious assumptions about and historical framings of, a given discipline and provide 'new and previously inaccessible ways of thinking' (Meyer and Land 2003: 1).

The three threshold concepts we have identified are critical for developing methodologies that approach humans and more-than-human interaction and co-production of convivial landscapes. We recognise that these threshold concepts are deeply interrelated in practice. However, for analytical purposes, we present them as separate concepts to illustrate how they can enable more symmetrical participation of humans and non-humans in conservation research (Bastian et al. 2016). We discuss each of these below.

Affect

Although Actor-Network Theory has drawn attention to the agency of non-humans, some scholars have argued that the concept of agency does not sufficiently capture inter-subjectivity between humans and non-humans. They have instead put forward the notion of 'affect' which can encompass the inter-subjectivity of more-than-human participation in research (Bennett 2010; Latimer and Miele 2013). Affect is understood as a shared or relational 'force' 'in terms of "attachment" [or engagement] on the one hand and being 'moved' on the other' (Latimer and Miele 2013: 8). In general, affect refers to the way that a relationship influences or 'affects' both humans and more-than-human beings in terms of what they can do, and how they can act, move or think. This can involve experiences such as feeling, touching, or smelling but it can also involve experiences such as growing, flowering, and dying (Gregg and Seigworth 2010). Affects emerge from the interaction between entities and influence the capacities attributed to the participating entities. The concept of affect allows researchers to analyse how encounters between humans and non-humans (animals, plants, and the environment) often leave both of them changed in one way or another. Affects, in other words, encourage effects (Lorimer 2008; Despret 2016).

Nygren and Jokinen (2013: 87), for example, found the notion of affect helpful to capture the surveying of the elusive and strictly protected Siberian Flying Squirrel *Pteromys volans* in Finland. In their case of surveying the surveyors of nocturnal flying squirrels, they show that 'the emergence of affect in encounters between field surveyors and flying squirrels is at the core of survey practices'. They observe that each surveyor develops their own way of co-operating with the flying squirrels to obtain the required field data for nature conservation. The various ways of surveyor-flying squirrel co-operation arise from the affect of these encounters. Affective knowing is core for generating the required data to protect the animal. Nygren and Jokinen (2013) discuss the tension between the need for accurate and unambiguous information in nature conservation and the high uncertainties involved in surveying the flying squirrels. They note that the focus on affect provides the means to deal with this tension.

Candea (2010; 2013) uses the notion of affect in navigating 'the complex landscape of mutual modification' in their scientific field study of meerkats. To study meerkats, both meerkats and observers needed to modify their behaviour. These mutual modifications aimed to interact with these meerkats for collecting the necessary data. The observers tried to get the meerkats to become interested in the carefully positioned eggs on scales so that they could be weighed without being touched. Candea (2010: 251) notes that affect played a key role in the field study and was 'premised on a careful balancing act between engagement and detachment'. Both observers and meerkats learned from each other's behaviour and the 'language' that was produced from their encounters (Candea 2013). For instance, when a meerkat had been unintentionally alarmed by an observer, the latter used a call—described as 'a message conveying peaceful intentions' (Candea 2010: 246)—which had a calming effect on the animal. Even though detailed knowledge about the engagement and learning of the meerkats remains elusive, Candea's work highlights the critical role of affective field practices for both conservation researchers and the non-human beings they study.

The foregoing examples illustrate the different ways in which the concept of affect allows more inter-subjective engagement between humans and non-humans in conservation research. In the case of Nygren and Jokinen (2013), affect helps to understand the ongoing processes and experiences between human and animal, and how inclusive knowledge about nature conservation is produced and shaped by interpretations of traces/signs (see also Mason and Hope 2014). The example of Candea (2010, 2013) illustrates affect in terms of the capacity of bodies to act, move and think. This also resonates with our own experience in nature conservation (see Box 1).

Reflecting on his field research during a project meeting, Neil Powell recounts how the local people in Kaokoland wanted the local elephants to participate as stakeholders in the action research on the harvesting of the Marula trees Sclerocarya birrea in the area. People and elephants affected each other by competing for the same resources, namely the fruits of the Marula trees. According to the local community, they had an institutional arrangement with the elephants regarding the use of the Marula trees. Neil Powell remembers that the local people had negotiated with the local elephants that some Marula trees are 'people trees' and some Marula trees are 'elephant trees'. They had agreed that people only harvest fruits from 'people trees' and elephants only eat fruit from 'elephant trees'. As such the elephants and the people in the area formed affective multi- species partnerships that allowed for the Marula fruits to be divided between the elephants and the people and this allowed them to collaborate and coexist. All was well until a borehole was created by a community-based conservation project. Whereas before water had only been available seasonally, with the borehole water was now available throughout the whole year. This sudden year around water supply attracted a new group of elephants to the region. These new elephants were unaware of the institutional arrangement regarding the Marula trees and they ate the fruits of both the people trees as well as the elephant trees. When the original group of elephants returned to the region after their yearly migration, they found their trees empty. They blamed the people and in retaliation, they destroyed all the 'people trees'.

'/Ai!ae [one of the community members] said in this case he was convinced that he had left the correct trees with sufficient Marula fruit for the elephants. He, therefore, attributed the elephant's revenge to the influx of new elephants into the area caused by the opening of a new permanent water point by the MET [Ministry of Environment and Tourism]. These new elephants, he said, had not had any dialogue with the people and therefore had not been included in the planning of Marula harvesting' (Powell 1998: 47).

Box 1: The unintended effects of overlooking affect in research on co-management in Namibia

Embodiment

Affect is an essential ingredient of embodied inter-subjectivities. Inviting the non-humans to be an active participant in research means that we need to consider how to understand the everyday lived experiences of humans and non-humans to consider how relations of responsibility between humans and non-humans might be practically accomplished (Brown and Dilley 2012: 38). Haraway (2008) explains that responsibility in multi-species encounters includes the ability to respond, which she calls 'response-ability'. Responding is an emotional and bodily experience that may or may not include logical, intellectual reasoning. Some scholars have found the notion of 'embodiment' helpful (e.g., Lorimer 2008; Locke 2012) to capture the idea of responding through lived experience. Embodiment is about 'perceptual experience and the mode of presence and engagement in the world' (Csordas 2002: 241). It is the way in which 'the body' enables an inter-subjective lived experience of the world. Embodied experience is something that humans and non-humans deeply share and the concept of embodiment offers a way to describe lived experience in a more symmetrical way than language can.

As with affect, the mutuality of embodiment between humans and non-humans is critical in establishing the inter-subjective relationship. For example, in describing their research on wild wolves in Romania, O'Mahony et al. (2018: 124) note that in nature conservation research, the bodies of researchers and wildlife often do not interact in real time. Instead, 'rather than researchers becoming with wolves, [...] relationships are more ones where researchers grasp for "partial affinities", shards of molecular closeness, that might emerge through emplacement and a sensorium of congealing experiences'. They illustrate how embodiment in their research is about interacting with partial wolf elements (footprints, wolf droppings, howls) while the wolves themselves 'remain at a distance' (ibid). While tracking wolves, the bodies of the researchers become the tool which allows them to attune to the wolves by means of sight, smell, sound, or feelings. Over time, researchers become more skilled at attuning themselves, amplifying their responsiveness to the signs of the wolves in a particular environment. These skills are acquired solely through embodied experiences and prolonged engagement. Likewise, the wolves become equally attuned to signs of humans in the landscape, similarly acquired by means of embodied experiences. O'Mahony et al. (2018) point out that the behaviour of any other wildlife, including wolves, can be influenced by 'unseen human vapours and artificial scents residual…and lingering around trees' (ibid: 121). So multi-species sense-making is an embodied interactional process that goes both ways.

The role of embodied skills is also highlighted by Mason and Hope (2014) in their research on tracking the presence of bats around the Greywell Tunnel in Hampshire, UK. They observe that bodily skills and bodily learning are important to become sensitive to non-human performances. They explain that 'once tracking begins, it is necessary to become absorbed and aligned with the movements of one individual, remaining focused on this bat until it re-enters the tunnel or an alternative roost' (ibid.: 112). Although surveyors might observe a glimpse of the bat themselves, most of the tracking occurs by radio. They describe a specific—triangulation—technique, which allows surveyors to map the bat's choreography: 'Two or more surveyors assume fixed positions and take simultaneous bearings in the direction of the strongest signal at regular intervals. These timed bearings are then plotted on a map and the bat's location is deduced from the intersection of the lines' (ibid.: 113). This technique requires the surveyor to be 'continually attentive to the bat's movements' (ibid.: 113) while simultaneously remaining aware of their own body in relation to the bat in order to plot the bat's location. As pointed out by O'Mahony et al. (2018), the bat surveyors grasp for 'partial affinities' through bat movements. They developed and refined their embodied skills by honing their senses and using radio technology to become sensitive to the presence and behaviour of different bats.

Both these examples illustrate how the concept of embodiment can capture what happens when bodies come together or remain at a distance but always influence each other in sense-making processes. Our own research experiences also show how embodiment can offer insight into how humans and non-humans respond to each other when they meet (see Box 2).

Box 2: Weaving together embodied interaction with wild boars

Multi-sensory communication

Embodiment is a key part of multi-sensory communication. We find the notion of 'multi-sensory reading and writing' helpful to capture the communication between humans and non-humans. Boonman-Berson et al. (2016) introduced this concept in their research on interactions between humans and black bears in Colorado. Drawing on Hinchliffe et al.'s (2005) work on water voles, they describe multi-sensory communication as the ways in which 'signs (visual, olfactory, auditory, tactile), materialised in words, signals or things, are communicated between humans, between wild animals, and between humans and wild animals through the writing and reading of these signs in the landscape' (Boonman-Berson 2016: 194). Although Hinchliffe et al. (2005) focused on how water voles 'write' footprints in the landscape which are then 'read' by humans, Boonman-Berson et al. (2016) approach this as a two-way interaction in which humans also leave signs in the landscape which can be read by animals. For example, black bears communicate their presence to people by tipping over trash cans and leaving scratch marks. In turn, people communicate to black bears that their presence is unwanted by using scent (ammonia) and tactile signals such an electrical mat that will 'zap' the bears as they try to enter a building. Black bears sense this olfactory and tactile communication and learn to modify their behaviour. Local surveyors in the practice of black bear management explicitly remarked that black bears differ from each other: each bear has his/her 'own, individual "method"' (Boonman-Berson et al. 2016: 198).

Gaining insight into the multi-sensory communication repertoire between humans and black bears involves the use of all senses (which might differ between both) as well as the continuous process of ongoing interpretations between them. This requires, for example, the researcher to perceive the—individual—bear as a co-constitutive participant in communication as well as describe the 'lived experiences' of people and black bears living closely together and sharing the same landscape (see Box 3). Yeo and Neo (2010) describe how both humans and macaques in urban Singapore communicate and negotiate urban space. They note that both macaques and humans have developed a way of shared understanding through ongoing non-linguistics—multi-sensory—forms of communication. To live with the macaques, humans need to adjust their daily behaviour, as one resident describes: 'when I come home around 6 pm (when macaques usually appear), I have to carry my groceries above my shoulders to prevent them from snatching it away' (Yeo and Neo 2010: 692). Also, macaques seemed to adjust their behaviour to their human co-residents; as another resident stated: 'I once reprimanded a monkey for attempting to snatch my bag from me. It seems to understand my reaction, like raising my voice, pointing a finger at it, and it backed off' (ibid.: 693).

Such examples show how humans and animals communicate, negotiate, and seem to deliberate with each other (Meijer 2013; Driessen 2014). They illustrate that animal cooperation and animal resistance can be seen as a response to 'proposals for alternative modes of shared living' (Driessen 2014: 99). Recognising this type of common sensing involves seeing participation to occur at unexpected, mundane sites in our own research experience. Although it is difficult to confirm whether the animals were aware of their power to negotiate, it opens up the idea of participation, communication, and negotiation as something that happens between humans to something that happens between humans and non-humans as well.

A Bear Aware Volunteer describes what happens when he receives a call from a resident after a bear sighting near their house.

'When I get a call then I go see what is happening and try to figure out then how they deal with it [the bears]. You know and it could be several different things that we might try before we hit the one that works the most. First of all, we try to get the people to remove or whatever they attracted it with. And then secondly if we have to condition the bear there is all kinds of different ways. You can put security things on top of the dumpsters and the trash that the bears do not like and that will turn 'em away. Then we can try to negative condition the bear to this place. We can use paintballs and there is a rubber buckshot, a rubber and a beanbag that comes out of a shotgun, and that'll sting 'em but it doesn't hurt.

And of course we can make a lot of loud noise you know, I use an airhorn that is used by mariners. This is compressed air and you know you push the button it just blasts. In general, that works quite well at first. But then bears get used to that you know. And it scares them if they are close but if they are not very close, they just look at you. Pepper-spray I use a lot of times. Well, pepper-spray, paintball, rubber buckshot you know all of those things work. Mostly it is educating the people. That they remove any attractant. And writing tickets to some people might help too. We just want to prevent killing bears'.

Box 3: A toolbox full of multi-sensory communication tricks

Threshold Methodology: Promiscuous Methods and Methodology

Conventional conservation science research tends to follow the nature–culture divide and maintains implicit anthropocentric beliefs that keep this divide in place, thereby making collaborations between natural scientists and social scientists difficult in practice. More-than-human participation in research not only challenges existing categories and concepts, it also challenges the methods that are normally used in research. The classical social science tools—such as interviews and participant observation—that are used for studying the practices of people do not always work sufficiently for studying more-than-humans. As illustrated by our opening example of wild dogs and sheep, these methods still leave open the question of how much the researchers actually understand non-humans experiences/perceptions and to what extent they may be projecting their own views on them.

To create in-depth and trustworthy accounts and to create a more nuanced understanding of the relations between human and non-humans, researchers have argued for methods and methodology that transcend the boundaries and borders between natural sciences, social sciences, philosophy and art (Swanson 2017). We refer to these as so-called promiscuous methods. This is similar to what others have termed 'bio-geographies' (Lorimer 2010; Barua 2014), trans- or multi-species ethnologies (Hurn 2012), anthrozoography (Madden 2014), ethnoelephantology (Locke 2013) or combining ethnographic with ecological/ethological records (Hodgetts and Lorimer 2015).

Hodgetts and Lorimer (2015) suggest three methods to explore interactions between humans and non-humans: 1) tracking and data collection devices; 2) technologies for investigating animal communicative practices that fall outside the range of human visual and aural practices; and 3) methods of genomic analysis, including phytogeography. Swanson (2017), in her research on salmon landscapes and salmon lives, used tracking methods to understand what happened to the salmon when they migrated. In the salmon hatchery she was able to use traditional social science methods of observation to understand how salmon interacted with their environment. But when the juvenile salmon were released and migrated to the ocean, she was not able to follow them anymore. Therefore, she learned to read salmon scales from natural scientists. Salmon scales have lines like tree rings which can provide information about the age of the fish and how much time it spent in different habitats. Reflecting on this, she states:

> Nearly every anthropologist I know ends up doing archival research despite the fact that very few of us have extensive formal training in historical methods. We depend on our ability to learn the methods of another discipline, in this case history, and to integrate them with our own. (Swanson 2017: 89)

The reading of salmon scales allowed Swanson (2017) to reconstruct the lived experiences of the salmon.

Mason and Hope's (2014) research on bats illustrates how engaging with affect in multi-species research may require the use of technical devices that augment human senses. It is difficult for humans to imagine 'being a bat', since the 'sensory apparatuses' of humans and bats differ too much. Bats make use of echolocation to navigate and forage. They emit a call—between 11 and 212 kHz— in their environment and listen to the echoes of this call reflected by various objects in their surroundings. The upper limits of human hearing, however, is generally around 20 kHz. Technology that enables hearing high frequency bat calls provides surveyors the ability to identify and interpret calling patterns. It bridges the sensory experiences between human and bats and allows interspecies communication and affective relations.

Finally, the research by O'Mahony et al. (2018) on wolves in Romania illustrates the way in which genomic analysis can help to mediate affect between researchers and wolves. By analysing samples of fur and excrement, the researchers were able to determine sex and family relationships. Similar to the analysis of the fish scales by Swanson (2017), the analysis of genetic material allowed researchers to identify individual wolves and piece their stories together.

These examples illustrate the idea of promiscuous methods and methodology in which social scientists incorporate natural science methods in their social science research practices. Van Dooren et al. (2016: 11) note that 'collaborative associations are starting to move beyond earlier approaches in science studies that put biologists themselves under the microscope, to create projects with scientists that might frame experiments addressing shared questions and concerns or re-craft existing empirical methods. Biologists and ecologists have become "critical friends" for multi-species scholars'.

Towards Conviviality in Nature Conservation Research

As more-than-human participation in research challenges the divide between humans and non-humans, it is not surprising to see new interdisciplinary approaches to research emerging that are engaging natural sciences and social sciences in a constructive dialogue. This is especially relevant for pursuing the idea of convivial conservation, which seeks to 'live with nature' and promote a variety of conversations (Büscher and Fletcher 2019; Staddon 2021). While we started our investigation of how researchers engage with more-than-humans by relying on multi-species work, we think that the ongoing work associated with convivial conservation may also offer new ideas for collaborating with multi-species scholars.

We have argued that a convivial approach to research which acknowledges non-humans as inter-subjective participants in research is an important element of the praxis of conviviality. The commitments of convivial conservation—to a wider recognition of agency, embeddedness, and an expansive sense of situated knowledge—should include more-than-humans in research. But in order to engage the subjectivities of non-humans, researchers need to learn new ways of 'hearing' and including the needs of more-than-humans. The promiscuous threshold methodology we have articulated through three interrelated concepts of 'affect', 'embodiment', and 'multi- sensory communication', transcends the binary between social sciences and natural sciences. Affect runs through embodied inter-subjectivities, and embodiment is a key part of multi-sensory communication.

More-than-human participation in research is not only a call for a multi-species co-production of knowledge process. As participation has the power to create communities, more-than-human participation in research can also create 'situated connectivities that bind us into multi-species communities' (Rose 2009: 87). Learning to listen to more-than-humans will make for more interesting forms of conviviality in the Anthropocene. As Driessen (2014) thoughtfully remarks, more-than-human participation in research can even be driven by anthropocentric motives: learning to coexist with more-than-humans—in nature, in farming practices and perhaps in our homes—is the key to surviving as humans on this planet.

Research has an important role to play here because of its performative nature. The stories that researchers write do not offer simple descriptions but 'perform' certain realities (Pickering 1995; Mol 1999; Law 2008). Choices are made with regard to the questions we ask, the methods we use, and the stories we tell, including the ones that non-humans tell us. These choices are ultimately political because different knowledge practices bring different worlds into being (van Dooren et al. 2016). As Fawcett (2000: 136–137) notes, 'the choices we make and the actions we take on any environmental problem depend on the quality and reflexivity of our knowledge making'.

Convivial world-making requires full collaboration between (research) partners. If convivial conservation is to be made a living practice that acknowledges and highlights non-human subjectivities, then it will also need to deal with potential tensions centred on the concerns of marginalised people in communities who may have formed a diverse range of relationships with non-humans. In such situations, a convivial conservation approach will need to carefully engage with who or what is given precedence in the relationships and how they are allowed to 'flourish' (Haraway 2008).

There are, of course, important questions that will be raised regarding this collaborative approach to conservation research. After all, it is humans who are designing the research, choosing to interact with the non-humans using various sorts of technology they have created, and reporting on the results to other people in their own authorial voices. This is a form of communication that excludes participation of non-humans in a meaningful way as non-humans do not speak or write words. There is also the question of 'epistemological circularity' (Hamilton and Taylor 2017): those that argue for challenging anthropocentrism and human exceptionalism in research still end up reproducing human authority and interspecies inequality in their research practices and accounts. This leads to the question if the aspired symmetry in research is ever possible. Although we do not have answers to these methodological questions, the acknowledgement of the need for more-than-human participation in research has opened up the debate over the conventional epistemology, methods, and ethics and made them changeable. We believe the best way of answering these questions is by developing promiscuous methods for engaging the subjectivities of more-than-humans in conservation research and generating new understandings of living and flourishing in proximity. This is the way that more-than-human participation in research can contribute to truly transformational conviviality in conservation practice.

PART IV

Alternative Governance and Financing Mechanisms

Chapter 11:

Conservation Basic Income: A Non-market Mechanism to Support Convivial Conservation[*]

By Robert Fletcher and Bram Büscher

Introduction

Conservationists have increasingly questioned the efficacy of neoliberal conservation strategies centred on promotion of market-based instruments (MBIs). Whereas a decade ago these were seen as the most sensible and realistic conservation policies by mainstream conservation organisations, this aura is now gone. Some conservationists even assert that market-based conservation will not get us out of the current environmental and extinction crisis (Cafaro et al. 2017). Based on our own research, we too have suggested that conservationists might 'begin taking the market out of conservation altogether and moving toward redistribution' instead (Fletcher et al. 2016). Few scholars and practitioners, however, have seriously conceptualized what this means and what concrete steps might be taken to transition towards a different strategy for financing conservation. In this chapter, we propose one potential mechanism that could help trigger such a broader transition: a conservation basic income (CBI). We situate this proposal within an overarching approach to transforming biodiversity policy and practice globally that we call convivial conservation (see Büscher and Fletcher, 2019). Convivial conservation is 'a vision, a politics and a set of governance principles that... proposes a post-capitalist approach to conservation that promotes radical equity, structural transformation and environmental justice' (Büscher and Fletcher

[*] Originally published as: Fletcher, R., and B. Büscher. (2020). Conservation basic income: A non-market mechanism to support convivial conservation. Biological Conservation 244: 108520.

2019: 283). The approach seeks to challenge and transcend both reliance on neoliberal capitalist markets *and* the strict separation between humans and nonhuman nature via protected areas (PAs) in pursuit of conservation policy and programming that foregrounds the principles of justice and equity.

We detail our convivial conservation proposal in great depth elsewhere (see Büscher and Fletcher 2019; 2020). There we also briefly advanced CBI as a concrete means of operationalizing part of the approach. Here, we seek to outline this potential funding mechanism in in greater detail and specificity as the basis for future research and experimentation concerning its possible implementation in conservation-critical areas.

This proposal is timely in multiple ways. First, it builds on growing discussion concerning the potential to implement universal basic income (UBI), a discussion that builds on the rapidly growing operationalization of cash transfer programs (CTPs). Challenging bureaucratic, top-down interventions, CTPs and UBI aim to ensure a basic, decent living for all and so create conditions for bottom-up forms of pro-poor development. CTPs have been widely implemented worldwide in various forms while despite some partial operationalization UBI remains largely hypothetical. Within these discussions, however, attention to environmental issues including biodiversity conservation has been largely absent thus far. We believe CBI can rectify this omission, by bringing discussion of CTPs and UBI into dialogue with a parallel stream of research concerning payments for environmental or ecosystem services (PES) and REDD+ schemes that have spread throughout the world to promote conservation specifically.

While these programs originated, and continue to be promoted, as quintessential MBIs, in practice most have instead become forms of (primarily state-based) resource appropriation and redistribution or 'results-based aid' (Angelsen 2017). Even so they have largely failed in their aim to achieve significant biodiversity conservation while also reducing poverty. We therefore explore how this experience of 'actually existing' MBIs might be integrated with UBI to create novel forms of CBI. Conceptualized in this way, we believe that CBI can help move conservation policy beyond MBIs that are currently still dominant but failing to both conserve biodiversity and challenge unsustainable forms of development.

We begin by outlining the rationale for CBI, charting the disappointing performance of conservation MBIs over the past several decades. We then synthesize the research exploring CTPs and UBI, followed by an explanation of how PES and REDD+, have evolved to become de facto redistribution mechanisms. We show how integrating the different mechanisms could provide the basis for a synthetic CBI instrument that would go beyond currently existing conservation funding schemes in potentially interesting and productive ways. We conclude by briefly outlining what such a CBI might look like in practice as part of a broader transition towards convivial conservation.

The Problem

Over the past several decades, the global conservation movement has increasingly embraced MBIs as the basis for interventions in pursuit of biodiversity protection (McAfee 1999; Büscher et al. 2014; Corson et al. 2014). Common MBIs include bioprospecting, ecotourism, biodiversity offsetting, and wetlands banking, in addition to PES and REDD+. While the specifics of MBIs vary widely (Pirard 2012), they tend to share a common logic: to harness economic markets as a means to attach sufficient monetary value to biodiversity (understood as comprising 'ecosystem services' or 'natural capital') to cover the opportunity costs of alternative land use and thereby incentivize conservation over resource extraction. They are also widely promoted as a means to 'internalize' environmental (and social) costs previously externalized from economic markets so that these can be rationally managed as part of the production process. In this way, MBIs are intended to reconcile economic development and environmental protection by harnessing conservation as a form of income generation. A substantial body of research investigating the impact of MBIs in sites throughout the world is now reaching consensus that despite decades of implementation and development they have, with rare exceptions, largely failed to achieve intended aims (McShane et al. 2011; Büscher and Fletcher 2015; Dempsey and Suarez 2016; Holmes and Cavanagh 2016; Dunlap and Sullivan 2020). Moreover, as we explain below, many mechanisms have evolved into forms far removed from the market-based approach they were intended to implement. Deficiencies of MBIs for purposes of biodiversity conservation in particular have indeed been highlighted by a growing number of recent commentaries (e.g. McCauley 2006; Chan et al. 2007; Child 2009; Ehrenfeld 2008; Peterson et al, 2009; Redford and Adams, 2009; Walker et al. 2009; Redford et al. 2013; Fletcher et al. 2016; Dunlap and Sullivan 2020).

MBIs have been frequently characterized as components of a general approach to policy and practice termed 'neoliberal conservation' (Büscher et al. 2012; Büscher et al. 2014). From this perspective, they are considered part of the overarching hegemony of the neoliberal economic paradigm that has come to dominate the global economy since the 1970s (Harvey 2005; Peck 2010). While neoliberalization has been enacted differently in various societies (Brenner et al. 2010), its promotion has generally pursued a common set of principles that Castree (2010) summarizes as: 1) privatization; 2) marketization; 3) deregulation and reregulation (both away from and through state actors); 4) commodification; 5) use of 'market proxies' in state processes; and 6) encouragement of civil society 'flanking mechanisms'. All of these principles can be observed in the promotion of MBIs as a component of neoliberal conservation more generally.

The neoliberal paradigm shaping conservation MBIs has been subject to growing critique for its failure to achieve the 'free' markets it pursues. Hence Peck (2010, page xiii, emphasis in original) describes the history of neoliberalization as a series of 'repeated, prosaic, and often botched efforts to *fix* markets, to build quasi-markets, and to repair market failure'. In the process, neoliberal policies have instead greatly exacerbated economic inequality (Harvey 2005; Wilkinson and Pickett 2010; Piketty 2014; Hickel 2017). Evidence of this dynamic has mounted to the point that even representatives of the International Monetary Fund (IMF), one of the foremost (past) proponents of neoliberalization, recently admitted that 'the benefits of some policies that are an important part of the neoliberal agenda appear to have been somewhat overplayed' (Ostry et al. 2016: 40).

Substantial research demonstrates the pervasive negative consequences of inequality for human health and wellbeing (Wilkinson and Pickett 2010; Stiglitz 2012). There is strong correlation between inequality and biodiversity degradation as well (Mikkelson et al. 2007; Holland et al. 2009; Hicks et al, 2016). According to the IMF, consequently, 'evidence of the economic damage from inequality suggests that policymakers should be more open to redistribution than they are' (Ostry et al. 2016: 40, 41). A key question then becomes: what would such redistribution look like in the realm of environmental conservation policy as a corrective to the ineffective MBIs widely promoted over the last several decades?

Ultimately, given the extent of uneven development throughout the world grounded in primitive accumulation and other processes of violent expropriation (Dunlap and Sullivan 2020), a truly transformative programme seeking to redress inequality at its roots would need to move beyond mere wealth redistribution to pursue to re-appropriation of physical space for collective use is some form – what Shaw and Waterstone (2019: 104) call pursuit of 'geographic justice'. As these authors argue, 'Without the appropriation of space, we can only tinker with capitalism's circuits' (Shaw and Waterstone 2019: 99). It is also clear that effective conservation policy must not only find ways to support the livelihoods of people living in conservation-critical areas, but must also address head on the main root causes of biodiversity loss in: 1) the expansion of extractive industries driven by dynamics of capital accumulation;

and 2) associated resource overconsumption by the relatively wealthy segments of society who usually live far from conservation areas themselves.

In our overarching convivial conservation proposal, we advance a two-pronged strategy that combines long-term development of postcapitalist spaces and forms of organization that confront destructive capitalist industries, such as Shaw and Waterstone (2019) highlight, with pursuit of concrete short-term practices that can address immediate problems and concerns as a step towards more profound structural transformation (Büscher and Fletcher 2020). In terms of this two-prong strategy, what might be done to promote wealth redistribution in support of conservation within impoverished rural communities in the present? We address this key question in the remainder of the paper.

Cash Transfer Programs

According to the World Bank, as of 2014, cash transfer programs—in which currency is given directly to recipients to spend on goods and services—encompassed 720 million people in 130 countries (World Bank 2015). CTPs are commonly distinguished between 'conditional' programs, in which payment requires recipients to comply with some type of behavioral requirement (typically health care visits or school attendance), and 'unconditional' ones, with no requirements. As of 2014, approximately 60 of the world's CTPs were conditional with the rest unconditional (World Bank 2015). Even so, conditional programs tend to be larger than unconditional ones, which typically target just one social group (i.e. elderly people or children) rather than all poor people as conditional CTPs often do. There is obviously a grey area between these two modalities, with some unconditional programs still imposing restrictions on funding use and some nominally conditional programs, such as Brazil's well-known *Bolsa Familia*, being notably lax in their enforcement of conditionality (Peck and Theodore 2015; Standing 2017).

Beginning in the 1990s, CTPs were introduced as a corrective to problems produced by neoliberal interventions associated with structural adjustment policies (SAPs) widely promoted in low-income societies in the 1980s. Initially, international financial institutions like the World Bank and IMF that had championed SAPs were quite skeptical of CTPs due to their apparent revival of the state-based redistribution mechanisms SAPs sought to dismantle (Peck and Theodore 2015). In their popular book *Just Give Money to the Poor*, Hanlon and colleagues (2010) thus term CTPs a 'development revolution' originating in the Global South. Yet precisely how revolutionary CTPs are has since been debated extensively. Due to initial skepticism concerning CTP effectiveness, programs have been subject to rigorous evaluation procedures to test the extent to which they succeed in their aims to combat poverty and enhance wellbeing. Increasing evidence of CTPs' effectiveness documented by such procedures eventually convinced the World Bank to reverse its position, after which it became one of the most enthusiastic promotors of CTPs as a novel development strategy (Peck and Theodore 2015). Consequently, CTPs proliferated dramatically in the first decades of the twenty-first century, introduced by regimes from across the political spectrum (Pena 2010).

Far from a departure from neoliberal policy, therefore, critics contend that conditional CTPs, at least, remain squarely neoliberal. Saad-Filho, for instance, asserts that conditional CTPs are 'the social policies naturally associated ("best fit") with neoliberalism', in that:

> Even though they can assist the target groups at the margin, they are, by design, insufficient to transform the economic, social and political structures perpetuating poverty. CCTs [conditional cash transfers] also introduce commercial mediations and arbitrary limitations to the rights of citizens, manage poverty only within narrow limits, and provide subsidies to capital that, ultimately, reproduce poverty rather than supporting its elimination. (2016: 76)

Indeed, CTPs are often described in quintessential neoliberal terms: as an 'investment in human capital' intended to combat the chronic dependency created by extreme poverty. They are framed as a counter to the 'nanny' state; not a 'safety net' but a 'springboard' to self-sufficiency designed to avoid cumbersome state bureaucracies and decentralize governance by harnessing the power of individual choice and responsibility (Ferguson 2010; Van Parijs and Vanderborght 2017).

While largely agreeing with this characterization of conditional CTPs as a neoliberal effort to 'pay for good behavior', Peck and Theodore assert that unconditional programs are 'anathema to neoliberal policy-makers' (2015: xxi) due to their lack of behavioral modification requirements. By contrast, Ferguson (2010, 2015) considers both conditional and unconditional CTPs creative 'uses of neoliberalism' for alternative ends that may illustrate of 'a new politics of distribution' growing within international development policy.

Notwithstanding their enthusiastic embrace of conditional CTPs, the World Bank and other international financial institutions have remained skeptical of unconditional programs. This is despite the fact that research concerning CTP effectiveness demonstrates that in most cases unconditional programs are equally—or at least nearly—as effective in achieving the same positive outcomes as conditional ones (Hanlon et al. 2010; Bastagli et al. 2016; Standing 2017). Given such evidence, critics have argued that conditionality is both ineffective and unnecessary and should therefore be eliminated (Hanlon et al. 2010; Standing 2017).

In sum, the rise of conditional and unconditional CTPs throughout the Global South over the past three decades seems to have precipitated a major transformation in international development policy that has produced well-documented success with respect to a range of objectives. As Standing summarizes, 'the vast literature generated by evaluations of cash transfers... shows convincingly that cash transfers result in lower poverty and achieve many of the outcomes desired by policymakers, such as improved school enrolment and attendance, better nutrition, better health and more income-generating activity' (2017: 221).

Universal Basic Income

A particular variant of unconditional CTP is commonly termed universal basic income. Similar approaches come under a variety of different labels, including 'unconditional basic income,' 'basic income grant,' 'citizen's income' and 'social dividend', while related mechanisms have received other monikers, including a 'negative income tax,' 'capital grant' and 'participation income' (see Standing 2017 for an overview). Here, we focus on UBI defined as *universal* basic income since this approach is most comprehensive and most conducive to the proposal here.

UBI is commonly considered to comprise several core features that distinguish it from most existing CTPs. First and foremost, it must be *universal*, granted to everyone within a given social group. By contrast, CTPs are usually given only to (specific groups within) the poor, on the basis of means testing. Second, UBI must be *individual*, given equally to each person of all genders within a given age range (rather then distributed by household, as many CTPs are). Third, UBI must be *basic*: sufficient for an individual to survive on (which is not the same as living comfortably). Most existing CTPs, in contrast, pay less than a basic living standard. Fourth, like all unconditional CTPs, UBI must be *unconditional*, allowing recipients to spend funds on whatever they deem appropriate. Fifth, UBI should be *regular, predictable, stable, permanent*, and *non-withdrawable* to facilitate long-term planning.

Conceptualized in this way, UBI has never been widely implemented, even though it has been periodically promoted by a variety of advocates in many places for several centuries (see Standing 2017: Van Parijs and Vanderborght 2017). A number of pilot projects resembling UBI have, however, been implemented in the past, generating compelling evidence of its more widespread potential. Moreover, as Standing asserts, ''Cash transfer schemes that at present are overwhelmingly targeted at "the poor" have the potential to prepare the way for basic income' (2017: 220). And since the 2008 economic crisis, public discussion of UBI has expanded dramatically, encompassing a growing collection of researchers (many within the Basic Income Earth Network (BIEN); https://basicincome.org/) as well as politicians and business leaders (Standing 2017).

In recent years, a number of new UBI pilot studies have been implemented in high income societies like Canada, Finland and the Netherlands as well as lower income countries including Kenya, India and Namibia (Bregman 2017; Standing 2017). The closest approximation to an UBI currently in widespread operation is the Alaska Permanent Fund (APF), instituted in 1976, which provides every official resident of the state with a direct yearly dividend from revenues on oil production within the territory (which fluctuates but is often around US $2000/year). While this payment is not enough to make the fund qualify as truly *basic*, the APF 'has long appealed to advocates of basic income within the BIEN community and can be regarded as a nascent fund for payment of either basic capital grants or basic incomes' (Standing 2017: 151).

Few advocates of UBI claim that it can function as a lone silver bullet for redressing inequality and social injustice; it must be combined with other programs and within an overall policy framework that redistributes and changes political-economic power. Yet proponents assert that UBI can achieve important gains far beyond current social relief programs. Like CTPs, it would reduce overhead to a minimum, thereby delivering maximum funding into the hands of program recipients. By providing payments to everyone it would stop perverse incentives for people to remain (or feign being) poor to continue receiving means-based payments. Lack of behavioral requirements would eliminate oversight, help to preserve recipients' dignity, and allow them to focus energy on using funding to maximum advantage rather than on reporting requirements. Offering secure long-term funding would allow recipients to forego low-wage or degrading jobs, potentially augmenting wages and working conditions overall. Contrary to common concerns about wasting funding on already comfortable recipients, payments given to wealthy people would be recovered in the higher taxes likely needed to fund the program. Strong evidence from CTPs, meanwhile, allays widespread fears that UBI would be spent on frivolous luxuries rather than basic needs and activities to build long-term security.

Like CTPs, UBI has been asserted by some proponents to be a 'radical' or 'revolutionary' proposal (Bregman 2017; Standing 2017; Van Parijs and Vanderborght 2017). Yet others have questioned this perspective, asserting that UBI can itself be used as an instrument of neoliberal reform (Clarke 2017; Kapoor 2017; Shaw and Waterstone 2019). Clarke cautions:

> The hope of a social policy solution to the problems created by neoliberalism and the attacks associated with it is profoundly dangerous because that very 'solution' can so readily assume a form that furthers the very agenda that left [U]BI advocates hope to escape. The institutions of global capitalism are taking an interest in Basic Income and the Davos crowd are even considering it. (https://socialistproject.ca/bullet/1438.php; accessed 11/11/2017)

UBI has indeed been endorsed by proponents across the political spectrum, including foundational neoliberal thinkers like Milton Friedman (1962) and Friedrich Hayek (1979). In its neoliberal framing, therefore, UBI may be merely 'intended to provide political cover for the elimination of social programs and the privatization of social services'[1]. UBI, after all, switches the focus of political action from the traditional left emphasis on gaining greater control over the means of production to appropriating more of the surplus, something Ferguson (2015) finds evident of this 'new politics of distribution' more generally.

Yet as Standing (2017) and others point out, this is not intrinsic to UBI design, which can be structured to combine with—rather than replace—other social welfare programs to build a 'social floor' rather than removing the 'safety net'. Depending on how it is conceived and implemented, then, UBI can be employed in quite different ways: from an instrument of individual 'freedom' to a vehicle of social justice and protection. From all of these perspectives, however, UBI is understood primarily as a mechanism to address poverty, while the question of environmental protection is, with exceptions (discussed below), rarely addressed. It is to this question that we now turn.

Payment for Ecosystem Services

The same period during which CTPs proliferated has seen rapid expansion of PES programs, in which landowners are paid to conserve biodiversity. Currently more than 550 such programs operate throughout the world with annual payments totalling more than US$36 billion (Salzman et al. 2018). PES was originally envisioned as an MBI (esp. Pagiola et al. 2002). As an external evaluation of Costa Rica's program—widely considered to have 'pioneered the nation-wide PES scheme in the developing world' (Daniels et al. 2010: 2116)—describes, the mechanism was explicitly intended to move forest conservation policy 'away from deficit-plagued, subsidized operations that are only able to survive with the aid of state 'alms' and toward a form of profitable, competitive land use based on sound business principles' (Heindrichs 1997: 23). Yet a growing body of research has revealed that most existing programs have departed, often quite dramatically, from this neoliberal framing to instead resemble the state-centred 'command and control' mechanisms they were intended to replace (Fletcher and Büscher 2017). Vatn summarizes this consensus as demonstrating that 'a very large fraction of transactions between public intermediaries and "providers" does not take the form of trade but are better characterized as subsidies... we can therefore conclude that a substantial part of PES is non-market. Where markets exist, they are mainly of the incomplete kind' (2015: 229).

Similar dynamics are evident in REDD+. Like PES, REDD+ was

envisioned as an MBI relying on global carbon markets to mobilize funding for payments to incentivize local forest conservation. Yet a decade on, the international market for REDD+ payments is still quite small, operating mostly through voluntary offsets, and hence like PES it has progressively shifted from an MBI to a non-market mechanism for centralized appropriation and redistribution of resources (Angelsen 2017). The Centre for International Forestry Research (CIFOR) concludes:

> While the scheme was initially conceived as a market-based instrument that would be funded by a massive global carbon market, that vision no longer fits reality. In the absence of that market, REDD+ has since evolved into a form of results-based aid, with various kinds of financing from governments, civil society, and the private sector. (https://forestsnews.cifor.org/49642/its-too-soon-to-bury-redd?fnl=en; accessed 11/7/2017)

This common evolution of PES and REDD+ results in large part from these mechanisms' failure to generate sufficient revenue via market engagement to achieve either conservation or poverty reduction on a significant scale. We have argued that this is due to MBIs' intrinsic inability to compete with much more lucrative extractive activity within neoliberal markets (Fletcher et al. 2016). In trying to spend limited funding most 'efficiently,' moreover, they frequently channel payments to wealthier landowners, thus also exacerbating the inequality they seek to redress. To address these problems requires continued intervention to directly allocate resources. While such intervention has allowed these mechanisms to achieve some gains, they remain hobbled by their inability to generate needed funding. This is why we propose CBI as a potential alternative funding mechanism that does not rely on the sort of direct market engagement that has proven inadequate for this aim.

Comparing PES and CTPs

Despite differences in how the two mechanisms are financed

and payments distributed, in implementation PES and CTPs may be quite similar. While often framed in neoliberal terms, as noted earlier, in practice CTPs—even conditional ones—are still essentially forms of redistribution, usually administered by the national government via taxation (Hanlon et al. 2010). Consequently, they can be seen to operate quite similar to how PES and REDD+ tend to also function in practice. While Ferguson (2010) considers CTPs a creative use of neoliberalism for progressive ends, they could thus equally be viewed, like most PES programs, as a 'subsidy in disguise' (Fletcher and Breitling 2012).

Resemblance between PES and CTPs has been highlighted by previous research (Alix-Garcia et al. 2009; Rodriguez et al. 2011; 2013; Persson and Alpizar 2013; Le Velly and Dutilly 2016; Wilebore et al. 2019). Some indeed define PES as a form of conditional CTP in providing payments contingent on conservation behavior (Alix-Garcia et al. 2009; Le Velly and Dutilly 2016; Wilebore et al. 2019) – even suggesting that PES programs can function as de facto unconditional CTPs when enforcement of conditionality is weak or lacking (Wilebore et al. 2019). Others have drawn lessons for effective PES design from CTP implementation (Loft et al. 2014). Yet to date, surprisingly, there has been little initiative to directly combine the two mechanisms. In some cases, PES and CTPs may in fact target the same households with no direct connection between the payments nor organizations administering them (Isquierdo Tort 2018). Moreover, the limitations of pursuing one mechanism in the absence of the other have been recognized. PES predominantly focuses on environmental protection and hence has been criticized for neglecting poverty concerns (Pagiola et al. 2005), Focused on poverty alleviation, conversely, CTPs may actually exacerbate negative environmental impacts if not specifically mitigated (Alix-Garcia et al. 2013).

Acknowledging all of this, researchers including World Bank staff have suggested combining the two mechanisms in an aggregate 'payment for environmental services and poverty alleviation'

(PESPA) scheme (Rodriguez et al. 2011; 2013). Yet this approach has never been implemented. To our knowledge, only one existing PES program—*Bolsa Floresta* in the Brazilian Amazon—includes a specific component for poverty reduction (Bakkegaard and Wunder 2014). However, this program, like the integrated PESPA proposal, emphasizes the type of conditional payments whose necessity has been questioned within the wider CTP debate. Additionally, neither PES nor CTPs—even when operating in parallel—offer payments sufficient to constitute a *basic* income.

Conservation Basic Income

Building on the different bodies of research outlined above, we propose a fully unconditional payment scheme able to cover recipients' basic needs – a conservation basic income. This would combine the social benefits of UBI with PES's focus on environmental protection and hence address shortcomings present in both mechanisms operating independently. Important questions remain concerning exactly what CBI would look like in practice, but many of these can already be addressed to a degree by drawing on current discussions concerning CTPs and UBI.

CBI would need to be applied equally to all individuals within a given community. In this sense, it would not be truly 'universal,' as UBI intends, since it would be restricted to only members of groups living in conservation-critical areas. As UBI has become a subject of serious discussion within many institutions, in the future CBI might be able to be reduced to merely supplement the basic income participants already receive as residents within an overarching society. Whether groups receiving CBI should be communities located in geographical space or instead those comprising users of key resources remains a key question to be discussed and resolved. Length of residence needed to qualify for payments is another important consideration but five years is commonly suggested (Standing 2017; Van Parijs and Vanderborght 2017). Appropriate levels of funding would have to be determined by context. As a general rule, Van Parijs and Vanderborght (2017) suggest payments of one quarter current per capita GDP, but payments should always be at least the US $5 per day considered minimal for healthful living (UN 2014; Hickel 2017). In delivering payments by individual rather than household, CBI could act as an instrument of women's empowerment (Van Parijs and Vanderborght 2017). The necessity of additional payments for children is debated among UBI proponents. If provided they should be given to the primary adult caregiver. Recipients could be identified through GIS mapping of areas important to biodiversity hotspots, as occurs in some PES programs (Zhang and Pagiola 2011). Payment targeting could entail partnership with the Indigenous and Community Conservation Area (ICCA)[2] consortium to help channel CBI.

Different proponents propose a variety of means through which funding for UBI could be generated, from increased state taxation through redirection of existing public resources from other programmes through cracking down on tax havens to which potential current revenue is diverted (see e.g. Standing 2017; Stern 2017). Using such proposals as a springboard, and particularly by redirecting resources from other existing programs offering seed money to (unsuccessfully) establish conservation markets, it might be possible to finance CBI with little new fundraising. Alternatively, new funding could be raised through innovative sources, such as the (substantial) carbon tax increasingly advocated by climate activists and occasionally proposed as a basis for UBI (Standing 2017). In this way, CBI would achieve a double benefit, both promoting conservation in target communities and reducing environmental impact globally. This would be especially useful given the grave threat climate change poses to existing conservation areas that cannot be mitigated through local initiatives only (Thomas et al. 2004). In our larger convivial conservation proposal, we advocate pursuit of funding 'a diverse set of revenue sources combining state-based taxation (including public bonds), grants from international donors and individual patrons, insurance schemes, long-term engagement fees, sale of sustainable products, crowdsourcing campaigns, new blockchain technologies, and whatever else can be harnessed in the interest of' the campaign (Büscher and Fletcher 2020: 197). All of these could comprise the finance base of CBI specifically as well.

Clearly, there are many issues that must be thought through further than space affords here. One important outstanding question is whether CBI might paradoxically contribute to biodiversity loss by increasing people's income. Globally, income levels are strongly correlated with environmental impact (Caron and Fally 2018), while research has also documented cases where increased income (via ecotourism, for instance) leads to resource degradation by allowing recipients to purchase better land-clearing equipment (Stem et al 2003). With respect to CTPs specifically, researchers have also found evidence of correlation between nominally unconditional payments and (moderately) increased land clearing, at least in the short term (Wilebore et al. 2019).

Yet provision of basic payments might also reduce resource use by allowing recipients to forgo other income generating activities entailing destructive extraction – for instance, employment in mining or logging operations in places where few other options exist. Payments' unconditionality would at least assuage concerns about the 'crowding out' effects on intrinsic conservation values often associated with incentive-based initiatives (Rode et al. 2015). Indeed, evidence from CTPs suggest that even without conditionality payments might produce 'crowding in' effects on intrinsic motivation if payments are merely rhetorically connected with conservation; one study found that 'simply labelling an *unconditional* transfer as an education grant increases the likelihood that behaviour would be directed towards that goal' (Standing 2017: 224; Benhassine et al. 2015).

This is an issue that would need to be closely monitored and evaluated in any piloting of CBI, and steps taken to redress any increase in resource extraction if this were found to occur. As in most UBI piloting (Standing 2017), such considerations can likely be proactively pre-empted to some degree by combining payments with other forms of community engagement intended to inspire ethics-based forms of conservation commitment (e.g. environmental education) to help channel payments into beneficial activities. A related issue concerns the potential that funding of this sort might draw new migrants to conservation areas. This dynamic is ostensibly demonstrated by Wittemyer et al.'s (2008) mapping of the global correlation between protected areas and population growth. But detailed social scientific research in some of the areas included in Wittemyer et al.'s study have complicated this picture, demonstrating that the connection between income opportunities associated with protected areas and inmigration is quite spurius (Hoffman et al. 2011). Future research would need to address whether such issues need consideration in CBI.

A third significant question is whether cash money is the best medium of exchange in all contexts. Proponents of UBI generally advocate cash as it affords recipients maximum control, allowing them to decide for themselves how they will use the benefits provided. Yet it is widely acknowledged that cash is useless if there are no effective provision of the various good and services (from consumer markets to health care and education) stakeholders need to access. Hence cash benefits must be complemented by attention to the effectiveness of social services and infrastructure in target communities. An additional concern in relation to cash transfers regards their implications for cultural groups for whom use of money is rare or absent. After all, a common critique of MBIs concerns their potential to impose a monetary logic on resources or practices previously valued in culturally-specific ways, and hence to encourage commodification (Sullivan 2009; Büscher et al. 2012).

Considering issues such as this, Coote and Yazici caution, 'If cash payments are allowed to take precedence, there's a serious risk of crowding out efforts to build collaborative, sustainable services and infrastructure – and setting a pattern for future development that promotes commodification rather than emancipation' (2019: 31). Such considerations lead some to advocate providing 'universal basic services' rather than income (Coote et al. 2019). Yet there are dangers in this approach as well. For one, it usually requires a strong state capable of providing effective services – something conspicuously absent in many places where conservation interventions are most needed. It is for this reason we do not generally advocate a return to the type of state-based 'command-and-control' strategies for environmental governance that some others (e.g. Klein 2015) do in challenging neoliberal approaches, save in societies in which states have proven capable of executing this function effectively. In other places, coalitions of non-state actors are likely needed to deliver both CBI and the social services this will be spent on. In such situations, cash transfers may be something of a 'least evil' for local residents who been largely abandoned by agents of the states in which they live. And even if services are capable of delivery by nonstate actors, they still hold potential to replicate the pattern of paternalistic external control that UBI is intended to combat. As Coote qualifies, 'everything turns on how much money is paid, under what conditions and with what consequences for the welfare system as a whole'[3]. Consequently, how CBI, or variations upon it, are designed and implemented will require sustained attention to the particularities of local contexts as well as active collaboration with intended recipients. It also requires connection to broader convivial conservation efforts that aim to provide a conducive overarching environment for local initiatives to succeed.

In terms of framing, rather than a payment for 'ecosystem services,' CBI could be considered a form of compensation for the impact of conservation interventions on recipients' lives. In this way, CBI could contribute to developing non-instrumental or -utilitarian means of relating with nonhuman natures in dramatic contrast with that promoted via ecosystem services and natural capital approaches. Moreover, CBI could be considered a form of decolonial reparation for the damage inflicted on communities by previous conservation efforts. By displacing millions of people to create protected areas, conservation has deprived many of access to resources from which they previously derived livelihoods (Dowie 2009). Providing reparations for past harm is part of the demand for UBI recently advanced by the Black Lives Matter alliance (Standing 2017: 287) and something we advocate more generally in our convivial conservation proposal (Büscher and Fletcher 2019). All this could help to further decolonize conservation and render it more legitimate for the historically dispossessed.

Conclusion

Notwithstanding persistent attempts to develop a global market for generating finance, in practice conservation funding has come to increasingly rely on (often covert) forms of redistribution. This is true, we have shown, of many PES and REDD+ programs. In their recent review of the global experience of neoliberal conservation, Dempsey and Suarez (2016) demonstrate this pattern more generally. In line with PES research, they show that despite widespread promotion of measures to incentivize conservation around the world over the past decades, in reality very little actual market exchange has taken place and the majority of trade that does occur is directed by states. Hence, they describe genuine market transactions among private parties as merely 'slivers of slivers of slivers' of overall finance (Dempsey and Suarez 2016: 654).

In sum, much biodiversity conservation has to date functioned mostly as a (global) subsidy system, redistributing resources to support conservation rather than developing genuine market mechanisms (Fletcher and Breitling 2012). What if we chose to call a spade a spade and simply followed this logic in framing and administering conservation funding as explicit versions of the subsidies it actually provides in practice? As we suggested previously, in acknowledging this reality '[m]ight one instead experiment with providing subsidies (state supported or otherwise) to resource-dependent communities based on direct taxation of extractive activities of the type that are already in some cases covertly supplied through MBIs?' (Fletcher et al, 2016: 675).

CBI is one potential mechanism by which this broader strategy could be cultivated. We propose it here as the basis for a future research and policy agenda that should seek to assess its viability and appropriate forms of design. Among other issues, such research should address the following questions:

1) How recipient communities receiving CBI should be defined;

2) Whether payments need be conditional or not;

3) What level of payments are needed to be both effective and just;

4) Whether cash is the most appropriate medium of payment, or whether services and/or other benefits are preferable;

5) Whether payments are likely to compel in-migration, and if so how to address this;

6) Whether payments encourage increased resource use, and if so how to remedy this;

7) How to use this mechanism as part of a broader political discussion to achieve broader 'transformative change'.

We invite others to contribute to this important discussion in pursuit of a more equitable and convivial future for conservation.

Chapter 12:

Conviviality in Disrupted Socionatural Landscapes: Ecological Peacebuilding around Akagera National Park*

By Elaine (Lan Yin) Hsiao

Introduction: Bringing Conservation Back to Conviviality

Different spatial and ideological contemplations of how human and non-human species can or should cohabit this Earth, ranging from fortress conservation to convivial conservation, are at the forefront of debates in the conservation community. Conviviality requires day-to-day coexistence and management of conflicts between human and non-human species, otherwise known as human-wildlife conflicts. These conflicts are often experienced as a tension between human ideologies about how we should coexist with other species. As a result, human-wildlife conflicts are frequently managed by conservationists in a variety of ways intended to appease species-impacted human populations. These include barrier mechanisms to separate people or their property from wildlife, financial schemes, including compensation for damages caused by wildlife or investments in community development, or education programs about the value and practicalities of living with wildlife. These human-wildlife conflict interventions may make sense from the perspective of the conservation community's interests in reducing the negative impacts of wildlife on people or vice versa, and especially towards improving people's perceptions of wildlife and environmental conservation. In this chapter, I examine these interventions from a peace perspective in order to situate different

* Originally published as: Hsiao, E. (2022). Conviviality in disrupted socionatural landscapes: Ecological peacebuilding around Akagera National Park. Conservation & Society 20(2): 79-91.

conservation approaches within understandings of harmonious socioecological relations.

Although human-wildlife conflicts use the terminology of conflict, peace and conflict theories have rarely been applied to understand or evaluate their management and resolution. Published in 2008, the Special Issue of the *Journal of International Wildlife Law and Policy* was dedicated to the topic of 'Human-Wildlife Conflict and Peace-building Strategies', but none of the articles provided a conceptual framework for what peace means in context of human-wildlife conflict or what kind of peace the different peacebuilding strategies are intended or in effect achieve (Jaireth 2008). More recently, some effort has been put into understanding human-wildlife conflict through the practices of conventional conflict-analysis (E.g., Zimmermann et al. 2020), but human-wildlife conflict interventions have not yet been considered through peace theory. Since so many human-wildlife conflicts are seen as social conflicts between humans, I suggest that peace theory is well-suited to understand where interventions and their outcomes align with different types of peace and that this can offer human-wildlife conflict 'managers' another framework to assess and prioritise the actions they take. Also, this raises an opportunity to apply peace theory in the context of human and non-human relations or ecological peace, which emphasizes the value and challenges of convivial conservation amongst the many approaches to conservation that seek more harmonious interspecies coexistence.

In the first section of this chapter, I define ecological peace in terms of Galtung's (1969) theory of negative peace (freedom from direct physical violence) and positive peace (freedom from physical, cultural, and structural violence) as applied to relations between human and non-human species. I argue that convivial conservation is a vision of positive ecological peace based on radical coexistence and interspecies cooperation and that this perspective is even more applicable in disrupted socionatural landscapes. Akagera National Park in Rwanda (ANP or Akagera) represents a disrupted socionatural landscape where human and non-human species have been displaced and the relationships between them have been disturbed by violence and conflict. Socionatural disruption exists in varied degrees in nearly every community around the world, with the potential exception of uncontacted Indigenous Peoples. Therefore, a Whole Earth approach to convivial conservation requires us to understand how socionaturally disrupted communities (human and non-human) can transition towards positive ecological peace. This section frames the case study that follows.

In the second section, the case study of Akagera is introduced to illustrate how different human-wildlife conflict interventions can have different outcomes for ecological peace. In the third section, I show how an electric boundary fence may be an attempt to build social peace between the protected area management and local communities, but for humans and wildlife it offers only negative peace, rife with injustice. Meanwhile, in the next sub-section, the park's compensation schemes and revenue sharing programs apply liberal peace strategies that fall short of positive peace. Traditional biocultural knowledge, however, has the potential to build positive ecological peace and as the next sub-section suggests, is endangered but carries the possibility of revitalization. The Akagera case study offers potential for culture-based coexistence between historically-displaced and locally-settled people and the wildlife they cohabit with, if the park's human-wildlife conflict interventions do not undermine these positive ecological peacebuilding opportunities in the meantime. In concluding this chapter, I reiterate how important it is to evaluate different human-wildlife conflict mechanisms from the perspective of peace for the realisation of convivial conservation in a world of complex disrupted socionatural landscapes. In the face of conservation agendas seeking to expand conservation territorialities, this is not only critical for ecological peace, but also for conflict sensitive conservation.

Human-Wildlife Conflict Management from the Perspective of Peace

The 2030 international policy agenda for environmental protection is ambitious in its targets for area-based conservation, eying approximately 30% of the Earth's territorial lands and seas for conservation management by 2030 while many are proposing 50% for the 2050 Vision for Biodiversity (CBD 2020a; 2020b). In response to the Nature Needs Half movement (Locke 2013), social justice organizations have raised alarm around an aggressive area-based expansion of conservation territorialities (Minority Rights Group et al. 2020). Conservation territoriality, or the territorialisation of protected areas, 'involves delineating a particular space, determining what behavior and activities are and are not allowed within it, giving it particular political and social meaning, and communicating this delineation and meaning to others' (Holmes 2014: 1). Studies indicate that more than one billion people could be impacted by a 50% agenda and specifically, as many as 1.65–1.87 billion Indigenous, local and Afro-descendant communities (Schleicher et al. 2019; Rights and Resources Initiative 2020). Impact in these cases can range from conservation restrictions on individual activities (e.g. hunting bans) to forced displacement (e.g. evictions) in newly designated conservation areas – all of which trigger red flags for human rights violations (Brockington and Igoe 2006; Tauli-Corpuz et al. 2020). These kinds of grievances frequently underlay human-wildlife conflicts that serve as manifestations of antagonism by local communities against protected areas and their expansion. This is illustrated in Akagera through the positioning of responsibility for problematic wildlife on park management and highlights the need for just conservation.

A counter proposition to expanding conservation territorialities is a Whole Earth approach through convivial conservation. Half Earth vs. Whole Earth is a debate that has emerged between largely conservation biologists who argue that the survival of non-human life on Earth hinges on sufficient levels of habitat protection and conservation social scientists who believe that this expansion of conservation territoriality will not only impact on already vulnerable peoples, but it also fails to address the root causes of environmental degradation and climate change deriving from capitalism and overconsumption (Büscher et al. 2016; Cafaro et al. 2017). Convivial conservation is a movement towards Whole Earth premised on reconciling these two problems – social injustice and growth-driven capitalist economic systems (Büscher and Fletcher 2019). These different approaches to protecting (human and non-human) life can be understood through peace theory and its different approaches (e.g. liberal, cultural), and are explored in the case study of ANP. In the paragraphs that follow, the pros and cons of common theories of peace, in this case Galtung's positive and negative peace or liberal peace, are elaborated for a socionatural context where human relationships transgress species (i.e. ecological peace).

We often think of coexistence as peace, but the ways we achieve coexistence impact on the nature of the peace produced. To illustrate this, I draw from Galtung's (1969) theory of peace, wherein peace is not the absence of conflict, but rather the absence of violence, and notably particular forms of violence. Negative peace represents the absence of direct violence (personal, physical), while positive peace represents the absence of direct and indirect (structural and cultural) violence (Ramsbotham et al. 2011). Structural violence originates from human social structures (e.g., when immigrant children in the U.S. die from lack of care in deportation centres), whereas cultural violence is 'any aspect of a culture that can be used to legitimize violence in its direct or structural form' (Galtung 1990: 291). Where direct physical violence is no longer present, but structural violence or injustice remains, there is only negative peace. Positive and negative peace were first conceptualised by Galtung, but continue to endure as essential theory in peace and conflict studies, which makes it meaningful to draw upon for a reflection on interspecies conflicts, namely between humans and other species.

Positive peace is also important in the context of convivial conservation, which stresses the need for just and integrated coexistence, moving away from ghettoised segregation (negative peace) between human and non-human nature (fortress conservation) towards 'long-lasting, engaging and open-minded relationships with nonhumans and ecologies', but is not yet conceptualised through this framing of positive and negative peace (Büscher and Fletcher 2019: 286-288). Through the case study of ANP, I suggest that human-wildlife conflict mechanisms that rely on barriers to prevent direct violence between human and non-human species (e.g. prevent poaching or crop-raiding) can achieve no more than negative peace, falling short of both positive peace and convivial conservation. Similarly, compensation or financial mechanisms designed to offset the costs of living with wildlife and to assuage any animosity towards non-human species or conservationists (sometimes seen as wildlife-preferring humans) are comparable to a form of negative peace known as liberal peace.

Some argue that a powerful incentive to maintain negative peace (i.e. avoid militarized interstate disputes), especially in democratic states, is economic interdependence or growth in trade (Oneal et al. 1996; Gelpi and Grieco 2008). Liberal peace is favored by those who see peace as economically- or development-driven (Gartzke and Weisiger 2014); the same ideology pervades human-wildlife conflict where coexistence is framed as a cost-benefit analysis for people living near protected areas (Barua et al. 2013). Critiques of liberal peace, which also apply to neoliberal conservation (Heynen et al. 2007), point to its reliance on the globalisation and neoliberalisation of markets and growth-hungry capitalism that exacerbate socio-economic inequalities and the anthropogenic drivers of environmental change, including climate change, resulting in negative peace wrought with injustice (Gonzalez-Vicente 2020; Nixon 2011). Nixon describes 'antihuman conservation practices... that disproportionately jeopardise the livelihoods, prospects, and memory banks of the global poor' as an example of slow violence resulting from neoliberalism (Nixon 2011: 2, 5). Liberal peace approaches to human-wildlife conflict resolution can result in a culture of monetisation of human and non-human relations, as witnessed in the measure of human-wildlife conflicts through compensation claims, and can produce slow violence, including forced displacement of species and growing acceptance of human-wildlife segregation, which aligns it with negative peace rather than convivial conservation's goals of 'equity, structural change and environmental justice' (Büscher and Fletcher 2019: 286).

Ecological peace is unique in that it unifies threads of conventional peace theory, convivial conservation, environmental peacebuilding and the more-than-human Whole Earth. It refers to non-violent relations between humans and the rest of nature in the same way that convivial conservation is a celebration of human and non-human nature, not as a dichotomy, but rather as 'exceptional and unique' aspects of a Whole Earth (Büscher and Fletcher 2019: 287). It is different from environmental peacebuilding, which is premised on cooperation between people for improved human-human or inter-state relations (Conca and Dabelko 2002), and instead 'reflects a state of harmony or "species cooperation" between humans and the rest of nature premised on an ethic or relationship of mutual care and respect' (Hsiao and Le Billon 2021: 30). Applying Galtung's theory of positive and negative peace, we can think of negative ecological peace as freedom from direct forms of physical interspecies violence, focusing particularly on the human to non-human dichotomy, such as people clear-cutting or fire-bombing forests. Positive ecological peace would mean freedom from structural violences, such as human exploitation of non-human nature within capitalist economic systems, as well as cultural violence, such as human ideologies of species elitism and domination. This may be visible in thriving Territories of Life, where socio-ecological wellbeing are entwined. In these places, coexistence is sought through non-violent and just forms of mutual care between species.

Ecological peace differentiates itself from human-centered concepts of peace, i.e. international peace (between states) and social peace (between humans), in that it incorporates the non-human and therefore, recognises that some physical violence is inherent to nature. The natural laws of ecosystems demand that predators kill prey to sustain life and permit parasitic species to persist. Even vegetarian species consume plant life and plants consume nutrient matter, sometimes in competition with other species. Human and non-human species have also always killed each other, but as De Silva and Srinivasan (2019: 188), citing Dempsey (2010) and others, have noted, the existence of most wildlife is now precarious and the nature of that killing has changed to one which exceeds 'moments of need or dangerous encounter'. As Le Billon and I note, 'ecological peace does not assume that all species will be free of all violence, but rather, focuses on a sustainable relationship between humans and the rest of nature and more specifically, on the kinds of violence and conflict that exceed a threshold that sustains the wellbeing of all life (e.g., anthropogenically-induced extinctions)' (Hsiao and Le Billon 2021: 31). When these thresholds are exceeded, for example with the unsustainable killing of non-humans by humans (e.g. overfishing) or even the introduction of invasive species which extirpate endogenous species, it would be considered direct violence, and therefore an absence of negative ecological peace.

Ecological peace can be impacted by intra-human conflicts resulting in socionatural disruption. Socionatural refers to the 'inextricably intertwined domains of human action and physical environment' that are inherent to ecological peace and convivial conservation (Siegel 2018: 338). On one hand, this captures the interconnectedness of nature and culture or human society, on the other, it speaks to the interlinked social and ecological change that shapes the co-evolution of nature and culture or society. Integrated socionatures are perhaps most stereotypically observed in Indigenous and traditional societies whose social systems are imbued with traditional ecological knowledge that simultaneously sustains human and non-human wellbeing (Gadgil et al. 1993). It is also visible in the scale of anthropogenically-induced environmental change that has inspired the term 'Anthropocene'. Even long coeval socionatures are vulnerable to disruption and over time can result in loss of ecological knowledge and degradation of either or both human and ecological well-being (Costanza Torri 2011). These processes alter the ways in which humans manage coexistence with wildlife, shifting from traditional practices that may have included mutual respect, taboos, knowledge of wildlife behaviour, culturally moderated forms of hunting, or the designation of no-go zones, to more contemporary mechanisms of human-wildlife separation and neoliberalism. In this chapter I argue that the former supports more positive ecological peace, while the latter may only attain negative ecological peace.

Socionatural disruption can occur for many reasons – colonisation, industrialisation, conservation, development, and as noted above, from civil war, genocide, and armed conflict. The colonial modus operandi of fortress conservation has been one of the most disruptive processes for socionatures, severing communities from both natural environments and governance of those territories (Tauli-Corpuz et al. 2020). Armed conflicts can have the same effect, creating crises that compel displacement and settlement, temporarily or permanently, in other locales. In the case of Rwanda, both the creation of protected areas and violent conflict have uprooted people time and again, resulting in the country's mosaic of local communities often made up of people with fractured connections to the villages or ecosystems they currently inhabit – some may have ancestral connections, but they were born and raised elsewhere only to return after the genocide of the Tutsi, while others are refugees settled in an area designated for them by the government. As a village leader in Ndego (south of ANP) observed, a local person may have limited knowledge of the species they coexist with or how to coexist with them, because the ecosystem is different from where they were raised (Umudugudu Chief 2020). Even resettled refugees who have returned to their families' former homelands may have spent one or more generations away, growing up with a different set of species and landscapes—most refugees in Rwanda fled around 1959 or 1994 to return some time after 1997—leading to different levels of knowledge erosion. Some may encounter traditional ecological knowledge in stories alone. Ecological peace in a disrupted landscape requires reconciliation between these groups of locally displaced to restore a land ethic, and those who were displaced from elsewhere to cultivate coexistence in their new habitat (Martin 2005; see also van Holstein and Head 2018).

Socionatural disruption shapes human-wildlife interactions and perceptions, which impact on ecological peace. Increasing violence between humans and non-human species is both real and perceived. Shifting perceptions can result from a diminishing practice of cohabitation or a diminishing desire to cohabit. Humans now seek to eradicate or separate ourselves from certain species with whom we have co-evolved, but now consider pests, and when we are no longer around certain species, we lose our knowledge of how to coexist and cooperate (i.e. mutual care). De Silva and Srinivasan (2019) note that this reinforces nature-society divides in two ways: 1) separating people from wildlife by creating exclusive protected areas and 2) separating wildlife from people by creating wildlife-free spaces in human settlements. They argue that social natures 'require the equitable sharing of landscapes with nonhuman others and entails mutual risk', which can include acceptance of certain thresholds of harm to crops, livestock, or even physical wellbeing (De Silva and Srinivasan 2019: 188). Convivial conservation may allay some of that risk by cultivating local ecological knowledge, practices and systems that minimize negative human-wildlife encounters, and involve less violent means than the separation characteristic of conservation territoriality (Duffy et al. 2019).

In order to capture the Whole Earth, convivial conservation rejects nature-people or nature-culture dichotomies, and promotes radical coexistence in its vision that 'all people have to be able to (potentially) live with all nature' (Büscher and Fletcher, 2019: 288). What convivial conservation does not dictate is how all people can live with all nature, leaving the modalities of coexistence to the imagination. While barrier mechanisms like the park's electric fence can reduce incidences of illegal hunting and crop/livestock damage and its compensation scheme can dissuade people from retaliating against wildlife (negative ecological peace), they do not restore critical elements of culturally governed coexistence and integrated socioecological well-being (positive ecological peace). The ANP case study in the next section distinguishes between human-wildlife conflict interventions in terms of negative and positive peace, in order to understand how certain solutions align or do not align with convivial conservation's more transformative goals.

ANP as A Case Study of Ecological Peace and Conviviality

This case study is based primarily on a review of literature and consultations with the Rwanda Development Board (RDB) and Akagera Management Corporation (AMC) staff, as well as cumulative knowledge over years of research in the region. Due to pandemic restrictions, field visits were only made to the park headquarters, including a 'Behind the Scenes' tour of the park in March 2019, and Gasabo and Mucucu villages (see map) between February and March 2020 for interviews with eight local government representatives, village leaders, and local healers. These were identified as 'villages of interest', along with Karangazi and Rwimiyaga sectors from the Nyagatare District in the north, through consultations with park staff looking at their reports of human-wildlife conflict claims in the preceding months (Fiston Ishimwe, 2020). The study also draws from a human-wildlife conflict study of the 'Socio-economic and Ecological Dimensions of Restoring Akagera National Park, Rwanda' by Treves et al. (2019) (hereinafter Akagera HWC Report), which produced the map (Figure 1), illustrating the geographic distribution of compensation claims made based on wildlife damage to crops, livestock, or humans between 2014 and 2018).

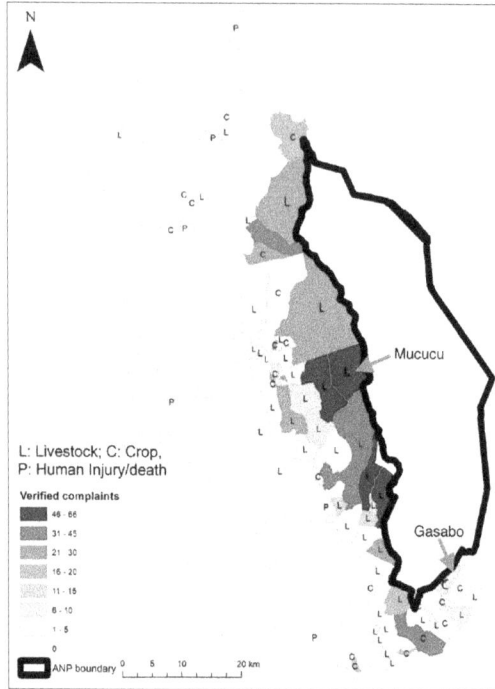

Figure 1: Geographical distribution of verified complaints about wildlife damage around Akagera National Park, Rwanda recorded by park management in 2014-2018 by village. Background colors estimate the total number of verified complaints by all species, as per the legend, where the dominant type of wildlife damage in that village is mapped by letter (C=crop, L=livestock, P=human injury/death) (Treves et al. 2019, 11).

Before the park was established, it was sparsely populated with pastoralists utilizing mainly grassland areas in the northern Mutara rangelands (e.g., Bahima) and living in the eastern region along the Akagera riverbank (e.g. Banyambo) (Hall 2014). The woodlands were avoided because of tsetse flies, as were the marshy wetlands, leaving the south and central regions uninhabited. Civil war and genocide changed the human geographies of Akagera dramatically, bringing in refugee populations from different parts of the country. Approximately two million refugees and another one million were internally displaced during the genocide years (Prunier 1995: 312–313). Before that, Akagera had already been turned into a humanitarian site for mostly Ugandan refugees, with over 45,000 people (sometimes as many as 1,500 arriving per day) and 50,000 cattle brought to camps in Kanyinya, Mahega, and Kibondo in and around ANP (US House of Representatives 1984). After the plane crash of President Habyarimana, ANP became a through-way/battleground for the Rwanda Patriotic Front's liberation army entering from Uganda (Kuperman 2004: 23).

Today, AMC estimates there are over 300,000 people living around the park, though it is still the least densely populated region in the country (African Parks 2021a). According to park staff, lands outside the northern sector are dominated by historically-rooted pastoral people with a long-established connection to the ecosystem and constituent species and typically reports the lowest number of human-wildlife conflict incidences or cases of damages caused by wildlife (Fiston Ishimwe, 2020). The central sector also features large landholding pastoralists, often with hundreds of cows, but many originate from other parts of the country and fled Rwanda until they were granted property in former parklands as part of post-conflict repatriation (AMC Staff, 2019). Observable in Figure 1, this area is a hotspot for human-wildlife conflict claims. Around the southern sector are repatriated, largely agricultural communities, typically with smaller herds of livestock, while some are tenant farmers working for remote landowners (Fiston Ishimwe, 2020; Umudugudu Chief, 2020).

ANP was gazetted in 1934 (Decree of November 26, 1934), establishing one of the largest wetland protected areas in Africa to encompass the Akagera River watershed, as part of the Nile River Basin, and its wildlife (Treves et al. 2019). It is Rwanda's only 'Big 5' game park, a title reclaimed in 2017 with the reintroduction of Eastern Black Rhinos (*Diceros bicornis ssp. michaeli*) from South Africa (Gill 2019). Initially the park included multi-use zones where some human activities were allowed, but the core was strictly reserved for 'leave no trace' scientific research – even tourists were not allowed (Hall 2014).

ANP is an excellent example of interlinked socio-ecological

disruption, with its wildlife and size rising and falling with the stability/insecurity of its socio-political context. Originally 252,000 hectares, it saw some years of ecological expansion; recorded at 267,000 hectares in 1960 with its lion population doubling from 150 to 300 between 1969 and 1990 (Ministry of Lands, Resettlement and Environment 2003: 13–42). A field visit by the Association pour la Conservation de la Nature au Rwanda (ACNR) in 1993 estimated that ANP had lost 90% of its large mammals with important changes to its habitats (Kanyamibwa 1998: 1402). In 1997, it was regazetted at half its original size (112,193 hectares) (Decision No. 3 of the Cabinet meeting on July 29, 1997) in order to accommodate large populations of refugees settled inside of the park and neighboring Mutara Hunting Fields (Ministry of Lands, Resettlement and Environment 2003: 23).

With the park size dramatically decreased and dramatically increasing human population, human-wildlife conflicts abounded in the decade following the 1997 regazettement. Retaliatory poisoning and illegal hunting led to the extirpation of lions by 2006 and rhinos around 2007 (Rwanda Environment Management Authority 2016: 27). ANP's boundaries were redrawn again in 2010, this time with a 967 ha buffer zone (Law No. 33/2010 of 24/09/2010 Establishing Akagera National Park 2010: 33). As of 2019, ANP covers 108,363.7 hectares with a 1,153.3 hectare buffer zone (Law No. 68/2019 of 29/10/2019 Governing the Akagera National Park 2019) and the government is now keen to extend its connectivity to include the remnant Ibanda-Makera Forest (Rwanda Environment Management Authority 2016: 59–60). Figure 2 provides a timeline of ANP's ebb and flow in terms of territorial size and key figures in terms of lion and rhino extinctions and reintroduction, as well as poaching indicators, and key events in its establishment and management.

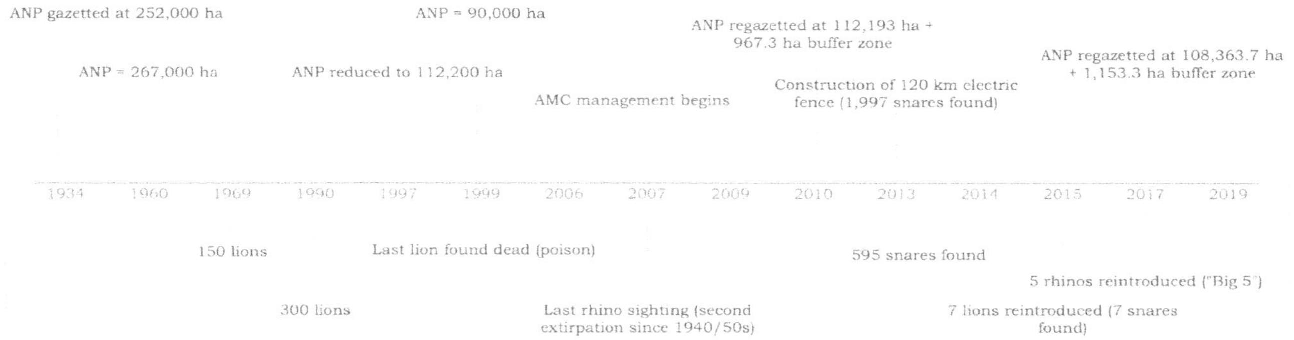

ANP gazetted at 252,000 ha

ANP = 90,000 ha

ANP regazetted at 112,193 ha + 967.3 ha buffer zone

ANP regazetted at 108,363.7 ha + 1,153.3 ha buffer zone

ANP = 267,000 ha

ANP reduced to 112,200 ha

Construction of 120 km electric fence (1,997 snares found)

AMC management begins

1934	1960	1969	1990	1997	1999	2006	2007	2009	2010	2013	2014	2015	2017	2019

150 lions

300 lions

Last lion found dead (poison)

Last rhino sighting (second extirpation since 1940/50s)

595 snares found

7 lions reintroduced (7 snares found)

5 rhinos reintroduced ("Big 5")

Figure 2: Akagera National Park Size and Selected Statistics (1934-2019)

In the years after lion and rhino extirpation, Akagera's management transitioned from state authority to a public-private partnership between African Parks and RDB under the AMC. Amongst the AMC's primary goals was to ensure the security of park wildlife, which includes the boundary fence, specially trained law enforcement rangers, and a canine team, plus upgraded surveillance technologies. Another target is to increase the economic productivity of the park through tourism investments, including the re-introduction of lions and rhinos, construction of roads and hotel infrastructure, and support to communities, especially those who contribute to one or both of these goals (e.g., renouncing poaching, producing supplies for park hotels, or guiding and entertaining tourists). Even the state's compensation scheme for wildlife damages are considered an offset of the costs of living with wildlife, and thus contribute to economic enhancement. As presented in the section that follows, these human-wildlife conflict interventions offer only negative ecological peace for human-wildlife coexistence.

From Fences and Funds to Totems and Taboos

Day-to-day practices of negative and positive ecological peace present different approaches to conviviality in Akagera's local communities, reminding us that the local community is neither homogenously heroic nor threatening, but will seek conviviality through the tools of individual circumstances and that individual strategies may differ from those of others within their same community. This presents itself in the park management's decision to construct a physical barrier at the boundary line between park land and community land in order to minimize conflicts between people and wildlife, and the government's policy to compensate wildlife damages to mediate conflicts between the park and people. As an alternative, local ecological knowledge, including cultural systems of totem species and related taboos, could help to transform cultural violence between human and non-human species (Brackhane et al. 2019; Kimenyi n.d.). These different approaches to human-wildlife coexistence bring further understanding to the kinds of peace (negative, liberal, and positive, respectively) that may be expected.

Fencing Nature: An Imperfect Fortress of Negative Ecological Peace

The reintroduction of apex predators like lions and critically endangered high-value species like rhinos into socionatural landscapes can compel a re-fortressing rather than positive ecological peacebuilding that can ensure long-term convivial conservation. For a country like Rwanda with a limited national budget, the purchase of lions and rhinos from other countries in Africa and zoos in Europe presents a large investment that needs to be safeguarded to yield returns in tourism revenues. While the European zoos saw this as an opportunity to return the descendants of captive rhinos 'back to their homeland', they wanted to know that the animals would be safe in a country where they had been wiped out twice before (Gill 2019). This effort towards decolonizing ex-situ conservation resulted in a re-colonization of fortress conservation in ANP. To heighten rhino and park security, AMC put into place a series of anti-poaching measures, which included ranger training, introduction of bloodhounds, surveillance technologies, and protective infrastructure (African Parks 2021b). As described during a 'Behind the Scenes' tour of the park in 2019, Akagera's rhinos are monitored constantly by a special ranger unit and rarely leave the safety of the northern sector of the park. In order to reintroduce the lions, however, the park management needed to assure the surrounding human populations that the animals would not be another threat to their lives and livelihoods (AMC Staff, 2019). Two years before their reintroduction, the electric boundary fence was installed and afterwards, neighbouring communities were taught how to upgrade their livestock infrastructures as well (AMC Staff, 2019; Sameul Rugamba and Kellen Sanyu, 2020). Altogether, the reintroduction of lions and rhinos in ANP has resulted in more fences, not only around the park itself, but also for domesticated animals, not considered wildlife.

Barrier mechanism like Akagera's electric boundary fence

and bomas for rhinos or livestock, at their best offer negative ecological peace by providing certain protective benefits. In human-wildlife conflict 'hotspots' around ANP like Gasabo and Mucucu, community members credit the fence for a reduction in crop-raiding, livestock killings, not to mention human injuries, and consider it one of the positive benefits deriving from the park (Benon Gashayija, 2020; Martin Rwakabogo, 2020). 'There is a huge difference, before they fenced the park, wild animals would kill people. They would come all the way from the park and damage communities' crops, and kill people. But now, it's different' (Posiyani Ntibagirirwa, 2020).

According to park management, the fence correlates with a significant reduction in poaching incidents inside of the park – during the 'Behind the Scenes' tour in 2019, a park ranger observed that throughout earlier years they would find hundreds of wire snares, while in the recent year or two they located only a handful. A traditional healer in Gasabo said that they used to go inside the forest to collect medicinal plants, but 'are now aware that the park is guarded, it has a fence, there is literally a frontier between people and the park' (Lenatha Mukamusoni 2020). These reductions in direct violence between humans and non-humans may have helped to improve social conflict between park authorities and local communities by providing a physical solution to the problems of property damage and risk to human and non-human life, but none of these problems will go away completely. Since the fence there have been 22 reports of wildlife-caused human injury and eight cases of human deaths, while evidence of poaching also continues (Treves et al. 2019: 11). Fences are also lacking in terms of the cultural and structural non-violence of positive ecological peace.

Even as a physical barrier to protect negative ecological peace, boundary fences are not impervious and can institutionalize a false sense of separation between people and other species. Research on the electric fence indicates that for most species, physical separation between humans and non-humans is largely an assumption and not absolute (see Treves et al. 2019). In other words, most of the species found inside the park also exist outside, with the exception of lions and rhinos, which were only reintroduced in Rwanda inside of Akagera's fenced boundary. Smaller species (e.g. baboons, vervet monkeys, and young leopards) can move in and out of the fenced boundaries, but not larger mammals (see Bariyanga et al. 2016). Human settlements have also been constructed inside ANP to house park staff and tourists. Compensation for crop raiding or livestock killings is premised on an attribution of the animal's origin to the park and thus, responsibility for managing that wildlife and reimbursing for its damages goes to state authorities (Minister of Trade and Industry 2012 art. 2(2)). The park's territorial demarcation and construction of a fence creates a false attribution of animal origin, making all wildlife, park wildlife. Ultimately, wildlife that continues to live on lands outside of ANP create a *de facto* area of human-wildlife cohabitation, while the park creates a *de jure* area of human-wildlife visitation. However, the impacts of these territorial distinctions and resulting quality of cohabitation is what the lens of negative and positive ecological peace brings into focus.

This false sense of separation between human and non-human nature can degrade local communities' desire for conviviality, evidenced by the dissonance between species that are considered desirable or undesirable, based on which side of the fence they are found (Treves et al. 2019: 18). In AMC's human-wildlife conflict study, 27.89% of the respondents listed elephants as one of their favorite species inside the park, but none listed it as a species they preferred to see on their own property (Treves et al. 2019). Two of the women interviewed in Mucucu expressed a common sentiment concerning 'problem animals' outside of the park: 1) wild animals should be taken 'back' to the park and 2) domestic species should be protected by building fences (e.g., bomas for livestock) (Faith Mukabaranga and Jolly Bafuruka, 2020). The challenges of human-wildlife conflict around ANP demonstrate that physical separation is counter-productive for positive ecological peace in at least a few specific ways. Notably, it facilitates a cultural violence of separation in the belief that humans and wildlife should be kept apart (species apartheid) and a structural violence of institutionalised segregation implemented by park management and law enforcement rather than acknowledgement that wildlife has always existed inside and outside of the park alongside humans.

In human-wildlife conflict 'hotspots', the separation between humans and species considered pests or frequent culprits of human-wildlife conflict are reinforced through physical relocation from outside of the protected area to inside – 'returning' the animals to where they belong. Just before the fence was first completed (June 2013), 452 buffalo, 508 zebra, 46 impala, 13 waterbuck and two giraffe were 'driven back into the park" (Bariyanga et al. 2016: 185). Community members want wildlife to be 'taken back to the park', regardless of whether the animals had originated from inside or not (Faith Mukabaranga and Jolly Bafuruka, 2020). Elephants, hippos, hyenas, leopards, and buffalo continue to be herded by helicopters through temporarily opened sections of the electric fence or trapped by local community members and translocated by park staff (AMC Staff, 2019; Moses Karenzi, 2020). These interventions frequently occur at the request of communities, as described by the Mucucu village chief, '[Buffaloes...] sometimes come here, and we call the sector's office, and they call you guys [park management] and they bring helicopters to bring them back to the park' (Samuel Rugamba and Kellen Sanyu, 2020). In Gasabo, a local cooperative was set-up to help trap and release hyenas: 'They use traditional snares. They were forbidden from killing them. When hyenas get trapped in the snare, the cooperative calls park people and they pick it up. After this initiative started, hyenas stopped coming in the area' (Lenatha Mukamusoni, 2020). The belief in and constant enforcement of separation between humans and wildlife represent cultural and structural ecological violence that undermine positive ecological peace, and I would argue that it therefore also falls short of convivial conservation.

The fence's reinforcement of cultural and structural violence, which is markedly different for larger species that are unable to cross (as) freely between the two spaces and require physical relocation, is augmented by the compensation scheme, which places human-wildlife coexistence into the realm of liberal agendas not in congruence with convivial conservation's critique of capitalist economies and vision for degrowth.

Fences and Funds: The Liberal Peace Approach to Negative Ecological Peace

The separation that is most tangible is between larger 'problem' species (e.g., elephants, hippos, buffalos, hyenas, and leopards) fenced inside the park and those outside, especially in terms of the ways they can affect income for humans. Typically, human-wildlife conflicts and their interventions are conceived of as an economic cost-benefit, with proximity to certain wildlife seen as an economic cost which must be reconciled in terms of compensation for losses and incentives for alternative livelihood development (Dickman et al. 2011). As a few authors have noted, negative perceptions about damages caused by protected wildlife or wildlife perceived to be under the management of authorities are often augmented in comparison to actual damages by other non-human species (e.g. elephants vs. rats) (Naughton-Treves and Treves 2005). Yet, when the park staff relocate problem animals from community lands to park lands, it is seen as a win-win that potentially reduces future incidences of human-wildlife conflict, places them under the safe watch of park authorities, and increases species populations inside the park, a draw for ecotourism revenues. Funds for the Rwandan compensation mechanism originate from park revenues, meaning tourism of animals inside the park pay for damages caused by animals outside the park – another good reason to relocate 'problem' animals inside park boundaries. As the Mucucu village chief describes, 'they should just be in the park, where they belong. Which is nice, for tourism, for us and our kids, we go there to

293

visit them, this is nice for the country, but having them outside, in the communities, then that's a problem' (Samuel Rugamba and Kellen Sanyu, 2020). This removes the animal as a life with which we must seek convivial coexistence and captures it as a subject of environmental capitalism.

In a study of compensation claims around ANP, one landowner filed 14 verified complaints about livestock losses to hyenas, yet continued to do nothing to prevent or minimize damages (e.g. use bomas or night guards) (Treves et al. 2019). If all his complaints were approved, he could receive RWF 5.3 million (approximately USD 5,200) for his livestock. This landowner presents the possibility that reporting incidences of human-wildlife conflicts can be profitable and that compensation schemes provide new ways for system-savvy people to earn money from wildlife. In this case, the landowner is known to have relatives in Kigali and is accustomed to traveling between the capital and the countryside (AMC Staff, 2019), distinguishing him from other local villagers who may be less mobile and adept at accessing state systems. Between the cost-benefit approach to conflict resolution, its potential manipulation for individual profit, and the commercialisation of wildlife that it depends on, I propose that compensation schemes are better conceived of as a liberal peace approach to negative ecological peace. Even if this manages to monetarily incentivize some degree of coexistence, it falls short of convivial conservation because it relies on relocation and separation, as well as commodification of the 'other'.

From the perspective of positive ecological peace, wildlife relocation is problematic. Relocation commonly involves capture and release or herding, including by aerial pursuit, from human-wildlife conflict 'hotspots' into protected areas – it is akin to forced displacement. As an example, we can look to the elephants found in ANP today, which originated elsewhere. Reports of Rwanda's elephant populations have historically situated larger populations in the western regions, with smaller populations in the north around Volcanoes National Park and Bugesera (Spinage and Guinness 1971).

In 1975, a herd of approximately 150 elephants around Bugesera were 'continually coming into conflict with local communities', and while there were no elephants in Akagera at the time, Akagera was believed to be part of a historic corridor from Bugesera to Uganda and thus, it was deemed ecologically viable to transfer 26 of them by military 'trucks, helicopters, all-terrain vehicles, cages, and strong boats' into the park (Hall 2014). The photo in Figure 3 by Jacky Babilon is of a young elephant being transported by helicopter from Bugesera to Akagera NP in 1975 (Root 2016).

Figure 3: Photo by Jacky Babilon in 1975 of a young elephant being transported by helicopter from Bugesera to Akagera NP (Root 2016).

The elephants more than eight years old were considered too large to transport, so they were shot and killed (Sullivan 2014). Four of the young elephants had to be bottle-fed on arrival because they were too young to even wean from their mothers (Hall 2014). The trauma of this violent decimation of an elephant herd and forced displacement of their survivors is masked in the celebration of this event at the time as a 'a ground-breaking conservation effort to eliminate human-wildlife conflict' (African Parks 2018). Translocation practices have evolved since then, allowing entire families to be moved, but this can still be a traumatic dislocation. The reintroduction of elephants and other previously extirpated species like lions and rhino have certainly been important for Rwanda's return to Africa's 'Big 5' tourism, but this only emphasizes the neoliberalism in the fences and funds approach to human-wildlife conflict management.

When 'problem' species are moved out of the *de facto* areas of convivial conservation to *de jure* areas of fenced management, it limits their freedom in terms of geographic as well as genetic dispersal across the larger ecoregion. This could present a form of slow ecological violence that compromises a species' agency, freedoms, and long-term resilience as increasingly isolated populations – especially when we consider, for example, the case of large migratory species which used to transect continents and are now increasingly constrained within ecosystem remnants with securitised borders. As species populations grow in Akagera and push at the carrying capacity of the park, the ongoing practice of compensation and relocation could lead to increasingly insecure populations. When the last of a species are geographically limited, they are more vulnerable to existential threats (e.g. disease or sudden-onset events) and at worst, to extinction or extirpation. Alternatively, healthy populations could find themselves overextending the park's carrying capacity, but trapped and unable to find other spaces for survival (see e.g. Byishimo 2021). As Nixon describes, slow violence is 'a violence that occurs gradually and out of sight, a violence of delayed destruction that is dispersed across time and space, an attritional violence that is typically not viewed as violence at all' (Nixon 2011: 2). Even as an attempt at negative ecological peace, wildlife relocation and hard-bordered isolation could actually represent slow violence targeting certain species (i.e. speciesism) and undermines long-term positive ecological peace.

This kind of segregation also creates a perception and reality that coexistence with certain species of wildlife is limited to income-generating viewing inside of park boundaries and not deeply convivial. Compensation schemes represent a liberal approach to negative peace, but not positive ecological peace.

Culture and Traditional Knowledge: Conviviality Through Positive Ecological Peace

The make-up of local communities around ANP reflect different socionatural relations between people and wildlife that are constructed by historical connections, traditional knowledge, and learned cohabitation with ecosystems. In Gasabo, the *umudugudu* (village) chief indicated that their community is made up of refugees who had fled Rwanda in 1959 and none of whom had lived there before. Though they may have been from nearby villages (e.g. Rukira, Nyarubuye, Kigarama), the ecosystem was different enough that the Indigenous trees were unfamiliar to them and they found it hard to adjust to the new environment at first. Their people were used to eating bananas, which do not grow well in the local soil, and the traditional plants they used for firewood or construction were also not available. They did not know the species they encountered in their new territory, but a few from close-by places were able to teach them. Another Gasabo villager shared a similar experience about his lack of exposure to hippos in Kigali, where he had lived before: 'No, there were no hippos. But you see, when you move to a new area, people teach you different tricks on animals' behavior, and you start being careful' (Posiyani Ntibagirirwa, 2020).

In some cases, these historically uprooted communities are able to carry-over ecological knowledge from the places where they lived before. The *umudugudu* chief of Ndego had been a refugee in Tanzania living alongside hippos, which also frequent the lakes and wetlands common to the southern sector of ANP. He was familiar with their patterns, their late-night crop raiding and 3 AM return to the lakes, and he knew how to build platforms for fruit trees to prevent them from being eaten. These transferrable forms of ecological knowledge can mitigate human-wildlife conflict and enhance conviviality (Anonymous. 2020a). The chief's family totem is also the lion (*intare*), which he observed is not in the village anymore, but can be found in the park. Many elders, like him, still retain traditional knowledge around totem species. Totem species are found in many Indigenous cultures around the world, typically a species 'which is symbiotically linked to the clan historically, physically and spiritually' and with whom a relationship of mutual care exists (Kimenyi n.d.). One *muzee* (an elder man) who joined my conversation with the umudugudu chief explained that his totem is also the lion, which he can never kill, and described a small frog, the totem of his wife, which he also protects as the 'relative of his in-laws' (Umudugudu Chief, 2020). That small frog is not native to the Akagera region, but he noted this cultural practice spills-over to include other frogs that he may encounter nearby. In this way, community members can retain a convivial connection to species within their new ecosystems.

This knowledge is diminishing however, with younger generations no longer aware of their totem species and the intricate normative systems of taboos and cultural practices around them. One villager in Gasabo lamented that 'the more Indigenous forests are cut, the quicker the traditional knowledge decreases' (Community Member, 2020). The same can be said of Indigenous or local fauna – the less they are present, the less local knowledge about these species persists. Totem-driven convivial conservation can also be eroded when the responsibility to protect a species shifts from the clan to the state or other conservation authority. As elaborated in previous sub-sections, hard-bordering of protected areas with physical infrastructure, such as ANP's electric fence, and wildlife damage compensation schemes that attribute the animal's origin to the park, enforce the concept that wildlife is the mandate of park authorities and not of local peoples' concerns. One of the villagers from Kayonza joked that 'I even think the government should bring these animals that live outside back to the park, or just build another fence and keep them there well [laughs]' (Pastoralist, 2020). Taking on this responsibility, the park's chief warden, Jes Gruner, once said, 'we were constantly chasing our herd of elephants who were eating their crops', which distinctly associates the elephants to the park and others the local people as 'they' (Bax, 2019).

In the absence of traditional knowledge, environmental education has been another angle on human-wildlife conflict management around Akagera, but it may be (unintentionally) reinforcing negative ecological peace rather than cultivating positive ecological peace. Park rangers currently teach the villagers how to build protective structures for their livestock and crops and other barrier mechanisms, like trenches, to minimise human-wildlife interactions. They also promote positive economic benefits deriving from park tourism, including revenue-sharing from park entry fees or the construction of roads and schools. Over time, this can create a financially-incentivised system of barrier and segregation-based ecological knowledge, replacing other potentially more non-violent means of coexistence. In other words, it teaches local communities to use strategies of separation (negative peace) and commodification (liberal peace), rather than establishing a culture of harmonious integration (positive peace). Instead, environmental education should seek to revitalise local ecological knowledge that offers strategies of non-violent cohabitation between species. It can draw from existing traditional knowledge or it can innovate new systems of local ecological knowledge and human-wildlife conflict resolution; for example, using participatory predator monitoring technologies via SMS alerts or mobile apps.

Positive ecological peacebuilding around ANP can also draw from the experiences of Territories of Life, where convivial conservation is an outcome of culture, livelihoods, and wellbeing (Borrini-Feyerabend et al. 2012; Sajeva et al. 2019). As the definition of ecological peace connotes, conviviality needs to be premised on a relationship of mutual care. In the field interviews, local people described how they would not cut large trees that provide shade for their livestock or rain for their crops and even plant medicinal species for healing various ailments (Moses Karenzi, 2020; Lenatha

Mukamusoni, 2020; Faith Mukabaranga and Jolly Bafuruka, 2020). One villager living in Akagera's southern sector explains the reasons they protect certain species:

> We also have native species in our farms. These were there when we got here and I didn't cut all of them. [...] Because, for example, the tall trees called '*imikobakobe*', you can even put in a beehive. A beehive for bees. You can conduct horticulture and harvest honey to eat, so you can't cut those. And for palm trees, these craftswomen use it [...]. That's why you can't cut these trees. (Posiyani Ntibagirirwa, 2020)

This relationship of positive ecological peace between humans and other species is premised on interdependence, traditional knowledge, and on-going connections. Hence, the need to reconsider human-wildlife conflict interventions for their approach to ecological peace to ensure that they do not undermine positive peace between species.

Conclusion

In a small country like Rwanda, which constitutes an important ecological corridor of the Albertine Rift biodiversity hotspot, and which features an increasingly dense human populated landscape, protected area expansion through conservation territorialities will prove sociopolitically challenging. A more ideal alternative, particularly in terms of positive ecological peace, is convivial conservation, which includes Indigenous or traditional custodianship and governance of Territories of Life. However, in socionaturally disrupted landscapes like Rwanda and the broader Albertine Rift, local communities are not homogenous entities. Conservation internationally has often been susceptible to a highly dichotomized view of the 'local community' as either a hyper-romanticized people living in harmony with nature or a hyper-stigmatized people out to destroy nature. These perspectives lose sight of the complex disrupted socionatural landscapes we live in today.

In the Rwandan case study presented in this chapter, I refer to the socionatural disruption caused by colonial conservation practices and genocide. More specifically, in the context of conviviality or human-wildlife coexistence, I consider dynamics between ANP's historically rooted pastoralists and post-conflict settlement of historically uprooted refugees and human-wildlife conflict interventions, namely the electric fence and compensation scheme. These mechanisms are coupled with other processes, including active relocation of non-human species from community lands to park lands, which erode socionatural relations and ecological knowledge that support convivial conservation. They also represent negative peace and liberal peace approaches to coexistence between human and non-human species, rather than the radically integrated coexistence of convivial conservation. For disrupted communities settled in new ecosystems or even long-standing traditional communities, these kinds of human-wildlife conflict interventions may erode the possibility of convivial conservation in the long-run. Fences and funds might ease human-wildlife conflict dynamics in the short-term, but when evaluated through a peace perspective, they fall short of positive ecological peace.

This chapter has brought conventional peace theory (Galtung's positive and negative peace) to more-than-human relations by looking at human-wildlife conflict management around ANP. This provides a framework for evaluating common approaches to human-wildlife conflict resolution (such as fences, funds) and in particular, to identify the indirect violences (structural or cultural) they may entail, to open a discussion on non-violent culture-based approaches, and to evolve our concepts of peace to move beyond negative or liberal peace towards positive ecological peace. Opportunities to embed positive peace approaches to ecological peace can diminish with the disruption of socionatural landscapes and human-wildlife relations, thus it is important to revitalize ecological knowledge and local environmental governance systems that can foster positive ecological peace and convivial conservation. Further research could explore the effects of different non-violent culture-based approaches for positive ecological peace around Akagera as its management and surrounding communities continue to evolve their strategies for conviviality.

Chapter 13:

Micro-Politics and the Prospects for Convivial Conservation: Insights from the Corbett Tiger Reserve, India[*]

By Revati Pandya

Introduction

Conservation has been long critiqued for its top-down and market-centred emphasis (Igoe and Brockington 2007; Dempsey and Suarez 2016). Consequently, there are increasing calls for alternative forms of conservation policy and practice that foreground social justice and equity. Convivial conservation is one such proposal rooted in political ecology that critiques propagation of capitalist economics and nature-culture dichotomies through Protected Area (PA) creation and other forms of conservation programming (Büscher and Fletcher 2019; 2020). While proponents of the idea recognise that dimensions of difference within local communities can shape the micro-politics of conservation, they have not yet critically engaged with how these differences intersect to create a differentiated landscape of ownership, access rights, and livelihood opportunities in the vicinity of conservation areas. To address this gap, this paper draws on feminist intersectional research and feminist political ecology (FPE) (Harris 2015; Scoones et al. 2018; Nirmal and Rocheleau 2019) to argue that the convivial conservation concept needs to explicitly engage with the ways that intersections of class, gender, caste, and other identity positions in local communities shape power dynamics around land rights and opportunities to benefit from conservation interventions. It thereby joins Krauss

---

[*] Originally published as: Pandya, R. (2022). Micro-politics and the prospects for convivial conservation: Insights from the Corbett Tiger Reserve, India. Conservation & Society 20(2): 146-155.

(2021) and Collins (2021) in calling for more explicit focus on gender and power differences in the convivial conservation concept and its translation into practice.

I illustrate my argument by examining the ways that land rights have shaped the differentiated socio-ecological context of everyday life and livelihood opportunities for people in villages adjoining the Corbett Tiger Reserve (CTR) in India. Named after Jim Corbett, a British colonial official who turned from tiger hunting to tiger conservation, CTR is one of the first Tiger Reserves (TRs) to be established in India (in 1973). It has served as the model for subsequent tiger reserves established in other parts of the country. It is also home to the highest number of tigers within a defined Wildlife Protection Area in India (Jhala et al. 2020). The substantial tiger population in CTR has propelled tourism promotion by the state, resulting in a booming industry shaped by both the state forestry agency and private enterprise. However, accessing the economic opportunities associated with tourism is strongly influenced by the intersection of differentiated land ownership and access rights in relation to micro-politics emerging from caste, class and gender differences within households in adjoining villages. My study of the intersectional feminist political ecology of CTR, thus, offers a critical contribution concerning the potential of the overarching convivial conservation proposal to generating transformative change in mainstream conservation thinking and practice.

In the following sections of the chapter, I begin by outlining the key elements of the convivial conservation proposal and then provide a short overview of feminist research which addresses the political ecological dimensions of conservation in terms of understanding local difference and micro-politics around land rights and forest access. I use the example of the Corbett Tiger Reserve to illustrate the way intersections of class, caste and gender articulate local differences in land rights and livelihood access. Engaging with learnings from recent implementation of progressive legislation via the Forest Rights Act (FRA), this chapter explores how micro-politics affect access to rights in relation to this development. My analysis suggests that the FRA represents potential to further a convivial vision in local people's engagement with CTR as long as these important micro-politics are sufficiently acknowledged and addressed. I highlight the importance of paying explicit attention to the micro-politics of access and equity in pursuit of a just and equitable conservation landscape that embodies the values and aspirations expressed in the convivial conservation proposal.

Convivial Conservation and its Conceptualisation of Local Power Dynamics

The concept of convivial conservation was put forward by Büscher and Fletcher (2019; 2020), in response to the neo-preservationist (Wilson 2016) and new conservation (Kareiva et al. 2012) proposals, to address the growing problem of global loss of biodiversity. The neo-preservationist proposal privileges and reinforces the separation between non-human nature and human society by expanding PAs, ideally to cover at least half the earth's surface while largely excluding any economic activities within them. The new conservationist proposals, on the other hand, promote explicitly capitalist approaches in integrating economic development into conservation programming, even as they seek to go beyond nature-society dichotomies embodied in PAs by calling for integrated spaces in which humans and non-humans overlap. In contrast to both of these perspectives, the proponents of convivial conservation call for radical transformative change in conservation thinking and practices grounded in post-capitalist politics and a co-constitutive understanding of nature and society.

The convivial conservation perspective draws on a growing body of scholarship that similarly argues for alternative frameworks for conservation policy, programmes, and practices. This scholarship calls for equity and justice in conservation based on recognising cultural diversity (Kothari et al. 2014), building self-reliant regional economies (Shrivastava and Kothari 2012; Büscher and Fletcher 2019), and pursuing redistribution and reduction in both production and consumption (Demaria et al. 2013). The overarching vision for convivial conservation entails moving beyond monetary valuation of nature and redefining value in terms of the social, cultural or affective ways that people live with, and relate to, nature in everyday life (Büscher and Fletcher 2020). This entails a focus on both short-term and long-term change, as well as engaging different groups of actors involved in conservation. Büscher and Fletcher (2020) argue that conservation interventions continue to disproportionately target rural or forest dwelling communities who are least responsible for the capitalist accumulation and resource extraction threatening conservation both locally and globally. Their critique is thus directed partly towards political and economic elites who are responsible for and promote capitalist approaches to both economic development and the conservation practice and governance intended to counter this. Their proposal, thus, calls for a radical transformation in conservation policy and practices that pursues both large-scale structural change and micro-level political organisation simultaneously.

Büscher and Fletcher (2020) outline several elements that articulate this vision across multiple scales ranging from macro governance structures to the level of local implementation. One of these key elements centres on moving away from 'protected' area thinking and towards 'promoted' areas wherein co-existence between humans and non-humans is encouraged. Another element concerns historical reparations for rural or forest-dwelling communities negatively impacted by past conservation interventions and other forms of uneven development. Potential forms of reparation include land distribution and co-ownership or co-management. Other elements address the need to move away from short-term voyeuristic tourism centred on charismatic wildlife towards long-term engagement with everyday nature; to reduce reliance on revenue from external tourism for conservation; and to introduce some basic welfare payments, such as a Conservation Basic Income, for households and individuals living in villages adjoining conservation areas.

Büscher and Fletcher (2020) recognise that contextual realities of local community politics matter in conservation interventions. They articulate the importance of a co-constitutive understanding of power that acknowledges micro-politics in relation to larger structural factors. They argue that while power is indeed situated within micro contexts and is complex, it is vital to also relate these complexities to the ways they are shaped and constrained by capitalist structures. Thus, they promote a co-constitutive understanding of structure and agency. They also call for the co-constitutive understanding of resistance movements, asserting that these must go hand in hand with movements that pursue broader structural change. Drawing inspiration from Gibson-Graham's (2006) community economies approach that highlights potential for cultivating post-capitalist practices and spaces within an overarching capitalist system, Büscher and Fletcher (2020) suggest that short-term and long term strategies to subvert capitalist logics at both micro and structural scales must be implemented simultaneously. They also relate issues with the separation of nature and culture and intensifying oppression along lines of race, gender, and coloniality.

While these are important points, here I suggest that the convivial conservation proposal warrants more explicit and substantial engagement with micro-contexts and the intersectional dimensions of difference they contain. I propose that a feminist intersectional lens is particularly suited for such analysis as it explicitly articulates and draws connections between these dimensions of micro-politics and the overarching societal structures in which they are situated.

Feminist Intersectional Perspectives on Micro-Politics and Conservation

Intersectionality involves viewing lived realities and identities as multidimensional (May 2014). A feminist intersectional lens recognises the multiple axes of power emerging the articulation of gender with other dimensions of difference including class, race and caste, which, depending on the local context, may intersect in different ways to shape patterns of access to and control of resources (Rocheleau et al. 1996; Nightingale 2011; Sultana 2011; Mollett and Faria 2013). Thus, a feminist intersectional framework provides insights into local social dynamics centred around patterns of differentiated access to resources and livelihoods as well as into larger community or regional resource management structures (Sultana 2021). For example, research on gender dynamics in India has shown that forest dependencies often vary based on dimensions of local difference such as gender, caste, and class, consequently impacting vulnerable groups' stakes in resource management (Agarwal 2009). Yet, despite the obvious intersections of these factors in shaping distributional outcomes, there is a tendency among scholars and policymakers to consider them as separate categories. Thus, Pan (2019: 36) argues that Dalit (a collective term used to refer to socially oppressed castes, also categorised as Scheduled Castes in the Indian Constitution[1]) politics and mainstream Indian feminism 'often suppress difference in order to magnify particular issues and impose universality'. Joshi (2011) notes similarly that water reform policies in India commonly consider caste and gender as separate categories, and hence that the benefits targeted on the basis of either caste or gender do not reach most Dalit women.

The invisibility and under-representation of women in forest access and management in India is well documented and points to the ingrained patriarchal relationships within communities and households. Agarwal (2001) argues that due to the combined influence of class and patriarchal power dynamics, community forestry groups often exclude women despite the official mandate to include women. Notwithstanding the fact that it is largely women in forest and rural areas who are the primary collectors of Non-Timber Forest Produce (NTFP), most women are represented through the men in their families (Sarin et al. 2003).

Feminist intersectional analyses concerning community dynamics and local participation in commons or forest management programmes in India reveals the ways that power dynamics between different caste groups can align to create strategic alliances for livelihood needs, but also end up perpetuating hierarchies wherein tribal community and women are dispossessed (Parthasarathy 2015). For instance, in a village in Odisha widely known for its forest protection, much of the work for protecting the forests was led by Scheduled caste women and men, yet after the forest regenerated, the village elites belonging to privileged castes asserted control over the management and extraction of resources by using their capital and gaining the support of state forest department officials (Sarin et al. 2003). Sarin and colleagues point out that the rights and interests of different groups within a village community are not congruent and that these differences are often institutionalised in their customary forms of forest governance and management systems. One major dimension of difference within any village community is class, which is directly related to land ownership status and size of holding and often overlaps with caste status and access to bargaining power. Naidu (2013) demonstrates that landholding not only defines access to benefits, but also facilitates circumventing restrictions on forest access or benefiting from alternative economic avenues. She points out that pre-existing class differences reinforce inequalities within a village and further marginalise the landless households who often belong to Scheduled castes.

Feminist political ecology (FPE) approaches have often integrated intersectional perspectives in their framework of analysis. FPE is 'more about a feminist perspective' than 'a single focus on women and/or gender' (Rocheleau 2015: 57). The emphasis of the approach is on environmental and social justice, focusing attention on local experiences of marginality, vulnerability and dispossession emerging from the intersections of gender, class, caste, race, and ethnicity (Baviskar 2001; Sundar 2001; Resurrección 2017; Joshi 2014; Shrestha and Clement 2019). It also examines the lived experiences of marginalised groups and situated knowledges which recognise multiple ways of relating to nature and place rather than only in terms of the strict nature-culture separation that state politics and modern science often promote (Rocheleau and Nirmal 2015). For instance, Aiyadurai (2018) demonstrates that the Mishmi community's spiritual kinship with tigers is challenged by conservationists' agenda of creating a tiger reserve to separate humans from tigers. Pandey (2017) examines how Dongria Kondh's legal battle against a mining corporation in Odisha remains a landmark case in the recognition of tribal communities' spiritual and material identities tied to their land. In this way, it represents the ongoing resistance of local and tribal groups to State prioritising corporate interests. Similarly, Baviskar (2004) examined the anti-dam movement in Narmada valley by highlighting the cultural relations of a tribal community to their land and river, revealing the discrepancies between identities used by the State to oppress and those embodied by the community. Other scholars have highlighted how social dynamics of caste are reflected in access to programmes and benefits within communities targeted for conservation and development projects (Rastogi et al. 2014; Kabra 2020). Kabra (2020), for instance, notes that when people in villages are displaced from their traditional homes for creating conservation areas, not only are the impacts of displacement varied but also that the demands for claims and settlements can differ based on historical access and dispossession.

A feminist intersectional perspective thus provides a valuable framework and grounded approach for understanding the landscapes of conservation that emerge from the interaction between broader policies and programmes and the micro-politics of rights, access, and opportunities available to various groups within areas adjoining conservation areas. In the following sections, I use this approach to illustrate the micro-politics of access, alienation, and dependencies in forest villages adjoining the Corbett Tiger Reserve in India.

The Corbett Tiger Reserve

Context

The Government of India instituted the Project Tiger in 1973 with the goal of stemming the dwindling tiger populations in the country and reviving their numbers through the creation of dedicated PAs for wildlife conservation (NTCA 2020). Project Tiger was inaugurated in Corbett National Park, making this site one of the first nine tiger reserves in India. CTR has a strong preservationist history. The CTR site was a hunting area before it was designated as the first National Park of India and of mainland Asia in 1936, during the British colonial regime. It is named after Jim Corbett, an officer of the colonial regime, who was known for being a hunter-turned-conservationist and who spent some years in the sub-Himalayan region before he left India. This history contributed to it being as an important site to launch the Project Tiger.

CTR is located in Uttarakhand State in the Shivalik foothill region of Indian Himalayas. It covers a total of 1,288.31 sq. km and encompasses a mix of montane areas and sub-Himalayan tracts called Terai-Bhabar which include grasslands, wetlands, riverine tracts, and moist deciduous forests (Badola et al. 2010). The forests comprise about 70% of the area with grasslands, wetlands, agriculture, and settlements occupying the remaining 30% (Government of Uttarakhand 2010). CTR contains a Core protected area of 821.99 sq. km which is exclusively maintained for the tiger population, and a Buffer zone of 466.32 sq. km surrounding the Core area (see Figure 1) within which some human settlement and livelihood activities are permitted and human-wildlife interactions can occur (NTCA 2012; 2020). The Buffer zone is also designated as an area where local communities are provided livelihood alternatives that reduce their dependence on forests. Ecotourism is promoted as a form of livelihood alternative employing the win-win narrative of simultaneously achieving conservation and community benefits (NTCA 2012).

The areas surrounding CTR are a combination of rural and forest landscape. Historically, livelihood activities in this region largely entailed subsistence agriculture, livestock keeping and forest resource use. Soon after it was designated a Tiger Reserve, the villages that existed within the demarcated boundaries were displaced and moved outside to the areas controlled by the State Forest Department (Lasgorciex and Kothari 2009). The growth of ecotourism since the early-2000s has heavily influenced land use and livelihoods. Today, the areas adjoining the south and eastern boundary of CTR have a high concentration of villages and hotels. The villages are distinguished by two formal classifications: revenue villages and forest villages. Revenue villages are agricultural areas with definitive cadastral boundaries of private land ownership. These villages and fall within the jurisdiction of the district administration and the State's Revenue Department (Census of India 2011b). Forest villages are located within areas that come under the land ownership and jurisdiction of the State's Forest Department. Thus, individuals and households in these forest villages cannot obtain titles to own land nor set up permanent structures.

Methods

I conducted ethnographic research in the villages near CTR between August 2018 and August 2019. I used qualitative methods such as participant observation and interviews in villages located outside the south and south-eastern boundary of CTR. I employed a field assistant to assist me with identifying research participants and for interviews. I used a basic framework of questions on family history and relationship to CTR and the area, livelihoods and association with tourism to guide the interviews. When necessary, I repeated interviews with the same respondents. Participant observation was recorded in field notes. In addition, I collected data on CTR from secondary sources such as independent and government reports, newspaper articles, and published academic research. I analysed the field data through inductive coding and drawing themes that supported comparing and contrasting information (Bernard 2011).

For this chapter, I focus on forest villages of Amer and Beran (pseudonyms). Fifty-three (53) participants were identified through a combination of referral and purposive sampling based on their dwelling location, livelihoods, and socio-cultural backgrounds. I provided full information about the research project and sought respondents' verbal consent before proceeding with the interviews. I use pseudonyms for the two villages to ensure full anonymity and privacy for participants. I did not ask participants about their caste status and only made note of it when it was freely offered by them. I was conscious of my positionality as a non-local, urban woman researcher from a substantially different socio-economic background and sought to maintain reflexivity during data collection. The field assistant was a local male from a nearby town, and his gender and situated knowledge about local social dynamics was critical for mediating initial doubts or concerns expressed by participants when they arose.

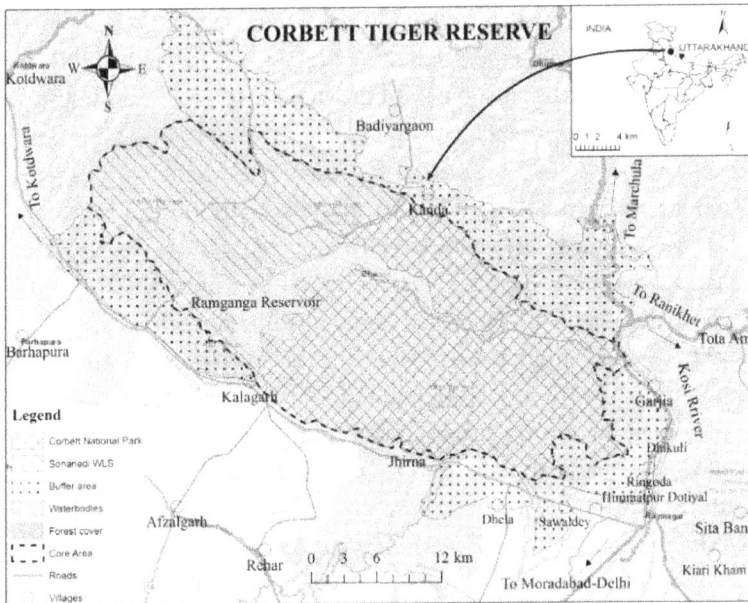

Figure 1: Corbett Tiger Reserve. Created by: Ecoinformatics Lab, ATREE

Amer and Beran

The forest village of Amer is located near the eastern boundary of CTR near the highway that runs along the Kosi River corridor. The village comprises 101 families, most of whom were relocated outside the PA after the area's designation as a Tiger Reserve in 1973. Relocation from inside the CTR area to land belonging to the State Forest Department outside the reserve boundary meant that the families held no legal rights to land ownership or forest access rights. The Forest Department initially employed people in the relocated settlement in plantation work in its Reserved Forests (Tiger Conservation Plan 2015). The majority of families in Amer are classified as falling within the officially defined low-income category (Tiger Conservation Plan 2015). Households in the village belong to privileged and Scheduled Castes (SCs). The average household size is 6 and approximately 90% of the households in the village rely on income from wage labour in tourism. According to information from field interviews, four individuals, all men belonging to privileged caste groups, have relatively stable daily wage jobs in tourism: one is a guide and three are safari vehicle drivers. Women are primarily involved in household care and forest resource collection. Some households maintain vegetable plots adjoining their homes, but most rely on purchasing their basic food requirements from local markets and government subsidised ration shops.

Beran is also a forest village located near the eastern boundary of CTR. It is home to nearly 500 families, all of whom fall under the category of SC and are identified as low-income households. Most of these households migrated to Beran from the nearby hill areas in the early-1970s to work as labourers for the forest department and seek employment in nearby urban areas. Since Beran is located within land owned by the State Forest Department, households do not have rights to own land. In addition, the CTR management plan has identified Beran as part of a wildlife corridor and has proposed the relocation of households to other sites. The majority of households depend on wage labour for their livelihoods, with nearly 80% linked to tourism. Men work as labourers in tourist lodges, for the forest department, in building and in road construction. Women are responsible for household care, firewood collection, and maintain small vegetable plots around their homes. Some women have found work in a local factory and piecework through local NGOs.

In comparison with these two forest villages, revenue villagers can own land, and many have sold their land to out-migrate or continue living on part of their land while leasing a section to tourism enterprises. The revenue villages near CTR have some of the densest tourism services. Revenue villages have a mixed composition in terms of class and caste, but are generally privileged class and caste owing to their land ownership status. Most households in such villages depend on or supplement income through tourism. Tourism work includes safari jeep drivers, safari guides, safari booking agents, homestays, guest house owners, restaurant entrepreneurs, souvenir shopkeepers and hotel staff. These villagers have relatively easier access to facilities as there are government primary schools, electricity and water access for farming in villages. Government schemes for supplementing livelihoods, such as silviculture, are also accessible to revenue villagers.

Corbett Tiger Reserve and the Politics Of Access

Variegated Access and Tourism Dependency

Amer and Beran are similar to many forest villages located around the Tiger Reserve where households' tourism dependencies through tourism-based work is increasing. However, the ability to gain better outcomes from tourism work is influenced by socio-economic status. A village elder from Amer pointed out that current restrictions on forest access is a contrast to his ancestors' time. His family, along with other villagers, was relocated in 1978 from the forest inside CTR with their agreement. While tourism has served as one source of income due to lack of options, it is also a form of restriction on villagers' lives:

They keep taking the tourists inside the forest and tell us to keep quiet. 30 safari jeeps go into the forest twice a day from the gate next to our village, but there is no issue with so many people going in. The issue is always with us entering the forest. All the kids from this village who work in tourism wash dishes. The better jobs go to people with contacts. (Respondent 1, May 9, 2019)

Steady employment, as per the Census definition (i.e. which provides income for more than six months of the year (Census 2011) in Amer is very low. At the time of fieldwork, only four men in Amer belonging to privileged caste groups held steady employment in tourism. Daily wage work, such as washing dishes, is most common in forest villages, followed by work for local businesses and government infrastructure projects. The village elder's assertion that better jobs in tourism go to those who are of higher socio-economic status and have direct access to powerful people or power brokers is repeatedly mentioned in forest villages. Other researchers refer to 'gatekeepers' who can influence the flow of benefits or funds as their social networks stem from their dominant caste position, thus allowing them to position themselves as links between the State and rural community (Kabra 2020).

The variegated access to steady employment and the type of work is more striking when households in forest villages are compared to revenue villages. In the latter case, more than 80% of the working population in the neighbouring revenue village were employed in farming their own land and had steady employment in tourism. For example, when CTR was being actively developed as an ecotourism destination in the early-1990s, the State Forest Department offered a safari guide training course for people from surrounding areas. The majority of trainees selected were from nearby revenue villages who later were worked for the State Forest Department or with private hotels. Some of these guides have since set up their own travel agencies, including safari booking agencies, as well as homestays. During the tourism boom in the 2000s, and after, landowning households in revenue villages were able to set up their own tourist accommodation facilities; one villager from a privileged caste, landowning family explained: 'we had land and set up a 16-room hotel' (Respondent 2, August 17, 2018). Other landowning households in revenue villages, since the 2000s, have built small shops on their land and some rent these out to tourism-related retail businesses, and set up restaurants. Since households in forest villages do not own titles to the land they occupy and are not permitted to build permanent structures on forest department land, they cannot set up similar businesses to take advantage of CTR tourism.

Access to Development Schemes, Infrastructure, and Benefits

In addition to the lack of land ownership, households in forest villages have little to no access to government schemes and subsidies, and infrastructure facilities such as electricity and water supply connections (Upadhyay 2019). Although road infrastructure in the area has improved, most forest village households point to the lack of electricity and water supply. A couple in Amer whose son works in a hotel spoke of the marginal change to their lives since they were relocated to the forest village: 'We were married here, we had children and now grandchildren, but no facilities over these generations. We don't even have an electricity connection' (Respondents 3-4, May 29, 2019). Although lack of electricity supply is a critical issue for forest villages, some settlements on forest land have been able to access electricity due to their proximity to major religious shrines or revenue lands purchased by wealthy outsiders. A resident of Beran village noted that its neighbouring settlement on forest land has been able to access electricity because 'Bania people (trading communities higher up the caste ladder) from a nearby town have bought land near the village' (Respondent 5, April 10, 2019). Another resident of Beran added 'there are people with contacts who have influence in that area which is why they got electricity access. There is a big temple there which attracts a lot of people, which is also why they get it [electricity]' (Respondent 6,

April 10, 2019).

Households in Beran also emphasised their disadvantaged position for access to formal education. Since most adult males work as daily wage labourers for construction or road work or as gardeners or guards in hotels, they see formal education as necessary for their children and grandchildren to gain access to better jobs. A teacher in the local primary school and resident of Beran said, 'We have been trying to get a high school set up here, it would be very good if we had one... We cannot ruin our children's future, but not everyone supports that idea even within the village' (Respondent 7, April 10, 2019).

Unequal access to development schemes not only affects households in forest villages near CTR, but also people belonging to lower socio-economic status within adjoining revenue villages. The village head, who is often a male from the dominant privileged castes, exercises power in decision-making for the village as a whole and functions as a gatekeeper for government schemes, grants, and subsidies that village household may be eligible to access. One member of a local women's association noted that,

> Most government schemes [for women's benefit] are not implemented in these [revenue] villages, unless you have contacts with the village head. But in a forest village there is no formal village head and so that is the biggest difficulty. Even in revenue villages, if a family who is well-off needs resources to rebuild their home or bathroom, they will be able to get resources to do so, but the poorest will not get the same.' (Respondent 8, May 14, 2019)

Access to Forest Rights and Community Mobilisation

Livelihoods based on forest access and resource collection are becoming more restricted for households in both forest and revenue villages. The restrictions imposed by the CTR management are more severely felt by forest village households in Amer and Beran since they lack tenure security. These residents, along with those from other forest villages on the periphery of CTR, have been seeking ways of accessing legal forest rights through existing legislation. However, finding common ground for demanding forest rights has been challenging. As one resident from Amer pointed out: 'Even within villages there are differences in coming together to demand for forest rights' (Respondent 1, May 9, 2019). Factors that influence differences include local elite alliances with political parties that attempt to secure 'vote banks' by promising benefits such as electricity supply, cooking gas, and food ration subsidies to village households. A resident of Beran remarked, 'this village has a two-party [political party] support' (Respondent 9, September 13, 2018), which resembles swing voting, and supporting political parties promising support and advocating for their rights, such as electricity connection. The villager also implied that people ally with political parties that have a chance of winning, with the hope of thereby building social capital through the parties' networks of influence. Nevertheless, despite divergent political allegiances, a Forest Village Association was formed to mobilise communities around CTR that lack security of tenure. The association threatened to boycott voting in the upcoming elections unless their demand for revenue village status was recognised (Upadhyay 2019). This demand has not yet been met.

Gender Dynamics

The insecurity of tenure for households in forest villages affects both men and women in terms of land ownership. However, women bear significant responsibility for cultivating food plots near their homes and collecting firewood and other produce from nearby forests. The restrictions imposed by CTR on forest access by local households have made it more difficult for women to carry out these activities. Due to gendered expectation and cultural norms, access to wage labour in tourism remains easier for men than women. Hotels are mostly unwilling to employ women from the villages, citing the inability of management to be responsible for their personal security and safety.

A forest village near Amer, and located close to the highway, has a number of small food stalls for tourists. Two women run such shops full time, while other women from the village may find temporary work or fill in for their husbands when they are otherwise committed. Several women from Beran worked at a local factory until the management changed and terminated their employment. About 10 young women from Beran received training in sewing and embroidery through a local non-government organisation. These women have been able to do piecework and contribute to their household income. Such work opens up avenues for income, but access to assets such as land remains impossible in forest villages, especially for women. While access to land ownership and better waged work remains a hurdle for male forest villagers, women remain more vulnerable due to the ingrained everyday practices of patriarchy.

Although revenue villagers are able to own land titles, land ownership titles are in the name of men in the family through a patrilineal system, except for widows who can claim ownership as a primary heir (Deo and Dubey 2019). In Uttarakhand state, rights to inheritance of agricultural land are secondary for daughters, and unmarried daughters have greater rights to land than married ones (ibid.). However, changes are taking place. The legal inheritance provisions have recently been clarified for the Hindu Succession Act of 2005, such that daughters will now have equal inheritance rights (Deo 2020). The Uttarakhand government recently supported women's co-ownership of land, specifically pointing out the imbalance in agricultural work between husband and wife (Das 2020). However, despite the existence of reformed inheritance laws, women's rights may continue to be curbed through the micro-politics of power and access to local economic opportunities associated with CTR.

Land Ownership and Forest Access: Intersectionality and the Micro-Political Dynamics of Conservation

The cases of Amer and Beran show the differentiated access to work and benefits, not only on account of landlessness but also in relation to intersecting dimensions of caste, class and gender. CTR's history as an exclusive space for elites has continued, although shifting from hunting grounds to ecotourism. Ecotourism in the form of safaris is one direct new restriction on use of forests that were previously home to the forest villagers. Such differentiated access follows and reinforces historical and ongoing oppression of SC and class groups. Tiger reserve governance and tourism has emphasised the lack of access to opportunities for work and use of space. The CTR forest is used for multiple jeep safaris every day, while forest villagers who were living in the same forest are restricted from using the same space. Job opportunities and economic mobility for forest villagers remain limited, except for those who are able to gain access through social capital. This takes place primarily through allegiance with those in power, which does not necessarily lead to benefits for the community as a whole with respect to rights or access. Most landowning villagers in revenue villages have been able to gain jobs in tourism, including as drivers, guides or entrepreneurs through use of their own farm land. Villagers who are able to train as guides and successfully become part of the guide association are rarely from forest villages. This is shaped by the historical disadvantage in the form of education, infrastructure and socio-cultural subjugation based on their landlessness, caste and class.

In the context of tiger reserve governance, forest villagers have been marginalised, most significantly because of landlessness. Forest resource access also remain restricted. To address the issue of historical injustice to forest dwellers and tribal communities in India, the Forest Rights Act was legislated. The Scheduled Tribes and Other Traditional Forest Dwellers (Recognition of Forest Rights) Act of 2006 (FRA) is a legal instrument for forest use reparations and land rights in India. In calling for redressing historical injustice suffered by forest dwelling and tribal communities, the FRA has forged a radical path for conservation and in many ways can be seen as a forerunner for convivial conservation. However, the implementation of this progressive legislation has faced hurdles emerging through micro-politics in local contexts which are discussed below.

Forest Access and Use: Institutions and Socio-Dynamics

The FRA is the outcome of a prolonged movement led by a grassroots and marginalised forest people's coalition; one that began in 2002 after a ruling by the Supreme Court of India on evicting forest dwellers (Kumar and Kerr 2012). The FRA was enacted by the State to address the historical injustices perpetrated on forest dwelling communities by providing them with legal rights to access and use forest produce, as well as the ability to cultivate land. I highlight the FRA in this context due to its relevance for forest dwellers around CTR and its potential to constitute one step towards enacting the convivial conservation vision. The provisions of the Act include recognition of forest rights in PAs, right to cultivate forest land, ownership, access and rights to the conversion of forest villages into revenue villages (Clause 3(1) (h) and 4(2) FRA, 2006). The FRA is a progressive legislation that encapsulates elements of the convivial conservation approach such as the idea of promoted areas. Through the recognition of rights in the FRA, communities have been able to generate revenue from forest harvest and create a self-sufficient model of livelihood while ensuring for ecological sustainability (Broome et al. 2017). For instance, after the recognition of Community Forest Rights titles, villages in Shoolpaneshwar Wildlife Sanctuary have been able to earn high revenue from sustainable harvesting and selling of bamboo, and have ensured their management plan is guided by their traditional knowledge (Kukreti 2018). FRA also promotes gender equity as it requires land titles for individual forest rights to be in the joint names of husband and wife, or a single household head regardless of the gender (CFR-LA 2016). In the state of Rajasthan, 60 women have filed rights claims as single women, and joint claims from 22 villages have the woman's name as the first claimant (ibid). It is precisely because of these radical possibilities of the FRA to revolutionise conservation that the conservation administration, particularly the tiger conservation apparatus, has hindered its implementation and actively sought to undermine it (Rai et al. 2019). There have been reports of violation of the FRA in TRs and a lack of state support even after rights are recognised (Fanari 2019; Gupta et al. 2020).

Despite the FRA being an emancipatory State intervention, local socio-cultural contexts have resulted in inconsistencies in its implementation. Kodiveri (2016) has recorded instances of discrimination against SC during the implementation of the FRA. Differences in local engagement, politics of identity, local bureaucracies and diverse local livelihood interests have also plagued FRA implementation and curtailed its emancipatory objectives (Bose et al. 2012; Kodiveri 2016; Sen and Pattanaik 2019). Similarly, Ramdas (2009) examined how the FRA officially recognised rights of women, yet the State ended up using tribal women's rights over land to promote plantation growth instead of their traditional farming practice. Local power dynamics influenced by identity differences and institutional cultures thus pose hurdles for implementing the FRA (CFR-LA 2016). These, in no way, diminish the crucial and necessary role of the FRA in recognising forest rights. Instead, they point to important issues that must be confronted in implementing progressive structural change, offering lessons that can be learnt by focusing on micro-politics and identity differences.

Connecting the Threads

I draw from experiences in the implementation of the FRA over the last decade to highlight how different community dynamics and social identities have implications on the outcomes of implementing such a legislation. I do this to illustrate the larger argument of the chapter regarding the need to focus on micro-politics, particularly those relating to caste, class and gender. The FRA presents a potential model or pathway for convivial conservation in undoing historical injustice and recognising legal rights of access and use. The FRA also provides valuable insights for implementing progressive legislation that explicitly tackles the micro-politics emerging from intersecting differences of caste and gender.

Conclusion

In this chapter I have examined the ongoing micro-politics in forest villages around CTR to demonstrate the possible hurdles that could emerge in the implementation of progressive conservation measures such as convivial conservation. I have emphasised the value of a feminist intersectional approach for understanding the micro-politics of difference within communities, and related issues of distribution of access and benefits while considering dimensions and divisions of caste, class and gender. Attention to differences emerging from the intersectionality of caste, class, gender will be vital for ensuring that interventions do not further marginalise but instead proactively benefit the most marginal in affected communities. I engage with FRA, as an existing legal measure to address historical injustice and recognise rights of forest dwelling communities, to demonstrate a potential form of convivial conservation measure aiming to redress these issues of marginalisation. By drawing out the issues concerning differential access based on caste or gender, however, I show that this progressive legislation has also faced hurdles in implementation related to similar dimensions of local micro-politics.

If the promoted areas element of convivial conservation were to be initiated in CTR, one of the key steps would be to pursue reparations with respect to land and forest access and use through the FRA. This would not only address the historical injustices of alienation experienced by forest villagers but also reveal the ways in which the micro-politics of conservation and ecotourism contribute to marginalisation of these groups by gender, class and caste. The value of an intersectional feminist lens for convivial conservation is in its explicit focus on confronting patriarchy and overcoming other forms of oppression in pursuit of social and ecological justice.

Chapter 14:

Convivial Conservation Prospects in Europe: From Wilderness Protection to Reclaiming the Commons[*]

By George Iordăchescu

Introduction

Current tendencies to support the strict protection of nature have prompted worries about justice and equity in global conservation. This chapter examines how Romanian forest commons can contribute to discussions around an emerging convivial conservation vision based on democratic governance and social justice. In September 2020, the *5th Global Biodiversity Outlook* published by the UN acknowledged that the international community has failed to meet all the Aichi Biodiversity targets set by the Convention on Biological Diversity in 2010 (CBD 2020b). Similarly, in the European Union (EU), the recent *State of the Environment Report 2020* shows limited progress from the 2010 baseline towards the 2020 targets, with Europe continuing to lose biodiversity at alarming rates (EEA 2019: 74). The EU Biodiversity Strategy to 2020 failed to deliver on its targets, and the continued deterioration of some habitats and species outweighed the improvements (EEA 2019). Despite these massive failures, both the CBD and EU have announced bold new targets for the current decade, of which increasing the percentage of protected areas (PAs) to 30% of landmass and seas and strong support for strict conservation are the most acclaimed. These proposals have already attracted serious criticism from academics, independent researchers, and other actors defending Indigenous peoples who question the lack of proper acknowledgement of these targets' environmental, social, and

* Originally published as: Iordăchescu, G. (2022). Convivial conservation prospects in Europe: From wilderness protection to reclaiming the commons. Conservation & Society 20(2): 156-166.

economic costs (Agrawal et al. 2021).

Aiming to respond to some of these challenges, Büscher and Fletcher recently advanced the convivial conservation vision. This proposal emerges from a stream of progressive movements such as radical ecological democracy (Kothari 2014), economic degrowth, and the commons' reinvigoration (Büscher and Fletcher 2019). This vision advances governance principles around social and environmental justice and structural transformation towards a new conservation politics (Büscher and Fletcher 2020a). The present paper contends that the convivial conservation proposal has the potential to shape biodiversity conservation within the EU by amalgamating already functioning rights-based conservation approaches such as the Indigenous and community conserved areas (ICCAs) championed by initiatives like the ICCA Consortium. Moreover, it argues that the current European political moment can constitute a window of opportunity for more socially equitable conservation approaches, a space for cross-fertilisation to remake conservation governance around conviviality (Büscher and Fletcher 2020a, engaging directly with Illich 1973) and rights-based approaches (Corson et al. 2020). By focusing on the EU, the paper aims to recentre the discussion on a region traditionally considered a source of various colonial forms of conservation to be imposed upon others, but not within its borders.

As part of the European New Green Deal (European Commission 2019), the Biodiversity Strategy for 2030 proposes bold conservation and restoration targets, including strict protection for at least 10% of the landmass and the complete protection of all old-growth forests hosted by the Member States (European Commission 2020). Although the document proposes an integrated approach to conservation, it constitutes the first binding policy which conditions the economy's relaunching to giving nature more space. This radical move builds upon more than a decade of attempts to increase the role of the strict protection of unfettered nature on the continent (WILD10 2015). This movement comprises mapping projects and documenting primary and old-growth forests, gazetting wilderness reserves, and establishing private PAs across the region (Promberger and Promberger 2015). The EU's current wilderness momentum is synchronous with the series of calls for transformative change in the governance of biodiversity conservation which advocate for increasing the percentage of PAs to 30% by 2030 (Waldron et al. 2020) or to half of the earth by mid-century (Wilson 2016). Multiple planetary crises and concerns about biodiversity decline and climate disruptions have been rightfully used to justify ramping up support for enlarging PAs. Still, critics point towards the social injustices coupled with these proposals (Schleicher et al. 2019) and to the fact that the real causes which triggered such crises are left unaddressed (Büscher et al. 2017).

In Europe, the growing anxiety about environmental collapse has made neo-protectionism enticing to the point that it is slowly becoming an official policy. While putting 'self-willed nature' at its centre, this move advocates for the expansion of PAs and stricter conservation law enforcement. As almost everywhere worldwide, European PAs overlap with territories inhabited by local communities and Indigenous peoples, who consider these lands central to their livelihoods and culture. Nevertheless, reserving more space for nature is considered the path to human wellbeing and economic recovery as an official policy of the European Commission (European Commission 2020).

For a long time now, the role of Indigenous peoples and local communities in conservation has been documented by rich scholarship (Stevens 2014), and it has been slowly recognised by international bodies like the UN or the CBD (Borrini-Feyerabend et al. 2004; Kothari et al. 2013). In Europe, community-conserved areas have started to be examined as ICCAs only recently (Vasile 2019), while these institutions have a long history in all biogeographic regions (RRI 2020) and literature on the functioning of European commons is well developed (Sikor 2004; Bravo and De Moor 2008). I turn to the example of Romanian commons to show how historical bylaws and cultural resilience have made these institutions important but unacknowledged conservation actors. These commons are juridical institutions representing historical associations of commoners governing natural resources according to customary principles which survived over centuries (Stahl 1998). They re-emerged during post-socialist land restitution reforms (Vasile and Mantescu 2009) and currently play an important role in governing human–environmental relations in many rural areas (Vasile 2019). While they feature a multitude of democratic governing principles and are, in most cases, examples of the successful conciliation of human and nonhuman needs, commons could offer important lessons for the development of the convivial conservation vision in Europe centred on justice and democratic governance.

I begin with a brief description of the methods and data which inform the analysis. Next, I revisit some of the theoretical tenets of convivial conservation proposals relevant to this radical proposal's future progress within the EU. A discussion of the current wilderness momentum in the EU and further consideration of the role played by ICCAs in biodiversity conservation will offer more context to the analysis. I then provide empirical material on the rich experiences of governing commons in Romania, focusing on their conservation efforts. The discussion section will outline possible synergies and cross-fertilisation between the convivial conservation proposal and the already existing ICCAs in Europe.

Methodology

This chapter is partially based on ethnographic fieldwork undertaken between May 2017 and March 2018 with members in the commons around Făgăraș Mountains in the Southern Carpathians, Romania. That research aimed to understand the contention around establishing a large private wilderness reserve in a region considered a biodiversity hotspot and home to a dozen community-based institutions which have governed the environment for many centuries. Aside from conducting participant observation, semi-structured interviews, and policy analysis, I spent the period walking the land accompanied by locals, foresters, and rangers alike (Ingold and Vergunst 2008). Previously, from August 2016 to March 2017, I was part of a team which documented Romanian commons' diverse history, governance, and livelihoods using a mixed methodology which included archival research, multiple field surveys, and in-depth interviews with commons representatives. In addition to this research spread over many years and projects, I conducted three interviews with representatives from Crăciunel commons in January 2021, the case which informs the vignette in Section 4. The short research in the Transylvanian village was part of a larger ongoing project documenting emblematic ICCAs across Europe under the ICCA Consortium's auspices (ICCA Consortium 2021).

Revisiting Convivial Conservation

This section will discuss the central tenets of the convivial conservation vision as advanced by Büscher and Fletcher (2019) and will situate its emergence as a response to the recent shift towards strict protection in global conservation debates. Despite vast scholarship evidencing the vital role of community-led governance of PAs, Indigenous peoples have been acknowledged as important actors in the global conservation relatively recently, with firm support emerging after the 2008 IUCN Congress (Kothari et al. 2013). Mainstream conservation has been for a long time reluctant to admit that local people have the knowledge, skills, and capacity to care for the environment, despite the significant overlap between biodiversity hotspots and the territories managed by Indigenous peoples (RRI 2015). This super-imposition of state or private conservation over lands owned or managed by Indigenous Peoples and local communities left these groups cornered by PAs, remaking their customary governance and limiting their access to vital resources (Tauli-Corpuz et al. 2020). Since the publication of the IPBES Global Assessment Report in 2019, the international conservation community has been compelled to acknowledge that locally adapted governance practices are associated with high biodiversity rates and healthy ecosystems (IPBES 2019), but the progress towards full recognition and respect is still very slow. Furthermore, the rising popularity of strict protection embodied in visions such as 30x30 or Half-Earth hints that we are heading back to neo-protectionism (Wilson 2016). As a neo-liberal project, neo-protectionism has morphed into numerous reiterations within the Global South (Brockington 2002; Igoe and Brockington 2007; Heynen et al. 2007). Proposing that biodiversity protection succeeds only in isolation from any human influence, this model has been tested repeatedly across multiple geographies and is still alive and dynamic (Büscher et al. 2012).

More recently, European conservation has brought the model back home in an attempt to find a remedy for multiple environmental crises by putting under strict protection large areas and charismatic habitats (i.e. old-growth forests). A private project heralded as a model for the future of conservation in the region is already taking shape in eastern Europe, advertised as the European Yellowstone and supported by global green philanthropists (Iordăchescu 2018; 2021). Mandatory targets for strict protection will inevitably clash with centuries-old traditional land uses. Enclosing commons under the pretext of biodiversity protection, be it by public or private actors, has international ramifications and is considered by many to be a global phenomenon (Peluso and Lund 2011; White et al. 2012; Corson and MacDonald 2012). Many scholars have approached these enclosures as green grabbing and have shown how it supposedly takes the nature out from the market and reserves it for ecotourism and the development of green businesses (Fairhead et al. 2012; Ojeda 2012).

However, this strict protection momentum has not yet become hegemonic in creating PAs. More inclusive models have emerged in some European countries following democratic decision-making processes and centred around the sustainability of traditional livelihoods (e.g. Barronies Provençales Regional Parc created in 2014 in France). In particular cases, even if the creation of PAs emerges as a bottom-up process, public distrust in neoliberal conservation leads to the rejection of parks, as the recent case of the Parc Adula in Switzerland illustrates (Michel and Bruggmann 2019).

As it builds upon many transformative movements and radical initiatives, the convivial conservation vision comes with a generous set of propositions to move beyond pursuing economic growth and reinforced nature–culture dichotomies (Büscher and Fletcher 2020a). These include a move to celebrated or promoted areas, long-term visitation, everyday environmentalism, democratic engagement, and wealth-sharing for the wellbeing of humans and nonhumans alike (Büscher and Fletcher 2019). This repertoire is flexible enough to inspire conservation across scales while nurturing local governance systems which favour sharing and commoning over top-down imposed conservation. Since this paper aims to illustrate how commons and community governance can boost convivial conservation in Europe, it is essential to reaffirm the importance of egalitarian decision-making and fair resource allocation doubled by proper recognition and respect (Kothari 2014).

The convivial conservation proposal can address some of neo-protectionism's shortcomings by putting local people at the centre of decision-making processes, thus turning them from intervention targets to active actors in charge of fashioning conservation according to their own values (Büscher and Fletcher 2019). In Europe, this decentring can be read as an attempt to decolonise nascent conservation policies which show a complete disregard for local bio-cultural systems and landscapes. Considering the history of one-size-fits-all approaches, it is vital that the convivial conservation vision remains open to building upon the teachings, successes, and struggles of local communities who devised efficient institutions to maintain their wellbeing while being stewards of forests, pastures, or wetlands.

Wilderness in the EU: Reasserting Fortress Conservation

This section will revisit the crucial political moments which marked the emergence of wilderness protection in the nature conservation frameworks of the EU, and will show how this strict protection comes at odds with the convivial conservation vision. From a relatively marginal approach among conservationists, the strict protection of 'untouched nature', generally identified as *'wilderness'*, has been propelled over the last decade among the most intensely discussed environmental topics by scientists, politicians, and civil society (Wild Europe 2019). From the extensive mapping of remaining wilderness to important signs of progress in the EU legislation, proposals for the strict protection of supposedly undisturbed natural areas have set the ground for many continent-wide alliances permeating national and institutional boundaries (Bastmeijer 2016). Although merely a decade old, such conservation approaches previously unpopular in Europe already trigger important changes in socio-environmental relations. The EU Biodiversity Strategy is the most recent example of a legal document which reinforces this ontological dualism between undisturbed nature and the human realm (European Commission 2020). In parallel, prominent environmental NGOs work towards identifying the last areas of 'unspoiled' nature, demanding their strict protection as part of domestic legislation (Wild Europe 2019). Additionally, important efforts are directed towards finding mechanisms to turn wilderness conservation into a profitable business through its commodification within ecotourism operations and as part of climate change mitigation strategies (Wild Europe 2018). The promoters of the convivial conservation vision identify this pro-market orientation as one of the most significant shortcomings of neo-protectionism (Büscher and Fletcher 2020a). Moreover, a revaluation of old-growth forests has made the region a prime focus for new financial mechanisms for carbon sequestration and new green-growth opportunities (European Commission 2020; Iordăchescu 2021)

Intensely lobbied for by a coalition of environmental NGOs, scientists, and philanthropists, wilderness debuted on the EU political scene with the European Parliament's adoption in 2009 (European Parliament 2009). The resolution called on the European Commission to define wilderness by addressing ecosystem services, conservation value, climate change, and sustainable use as the main elements (European Parliament 2009: Art 1). Lastly, the Parliament requested that wilderness be given a central role in the Natura 2000 network (Art 20), proposing a radical change from the official approach to conservation which stressed the role of traditional land uses in protecting biodiversity.

The next significant EU political moment for wilderness protection was the European Commission's release of the *Guidelines for Wilderness in Natura 2000* in 2013. If previously the Habitats and the Birds Directives strongly advocated for a continuation of traditional land uses (Neumann 2014), including marginal agriculture and other historical or customary practices essential for maintaining European landscapes, now it clearly stated that a strict separation of an allegedly wild nature could be more effective for biodiversity conservation. These guidelines were not binding but constituted an essential precedent for opening the path towards mandatory targets for the strict protection of nature.

In 2020, the time was ripe for a new EU Biodiversity Strategy, which in an attempt to put nature at the centre of Europeans' wellbeing, proposed a radical increase of EU's PAs to 30% of the landmass and seas, including 10% of the territory under strict protection. Seen as an attempt to give 'nature the space it needs' (European Commission 2020: 1), the Strategy did not offer any details on the socio-economic impact of such a proposal, but suggested nevertheless that 'there should be a specific focus on areas of very high biodiversity value or potential' (Idem: 5). Coupled with the proposal to set mandatory targets for ecosystem restoration and enact the complete protection of all remaining old-growth forests, but without offering adequate financial or legal mechanisms, the Strategy risks to set the ground for increased restrictions to affect traditional land uses and marginal agriculture in areas which are rich in biodiversity, but affected by poverty and economic inequalities (Iordăchescu 2021). The practical aspects of translating these targets into domestic legislation fall on Member States' shoulders, potentially widening the biodiversity protection gaps across Europe's biogeographic regions.

As a new Common Agricultural Policy and a European Green New Deal are implemented, conservationists have suggested that a growing interest in strictly conserving 'untouched' nature will mark a new era in intergovernmental cooperation and will conclude with the introduction of 'wilderness' values in sectors such as agriculture, energy, and infrastructural developments (Wild Europe 2019). In various peripheral regions of the EU or its close vicinity, notable wilderness-related initiatives are already drawing critical financial resources, from the establishment of Cabo de Gata-Nijar National Park in the south of Spain (Cortéz Vásquez 2012) to the emerging 'European Yellowstone' in the Romanian Carpathians and beyond (Iordăchescu 2021). Although very heterogeneous, these projects share a few standard features: they come as a response to degradation narratives or land abandonment and propose wilderness conservation as a fix; they advocate for a strict protection approach as opposed to an allegedly failing marginal agriculture; they legitimise interventions by appealing to western scientific knowledge; and lastly, they glorify past ecological riches which western Europe has lost, thus augmenting the urgency to act. The problematic separation of humans and nature advanced by these initiatives is echoed by the European Commission's latest proposal around strict protection targets, which leave unquestioned the costs of promoting a neo-protectionist approach.

In this context, challenging the new dawn of fortress conservation in Europe is necessary, and the turn towards more convivial approaches is timely. The present wilderness political momentum can potentially open the region to green grabbing and further socio-environmental injustices.

ICCAS in Europe

Many of the challenges posed by the current wilderness momentum could be addressed by scrutinising alternative approaches to conservation centred on equity and justice, a task this section aims to achieve. Across Europe, there is an intimate relationship between historical forms of land stewardship and the culturally rich and biodiverse landscapes (Samojlik et al. 2013; Neumann 2014; Drenthen 2018). In areas such as the Carpathian Mountains, freeholders' associations which function as commons have governed natural resources for many centuries (Vasile 2009; 2015; 2018; Dorondel 2016). The current high levels of biodiversity result from their affective labour and care for the environment (Crumley 2017; Singh 2018). Similar governance regimes exist in many other European regions, from the *comunales* in northwest Spain to the Sami *territories of life* beyond the Arctic Circle or the 'beni communali' in northern Italy. Research on various European forms of commoning is currently witnessing a resurgence as concurrent planetary crises have triggered increased interest in learning from more inclusive forms of governance. The Alpine collective-management institutions (Landolt 2019) and the various commons around the Mediterranean (Daici 2021; Guerrini 2021) are given as examples of resilience and adaptation and models of bottom-up institution building (Lätsch 2019). Yet, while neo-institutional approaches to such rich commoning traditions prevail (Haller 2019), more research is needed to understand how commons can contribute to current debates about the future of nature conservation.

Considered the most exciting conservation development of this century (Kothari et al. 2012), the recognition and support of community-conserved areas and territories are already becoming a global phenomenon. ICCAs have been recognised by the parties to the CBD since 2004 and several IUCN resolutions and recommendations over the last decade (Kothari and Neumann 2014). Although ICCAs sometimes function as other effective area-based conservation measures (OECM), in many countries, their territories are overlapped by public or private PAs which superimpose governance or management systems which are detrimental to the livelihoods and culture of the guardian communities (Stevens et al. 2016). In the European context, the OECM umbrella term represents a valuable opportunity to recognise ICCAs as these do not necessarily have the conservation of biodiversity at the core of their functioning, and OECMs are widely recognised by the CBD under Aichi Target 11 and by the IUCN (IUCN-WCPA 2019).

The ICCA Consortium is a platform and an organisation whose members work intensely to bring together and make visible the conservation efforts of hundreds of ICCAs from very different geographical regions, which are on the frontlines of the struggle to defend and protect their territories (ICCA Consortium 2021). As these lands are considered the heart of their identity, culture, and livelihoods, they are collectively defended against attempts of enclosures by governments, companies, and commercial enterprises (Borrini-Feyerabend and Hill 2015). For such an area to be qualified and registered as an ICCA, there should be a strong link between the territory and the livelihoods of the community; the community should have some sort of governance mechanism in place; and the primary outcome of this governance should be conservation through sustainable use (Stevens et al. 2016)—all these elements are central to the development of the convivial conservation vision as discussed above.

The process of recognising and registering potential ICCAs in Europe has started recently, and it can be rightfully claimed that some of the commons which still exist in the Western Balkans, in some Mediterranean areas but also in the Carpathians, satisfy all criteria to be considered as ICCAs (Vasile 2019). The struggles of ICCAs in Europe are manifold, from collision and the lack of recognition by states to green or military grabbing (Domínguez 2020). ICCAs are very effective as PAs and continuously invest in conservation because the stewardship of resources directly impacts their livelihoods (Borrini-Feyerabend and Hill 2015). External sources of funding do not condition this stewardship, and it happens even in countries where public funds are scarce, although ICCAs have no appropriate legal standing in most jurisdictions (Tauli-Corpuz et al. 2020). The recently published *Territories of Life 2021 Report* shows that currently one of the biggest opportunities to boost transformative change from the local to the global level is by recognising the ICCAs worldwide (ICCA Consortium 2021).

While arguing for the recognition of ICCAs as OECMs, it is important to remember that they are also institutions for voicing political dissent and mobilisation against social and environmental injustice. Far from embracing a strict separation between their livelihoods and autonomous nature, their conservation work involves mobilising financial resources, affective labour, and a plethora of regional alliances (Tran et al. 2020). Since it is currently crystallising as a revolutionary conservation approach, the convivial conservation proposal has plenty to learn from the struggles and successes of ICCAs. During this cross-fertilisation process, the convivial conservation proposal can assess the suitability of many of its theoretical tenets: switching from protected to promoted areas, experimenting with various governance models, and bridging the human–nature divide. Similarly, the recognised or potential ICCAs can find new inspiration to experiment with conservation basic income (CBI) and foster new alliances beyond for-profit conservation schemes.

Romanian Commons: Potential Paths to Conviviality

In this section, the rich experiences of governing commons in Romania will be highlighted to illustrate how local historical institutions increased their conservation efforts to meet the challenges posed by top-down conservation. The case of Crăciunel commons will be used as an example of a possible path towards conviviality.

Historical forest and pasture commons have been recently re-established in Romania, becoming efficient examples of decentralised governance of local resources to satisfy the needs of their members (Vasile 2009; 2018). Most of them could be considered veritable conservation actors similar to other institutions united under the ICCA umbrella term. Locally named 'obşti' or 'composesorate', most of these commons satisfy the three features of ICCAs: a transparent democratic governance system, a strong bond with the environment, and having conservation and sustainable use of resources as a primary goal. Commoners affinity to their territory expressed through sharing and caring for the land point to a convivial future for conservation within the European continent.

Crăciunel

Crăciunel village (Karácsonyfalva in Hungarian) is located in the heart of the Székely Land, an ethnocultural region of Transylvania and a rural area rich in deciduous forests and woody pastures which have shaped locals' livelihoods over centuries of continuous use. During the post-socialist land reforms, the community successfully claimed the collective ownership of 1,100 hectares of forestlands and pastures and re-established the historical governance regime (közbirtokosság) which communist authorities had previously dissolved in 1948. As with other commons in the country, the community maintains a robust bond with the territory and uses both tradition and official documents to attest to their customary governance. Although their collective ownership had been formalised by the end of the nineteenth century and recognised by the Austro-Hungarian and Romanian governments (Vasile 2019), the post-WWII nationalisation restricted their capacity to manage and care for the environment according to their historical bylaws. In 2000, at the moment of its re-establishment, the commoners faced a series of obstacles from the local and regional authorities related to recognising their rights. As the country was undergoing serious agrarian transformations, which quickly escalated in misappropriation of lands and decimation of forests (Dorondel 2016), the commoners of Crăciunel swiftly moved towards securing their rights and strengthening the management of their resources according to sustainable-use principles. They were the first commons in the region to approve a forest management plan, which guaranteed their forest conservation according to scientific forestry prescriptions. More recently, the commons' elected body of representatives managed to file for the increased protection of 120 hectares of old-growth forest, a voluntary measure which will restrict this area's use and contribute to the permanence of a rich resource for future generations. Besides, another area of 60 hectares is already strictly protected as it constitutes a sessile oak seed reserve.

After Romania acceded to the EU, the Common Agricultural Policy offered the community the opportunity to adopt voluntary measures for the sustainable management of their grazing lands. Under these provisions, the use and maintenance of pastures were clearly regulated to prevent overexploitation and maintain high biodiversity. Concomitantly, the commoners received direct payments as a recognition for their care. The woody pastures are remarkable examples of silvopastoral systems, once spread everywhere in central Europe, but currently declining owing to intensive agriculture, the abandonment of traditional animal husbandry, and rural depopulation (Hartel et al. 2013). They are considered an important biodiversity hotspot and are valuable cultural landscapes (Hartel et al. 2015). Woody pastures are veritable examples of shared landscapes and attest to local patterns of conviviality.

Crăciunel közbirtokosság stands out from other neighbouring commons for its efforts to conserve the rich bio-cultural values of the territory. After their re-establishment as a juridical institution, the commons council collaborated with local environmental NGOs and pieced together documents and environmental assessments to declare a couple of PAs of local importance. The first one is an ancient sweet chestnut orchard which has been a central cultural element of the community for generations, while the second, a complex of healing water springs located in a biodiversity hotspot, is not only of spiritual value but also a place to reaffirm the commoners' communitarian values during festivals and religious gatherings. The two PAs, of a size smaller than two hectares each, were declared despite opposition from the local municipality, as the commoners wished to prevent the areas from being subjected to future infrastructure developments. It has been often said that community-led conservation is often guided by instrumental and cultural values rather than exclusive care for biodiversity in itself (Stevens et al. 2016). While being conserved for their cultural relevance, these two PAs host a range of endangered and endemic species and habitats while providing the community with essential services. In the process of gaining traction in Europe, convivial conservation should play a crucial role in recognising the commons' role in conservation. Those who implement convivial conservation can build upon multiple valuation systems which underline custodians' skills, knowledge, and practices.

The governance of közbirtokosság in Crăciunel follows bylaws which have legal value, being registered by courts. Currently, the community comprises 347 commoners who are entitled to fixed quantities of timber and access to pastures for grazing cattle according to a transparent system of rights distribution. These clear rules of access and use function as a guarantee that grazelands are not overstocked and forests are not overexploited. Over the last decade, since compensation and direct payments constitute a critical revenue to the commons' budget, the annual quota of harvested wood has dropped, while commercial felling has almost disappeared. This shows how critical financial mechanisms are for the fair recognition of the community's conservation work. Aside from securing commons' institutional functioning, revenues are used to sponsor the local school, annual public festivities, renovation of historical buildings, and continued investment in the development of a public baths complex around the mineral springs. The commons is thus instrumental to both maintaining and enriching the biodiversity and promoting a harmonious relationship between the collective and the natural values (Enikő Benedek, commoner, 2021) in ways similar to those advanced by the proponents of the convivial conservation vision.

Since Crăciunel közbirtokosság turned to conserve the bio-cultural values of the territory, a significant return of wildlife has been observed by locals and biologists studying the area (Varga and Molnár 2014). Beavers (*Castor fiber*) repopulated the stream of Homorod, the black stork (*Ciconia nigra*) has nestled in the commons' forest, and the local game guards have spotted the elusive lynx (*Lynx lynx*). The commoners celebrate the return of wildlife and take pride in the ever-increasing number of storks (*Ciconia ciconia*), said to be a blessing for the village. Still, there are also cases when conflicts with wildlife bring feelings of frustration and powerlessness. In particular, the presence of brown bears (*Ursus arctos*) within the village constitutes a nuisance, as the central authorities rarely compensate locals for the damaged fields. Many farmers have abandoned distant fields and concentrated their subsistence agriculture around the households to reduce such conflicts, leaving thus more habitat to the bears. A Natura 2000 PA overlaps the entire territory, but for which no management plan has been approved by the government so far. The local commoners' sustained efforts make this land a hotspot of biodiversity (Csaba Orbán, commons representative, 2021). As in other country regions, locals were not consulted when the PA was declared in the late 2000s. Nevertheless, the community welcomes its existence and has put together a vision to expand the village's economic activity by developing it as an eco-touristic destination. Conviviality plays a significant role in this vision as sharing ecological knowledge with future tourists and engaged visitation are its central elements.

Commons like Crăciunel are spread across the Carpathians and function as safety nets for the less privileged community members; they invest part of their income in public infrastructures such as roads and power grids, and support the local school's functioning, churches, and even hospitals. Even if their governance model varies from one region to another, decisions are taken by democratic vote in general assemblies. A first step in building a more inclusive conservation for these mountains and expanding the convivial proposal would be to recognise commons' role across centuries in shaping and enriching the landscape. Proper recognition, support, and the promotion of forest commons in the Carpathians as socially and environmentally just conservation examples should be high on the convivial conservation agenda in this region. In the next section, we will discuss specific elements which can guide the development of convivial conservation in Europe.

Discussion: Lessons towards Conviviality

The current political turn towards strict protection pushes us to re-assert the role of alternative conservation models centred around social and environmental justice. In this context, how can the Romanian commons contribute to reimagining conservation governance within the convivial vision? In what ways could these institutions advance our understanding of resilient livelihoods? And lastly, how can the commons advance a conservation vision which emerges from the bottom-up and breaks free from market logic?

Self-governance

Exploring different governing conservation mechanisms is one of the biggest challenges set by the convivial conservation proposal (Büscher and Fletcher 2019: 191). The great variety of governance models featured by these commons can offer important lessons to future convivial conservation reiterations in Europe. Under Romanian law, commons are recognised as associations of owners. They are part of the national historical heritage, governing themselves independently from the state according to their bylaws and decision-making institutions (Vasile and Mantescu 2009). The law grants the ownership of the communal lands to the community of rights holders. All commoners assemble at least once annually to vote changes to bylaws, decide on grazing rights, and share monetary proceeds. The commons are represented by a president and a council of representatives holding office for four years and are elected democratically by the general assembly. Both the president and the council are supervised by a committee of auditors appointed by the assembly. In some regions, the communities of freeholders take pride in their common ancestry which often is associated with past struggles against enclosures which shaped their shared identity. Pride in a place is a powerful resource in conservation (Tran et al. 2020); therefore, commoners' care for the environment is rooted in local tradition and culture. The commons' bylaws contain precise details regarding membership, decision-making processes, and rules of access to the natural resources governed collectively.

Although the unequal distribution of rights promoted by this governance model might not be very appealing for the convivial conservation proposal, the Romanian commons can help convivial conservation proponents experiment with various democratic governance patterns. Imposing caps of resource use, voting on the sustainable allocation of pastures or timber, and the decision-making associated with the distribution of financial resources according to the community's needs have all been experienced by commons over generations and can yield important lessons for future reiterations of the convivial proposal. The flexibility shown by these commons in their democratic decision-making process has the potential to make convivial conservation a robust and realistic proposal in Europe. Simultaneously, their great variety can ensure that the proposal will not come at odds with local peculiarities across geographic, political, and cultural divides on the continent.

Livelihoods and Resilience

Aside from being a source of pride and self-identification, commons are primarily perceived as providing the commoners with access to timber, grazing, and monetary proceeds. All commons work together with state or private forestry districts responsible for guarding and administering the forest. More extensive commons, as well as those that are part of commons unions, have managed to establish their own independent forestry districts. Every ten years, a detailed management plan is submitted for approval, and timber exploitation is organised according to yearly quotas which allow for the regeneration and general health of the forest. Being the most important resource owned by the collective, the forests are perceived as productive, with the lumber being used for heating or building. Larger commons engage in commercial forestry, with the revenues being used to support the community or redistributed according to the rights system. In most villages, the functioning of schools and churches is financially supported by commons. Still, there are many cases where funds are directed to rural hospitals, fire brigades, cultural activities, or festivals. In the region of Vrancea, young families receive the timber to build their first home from the commons, and essential sums are allocated for supporting school children or the costs of funerals. Among more powerful commons, there is a recent tendency to develop other economic activities and to rely less on forest exploitation. Guesthouses, farms specialising in ancient cattle breeds, tree nurseries, and manufacturers for the processing of mushrooms and forest berries are examples of such enterprises (Opincaru 2020). By turning away from timber extraction activities to other income-generating opportunities, the commons show resilience and a great adaptation capacity coupled with care for future generations and the environment.

Commons' resilience is a well-researched topic, with a rich scholarship showing how property transformation (Vasile and Mantescu 2009), economic restructuring, or green investments (Achiba 2019) challenged commons to adapt, transform, and reinvent across time and geographies. In the Romanian context, these institutions survived repeated historical waves of enclosure (Stahl 1998), readjusted processes of internal governance and control, and accommodated increasing legal requirements from the state (Vasile 2018) while remaining central elements of local identity and pride and acting as platforms to voice political demands. Such great flexibility doubled by institutional robustness should be a central argument in raising support for their recognition as conservation actors and paths towards conviviality.

These commons show that funding local investments do not necessarily need to rely on market expansion, a point often raised by the proponents of the convivial conservation proposal. As shown above, the primary source of financial income is the proceeds from sustainable logging, grazing, direct payments, and other allocations through various EU schemes. Büscher and Fletcher have started a discussion around offering a CBI to communities living inside or in the proximity of conservation-critical areas (2020a: 187). They suggest that this redistribution logic should be unconditional, combine the socio-economic benefits of cash transfer programs, focus on environmental protection (2020b: 5), and apply to all residents. The commons discussed above already receive significant amounts of public money for adopting various land uses which enrich their landscapes, and this resource has contributed to the adoption of even further measures towards conservation, as shown in the case of Crăciunel. Nevertheless, the Common Agricultural Policy (CAP) direct payments and other agro-pastoral financial incentives received by commons are both conditional, and to a great extent, market-based, as they incentivise certain agricultural practices or function as compensations for unrealised profit from low-intensity use, thus departing from the CBI proposal. Yet, the positive conservation outcome of direct payments for commons is incontestable, contributes to members' wellbeing, and is a step towards recognising these institutions as conservation actors. Even if this falls short of the ideal CBI project, it forwards the acknowledgement of commons' contribution at broader scales than just 'conservation-critical areas' (Büscher and Fletcher 2020b: 5). With this mechanism already in place and in most cases functional, the convivial conservation proposal has all the tools necessary to push for further unconditional redistribution and Europe-wide CBI.

Conservation

PAs extend over 25% of Romania's territory and feature a diverse array of national and nature parks, scientific reserves, and natural monuments, with many of them being part of the EU Natura 2000 network (UNEP-WCMC and IUCN 2016). The most significant proportion of national parks and the entire network of Natura 2000 PAs were gazetted in Romania right before or immediately after the country acceded to the EU within a top-down process (Ioja et al. 2010). More than a decade after these PAs have been created, the government remains unable to ensure their proper functioning and financing so that the largest proportion of Natura 2000 PAs still have no approved management plans. Throughout the country, most rural communities living around or within PAs consider that the set of restrictions which came with the new protection regime are highly ineffective and a source of multiple conflicts—related to depredation by wildlife, access and property relations, violation of ownership rights, or even poaching and illegal logging (Knorn et al. 2012).

As most large PAs have been established over the last two decades, predominantly in the mountains where biodiversity is higher and habitats are less fragmented, it inevitably overlapped territories owned and managed by forest commons (Vasile 2019). The targets set by the new EU Biodiversity Strategy will put even more pressure on the communities living in or near these biodiversity-rich areas (European Commission 2020). Because the re-establishment of commons and the creation of most PAs happened simultaneously after 2000, clashes between commoners and PAs' administrators manifested almost instantly. In some regions, commons had to navigate complicated bureaucracy related to animal husbandry and pasturing rights, provisions concerning forestry, and pressures to expand commercial logging (Vasile 2019).

The distrust in conservation remains high and is sometimes accentuated by increased restrictions and the lack of fair or inconsistent compensation of economic losses associated with the strict protection of forests in the core areas of national parks (Aastrup 2020). Although commons are obliged to renew forest management plans every ten years to comply with the provision of sustainable forest management, to pay for the guarding of their forests, and to govern according to bylaws which set explicit use quotas for natural resources, they are never recognised as community-led conservation initiatives. As the ICCA denomination is currently unknown to national lawmakers and conservation practitioners, these commons are not regarded as other effective area-based conservation measures under the CBD's recommendation (IUCN-WCPA 2019), nor are there any registered ICCAs in the country. The contribution of the Romanian commons to biodiversity conservation as intentional or as a by-product of their governance is unquestionable and should represent a strong argument for recognising them as OECMs. While doing so, it is essential to remember that these commons have across history been more than self-governing institutions; they are essential instruments for securing political rights and reaffirming shared values and pride.

While laying the foundations of convivial conservation across the continent, its proponents should state clearly that the conservation done by commons must be understood as instrumental and relational. Commons livelihoods are not necessarily centred on conservation, but they are organised and function according to sustainable management principles sanctioned by internal bylaws, with exceptional care for future generations. The switch from protected (from humans) towards promoted areas, envisaged by the convivial proposal (Büscher and Fletcher 2020a: 163), must incorporate this reality and turn it into an instrument for making the proposal appealing to communities which struggled under top-down imposed conservation regime.

Commons and other ICCAs across Europe are large enough to turn conservation from focusing on charismatic species to more landscape-centred approaches, where vast swathes of land are promoted for their bio-cultural values rather than for their spectacular features or charisma. This departure not only will counter the EU's green colonialism but will also translate convivial conservation into concrete pathways for governing nature (Büscher and Fletcher 2020a: 191) beyond the commodification brought by nature-based tourism.

Lastly, the commons' long history and their ever-evolving relation with their territories hint at a change in the perception of temporality. The commons' functioning shows that conservation is a process marked by continuous democratic negotiations and enmeshed within valuation practices which might seem unrelated to species protection per se, rather than a time-bound project as most conservation practitioners and NGOs fashion it. The convivial proposal has already advanced the idea of long-term engagement (Büscher and Fletcher 2019), and therefore, a close examination of the history of commoning could boost its transformative potential in Europe.

Conclusion

The current political momentum towards strict biodiversity protection in Europe shows that the translation of the convivial conservation vision into concrete pathways is timely. While plans to increase the size and number of PAs on the continent are gaining traction, it is essential to scrutinise the potential of such proposals to cast unjust restrictions or bring new challenges to the livelihoods of those living in or near PAs. The paper discussed how potential ICCAs could offer valuable lessons for future convivial conservation reiterations, and it examined particular trajectories departing from the Romanian forest and pasture commons.

Although the commons' prevailing conception of nature is utilitarian, they have demonstrated remarkable resilience and flexibility for generations while committing to forest and pastures' stewardship. The care for both human and nonhuman wellbeing, the innovative conservation measures adopted for nurturing rich bio-cultural systems, and the opportunity to bring integrated landscape approaches to biodiversity conservation are all elements which resonate with the theoretical tenets of convivial conservation and can advance the proposal across Europe. Even if several elements within the commons' functioning differ from the convivial vision (mechanisms of exclusion, small-scale impacts, etc.), these institutions' diversity of commoning practices can contribute to the feasibility of convivial conservation vision in Europe.

In sum, even though there is strong backing for the strict protection of nature in Europe, important alternatives emerge which can lead to more just and democratic conservation models. These could be strengthened by learning from the efforts of various forms of commoning present across the continent. While taking the present moment as a window of opportunity to build more socially equitable conservation approaches, it is important to remember that the first step towards conviviality starts with increasing the support offered to commons and ICCAs and recognising their contribution to biodiversity conservation.

Chapter 15:

Why the Convivial Conservation Vision Needs Complementing to be a Viable Alternative for Conservation in the Global South[*]

By Wilhelm A. Kiwango and Mathew Bukhi Mabele

Introduction

Convivial conservation is presented as an anti-capitalist approach and alternative to current mainstream conservation as well as proposals for 'half-earth' and 'new conservation' approaches (Büscher and Fletcher 2019; 2020). While the ideas underlying convivial conservation are more compelling than the other proposed approaches, we argue that the concept is unlikely to have much influence in changing current conservation practices in countries that significantly rely on international wildlife tourism to fund both conservation and development projects. Using the case of conservation policies and practice in Tanzania, we show that path dependencies, reliance on international tourism, and competing political interests make it difficult to implement convivial conservation in any meaningful way.

In this paper, we review three new proposals which seek to address the current biodiversity crisis: half earth, new conservation, and convivial conservation. We go on to present a case study of the Rungwa-Ruaha ecosystem in Tanzania. We situate the case study within the context of mainstream conservation to explore how the path dependencies, political interests, and reliance on international tourism funding shape current conservation practices in Tanzania. In the fourth section we critically discuss the problems illustrated

---

[*] Originally published as: Kiwango, W.A., and M.B. Mabele. (2022). Why the convivial conservation vision needs complementing to be a viable alternative for conservation in the Global South. Conservation & Society 20(2): 179-189.

in the case study and how they undermine the vision of convivial conservation. We conclude by proposing a socio-ecological justice approach which is more likely to be effective in facilitating transformation of mainstream conservation in the global South. This approach includes three key features which are critically important for translating the idea of convivial conservation in the global South: promoting diversity of conservation knowledge and perspectives to embrace ecological integrity and social justice in policy and practice; promoting systemic recognition of the rights and responsibilities of different stakeholders in conservation agencies and benefits commensurate with the costs; and establishment of community-based conservation insurance as an alternative funding mechanism to reduce dependence on international tourism revenue.

Radical Proposals For Saving Nature

Biodiversity crises and environmental degradation generated by the expansion of human activities and exploitation of the biophysical world continue despite global efforts to address them (Ceballos et al. 2017). The Intergovernmental Science-Policy Platform on Biodiversity and Ecosystem Services (2019) has highlighted many of these problems and put forward concrete actions to reduce the intensity of the drivers of biodiversity loss. In the past decade, however, three radical proposals have been put forward to address the weaknesses of mainstream conservation and its inability to address the biodiversity crisis. These are 'new conservation' (Kareiva et al. 2012; Kueffer and Kaiser-Bunbury 2014), 'half earth' (Locke 2013; Wilson 2016; Dinerstein et al. 2017) and 'convivial conservation' (Büscher and Fletcher, 2019, 2020).

Mainstream conservation refers to the dominant strain in conservation which maintains the western ideological perspective of human/nature dichotomy and adopts a 'fortress conservation' model which is based on protecting nature from people (Brockington, 2002). It is premised on the close collaboration and intersection between state power, market-oriented approach, and philanthropic interests to generate revenue from tourism in protected areas (PAs) (Brockington et al. 2008; Büscher and Fletcher 2019).

The 'new conservation' approach argues that given the already great influence of people on nature, protecting biodiversity from people is a 'losing proposition' and the aim should be to protect a resilient nature *within* human populations (Kareiva et al. 2012; Kueffer and Kaiser-Bunbury 2014). The central argument is that human actions on nature are inevitable and the line that separates nature from humans is increasingly blurred. Hence it is necessary to think of shared landscapes between humans and nature and adopt alternative strategies such as rewilding to reduce biodiversity loss (Immovilli and Kok 2020). The proponents of new conservation support the promotion of economic growth and partnership with large corporations to minimise the impacts of development and steer it towards better conservation outcomes (Kareiva 2012).

The 'Half Earth' or 'Nature Needs Half' (hereafter 'half earth') proposal epitomises the neo-protectionist movement that proposes to flatten the curve of the current biodiversity crisis by returning to strict exclusion of humans from large parts of the earth (Locke 2013; Wilson 2016; Kopnina et al. 2018). It calls for urgent action to mitigate the ongoing 'sixth mass extinction' of species on a mass scale (Ceballos et al. 2017). Its proponents argue that in order to halt the biodiversity crisis, about half of the earth's area should be set aside for biodiversity conservation through a system of strict PAs (Dinerstein et al. 2017). This would ensure that human beings live justly and prudently on one half of the earth (Cafaro et al. 2017) while preserving the other half for 'other species' (Goodall, 2015). Other proposals in a similar vein include the Global Deal for Nature (Dinerstein et al. 2019) and the Global Biodiversity Framework (CBD 2020b) which set a target of bringing 30% of the earth under protection by 2030.

The half earth proposal has been criticised for 're-inventing the square wheel' (e.g. Wilshusen et al. 2002) and ignoring the root causes of biodiversity loss such as capitalist extraction and consumption, and for ignoring the enormous social costs of setting up such expanded PAs (Büscher et al. 2017). The new conservation proposal has been critiqued for relying on ineffective market-based instruments (Arsel and Büscher 2012; Fletcher et al. 2016), and for potentially exacerbating profit-driven changes in land uses (Caro et al. 2014).

Büscher and Fletcher (2019; 2020) draw on political ecology frameworks to show the flawed and the socio-ecologically problematic human/nature dichotomy underlying the neo-protectionist 'half-earth' approach and the capitalist rationale of the 'new conservation' approach that relies on continual economic growth via intensified consumerism. They put forward the alternative concept of 'convivial conservation' as 'a vision, a politics and a set of governance principles that realistically respond to the core pressures [of biodiversity loss] of our time. It builds on the politics of equity, structural change and environmental justice' (ibid: 283-284). They outline more equitable ways for transforming mainstream conservation into new just socio-ecologies for both humans and nonhumans (Massarella et al. 2021).

Büscher and Fletcher (2019) define their alternative concept of convivial conservation through five elements. First, they challenge the human/nature dichotomy inherent in PAs and propose a fundamental shift in thinking from 'protected' to 'promoted' areas. Instead of a conservation mentality centred on protecting nature from local people, they emphasise the need for creating areas which are promoted and conserved by and for the people without involving capitalist market mechanisms. Second, they propose a conservation approach that saves and equally celebrates both human and non-human nature. Third, they call for a move away from short-term voyeuristic tourism towards more long-term engagement with the 'wild'. Fourth, they emphasise appreciation of 'everyday' nature and environments rather than on tourism that focuses on 'spectacles of nature'. Finally, they envision a shift from a privatised conservation expert technocracy towards a common democratic engagement that enables all people to live with all nature.

Although the three proposed conservation approaches are presented as radically different from mainstream conservation, they cannot avoid some of its underlying features. While convivial conservation may be a more socio-ecologically preferred alternative to the half earth and new conservation proposals, it still reflects a global North perspective of conservation. It does not recognise three critical problems faced by countries of the global South for pursuing conservation. First, most conservation agencies in global South countries are burdened by institutional path dependencies that were established under European colonial rule according to the fortress conservation approach and have continued to do so in the post-independence era. Second, many of these countries heavily rely on generating foreign exchange earnings from the 'export' of nature tourism for funding national economic development. Third, there are various political interests at the national level which often undermine efforts to promote democratic governance and decision-making for conservation activities at the community level. Hence, from the perspective of the global South, we argue that convivial conservation is a promising 'work in progress' which needs to find new ways of addressing these critical problems. We thus ask: how can we build on the elements outlined in the convivial conservation proposal to address these problems of conservation in developing countries of the global South?

In the following sections, we illustrate these issues through the empirical case of the Rungwa-Ruaha ecosystem in south-western Tanzania. We selected the Rungwa-Ruaha ecosystem as our conservation case study due to its ecological, social, and economic significance at the ecosystem and national levels. Another important reason was the rich research experience gained by the first author over six years in understanding the Rungwa-Ruaha ecosystem and associated social, economic, and political dynamics. We reviewed and analysed the content of Tanzanian government policies, laws and regulations, media reports, and election manifestos related to national parks and wildlife conservation. We obtained data from reports published by the Ministry of Natural Resources and Tourism, the Wildlife Division, and Tanzania National Parks, and Wildlife Management Areas (WMAs).

The Rungwa-Ruaha Ecosystem

There are six categories of Protected Areas in Tanzania: National Parks, Game Reserves, Game Controlled Areas, Conservation Area, Ramsar/Wetland Sites and Wildlife Management Areas. However, four categories of PAs are represented in the Rungwa-Ruaha ecosystem: National Parks, Game Reserves, Game Controlled Areas and Wildlife Management Areas. *National Parks* represent the highest category of protection under the International Union for Conservation of Nature (IUCN, category II). In this category, main uses include photographic tourism, wildlife research, education, cultural and spiritual activities. Consumptive[1] uses such as tourist hunting are not allowed. *Game Reserves* represent the second category of PAs where wildlife utilization is allowed such as tourist and resident hunting, as well as photographic tourism. *Game Controlled Areas* represents an area outside village land and with definite boundaries where activities detrimental to wildlife such as livestock grazing and crop cultivation are not allowed. *Wildlife Management Areas* (WMAs) is a relatively new PA category, which comprises village land with significant resources that have economic value. WMA must form, or be part of, an ecologically viable ecosystem (MNRT 2012). The four categories of PAs are under different governance arrangements. While National Parks are under the Tanzania National Parks (TANAPA), the Game Reserves and Game Controlled Areas are under the Tanzania Wildlife Authority (TAWA) and the WMAs are under both the local governments and the central government through TAWA. These different conservation agencies shape management and use of these areas.

Rungwa-Ruaha forms an important ecosystem spanning an area of about 50,000km^2 in southwest Tanzania (Abade et al. 2020). It is located between 6°15'00" to 8°20'00" S and 33°45'00" to 35°50'00" E (Abade et al. 2020). It comprises several Protected Areas: Ruaha National Park (RUNAPA), Rungwa, Kizigo and Muhesi Game Reserves, Lunda-Mkwambi Game Controlled Area; Idodi-Pawaga (MBOMIPA), Waga and UMEWARUA Wildlife Management Areas (WMAs) (see Figure 1).

The climate of the Rungwa-Ruaha ecosystem is mainly semi-arid to arid with mean annual rainfall ranging from 500–600mm (Walsh 2000; SPANEST 2016). Rainfall occurs between December to January and March to April and tends to increase with altitude (Abade et al. 2014; SPANEST 2016). Temperatures range from 15°C to 35°C (Abade et al. 2014) but can occasionally reach up to 44°C (MBOMIPA 2014). The ecosystem is traversed by several rivers, the major ones being the Greater Ruaha in the south and Mzombe River in the north. These sustain the ecosystem by providing water for both wildlife and livestock, particularly during the dry season. The upstream PAs serve as catchment areas to ensure a stable flow of water throughout the year. The Rungwa-Ruaha ecosystem is critical for ensuring biodiversity connectivity between the different PAs. It encompasses migratory routes and species which would not otherwise be protected in isolated PAs (Abade et al. 2014; Kiwango et al. 2018). The Park is bordered by villages and WMAs. The WMAs form a buffer zone between the villages and the core PAs, and wildlife, including Elephants (*Loxodonta africana*) and large carnivores freely move between these two areas (Abade et al. 2020).

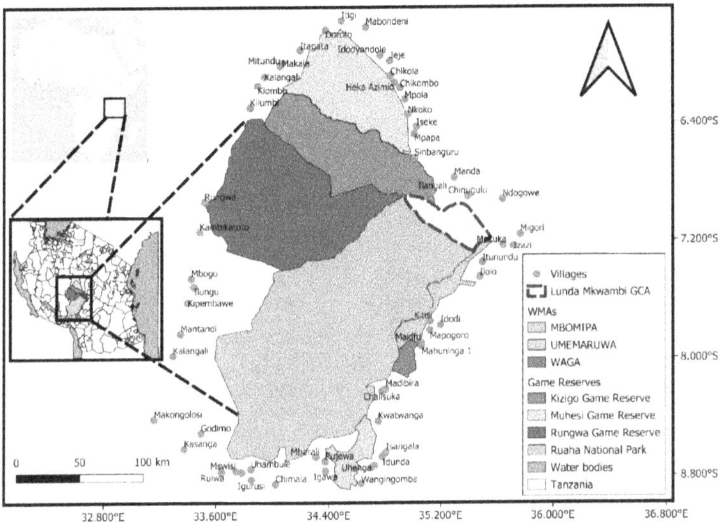

Figure 1: A map showing the Rungwa-Ruaha ecosystem with associated PAs. Black dots indicate villages surrounding the ecosystem Source: Field data, QGIS.

Since colonial times, Rungwa-Ruaha's uniqueness has been used to justify applications of coercive and repressive conservation policies that follow the 'fortress conservation' model (Brockington 2002). This is evidenced by the creation of the aforementioned PAs with different management regimes, but with the same principle of maintaining strict separation of humans from nature. Table 1 presents the categories and basic characteristics of the PAs that form the ecosystem. These PAs are classic manifestations of strict protectionist ideas.

Category of PA	Name	Size (Km²)	Year of gazettement	Type of use allowed/not allowed	Administered by
National Park	Ruaha National Park	20, 226	1964	Non-consumptive, human settlement not allowed	Tanzania National Parks
Game Reserves	Rungwa Kizigo and Muhesi (3)	15,000	Rungwa (1951), Kizigo (1972), Muhesi (1994)	Consumptive/ non-consumptive, human settlement not allowed	Tanzania Wildlife Authority (TAWA)/Wildlife Division (WD)
Game Controlled Area	Lunda Mkwambi (1)	1,000	1974	Consumptive/ non-consumptive, human settlement not allowed	TAWA/WD
Wildlife Management Areas	Idodi-Pawaga (MBOMIPA)	777	2007	Consumptive/ non-consumptive, human settlement not allowed	TAWA/WD, Iringa District Councils, MBOMIPA Authorized Association.
	Waga	315.27	2015	Consumptive/ non-consumptive, human settlement not allowed	TAWA, Mufindi District Council, TAWA, WD
	UMEWARUA	600.9	2015	Consumptive/ non-consumptive, human settlement not allowed	Wanging'ombe District Council, TAWA, WD

Table 1: Categories of protected areas, their governance structures and their land use classification in the Greater Rungwa-Ruaha ecosystem (GRRE). KEY: As per the Tanzanian Wildlife Conservation Act 5 of 2009, consumptive use means the taking of flora or the hunting or capturing of fauna, while non-consumptive use means the use of scenery, cultural and natural resources that does not involve taking any specimen from the PA, such as photographic tourism, walking safaris, hiking, canoeing, boating, scuba diving, mountaineering and any other similar or related activity. Source: Modified from MNRT 2013; Copollilo and Dickman 2007.

Path Dependencies and Intensified Protectionism

The concept of institutional path dependency offers a way of understanding how the PAs system shapes biodiversity conservation in Tanzania. Path dependency refers to the institutional practices and political cultures that become systemically entrenched to favour the interests of powerful actors (Berkes 2007). Although institutions are not static and change over time, powerful actors influence these changes to further their interests over the less powerful actors (Petursson and Vedeld 2015; 2017). The laws, rules, policies and practices that define PAs and their management in Tanzania were instituted under European colonial rule and reflected their values and interests in wildlife conservation (Adams and Mulligan 2003). This was manifest in the colonial government's use of militarised tactics and violent force to evict local farming and pastoral communities for creating PAs (Brockington 2002; Brockington and Wilkie 2015). After independence from colonial rule, the Tanzanian government agencies have continued to pursue the colonial protectionist paradigm in the name of economic development through wildlife tourism development and more recently through the narrative of biodiversity crisis (Adams 2020).

The Ruaha National Park (RUNAPA) which is at the heart of the Rungwa-Ruaha ecosystem exemplifies this path dependency. It was formally created in 1964 (MNRT 2013)[2], covering an area of about 10,300 km^2 by 1974 (Kashaigili et al. 2005; Zia et al. 2011). In 2008, the Usangu Game Reserve (9,926km^2) was annexed and added to RUNAPA, bringing its total area to 20,226 km^2 and making it the largest National Park in the country. The former Usangu Reserve included the Ihefu wetland, an important catchment area for the Great Ruaha River. In 2006, the government made the decision to evict a large number of livestock herders, mostly Sukuma agro-pastoralists, claiming that pastoral activity and rice cultivation was causing environmental destruction of the Ihefu wetlands (Sirima and Backman 2013; Walwa 2020). This led to a special operation by Park authorities to physically displace agro-pastoralists from seven villages and two hamlets (Sirima and Backman 2013) along with an estimated 300,000 cattle to Lindi and the Coast Regions (Walsh 2012). These displacements fuelled significant anger and resource conflicts between the agro-pastoralists and Park authorities and were condemned by civil society organisations in Tanzania and beyond (Walsh 2012; Walwa 2020).

Conflicts between livestock herders and the Park have persisted since the annexation of the former Usangu Game reserve into RUNAPA, and tensions remain high. While the Park authority has secured the boundaries, livestock incursions still occur, particularly in the Ihefu wetland area. This results in further eviction operations by the regional government administration. In January 2021, the Regional Commissioner for the Mbeya administrative region which includes the Ihefu wetland ordered voluntary relocations of livestock from the wetland within six days. He added that failure to comply would result in forceful eviction, even if it required using live ammunition by police or military troops to conduct the operation[3]. Although the majority of the herders removed their cattle within the specified period, about 200 cattle that remained in the wetland area were confiscated by the police force and park rangers (Lukonge 2021).

The government uses two main narratives to criminalise the use of the wetland by livestock herders. The first talks about protecting strategic national infrastructure for economic development. According to government authorities, the wetland is important because it contributes about 15% of the water requirement for power production in the Julius Nyerere Hydropower Project under construction on the Rufiji River as well as the Mtera and Kidatu dams located downstream (Lukonge 2021). The second narrative focuses on the seasonal drying of the river which is said to undermine (i) the Park's ecological integrity, (ii) conservation of Kilombero Ramsar site downstream, and (iii) the livelihoods of farmers who depend on river irrigation for rice production and livestock rearing (Lankford et al. 2004). Although the exact causes of the drying up remain contested (see Lankford et al. 2004; Mtahiko et al. 2006; Walsh 2012; England 2019), wetland degradation is mostly blamed on unregulated rice farming and the growth of human and livestock populations (Kashaigili et al. 2009; Kihwele et al. 2018). This narrative has been used by the government, international donors and conservation organisations like the World Wildlife Fund to develop projects for ensuring perennial flow in the river. In both narratives, the unregulated use of the wetland by livestock herders and rice farmers is criminalised and the state's use of militarised tactics and violence is justified to evict and displace them. It is, as Walwa (2020) points out, akin to 'licensed exclusion' by the government of the communities from their interests in the catchment.

Political Interests and WMAs

The need for development in rural communities has led to the promulgation of policies that address poverty along with conservation. This represents a turn in conservation policy where nature can 'pay its own way' by being conserved through capitalist market mechanisms in a win-win scenario such as the WMAs (Dressler et al. 2010; Green and Adams 2015).

Wildlife Management Areas in Tanzania were created in response to criticism of the PA 'fortress conservation' model and increasing advocacy for community-based conservation initiatives. The stated objective of WMAs is to achieve both conservation and livelihood improvements for communities that have set aside their village lands for conserving wildlife.

The Tanzanian government undertook several policy and legal reforms to implement the WMA approach. The 1998 Wildlife Policy of Tanzania (revised in 2007), the 2002 Wildlife Conservation (Wildlife Management Areas) regulations (revised 2005, 2012), and the 2009 Wildlife Conservation Act were reformed to include WMAs. The reforms recognise the important role of wildlife resources in contributing to economic growth and poverty alleviation through tourism and justify the need for the government to promote 'the development of village communities living in or close to wildlife and wetland areas... through facilitating the establishment of WMAs' (MNRT 2007: 27). These are conceptualised as areas for tourism investment where communities can enter into agreements with potential investors and economically benefit from these business ventures. WMAs are established through a declaration by the Minister of Natural Resources and Tourism which permits local communities to formally delineate and set aside village lands adjacent to core PAs for promoting conservation and generating consumptive and non-consumptive economic benefits through tourism (Nelson 2007; MNRT 2012; Kiwango et al. 2015). To date, about 38 WMAs have been created across the country, bordering National Parks and Game Reserves.

The Idodi-Pawaga WMA, commonly known as *Matumizi Bora ya Maliasili Idodi na Pawaga* (MBOMIPA, translated as Sustainable use of Natural Resources in Idodi-and Pawaga) is one of the PAs within the Rungwa-Ruaha ecosystem. It was one of the earliest pilot WMAs in the country, having benefited from funding and technical facilitation from an array of donors and conservation NGOs such as the former UK's Department for International Development, the World Wildlife Fund and the Wildlife Conservation Society. The MBOMIPA was modelled on the basis of experiences from other pilot areas in the Serengeti ecosystem and Selous Game Reserve in the 1980s and early 1990s. It consists of 21 villages spanning Idodi and Pawaga divisions in Iringa District. The WMA is located on the eastern side of the ecosystem, forming a buffer between the villages and the core PAs. It relies heavily on trophy or sport hunting to generate revenue which is shared between MBOMIPA (75%) and the government (25%) (MNRT 2012). However, as with the experiences of other WMAs (Igoe and Croucher, 2007), political interests have largely precluded the attainment of its objectives. Conflicts in revenue sharing, investment contracts and inadequate transparency and accountability have hampered the Idodi-Pawaga WMA's ability to operate profitably (Green 2016; Kiwango 2017). The significant losses in revenue prompted the Minister for Tourism and Natural Resources to dissolve the board in 2017 for its failure to deliver investment benefits from the WMA to local communities (TBC 2017).

WMAs represent the broader shift in government policies towards the neoliberal, market-driven approach to development and tackling poverty (Igoe and Croucher 2007). Conservation is viewed as part of business investment in wildlife tourism which can be promoted through partnership agreements between investors and local communities to maintain dedicated wildlife areas for economic benefit (Igoe and Brockington 2007). The WMAs thus operate on the same principles of the PA model which maintains a clear human/nature divide as the basis for conservation. Kiwango et al. (2015) regard WMAs as the fortress conservation approach in disguise, while Igoe and Croucher (2007) see the WMAs as a strategy of extending the core PAs by disciplining and excluding local communities from their own lands. Formo (2010) argues that despite being touted as community-based conservation alternatives to the PA approach, WMAs continue to function as instruments of power through which the economic and political interests of dominant conservation actors are consolidated. The economic benefits of the business partnership between investors and local communities promised by the MBOMIPA model have been largely elusive despite the expansion of total area under conservation in the form of protected migratory corridors, dispersal areas and buffer zones (Kiwango et al. 2015; Moyo et al. 2016). The driving market force in WMAs is the economic value of wildlife through the hunting system which creates rent-seeking opportunities for government officials (Benjaminsen et al. 2013; Humphries 2013). The WMAs have thus become the focus of power struggles as various officials and political elites seek ways to gain control over the substantial revenues generated from wildlife hunting and other related profitable activities (Humphries 2013).

The Role of International Tourism in Conservation

Tanzania's economy relies heavily on income from short-term visitations by international tourists. Tourism accounts for about 17.2% of the country's total GDP, a large component of which is from nature-based tourism (URT 2016). In 2018, out of 1,170,564 visitor arrivals in national parks, international visitors accounted for 62% of total visitation, while domestic arrivals accounted for 38% (MNRT 2018). About 12% of the total employed workforce in Tanzania is directly or indirectly employed by the tourism sector

(URT 2016). The government has progressively stepped up efforts to maximise tourism revenue and boost forex earnings. Its 2019-2025 target is to grow tourist numbers from 1.5 million to 5 million and tourism revenue from US$ 2.6 million to US$ 6 million (CCM 2020). Government agencies such as the Tanzanian Tourism Board and TANAPA are expected to play a major role in enhanced promotion of their 'tourism products' for both domestic and international tourists.

Tourism revenue is not only critically important for the national economy and development agendas, but the main source of financing for conservation. TANAPA, TAWA, and the WMAs rely on this revenue to operate and manage national parks, game reserves, game controlled areas and wildlife management areas for tourism and maintenance of related infrastructure. International tourists pay higher conservation fees per day to visit designated wildlife areas than domestic tourists. The differential pricing is aimed at encouraging domestic tourism by making park visitation affordable in line with local incomes. For example, an adult domestic visitor to RUNAPA pays US$ 2.16 as a conservation fee per day whereas an international visitor pays US$ 30 per day.[4] Despite reduced budget allocations by the government and declining support from international donors (Watson et al. 2014), TANAPA, and specifically RUNAPA is expected to primarily operate on a break-even basis with visitor income as the primary source of revenue. Hence there is greater pressure on TANAPA and other conservation agencies to attract and cater for the tastes of international visitors rather than domestic tourists.

The case of RUNAPA offers a clear illustration of the dilemmas faced by these agencies. Although the government has made allocations for the park in budget projections, it is expected to cover its entire operational expenses on a break-even basis with visitor income.[5] This has proved challenging for RUNAPA because it received roughly 2% of international tourists and about 3% of domestic tourists in 2018 (MNRT 2018). The low visitor numbers to the Park is due to its location in Tanzania's southern tourism circuit which has poor accessibility for international tourists compared with the northern tourism circuit. In addition, the Covid-19 pandemic drastically reduced international tourist visitations. As per the Central Bank of Tanzania data, foreign exchange earnings declined by 59.2% due to the drop in international arrivals from 1,527,230 to 616,491 for the year between December 2019-December 2020 (Ndalu 2021). The effects of this massive decline in foreign exchange earnings further complicates the possibility of RUNAPA operating on a break-even basis.

Discussion

The proponents of convivial conservation have highlighted the weaknesses of the 'half earth' and 'new conservation' proposals by demonstrating their continued reliance on the Protected Areas approach which uses a combination of capitalist market mechanisms and the regulatory power of state conservation agencies to maintain a strict separation between protected areas and local communities that live near them (Büscher and Fletcher 2019; 2020). While convivial conservation may be a welcome alternative to these proposals, it will prove challenging to implement its elements in a developing country context such as Tanzania.

First, although the suggestion to move from 'protected' to 'promoted areas' represents a radical shift in conservation thinking, it will need to confront the institutional path dependence of state agencies that have maintained the colonial era mentality towards local communities. The transformation to 'promoted' areas will need to be supported by all stakeholders, in particular the local communities that have largely borne the social and economic costs of PAs (West et al. 2006; Brockington and Wilkie 2015). Given the tensions between state conservation agencies and communities regarding natural resource use, livelihoods, conservation and management within and adjoining park areas, the process of creating 'promoted' areas may generate numerous disputes and conflicts.

As we have shown, the violent evictions of pastoralists from the Ihefu wetlands within the Rungwa-Ruaha ecosystem indicate the resolve of regional government administration and state conservation agencies to justify militarisation tactics by invoking narratives of national development, watershed and biodiversity protection. Indeed, the TANAPA has upped the ante for militarisation by transforming both their conservation and support staff into a full-fledged paramilitary system which is likely to have far-reaching consequences for conservation policy and practice (see Duffy et al. 2019).

Currently, about 40% of Tanzania's total area is under some form of protected status (URT 2015) and national parks represent the highest category of protected areas in Tanzania under the management of TANAPA. In addition, the Tanzanian government has committed to creating more PAs under the banner to protect biodiversity (Weldemichel 2020). It has established 6 national parks in areas previously categorised as game reserves. These include Nyerere National Park (occupying approximately two thirds of the former Selous Game Reserve), Ibanda-Kyerwa, Rumanyika-Karagwe, Burigi-Chato, Ugalla River, and Kigosi national parks. Although in 2019 the government degazetted a few conservation areas and recategorized them as village lands[6], it is likely to bring more areas under PA status and intensify its militarised approach as the pressure to address conservation issues mounts.

Second, the convivial conservation vision calls for 'radical ecological democracy' (Büscher and Fletcher 2019: 288), the strengthening of democratic engagement between human and non-human nature over technical expertise. While it is possible to consider the creation of WMAs as a preliminary step in this direction, the reality is that local democratic engagement and decision-making about the values of nature are already curtailed by state authorities who act in response to global market forces, national development agendas, and rent-seeking interests (Humphries 2013; Homewood et al. 2020). Hence, as with the MBOMIPA scheme in the Rungwa-Ruaha ecosystem context, the policy and practice underlying the WMA model reproduces the protectionist approach and its attendant power hierarchies and socio-ecological inequalities. The state's neoliberal market-driven approach which requires WMAs to generate revenue to cover operational costs, fund conservation activities[7] and local development initiatives makes it near impossible to promote any meaningful form of democratic engagement between all people and all nature. Although Büscher and Fletcher (2019) argue for renegotiating the value of nature beyond its 'capital' value, the combination of rent-seeking behaviour of local authorities, the control of WMA revenue by government technocrats, the poverty levels of local communities, and the prospect of economic profit from conservation as tourism enterprise make it difficult to look beyond the capital value of nature. Thus, despite being put forward as a community-oriented alternative to the PA approach, the WMA design and its reliance on partnerships with external investors for generating revenue from global tourism has been disappointing for local communities who bear the conservation costs.

Third, Büscher and Fletcher (2019) propose a more 'engaged' long term visitation that does not involve travelling long distances. This would encourage more democratic, long-term engagement and experience with non-human nature instead of short-term voyeuristic and commoditised tourism. However, as the preceding section illustrates, this approach cannot work in Tanzania and other global South countries which are heavily reliant on tourism revenue. While it may be possible to implement engaged visitation in global North countries, it is not possible to sustain conservation areas in Tanzania primarily from domestic tourism income. International tourism is a 'necessary evil' because foreign visitors pay a daily fee that is nearly 15 times more than what domestic tourists pay to visit PAs. The need for PAs such as RUNAPA to break even and contribute more revenue to the government coffers through tourism places a fresh impetus to expanding existing PAs and creating new ones. Although domestic tourists can potentially play a bigger role in long-term engagement with nature, attracting them is a greater challenge for national parks agencies due to remoteness, poor accessibility and affordable tourist infrastructure. It is only the relatively wealthy domestic elites who can afford long-term visits to these sites. Thus, conservation areas will continue to rely on short-term international voyeuristic tourists for the foreseeable future, at least in the global South context.

Finally, the proponents of convivial conservation advocate a *Conservation Basic Income* as a 'fully unconditional payment scheme able to cover recipient's needs' (Fletcher and Büscher 2020: 5). In this mechanism, all individuals of communities in a given geographical space adjacent to conservation areas should be equally entitled to an amount of not less than USD 5 a day for meeting their basic daily needs (Fletcher and Büscher 2020). Again, while this mechanism may be implementable in countries with well-established state welfare programs, it is unlikely to work in global South countries where there are high levels of economic disadvantage and issues of distributive justice and equity for welfare schemes. In the case of Tanzania, conservation agencies are unable to effectively fund their own operations and will be unwilling to set aside funds for payments of conservation basic income. In addition, the wildlife sector is already dominated by the political and economic interests of powerful actors who are likely to manipulate the mechanism to their advantage (see Humphries 2013; Kisingo and Kideghesho 2020). There is also no precedent to indicate whether such payments would encourage or discourage resource use by communities in conservation areas.

Conclusion

We agree with the proponents of convivial conservation that the 'half earth' and 'new conservation' proposals are more likely to exacerbate the biodiversity crisis than solve it. However, we have also shown that the convivial conservation approach they have outlined needs to be reframed to take into consideration institutional path dependencies, reliance on international tourism markets, and political interests which are embodied by the mainstream PA conservation paradigm. The three elements of the convivial conservation proposal, namely, 'promoted areas', 'radical ecological democracy' and 'engaged visitations', provide a good starting point for establishing socio-ecologically just alternative mechanisms to address the biodiversity crisis. But to make these elements implementable in countries like Tanzania, it is necessary to acknowledge that local communities experience the political, social, environmental, and economic costs and responsibilities of conservation in ways that are significantly different from those borne by communities in countries of the global North.

Based on our research and experience of conservation in Tanzania, we suggest four complementary ways to make the convivial conservation proposal more feasible for implementation in global South countries. The current debates regarding socio-ecological justice provide a useful way of introducing the idea of convivial conservation into the mainstream conservation paradigm without 'throwing the baby out with the bath water' (Büscher and Fletcher 2019: 4). These debates have highlighted the importance of articulating socio-ecological justice through the relational concepts of procedural, distributive, environmental, and recognition justice, which provide a framework for a systemic recognition of the rights and responsibilities of different stakeholders in conservation and benefits commensurate with the costs (Blaikie and Muldavin 2014; Gustavsson et al. 2014; Martin et al. 2016; Ruano-Chamorro et al. 2022). First, procedural justice entails how decisions are made, who participates and on which terms, across all institutional levels of conservation administration and management (Okereke and Charlesworth 2014; Martin et al. 2016). This will, for example, ensure that conservation areas such as the WMAs can be truly promoted by the relevant communities and their voices not overwhelmed by the interests of the state, its agencies, officials, investors, and international conservation technocrats. It will help reduce the violation of human rights and lack of trust that often prevails between local communities and state conservation agencies. Second, recognition justice entails giving respect for local knowledge and culture and embracing diverse understandings and perspectives on how to realise both conservation and development, (see Martin et al. 2016; Ruano-Chamorro et al. 2022; Mabele et al. 2022) instead of imposing ideas and cultures shaped by world views developed in the Global North (Gurney et al. 2021). Government and non-governmental conservation agencies and officials must recognise that local communities have a rich source of customs and traditions that have been integral for living with wildlife and part of managing the conservation landscape.

Third, distributive justice and equity requires conservation agencies to move beyond standardised blueprints and 'one size fits all' solutions and develop context specific strategies for implementing conservation and benefit sharing with local communities (Ostrom 2008). In the case of countries like Tanzania, this would involve deliberative processes between the national and regional government administrators, conservation agencies, and local communities for appropriate allocation of operating funds, tourism infrastructure improvements, and equitable distribution of economic development benefits. Finally, from the perspective of environmental justice, we propose a Community-based Conservation Insurance as a scheme to compensate any unforeseen risks, social costs, economic losses, or ecological degradation borne by local communities due to unintended consequences of maintaining PAs for wildlife tourism. This may be a more effective scheme than Fletcher and Büscher's (2020) conservation basic income, for protecting individuals and communities from the impoverishing effects of living in or around conservation areas, and possibly an alternative funding mechanism for a post-capitalist and convivial future for conservation in countries of the global South.

Notes

Chapter 2

1 https://conservationoptimism.org/.

2 See Harcourt and Nelson (2015), Bryant (2015) and Perrault et al (2015) for some recent, inspiring volumes highlighting political ecology scholarship.

3 https://entitleblog.org/2017/02/02/the-trump-moment-in-environmental-conservation/.

4 https://global.nature.org/content/environment2017 (accessed November 10, 2018).

5 We realise that we do not have the space here to give extensive evidence for this, and many other claims. We base them on our book, where we do provide extensive evidence for the claims made with respect to the different positions.

6 To a degree, it could be argued that this process had already started in the 1970s with the then radical critique of protected areas and top-down, colonial conservation. However, this process that led to manifold forms of community-based conservation was effectively cut short by a neoprotectionist revival and neoliberal restructuring.

7 We are not arguing here that 'protection' is *only* negative, as obviously protecting that which we love or care about is not something negative; our reason for moving away from the term 'protected areas' is a deliberate *political* move within the context of the political economic history and present of conservation.

8 https://www.iccaconsortium.org/; https://www.forestpeoples.org/en (accessed November 12, 2018).

9 This also does not mean that population (growth) is not important and should not be addressed. Yet, we believe, the only way to respectfully address the issue is by doing so in its multiple political economic and historical contexts, with a special emphasis on the historical colonial burden still deeply affecting non-western societies and people (Dawson 2016).

10 Obviously, desired natures, species or ecosystem traits are also protected from other, non-desired natures, species or ecosystem traits.

11 One of the main current empirical manifestations of this is the BBC's Planet Earth series which are, interestingly, criticised on exactly this point. See: https://www.theguardian.com/commentisfree/2017/jan/01/bbc-planet-earth-not-help-natural-world (accessed January 2, 2017).

12 See Harvey (2000: 263) for a proposal on how to organise power and livelihoods across scale in a postcapitalist society.

13 Key micropolitical practices to promote include the key degrowth proposals detailed earlier: truly 'green' production; elimination of perverse subsidies for unsustainable production; augmenting and redirection of public spending to support green production and community-based conservation; taxing CO_2 and financial transactions to generate the finance needed to do this; defusing competitive pressure; slowing down international trade; reducing advertising; promoting alternative cosmological visions and values; myriad household changes in terms of consumption, energy use, building materials, and so forth.

14 Crucially, this categorisation (in table 5) is meant as a heuristic, not to provide an adequate reflection of empirical reality in actual places.

15 Basic income grants can be structured in various ways, not all of them progressive. The key is to combine CBI with the other elements of convivial conservation to ensure that it functions as a transformative form of resource redistribution rather than a bulwark of the current social order (Fletcher and Büscher 2020).

16 See for example this recent pamphlet: https://d3n8a8pro7vhmx.cloudfront. net/rainforestactionnetwork/pages/17702/attachments/original/1497287352/ RAN_Every_Investor_Has_A_Responsibility_June_2017.pdf?1497287352 (accessed February 25, 2018).

Chapter 3

1 We hereby use 'southern Africa' to refer to the region comprising the sixteen member-states of the Southern African Development Community (SADC). See: https://www.sadc.int/member-states/.

2 Brockington et al. (2008: 9–10) describe mainstream conservation as the globally dominant mode of conservation in terms of ideology, resources, and practice. Its network building prioritises the interests of western and/or urban elites and businesses, while aiming to implement conservation strategies rooted in particularly the American conservation movement, such as strict protected areas.

3 With other linguistic variants values such as *Botho/Matho* in Sesotho, *Hunhu* in Shona, *Umuntu* in Bemba and *Vhuntu* in Venda, *Ubuntu* represents culturally contextualised environmental ethics in southern African societies (Gwaravanda 2019).

4 We acknowledge linkages to environmental justice, as our paper looks at similar dynamics common in the environmental justice literature. However, we do not delve into explicit linkages between environmental justice, convivial conservation, and *Ubuntu*, as this is beyond the paper's focus.

Chapter 5

1 For more discussion of the kindred concept of environmental justice, please see e.g. Martin et al. (2020) and Menton et al. (2020).

2 The aim is not to offer immediately implementable alternative indicators, since this would go against the participatory processes I highlight as important to drive alternative, social-equity-based notions informing funding and notions of progress. See Zafra-Calvo et al. (2017) for social-equity indicators in conservation and Hidalgo-Capitán et al. (2019), for the alternative 'Good Living Goals'). I acknowledge that my article stops short of using empirical material, like other decolonization literature. I hope to add to this discussion through empirically-based material in future.

3 I use the terms Global South, and Global North, cognizant that they lump together non-monolithic backgrounds with very diverse historical and contemporary experiences of conservation and justice. They need to be problematized so as not to exacerbate unhelpful binaries or to ignore context specificities and 'Norths within the South/Souths within the North' (cf. e.g. Dirlik 2007; Wa Ngugi 2012). I nevertheless use the terms to center the South and the Global South's experiences, given conservation's diverse implications – especially for lives and livelihoods in Southern contexts.

4 Anishinaabe author Gerald Vizenor defines 'survivance' as 'more than survival, more than endurance or mere response... survivance is an active repudiation of dominance, tragedy, and victimry' (Vizenor 1998: 15).

5 These principles can only be offered as starting points. To support a pluriversal approach, i.e. building a world in which many worlds fit (cf. Conway and Singh 2011; Demaria and Kothari 2017; Escobar 2011), these ideas are not meant to be prescriptive, but are to begin a conversation which avoids the risk of replacing one set of external agendas with another (Kothari 2021), a key concern for all decolonizing debates. Crucially, these conversations must bring together voices which have long been under-heard, i.e. Indigenous Peoples and local communities, women and marginalized voices including those of people with disabilities, in a way that respects non-Western knowledges and individuals. At the same time, reaching social agreements which respect the interdependencies of people, environment and future generations. Devising such a conversation process in itself will be challenging, as would implementing the outcomes.

Chapter 6

1 As a result, humans can reside only in 263 sq. km of land across four islands of the archipelago. This area amounts to 3% of the islands, or 0.2 of the entire archipelago, including its marine reserve. The centrality of the people-less, or

rather resident-less, element in conservation has continued despite the fact that the Galápagos have been a province of Ecuador since 1974, and currently 30,000 Ecuadorians live there. As late as 2002, conservation's ultimate goal was indeed to restore the islands to their condition before humans arrived there in 1532 (Bensted-Smith 2002).

Chapter 8

1 This constitutes the first part of a larger research project, involving case studies of three areas at different states of coexistence with wolves in Spain; see Pettersson et al. 2021.

2 https://www.lavalakelamb.com/lava-lake-story/conservation/

3 https://www.decadeonrestoration.org/

4 Phrased about wolves by Theodore Roosevelt in 'Hunting the Grisly and Other Sketches' in 1902.

5 See http://www.grupocampogrande.org/.

Chapter 9

1 While the research required no formal ethical review and clearance, potentially vulnerable groups such as these were protected through adherence to conventional ethical guidelines for ethnographic field research (see eg. http://www.aaanet.org/issues/policy-advocacy/upload/AAA-Ethics-Code-2009.pdf (accessed October 12, 2018).

2 European Commission Report, 2017: http://ec.europa.eu/environment/eir/pdf/factsheet_bg_bg.pdf (accessed March 22, 2018).

3 Traditional Bulgarian spirit made of grapes or plums.

4 http://roditel.bg/mechkata-i-loshata-duma-balgarska-narodna-prikazka (accessed October 12, 2018).

5 The saint, according to the religious narratives, managed to tame and defeat a bear, being able to control, in this way, the wilderness and uncultivated nature.

6 https://www.exodus.co.uk/responsible-travel (accessed October 17, 2018).

7 http://wildrodopi.org/wild-rodopi-mission (accessed November 12, 2018).

8 https://www.exodus.co.uk/bulgaria-holidays/wildlife/bulgaria-realm-brown-bear/wbb (accessed October, 2018).

Chapter 10

1 Following Haraway (2008), Hurn (2012), and Van Dooren and Rose (2016) we employ the terms non-humans and more-than-humans interchangeably to

refer to other (than human) subjectivities, such as plants, animals, rivers and mountains. With these terms we do not intend to emphasise the human and non-human binary we criticise. The terms are used both to align with commonly used terms in this field and to build our argument towards more-than-human participation in convivial conservation.

Chapter 12

1 https://www.opendemocracy.net/neweconomics/universal-basic-income-is-a-neoliberal-plot-to-make-you-poorer/ (accessed November 11, 2017).

2 https://www.iccaconsortium.org/ (accessed January 15, 2019).

3 https://neweconomics.org/2019/04/universal-basic-income-new-study-finds-little-evidence-that-it-can-live-up-to-its-promise (accessed June 28, 2019).

Chapter 13

1 Castes identified in one of the Schedules of the Indian Constitution for affirmative action; SCs continue to face enormous social stigma and oppression in the society.

Chapter 15

1 According to the Tanzanian Wildlife conservation Act no 5 of 2009, Consumptive use means the taking of flora or the hunting or capturing of fauna, while non-consumptive use means the use of scenery, cultural and natural resources that does not involve taking any specimen from the PA, photographic tourism, walking safaris, hiking, canoeing, boating, scuba diving, mountaineering and any other similar or related activity.

2 Government Notice (GN) number 464 (9500Km²). In 1974, 800Km² from south eastern part were added to the park (total 10,300Km²). GN number 28 of 2008 annexed the former Usangu Game reserve to RUNAPA, bringing the total area to 20,226Km². Sources: https://www.nemc.or.tz/uploads/publications/sw-1646119411-BROCHURE%20-%20THE%20ARUSHA%20MANIFESTO%202.pdf, RUNAPA park reports.

3 ITV news, 9th January 2021. The statement by the Regional Commissioner can be accessed here: https://www.youtube.com/watch?v=MRM5y1eEL4M (accessed February 26, 2021).

4 These tariffs are for the period 1st August 2020 to 30th June 2021, and are tax exclusive. The tariffs differ from one park to the other. They can be accessed here https://www.tanzaniaparks.go.tz/uploads/publications/en-1598856303-2020_2021%20TARIFFS%20Final%202%2011th%20August%202020.pdf.

5 The projected budget for RUNAPA in 2021 was US$ 4.3 million per year (about 10

billion Tanzanian shillings based on the exchange rate of 1USD = 2,310 Tanzanian Shillings). Other parks have their own break even targets. The requirement to break even was directed by the Minister for Natural Resources and Tourism to national park authorities in attempt to reach the national target of 6 million USD by 2025.

6 See for example https://therevelator.org/tanzania-farmers-livestock/. About 12 conserved areas have been degazetted totaling 707.6 acres. Further, 920 villages have been allowed to remain in the previous areas recognized as protected. More information can be found at https://habarileo.co.tz/habari/2019-09-235d89149d33ab2.aspx.

7 For example, the Wildlife Conservation (Wildlife Management Areas) (Amendment) Regulations, 2019 establishes the Community Wildlife Management Areas Trust Fund. The WMAs are required to contribute 5% of their annual gross income to the fund to be used for facilitation of various WMA activities by the WMA consortium.

References

Aastrup, M.L. (2020). Conservation narratives and conflicts over protected areas in post-socialist Romania. *Journal of Political Ecology* 27(1): 84–104.

Abade, L., J. Cusack, R.J. Moll et al. (2020). The relative effects of prey availability, anthropogenic pressure and environmental variables on lion (Panthera leo) site use in Tanzania's Ruaha landscape during the dry season. *Journal of Zoology* 310(2): 135-144.

Abade, L., D.W. Macdonald, and A.J. Dickman. (2014). Assessing the relative importance of landscape and husbandry factors in determining large carnivore depredation risk in Tanzania's Ruaha landscape. *Biological Conservation* 180: 241-248.

Abram, D. (2010). *Becoming animal: An earthly cosmology.* Toronto: Pantheon Books.

Achiba, G.A. (2019). Navigating contested winds: Development visions and anti-politics of wind energy in northern Kenya. *Land* 8(1): 7.

Adams, M. (2005). Beyond Yellowstone? Conservation and Indigenous rights in Australia and Sweden. Pp. 127-138 in *Discourses and silences: Indigenous peoples, risks and resistance*, G. Cant, A. Goodall, and J. Inns (eds.). Christchurch: Department of Geography, University of Canterbury, New Zealand.

Adams, W.M. (2003). Nature and the colonial mind. Pp. 16-50 in *Decolonizing nature: Strategies for conservation in a post-colonial era*, W.M. Adams and M. Mulligan (eds.). London: Earthscan.

Adams, W.M. (2013). *Against extinction: The story of conservation.* Oxfordshire: Earthscan.

Adams, W.M. (2015). The political ecology of conservation conflicts. Pp. 64-78 in *Conflicts in conservation*, S.M. Redpath, et al. (eds.). Cambridge: Cambridge University Press.

Adams, W.M. (2020). Geographies of conservation III: Nature's spaces. *Progress in Human Geography* 44(4): 789-801.

Adams, W.M., and M. Mulligan. (2003). *Decolonizing nature: Strategies for conservation in a post-colonial era.* London: Earthscan.

Adeyeye, Y., S. Hagerman, and R. Pelai. (2019). Seeking procedural equity in global environmental governance: Indigenous participation and knowledge politics in forest and landscape restoration debates at the 2016 World Conservation Congress. *Forest Policy and Economics* 109: 102006.

Aerts, S., B. Bovenkerk, and S. Brando. (2016). A philosophical and technical critique of zooanthropology as a moral and practical paradigm. Pp. 65-81 in *Food futures: Ethics, science and culture*, I. Olsson, S. Araújo, and M. F. Vieira (eds.). Wageningen, the Netherlands: Wageningen Academic Publishers.

African Parks. (2018). Mutware, Akagera's most well-known elephant, has died of natural causes at the ripe old age of 48. *African Parks News* (blog), October 2. Online at: https://www.africanparks.org/mutware-dies-natural-causes-ripe-old-age#:~:text=Mutware%2C%20Akagera's%20most%20well%2Dknown%20elephant%2C%20has%20died%20of,the%20wild%20landscapes%20of%20Rwanda (accessed February 13, 2021).

African Parks. (2021a). Community Involvement. *Akagera National Park, Rwanda* (blog). Online at: https://www.africanparks.org/the-parks/akagera/community-involvement (accessed January 7, 2021).

African Parks. (2021b). Poaching is at an all time low thanks to akagera's law enforcement efforts. Organization. *Law Enforcement* (blog). Online at: https://www.africanparks.org/the-parks/akagera/law-enforcement (accessed July 27, 2021).

Agarwal, B. (1997). Environmental action, gender equity and women's participation. *Development and Change* 28: 1-44.

Agarwal, B. (2001). Participatory exclusions, community forestry, and gender: An analysis for South Asia and a conceptual framework. *World Development* 29(10): 1623–1648.

Agarwal, B. (2009). Gender and forest conservation: The impact of women's participation in community forest governance. *Ecological Economics* 68(2009): 2785–2799.

Agrawal, A. (1995). Dismantling the divide between Indigenous and scientific knowledge. *Development and Change* 26: 413-439.

Agrawal, A., and C. Gibson. (1999). Enchantment and disenchantment: The role of community in natural resource conservation. *World Development* 27(4): 629-649.

Agrawal, A. et al. 2021. Open Letter to Waldron et al. Online at: https://openlettertowaldronetal.wordpress.com (accessed February 19, 2021).

Ahebwa, W.M. (2012). *Tourism, livelihoods and biodiversity conservation: An assessment of tourism related policy interventions at Bwindi Impenetrable National Park (BINP), Uganda.* Ph.D. Thesis, Wageningen University, The Netherlands.

Ahebwa, W.M., R. van der Duim, and C. Sandbrook. (2012). Tourism revenue sharing policy at Bwindi Impenetrable National Park, Uganda: A policy arrangements approach. *Journal of Sustainable Tourism* 20(3): 377–394.

Aiyadurai, A. 2018. The multiple meanings of nature conservation: Insights from Dibang Valley, Arunachal Pradesh. *Economic and Political Weekly* 53(39): 37-44.

Albó, X. (2011). Suma qamaña = convivir bien. ¿Cómo medirlo? Pp. 133-144 in *Vivir bien: ¿Paradigma no capitalista?*, I.H. Farah and L. Vasapollo (eds.). La Paz: CIDES-UMSA.

Albó, X. (2019). *Suma Qamaña* or Living well together: a contribution to biocultural conservation. Pp. 333-342 in *From biocultural homogenization to biocultural conservation*, R. Rozzi, R. May Jr., F. Chapin III, F. Massardo, M. Gavin, I. Klaver, A. Pauchard, et al. (eds.). Cham: Springer.

Alix-Garcia, J., A.D. Janvry, E. Sadoulet, and J. Manuel. (2009). Lessons learned from Mexico's payment for environmental services program. Pp. 163-188 in *Payment for environmental services in agricultural landscapes*, L. Lipper (ed.). New York: Springer.

Alix-Garcia J., C. McIntosh, K.R. Sims, and J.R. Welch. (2013). The ecological footprint of poverty alleviation: Evidence from Mexico's Oportunidades Program. *Review of Economics and Statistics* 95: 417-435.

Alphandéry, C., G. Ancel, A.M. Araujo, C. Attias-Donfut, G. Azam, A. Belkaid, Y. Moulier-Boutang, et al. (2013). *Manifeste convivialiste: Déclaration d'interdépendance*. Paris: Le Bord de L'Eau.

Alphandéry, C., G. Ancel, A.M. Araujo, C. Attias-Donfut, G. Azam, A. Belkaid, F. Brugère, et al. (2020). *Second manifeste convivialiste: Pour un monde post-néoliberal*. Paris: Actes Sud.

Álvares, F., J. Domingues, P. Sierra, and P. Primavera, et al. (2011). Cultural dimension of wolves in the Iberian peninsula: Implications of ethnozoology in conservation biology. *Innovation: The European Journal of Social Science Research* 24(3): 313–331.

Álvarez, L., and B. Coolsaet. (2020). Decolonizing environmental justice studies: A Latin American perspective. *Capitalism Nature Socialism* 31(2): 50-69.

Amaja, L.G., D.H. Feyssa, and T.M. Gutema. (2016). Assessment of types of damage and causes of human-wildlife conflict in Gera district, south western Ethiopia. *Journal of Ecology and the Natural Environment* 8(5):49-54.

Amir, A.P.H. (2019). Who knows what about gorillas? Indigenous knowledge, global justice, and human-gorilla relations. *Other Ways of Knowing* 5: 1–40.

Amit, R., and S.K. Jacobson. (2017). Understanding rancher coexistence with jaguars and pumas: a typology for conservation practice. *Biodiversity and Conservation* 26(6):1353-1374.

Ampumuza, C., and C. Driessen. (2021). Gorilla habituation and the role of animal agency in conservation and tourism development at Bwindi, South Western Uganda. *Environment and Planning E: Nature and Space* 4(4): 1601-1621.

Ampumuza, C., M. Duineveld, and R. van der Duim. (2020). The most marginalized people in Uganda? Alternative realities of Batwa at Bwindi Impenetrable National Park. *World Development Perspectives* 20: 100267.

Anadón, J.D., A. Giménez, R. Ballestaret, and I. Pérezal. (2009). Evaluation of local ecological knowledge as a method for collecting extensive data on animal abundance. *Conservation Biology* 23(3): 617–625.

Angelsen A. (2017). REDD+ as result-based aid: General lessons and bilateral agreements of Norway. *Review of Development Economics* 21: 237-264.

Arsel, M., and B. Büscher. (2012). Nature™ Inc.: Changes and continuities in neoliberal conservation and market-based environmental policy. *Development and Change* 43(1):53-78.

Asiyanbi, A. (2019). Decolonising the environment: Race, rationalities and crises. *Sheffield Institute for International Development* blog, August 7. Online at: http://siid.group.shef.ac.uk/blog/decolonising-the-environment-race-rationalities-and-crises/ (accessed August 21, 2020).

Asiyanbi, A., and J.F. Lund. (2020). Policy persistence: REDD+ between stabilization and contestation. *Journal of Political Ecology* 27(1): 378-400.

Atasay, E., and G.N. Bourassa. (2013). Illich Beyond Illich: Convivial tools for Illichean readings. A Rejoinder to UCLA's 2003 Roundtable on Illich. *International Journal of Illich Studies* 3(2): 75-79.

Atkinson, R., M.R. Gardener, G. Harper, and V. Carrion. (2012). Fifty years of eradication as a conservation tool in Galápagos: What are the limits. Pp. 183-198 in *The role of science for conservation*, M. Wolff and M. Gardener (eds.). Oxon: Routledge.

Badola, R., S.A. Hussain, B.K. Mishra, B. Konthoujam, S. Thapliyal, and P.M. Dhakate. (2010). An assessment ecosystem services of Corbett Tiger Reserve, India. *The Environmentalist* 30: 320–329.

Baker, J., and P. Brinckerhoff. (2015). *Research to policy: Building capacity for conservation through poverty alleviation.* Final Project Workshop, 19 to 21 January on *Enhancing Equity within conservation: Bwindi Impenetrable National Park.* London.

Baker, J., E.J. Milner-Gulland, and N. Leader-Williams. (2012). Park gazettement and integrated conservation and development as factors in community conflict at Bwindi Impenetrable Forest, Uganda. *Conservation Biology* 26(1): 160–170.

Bakkegaard, R.Y., and S. Wunder. (2014). Bolsa Floresta, Brazil. Pp. 41-57 in *REDD+ on the ground*, CIFOR (eds.). Bogor, Indonesia: CIFOR.

Bariyanga, J.D., T. Wronski, M. Plath, and A. Apio. (2016). Effectiveness of electro-fencing for restricting the ranging behaviour of wildlife: A case study in the degazetted parts of Akagera National Park. *African Zoology* 51(4): 183–91.

Barkin, D. (2019). Conviviality. Pp. 136-139 in *Pluriverse: A post-development dictionary*, A. Kothari, A. Salleh, A. Escobar, F. Demaria, and A. Acosta (eds.). London: Tulika Books.

Barragan-Paladines, M.J., and R. Chuenpagdee. (2017). A step zero analysis of the Galápagos Marine Reserve. *Coastal Management* 45(5): 339–359.

Barrett, M.J., M. Harmin, B. Maracle, M. Patterson, C. Thomson, M. Flowers, and K. Bors. (2017). Shifting relations with the more- than-human: Six threshold concepts for transformative sustainability learning. *Environmental Education Research* 23(1): 131–143.

Barua, M. (2014). Circulating elephants: Unpacking the geographies of a cosmopolitan animal. *Transactions of the Institute of British Geographers* 39(4): 559–573.

Barua, M., S.A. Bhagwat, and S. Jadhav. (2013). The hidden dimensions of human-wildlife conflict: Health impacts, opportunity and transaction costs. *Biological Conservation* 157: 309–16.

Bastagli, F., J. Hagen-Zanker, L. Harman, V. Barca, G. Sturge, T. Schmidt, and L. Pellerano. (2016). *Cash transfers: What does the evidence say?* London: Overseas Development Institute.

Bastian, M., O. Jones, N. Moore, and E. Roe. (2016). *Participatory research in more-than-human worlds*. London: Taylor & Francis.

Bastmeijer, K. (2016). *Wilderness protection in Europe*. Cambridge: Cambridge University Press.

Bauman, Z. (2013). *Liquid love: On the frailty of human bonds*. London: Polity.

Baviskar, A. (2001). Forest management ass political practice: Indian experiences with the accommodation of multiple interests. *International Journal of Agricultural Resources, Governance and Ecology* 1(3/4): 243–263.

Baviskar, A. (2004). *In the belly of the river: Tribal conflicts over development in the Narmada Valley.* 2nd edition. Oxford: Oxford University Press.

Bax, P. (2019). Africa's biggest conservation success was once a poachers' paradise. *Bloomberg*, January 7. Online at: https://www.bloomberg.com/news/articles/2019-01-07/africa-s-biggest-conservation-success-was-once-a-poachers-paradise (accessed January 6, 2021).

Bekoff, M. (2015). Rewilding our hearts: Making a personal commitment to animals and their homes. Pp. 144-153 in *Protecting the Wild*, G. Wuerthner, E. Crist, and T. Butler (eds.). Washington, DC: Island Press.

Benhassine, N, F. Devoto, E. Duflo, P. Dupas, and V. Pouliquen. (2015). Turning a shove into a nudge? A 'labeled cash transfer' for education. *American Economic Journal: Economic Policy* 7: 86–125.

Benjaminsen, T.A., M.J. Goldman, M.Y. Minwary, and F.P. Maganga. (2013). Wildlife management in Tanzania: State control, rent seeking and community resistance. *Development and Change* 44(5): 1087–1109.

Bennett, E.M., M. Solan, R. Biggs, T. McPhearson, A.V. Norström, P. Olsson, L. Pereira, G.D. Peterson, C. Raudsepp-Hearne, F. Biermann, and S.R. Carpenter. (2015). Bright spots: Seeds of a good Anthropocene. *Frontiers in Ecology and the Environment* 14(8): 441–448.

Bennett, J. (2010). *Vibrant matter.* Durham, NC: Duke University Press.

Bennett, N.J., R. Roth, S.C. Klain, K. Chan, P. Christie, D.A. Clark, G. Cullman, D. Curran, T.J. Durbin, G. Epstein, and A. Greenberg. (2017). Conservation social science: Understanding and integrating human dimensions to improve conservation. *Biological Conservation* 205: 93–108.

Bensted-Smith, R. (2002). *A biodiversity vision for the Galápagos islands.* A Report for the Charles Darwin Foundation and WWF. Puerto Ayora, Galápagos, Ecuador: Charles Darwin Foundation.

Berberoglu, B. (ed.). 2018. *The Palgrave handbook of social movements, revolution, and social transformation.* Cham: Palgrave.

Berkes, F. (2004). Rethinking community-based conservation. *Conservation Biology* 18(3): 621–630.

Berkes, F. (2007). Community-based conservation in a globalized world. *Proceedings of the National Academy of Sciences* 104(39): 15188-15193.

Berkes, F. (2008). *Sacred ecology: Traditional ecological knowledge and resource management.* 2nd edition. London: Routledge.

Berkes, F. (2021). *Advanced introduction to community-based conservation.* Cheltenham: Edward Elgar Publishing.

Berkes, F., J. Colding, and C. Folke. (2000). Rediscovery of traditional ecological knowledge as adaptive management. *Ecological Applications* 10(5): 1251–126.

Bernard, H.R. (2011). *Research methods in anthropology: Qualitative and quantitative approaches.* 4th edition. Berkeley, CA: Altamira Press.

Bhambra, G.K., K. Nişancioğlu, and D. Gebrial (eds.) (2018). *Decolonising the university.* London: Pluto Press.

Biggs, R., M. Schlüter, and M.L. Schoon. (2015). *Principles for building resilience: Sustaining ecosystem services in social-ecological systems.* Cambridge: Cambridge University Press.

Bishop, J., and S. Pagiola (eds.). (2012). *Selling forest environmental services: Market-based mechanisms for conservation and development.* Oxfordshire: Taylor & Francis.

Blackstone, A. (2012). *Sociological inquiry principles: Qualitative and quantitative methods.* Irvington, NY: Flat World Knowledge.

Blaikie, N. (2007). *Approaches to social enquiry: Advancing knowledge*: London: Polity.

Blaikie, P., and J. Muldavin. (2014). Environmental justice? The story of two projects. *Geoforum* 54: 226-229.

Blanco, J.C. (2017). Wolf management in Spain: Scientific debates on wolf hunting. *Arbor* 193(786): a418. https://doi.org/10.3989/arbor.2017.786n4007.

Blanco, J.C., and Y. Cortés. (2009). Ecological and social constraints of Wolf recovery in Spain. Pp. 41-66 in *A new era for wolves and people: Wolf recovery, human attitudes, and policy*, M. Muisani, L. Boitani, and P. Paquet (eds.). Calgary: University of Calgary Press.

Blomley, T. (2003). Natural resource conflict management: The case of Bwindi Impenetrable and Mgahinga Gorilla National Parks, southwestern Uganda. Pp. 231–250 in *Natural resource conflict management case studies: An analysis of power, participation and protected areas*, P. Castro and E. Nielsen (eds.). Rome: Food and Agriculture Organization of the United Nations.

Blythe, J., J. Silver, L. Evans, D. Armitage, N.J. Bennett, M-L. Moore, T.H. Morrison, and K. Brown. (2018). The dark side of transformation: Latent risks in contemporary sustainability discourse. *Antipode* 50(5): 1206-1223.

Bocci, P. (2017). Tangles of care: Killing goats to save tortoises on the Galápagos islands. *Cultural Anthropology* 32(3): 424–449.

Bocci, P. (2019a). Planting the seeds of the future: Eschatological environmentalism in the time of the Anthropocene. *Religions* 10(2): 125.

Bocci, P. (2019b). Utopian conservation: Scientific humanism, evolution, and island imaginaries on the Galápagos islands. *Science, Technology, & Human Values* (45)6: 1168-1194.

Bock, B.B. (2012). Social innovation and sustainability: How to disentangle the buzzword and its application in the field of agriculture and rural development. *Studies in Agricultural Economics* 114(2): 57-63.

Boitani, L., and J.D.C. Linnell. (2015). Bringing large mammals back: Large carnivores in Europe. Pp. 127–142 in *Rewilding European landscapes*, H.M. Pereira and L.M. Navarro (eds.). Heidelberg: Springer, Cham.

Boonman-Berson, S., C. Driessen, and E. Turnhout. (2019). Managing wild minds: From control by numbers to a multinatural approach in wild boar management in the Veluwe, the Netherlands. *Transactions of the Institute of British Geographers* 44(1): 2-15.

Boonman-Berson, S., E. Turnhout, and M. Carolan. (2016). Common sensing: Human-black bear cohabitation practices in Colorado. *Geoforum* 74: 192-201.

Borgerhoff Mulder, M., and P. Coppolillo. (2005). *Conservation*. Princeton, NJ: Princeton University Press.

Börner, J., K. Baylis, E. Corbera, D. Ezzine-de-Blas, J. Honey-Rosés, U.M. Persson, and S. Wunder. (2017). The effectiveness of payments for environmental services. *World Development* 96: 359-374.

Borrini-Feyerabend, G., and J. Campese. (2017). *Self-strengthening ICCAs: Guidance on a process and resources for custodian indigenous peoples and local communities - draft for use by GSI partners.* Geneva: The ICCA Consortium.

Borrini-Feyerabend, G., and R. Hill. (2015). Governance of the conservation of nature. Pp 169-206 in *Protected areas governance and management*, G.L. Worboys, M. Lockwood, A. Kothari, S. Feary and I. Pulsford (eds.). Canberra: ANU Press.

Borrini-Feyerabend, G., A. Kothari, and G. Oviedo. (2004). *Indigenous and local communities and protected areas.* WPCA Best Practice Protected Area Guidelines Series No. 11. Gland and Cambridge: IUCN/WCPA.

Borrini-Feyerabend, G., B. Lassen, S. Stevens, G. Martin, J.C. Riascos de la Peña, E.F. Ráez-Luna, and M. Taghi Farvar. (2012). *Bio-cultural diversity conserved by indigenous peoples and local communities: Examples and analysis.* Tehran: Cenesta for the ICCA Consortium, IUCN, UNDP GEF SGP and GIZ on behalf of BMZ.

Bose, P., B. Arts, and H. van Dijk. (2012). 'Forest governmentality': A genealogy of subject-making of forest dependent 'scheduled tribes' in India. *Land Use Policy* 29: 664–673.

Brackhane, S., G. Webb, F.M. Xavier, J. Trindade, M. Gusmao, and P. Pechacek. (2019). Crocodile management in Timor-Leste: Drawing upon traditional ecological knowledge and cultural beliefs. *Human Dimensions of Wildlife* 24(4): 314–31.

Braidotti, R. (2013). *The posthuman.* Cambridge: Polity Press.

Bravo, G., and T. De Moor. (2008). The commons in Europe: From past to future. *International Journal of the Commons* 2(2): 155–161.

Brenner, N., J. Peck, and N. Theodore. (2010). After neoliberalization? *Globalizations* 7: 327–345.

Bridgewater, P., and I.D. Rotherham. (2019). A critical perspective on the concept of biocultural diversity and its emerging role in nature and heritage conservation. *People and Nature* 1(3): 291–304.

Brockington, D. (2002). *Fortress conservation: The preservation of the Mkomazi Game Reserve, Tanzania.* Oxford: James Curry.

Brockington, D., E. Corbera Elizalde, and S. Maestre Andrés (2021). The challenges of decolonizing conservation. Special section of *Journal of Political Ecology* 28(1).

Brockington, D., and R. Duffy. (2010). Conservation and capitalism: An introduction. *Antipode* 42(3): 469–484.

Brockington, D., and R. Duffy. (2011). *Capitalism and conservation.* New York, NY: John Wiley & Sons.

Brockington, D., R. Duffy, and J. Igoe. (2008). *Nature unbound: Conservation, capitalism and the Future of Protected Areas.* London: Earthscan.

Brockington, D., and J. Igoe. (2006). Eviction for conservation: A global overview. *Conservation and Society* 4(3): 424–70.

Brockington, D., and D. Wilkie. (2015). Protected areas and poverty. *Philosophical Transactions of the Royal Society B: Biological Sciences 370*(1681): 20140271.

Brondizio, S., J. Settele, S. Díaz, and H.T. Ngo (eds.). (2019). *Global assessment report on biodiversity and ecosystem services of the Intergovernmental Science-Policy Platform on Biodiversity and Ecosystem Services.* Bonn: IPBES secretariat.

Broome, N.P., N.D. Rai, and M. Tatpati. (2017). Biodiversity conservation and Forest Rights Act. *Economic and Political Weekly* 52(25-26): 51-54.

Brown, K., and R. Dilley. (2012). Ways of knowing for 'response-ability' in more-than-human encounters: The role of anticipatory knowledges in outdoor access with dogs. *Area* 44(1): 37-45.

Brown, T. (2016). Sustainability as empty signifier: Its rise, fall, and radical potential. *Antipode* 48(1): 115-133.

Bruskotter, J.T., J.A. Vucetich, M.J. Manfredo, G.R. Karns, C. Wolf, K. Ard, N.H. Carter, J.V. López-Bao, G. Chapron, S.D. Gehrt, and W.J. Ripple. (2017). Modernization, risk, and conservation of the world's largest carnivores. *BioScience* 67(7): 646–655.

Bryant, R. (ed.). (2015). *The international handbook of political ecology*. Cheltenham: Edward Elgar.

Buller, H. (2015). Animal geographies II: Methods. *Progress in Human Geography* 39(3): 374–384.

Bunn, D. (2003). An unnatural state: Tourism, water and wildlife photography in the early Kruger National Park. Pp. 199–220 in *Social history and African environments*, W. Beinart and J. McGregor (eds.). Oxford: James Currey.

Büscher, B. (2016a). 'Rhino poaching is out of control!' Violence, race and the politics of hysteria in online conservation. *Environment and Planning A* 48(5): 979–998.

Büscher, B. (2016b). Reassessing fortress conservation? New media and the politics of distinction in Kruger National Park. *Annals of the American Association of Geographers* 106(1): 114–129.

Büscher, B., W. Dressler, and R. Fletcher (eds). (2014). *Nature^{TM} Inc.: Environmental conservation in the neoliberal age*. Tucson, AZ: University of Arizona Press.

Büscher, B., and R. Fletcher. (2015). Accumulation by conservation. *New Political Economy* 20: 273-298.

Büscher, B., and R. Fletcher. (2019). Towards convivial conservation. *Conservation and Society* 17(3): 283-296.

Büscher, B., and R. Fletcher. (2020). *The conservation revolution: Radical ideas for saving nature beyond the Anthropocene*. London: Verso.

Büscher, B., R. Fletcher, D. Brockington, C. Sandbrook, W. Adams, L. Campbell, C. Corson, et al. (2017). Half-Earth or whole earth? Radical ideas for conservation and their implications. *Oryx* 51(3): 407–410.

Büscher, B,, and T. Mutimukuru. (2007). Buzzing too far? The ideological echo of global governance concepts on the local level: The case of the Mafungautsi Forest in Zimbabwe. *Development Southern Africa* 24 (5): 649-664.

Büscher, B., and M. Ramutsindela. (2016). Green violence: Rhino poaching and the war to save southern Africa's peace parks. *African Affairs* 115(458): 1–22.

Büscher, B., S. Sullivan, K. Neves, J. Igoe, and D. Brockington. (2012). Towards a synthesized critique of neoliberal biodiversity conservation. *Capitalism Nature Socialism* 23: 4–30.

Büscher, B., and W. Whande. (2007). Whims of the winds of time? Emerging trends in biodiversity conservation and protected area management. *Conservation and Society* 5(1): 22-43.

Butler, J., E. Laclau, and S. Žižek. 2000. *Contingency, hegemony, universality.* London: Verso.

Butynski, T.M. (1984). *Ecological survey of the impenetrable (Bwindi) Forest Uganda and recommendations for its conservation and management.* New York: Wildlife Conservation International, New York Zoological Society.

Butynski, T.M., and J. Kalina. (1993). Three new mountain national parks for Uganda. *Oryx* 27(4): 214–224.

Byishimo, B. (2021). Volcanoes Park to acquire 10,000 hectares for expansion. *The New Times*, July 15. Online at: https://www.newtimes.co.rw/news/volcanoes-park-acquire-10000-hectares-expansion (accessed July 15, 2021).

Cafaro, P., T. Butler, E. Crist, P. Cryer, E. Dinerstein, H. Kopnina, R. Noss, et al. (2017). If we want a whole earth, nature needs half: A response to Büscher et al. *Oryx* 51(3): 400.

Caillé, A., Humbert, M., Latouche, S., and P. Viveret. (2011). *De la convivialité: Dialogues sur la société conviviale à venir.* Paris: La Découverte.

Cairns, R., and A. Krzywoszynska. (2016). Anatomy of a buzzword: The emergence of 'the water-energy-food nexus' in UK natural resource debates. *Environmental Science & Policy* 64: 164-170.

Calvopiña, M., E. Cruz, W. Tapia, and A. Izurieta. (2013). The management plan for the protected areas of Galápagos for good living: An innovative tool that contributes to the integrated management of the archipelago. Pp. 13-17 in *Galapagos Report* 2013-2014. Puerto Ayora, Galapagos, Ecuador: GNPD, GCREG, CDF and GC.

Camazón, A. (2020). La Justicia condena a la Junta de Castilla y León a pagar más de 800.000 euros por la caza de 91 lobos en 2016. *El Diario*. Online at: eldiario.es/cyl/tribunales/Justicia-condena-Junta-Castilla-Leon_0_980951973.html (accessed January 1, 2022).

Candea, M. (2010). 'I fell in love with Carlos the meerkat': Engagement and detachment in human–animal relations. *American Ethnologist* 37(2): 241–258.

Candea, M. (2013). Habituating meerkats and redescribing animal behaviour science. *Theory, Culture & Society* 30(7/8): 105-128.

Cannon, S.E. (2019). *Decolonizing conservation: A reading list*. Genève: Zenodo.

Caron, J., and T. Fally. (2018). *Per capita income, consumption patterns, and CO2 emissions* (No. w24923). Cambridge, MA: National Bureau of Economic Research.

Carter, N.H., and J.D.C. Linnell. (2016). Co-adaptation is key to coexisting with large carnivores. *Trends in Ecology & Evolution* 31(8): 575-578.

Castree, N. (2010). Neoliberalism and the biophysical environment: A synthesis and evaluation of the research. *Environ. Soc. Adv. Res.* 1: 5–45.

Castree, N., P. Chatterton, N. Heynen, W. Larner, and M. Wright (eds.). (2010). *The point is to change it: Geographies of hope and survival in an age of crisis*. New York: Wiley.

Castree, N., and C. Nash. (2004). Themed essay and responses on posthumanism. *Environment and Planning A* 36(9): 1341-1363.

Cato, M.S. (2013). *The bioregional economy: Land, liberty and the pursuit of happiness*. London: Earthscan.

Cavanagh, C.J., and T.A. Benjaminsen (eds.). (2017). Political ecologies of the green economy. Special section of *Journal of Political Ecology* 34.

Convention on Biological Diversity (2022) *Final text of Kunming-Montreal Global Biodiversity Framework available in all languages*. Online at: https://prod.drupal.www.infra.cbd.int/sites/default/files/2022-12/221222-CBD-PressRelease-COP15-Final.pdf (accessed February 26, 2023).

Convention on Biological Diversity (CBD). 2014. *Global Biodiversity Outlook 4*. Montreal: CBD Secretariat.

Convention on Biological Diversity (CBD). (2020a). *Updated synthesis of the proposals of parties and observers of the structure of the post-2020 global biodiversity framework and its targets. Note by the Co-Chairs CBD/POST2020/PREP/2/1. United Nations Environment Programme*. Online at: https://www.cbd.int/doc/c/ef28/32d6/883b8de693927c8baa2e4d0a/post2020-prep-01-inf-03-en.pdf (accessed November 18, 2021).

Convention on Biological Diversity (CBD). (2020b). *Update on the zero draft of the post-2020 Global Biodiversity Framework*. Online at: https://www.cbd.int/doc/c/30 64/749a/0f65ac7f9def86707f4eaefa/post2020-prep-02-01-en.pdf (accessed March 19, 2021).

Convention on Biological Diversity (CBD). (2021). *First draft of the post-2020 global biodiversity framework*. Online at: chrome-extension://efaidnbmnnnibpcajpcglclefindmkaj/https://www.cbd.int/doc/c/abb5/591f/2e46096d3f0330b08ce87a45/wg2020-03-03-en.pdf (accessed November 18, 2021).

Chama Cha Mapinduzi (CCM). (2020). *Manifesto for the 2020 general elections*. Dodoma: CCM.

Ceauşu, S., R.A. Graves, A.K. Killion, J-C. Svenning, and N.H. Carter. (2019). Governing trade-offs in ecosystem services and disservices to achieve human–wildlife coexistence. *Conservation Biology* 33(3): 543-553.

Ceballos, G., P.R. Ehrlich, A.D. Barnosky, A. García, R.M. Pringle, and T.M. Palmer. (2015). Accelerated modern human–induced species losses: Entering the sixth mass extinction. *Science Advances* 1(5): e1400253.

Ceballos, G., P.R. Ehrlich, and R. Dirzo. (2017). Biological annihilation via the ongoing sixth mass extinction signalled by vertebrate population losses and declines. *Proceedings of the National Academy of Sciences* 114(30): E6089-E6096.

Census of India. (2011a). *Uttarakhand district census handbook, Nainital, village and town wise primary census abstract (PCA)*. New Delhi: Government of India. Online at: https://cdn.s3waas.gov.in/s3ef575e8837d065a1683c022d2077d342/uploads/2018/03/2018031241.pdf (accessed June 2, 2021).

Census of India. (2011b). *Census terms*. New Delhi: Government of India. Online at: http://censusindia. gov.in/Data_Products/Library/Indian_perceptive_link/Census_Terms_link/censusterms.html (accessed January 16, 2022).

CFR-LA. (2016). *Promise and performance: Ten years of the forest rights act in India (Citizen's Report)*. Community Forest Rights-Learning and Advocacy Process (CFR-LA), India.

Chan, K., R. Pringle, J. Ranganathan, C. Briggs, Y. Chan, R. Ehrlich, P. Haff, N. Heller, K. Al-Krafaji, and D. Macmynowski. (2007). When agendas collide: Human welfare and biological conservation. *Conservation Biology* 21: 59–68.

Chandhoke, N. (2007). Civil society. *Development in Practice* 17(4-5): 607-614.

Chapron, G., P. Kaczensky, J.D. Linnell, M. von Arx, D. Huber, H. Andrén, J.V, López-Bao, M. Adamec, F. Álvares, O. Anders, and L. Balčiauskas. (2014). Recovery of large carnivores in Europe's modern human-dominated landscapes. *Science* 346(6216): 1517–1519.

Chapron, G., and J.V. López-Bao. (2016). Coexistence with large carnivores informed by community ecology. *Trends in Ecology & Evolution* 31(8): 578-580.

Chartier, L., A. Zimmermann, and R.J. Ladle. (2011). Habitat loss and human–elephant conflict in Assam, India: Does a critical threshold exist? *Oryx* 45(4): 528-533.

Chasek, P.S., and L.M. Wagner. (2016). Breaking the mold: A new type of multilateral sustainable development negotiation. *International Environmental Agreements: Politics, Law and Economics* 16(3): 397-413.

Chemhuru, M. (ed.). (2019a). *African environmental ethics: A critical reader.* Cham, Switzerland: Springer Nature.

Chemhuru, M. (2019b). Interpreting ecofeminist environmentalism in African communitarian philosophy and Ubuntu: An alternative to anthropocentrism. *Philosophical Papers* 48(2): 241–264.

Chibvongodze, D.T. (2016). Ubuntu is not only about the human! An analysis of the role of African philosophy and ethics in environment management. *Journal of Human Ecology* 53(2): 157-166.

Child, M. (2009). The Thoreau ideal as a unifying thread in the conservation movement. *Conservation Biology* 23: 241–243.

Chilisa, B. (2017). Decolonising transdisciplinary research approaches: An African perspective for enhancing knowledge integration in sustainability science. *Sustainability Science* 12(5): 813-827.

Chivaura, V.G. (2006). Hunhu/Ubuntu: A sustainable approach to endogenous development, bio-cultural diversity and protection of the environment in Africa. Pp. 229–240 in *Endogenous development and bio-cultural diversity*, B. Haverkort and S. Rist (eds.). Bern: Centre for Development and Environment.

Chua, L., M.E. Harrison, H. Fair, S. Milne, A. Palmer, J. Rubis, P. Thung, S. Wich, et al. (2020). Conservation and the social sciences: Beyond critique and co-optation. A case study from orangutan conservation. *People and Nature* 2: 42-60.

Cimatti, M., N. Ranc, A. Benítez-López, L. Maiorano, L. Boitani, F. Cagnacci, M. Čengić, P. Ciucci, M.A. Huijbregts, M. Krofel, and J.V. López-Bao. (2021). Large carnivore expansion in Europe is associated with human population density and land cover changes. *Diversity and Distribution* 27(4): 1–16.

Collins, Y.A. (2019). Colonial residue: REDD+, territorialisation and the racialized subject in Guyana and Suriname. *Geoforum* 106, 38-47.

Collins, Y.A. (2021). Book review: Bram Büscher and Robert Fletcher, *The conservation revolution: Radical ideas for saving nature beyond the Anthropocene.* *Antipode* 53(2): 1-8.

Collins, Y.A., V.A. Maguire-Rajpaul, J.E. Krauss, A. Asiyanbi, A. Jiménez, M.B. Mabele, and M. Alexander-Owen. (2021). Plotting the coloniality of conservation. *Journal of Political Ecology* 28(1).

Conca, K. and G.D. Dabelko (eds.). (2002). *Environmental peacemaking.* Washington, DC: Woodrow Wilson Center Press.

Congreso Nacional. (1998). *Ley de regimen especial para la conservacion y desarrollo sustentable de la provincia de Galápagos.* Ministerio de Medio Ambiente: Programa de Manejo Ambiental para las Islas Galápagos.

Connell, R. (2007). *Southern theory: The global dynamics of knowledge in social science.* London: Allen & Unwin.

Cons, J. (2018). Staging climate security: Resilience and heterodystopia in the Bangladesh borderlands. *Cultural Anthropology* 33(2): 266–294.

Convivialist International (2020). The second convivialist manifesto: Towards a post-neoliberal world. Civic Sociology 1(1): 12721.

Conway, J., and J. Singh. (2011). Radical democracy in global perspective: Notes from the pluriverse. *Third World Quarterly* 32(4): 689-706.

Coote, A., Kasliwal P, Percy A. 2019. *Universal basic services: theory and practice; A literature review.* London: Institute for Global Prosperity.

Coote, A., and E. Yazici. (2019). *Universal basic income: A report for unions.* London: New Economics Foundation and Public Services International

Coppolillo, P., and A. Dickman. (2007). Livelihoods and protected areas in the Ruaha Landscape: A preliminary review. Pp. 17-26 in *Protected areas and human livelihoods,* K.H. Redford and E. Fearn (eds.). New York: Wildlife Conservation Society.

Cornwall, A. (2007). Buzzwords and fuzzwords: Deconstructing development discourse. *Development in Practice* 17(4-5): 471-484.

Cornwall, A., and K. Brock. (2005). What do buzzwords do for development policy? A critical look at 'participation', 'empowerment' and 'poverty reduction'. *Third World Quarterly* 26(7): 1043-1060.

Corson, C., R. Gruby, R. Witter, S. Hagermand, D. Suarez, S. Greenberg, M. Bourqueg, et al. (2014). Everyone's solution? Defining and redefining protected areas at the Convention on Biological Diversity. *Conservation and Society* 12(2): 190–202.

Corson, C., and K. MacDonald. (2012). Enclosing the global commons: The Convention on Biological Diversity and green grabbing. *The Journal of Peasant Studies* 39(2): 263–283.

Corson, C., J. Worcester, S. Rogers, and I. Flores-Ganley. (2020). From paper to practice? Assembling a rights-based conservation approach. *Journal of Political Ecology* 27(1): 1128-1147.

Cortéz Vázquez, J.A. (2012). *Naturalezas en conflicto: Conservación ambiental y enfrentamiento social en el Parque Natural Cabo de Gata-Níjar.* València: Germania.

Cortez, D. (no date). *La construcción social del 'Buen Vivir' (Sumak Kawsay) en Ecuador: Genealogía del diseno y gestión política de la vida.* Programa Andino de Derechos Humanos. Online at: https://repositorio.uasb.edu.ec/bitstream/10644/2788/1/RAA-28%20Cortez,%20La%20construcción%20social%20del%20Buen.pdf (accessed 1 March 2022).

Costanza Torri, M. (2011). Conservation, relocation and the social consequences of conservation policies in protected areas: Case study of the Sariska Tiger Reserve, India. *Conservation and Society* 9(1): 54–64.

Cote, M., and A.J. Nightingale. (2012). Resilience thinking meets social theory: Situating social change in socio-ecological systems (SES) research. *Progress in Human Geography* 36(4): 475–489.

Creed, G. (1995). The politics of agriculture: Identity and socialist sentiment in Bulgaria. *Slavic Review* 54(4): 843–868.

Cretois, B., J. Linnell, B.P. Kaltenborn, and A. Trouwborst. (2019). What form of human-wildlife coexistence is mandated by legislation? A comparative analysis of international and national instruments. *Biodiversity and Conservation* 28(7): 1729–1741.

Cronon, W. (1996). The trouble with wilderness: Or, getting back to the wrong nature. *Environmental history* 1(1): 7-28.

Crumley, C. (2017). *Issues and concepts in historical ecology: The past and future of landscapes and regions.* Cambridge: Cambridge University Press.

Csordas, T.J. (2002). *Body/meaning/healing.* New York: Palgrave Macmillan.

Cumming, G.S., and C.R. Allen. (2017). Protected areas as social-ecological systems: Perspectives from resilience and social-ecological systems theory. *Ecological Applications* 27(6): 1709–1717.

Cussins, C. (1996). Ontological choreography: Agency through objectification in infertility clinics. *Social Studies of Science* 26(3): 575–610.

Daici, M. (2021). Common property and local development. Research elements for Friuli Venezia Giulia. *Journal of Alpine Research* 109(1): 1–14.

Daniels, A., K. Bagstad, V. Esposito, A. Moulaert, and C.M. Rodriguez. (2010). Understanding the impacts of Costa Rica's PES: Are we asking all the right questions? *Ecological Economics* 69: 2116-2126.

Das, K. 2020. Uttarakhand to give land ownership rights to women working in their husband's fields. *Hindustan Times*, July 22. Online at: https://www.hindustantimes.com/dehradun/uttarakhand-to-give-landownership-rights-to-women working-in-their-husband-s-fields/storysN52w0yhzzYYnKL4Z2wKYJ.html (accessed 10 December, 2020).

Dawson, A. (2016). *Extinction: A radical history*. New York: OR Books.

de Silva, S., and K. Srinivasan. (2019). Revisiting social natures: People-elephant conflict and coexistence in Sri Lanka. *Geoforum* 102: 182-190.

De Waal, F. (2016). *Are we smart enough to know how smart animals are?* New York: W.W. Norton.

Defenders of Wildlife (2019). The year of coexistence: What is coexistence? [promotional video]. Online at: https://www.youtube.com/watch?v=bF_gyhzLpUg&t=5s (accessed July 25, 2020).

Defenders of Wildlife. (2021). Promoting coexistence. Online at: https://defenders.org/issues/promoting-coexistence (accessed January 15, 2022).

DeGeorges, P.A., and B. Reilly. (2008). *A critical evaluation of conservation and development in Sub-Saharan Africa.* New York: Edwin Mellen Press.

Delibes-Mateos, M. (2020). Wolf media coverage in the region of Castilla y León (Spain): Variations over time and in two contrasting socio-ecological settings. *Animals* 10(4): 736.

Demaria, F., and A. Kothari. (2017). The Post-Development Dictionary agenda: Paths to the pluriverse. *Third World Quarterly* 38(12): 2588-2599.

Demaria, F., F. Schneider, F. Sekulova, and J Martinez-Alier. (2013). What is degrowth? From an activist slogan to a social movement. *Environmental Values* 22: 191–215.

Dempsey, J. (2010). Tracking grizzly bears in British Columbia's environmental politics. *Environment and Planning A: Economy and Space* 42(5): 1138–56.

Dempsey, J., and D.C. Suarez. (2016). Arrested development? The promises and paradoxes of 'selling nature to save it'. *Annals of the American Association of Geographers* 106(3): 1–19.

Deo, S. (2020). With a historic legal decision, India marks progress toward equal inheritance rights for daughters. *Land Portal 2022*. Online at: https://landportal.org/blog-post/2020/08/historic-legal-decision-india-marks-progress-towardequal-inheritance-rights (accessed January 1, 2022).

Deo, S., and A. Dubey. (2019). Gender inequality in inheritance laws: The case of agricultural land in India. *Landesa* 2019.

Deriu, M. (2014). Conviviality. Pp. 54-58 in *Degrowth: A vocabulary for a new era*, G. D'Alisa, F. Demaria, and G. Kallis (eds.). London: Routledge.

Despret, V., and B. Buchanan. (2016). *What would animals say if we asked the right questions?* Minneapolis, MN: University of Minnesota Press.

DeVore, J., E. Hirsch, and S. Paulson. (2019). Conserving human and other nature: A curious case of convivial conservation from Brazil. *Anthropologie et Sociétés* 43(3): 31-58.

Diaz, S., J. Settele, E. Brondizio, H.T. Ngo, M. Guèze, J. Agard, A. Arneth, A., et al. (2019). *Summary for policymakers of the global assessment report on biodiversity and ecosystem services of the Intergovernmental Science-Policy Platform on Biodiversity and Ecosystem Services*. Online at: https://www.ipbes.net/system/tdf/ipbes_7_10_add-1-_advance_0.pdf?file=1&type=node&id=35245 (accessed February 8, 2021).

Dickman, A.J. (2009). *Key determinants of conflict between people and wildlife, particularly large carnivores, around Ruaha National Park, Tanzania*. PhD thesis, University College London, London, UK.

Dickman, A.J., E.A. Macdonald, and D.W. Macdonald. (2011). A review of financial instruments to pay for predator conservation and encourage human-carnivore coexistence. *Proceedings of the National Academy of Sciences* 108(34): 13937–13944.

Dickman, A., S. Marchini, and M. Manfredo. (2013). The human dimension in addressing conflict with large carnivores. *Key Topics in Conservation Biology* 2(1): 110–126.

Dietsch, A., M.J. Manfredo, L. Sullivan, J.T. Bruskotter, and T.L. Teel. (2019). A multilevel, systems view of values can inform a move towards human-wildlife coexistence. *Human Wildlife Interactions* 13: 20-44.

Dinerstein, E., D. Olson, A. Joshi, C. Vynne, N.D. Burgess, E. Wikramanayake, N. Hahn, S. Palminteri, P. Hedao, and R. Noss. (2017). An ecoregion-based approach to protecting half the terrestrial realm. *BioScience* 67 (6):534-545.

Dirlik, A. (2007). Global South: Predicament and promise. *The Global South* 1(1): 12-23.

Domínguez, L., and C. Luoma. (2020). Decolonising conservation policy: How colonial land and conservation ideologies persist and perpetuate indigenous injustices at the expense of the environment. *Land* 9(3): 11–14.

Domínguez, P. 2020. The evolving crisis in Sinjajevina. Online at: https://www.iccaconsortium.org/index.php/2020/05/05/the-evolving-crisis-in-sinjajevina/ (accessed February 19, 2021).

Donati, K. (2019). 'Herding is his favourite thing in the world': Convivial world-making on a multispecies farm. *Journal of Rural Studies* 66: 119-129.

Dorondel, Ş. (2016). *Disrupted landscapes. State, peasants and the politics of land in postsocialist Romania*. New York: Berghahn Books.

Dorresteijn, I., J. Hanspach, A. Kecskés, H. Latková, Z. Mezey, S. Sugár, H. von Wehrden, and J. Fischer. (2014). Human-carnivore coexistence in a traditional rural landscape. *Landscape Ecology* 29(7): 1145-1155.

Dowie, M. (2009). *Conservation refugees: The hundred-year conflict between global conservation and native peoples*. Boston, MA: MIT Press.

Drenthen, M. (2018). Rewilding in cultural layered landscapes. *Environmental Values* 27(4): 325–330.

Dressler, W., B. Büscher, M. Schoon, D. Brockington, T. Hayes, C.A. Kull, J. McCarthy, et al. (2010). From hope to crisis and back again? A critical history of the global CBNRM narrative. *Environmental Conservation* 37(1): 5–15.

Driessen, C. (2014). Animal deliberation. Pp. 90–104 in *Political animals and animal politics*, M. Wissenburg and D. Schlosberg (eds.). London: Palgrave Macmillan.

Dryzek, J.S. (1995). Political and ecological communication. *Environmental Politics* 4(4): 13–30.

Dryzek, J.S. (2008). Green reason. *Environmental Ethics* 12(3): 195-210.

Dudley, N. (ed.). (2008). *Guidelines for applying protected area management categories*. Gland, Switzerland: IUCN

Dudley, N., H. Jonas, F. Nelson, J. Parrish, A. Pyhälä, S. Stolton, and J.E. Watson. (2018). The essential role of other effective area-based conservation measures in achieving big bold conservation targets. *Global ecology and conservation* 15: e00424.

Duffy, R. (2002). *A trip too far: Ecotourism, politics and exploitation*. London: Earthscan.

Duffy, R. (2014a). Waging a war to save biodiversity: The rise of militarized conservation. *International Affairs* 90(4): 819–834.

Duffy, R. (2014b). Interactive elephants: Nature, tourism and neoliberalism. *Annals of Tourism Research* 44: 88-101.

Duffy, R., F. Massé, E. Smidt, E. Marijnen, B. Büscher, J. Verweijen, M. Ramutsindela, et al. (2019). Why we must question the militarisation of conservation. *Biological Conservation* 232: 66–73.

Dunlap, A. (2020). Review of Bram Büscher and Robert Fletcher. 2020. *The conservation revolution: Radical ideas for saving nature beyond the Anthropocene*. New York: Verso. *Journal of Political Ecology* 27(1). doi: https://doi.org/10.2458/v27i1.23736.

Dunlap, A., and S. Sullivan. (2020). A faultline in neoliberal environmental governance scholarship? Or, why accumulation-by-alienation matters. *Environment and Planning E: Nature and Space* 3(2): 552-579.

Echeverria, P. (2020). Fog harvesting potential for domestic rural use and irrigation in San Cristobal Island, Galápagos, Ecuador. *Cuadernos de Investigacion Geografica* 46(2): 32-47.

Ehrenfeld, D. (2008). Neoliberalization of conservation. *Conservation Biology* 22: 1091–1092.

Eklund, A., J.V. López-Bao, M. Tourani, G. Chapron, and J. Frank. (2017). Limited evidence on the effectiveness of interventions to reduce livestock predation by large carnivores. *Scientific Reports* 7(1): 1–9.

England, M.I. (2019). Contested waterscapes: Irrigation and hydropower in the Great Ruaha River Basin, Tanzania. *Agricultural Water Management* 213: 1084-1095.

Escobar, A. (1996). Construction nature: Elements for a post-structuralist political ecology. *Futures* 28(4): 325–343.

Escobar, A. (2010). Postconstructivist political ecologies. Pp. 91–105 in *The international handbook of environmental sociology* (2nd ed.), M.R. Redclift and G. Woodgate. London: Edward Elgar Publishing.

Escobar, A. (2011). Sustainability: Design for the pluriverse. *Development* 54(2): 137-140.

Escobar, A. (2018). *Designs for the pluriverse*. Durham, NC: Duke University Press.

Espejo, R. (2011). Humanismo radical, decrecimiento y energia. Pp. 22-44 in *La convivencialidad*, by Ivan Illich. Barcelona: Virus editorial.

Etieyibo, E. (2017). Ubuntu, cosmopolitanism, and distribution of natural resources. *Philosophical Papers* 46(1): 139–162.

European Commission. (2013). Guidelines on wilderness in Natura 2000. *Technical Report – 2013-069*. Brussels: European Commission

European Commission. (2019). The European green deal. *COM(2019) 640 final* from December 11. Brussels: European Commission

European Commission. 2020. EU biodiversity strategy for 2030: Bringing nature back into our lives. *COM(2020) 380 final* from May 20. Brussels: European Commission

European Environment Agency. (2019). *The European environment state and outlook 2020*. Luxembourg: Publications Office of the European Union.

European Parliament. (2009). Resolution on wilderness in Europe. P6_TA(2009)0034 from 3rd February 2009. Online at: https://www.europarl.europa.eu/doceo/document/TA-6-2009-0034_EN.html?redirect (accessed February 19, 2021).

Ewuoso, C., and S. Hall. (2019). Core aspects of Ubuntu: A systematic review. *South African Journal of Bioethics Law* 12(2): 93–103.

Fagerholm, N., B. Martín-López, M. Torralba, E. Oteros-Rozas, A.M. Lechner, C. Bieling, A. Stahl Olafsson, C. Albert, C.M. Raymond, M. Garcia-Martin, and N. Gulsrud. (2020). Perceived contributions of multifunctional landscapes to human well-being: Evidence from 13 European sites. *People and Nature* 2(1): 217-234.

Fairhead, J., M. Leach and J. Scoones. (2012). Green Grabbing: A new appropriation of nature? *The Journal of Peasant Studies* 39(2): 273–261.

Fanari, E. (2019). Relocation from protected areas as a violent process in the recent history of biodiversity conservation in India. *Ecology, Economy and Society - the INSEE journal* 2(1): 43–76.

Fanon, F. (2002). *Les damnés de la terre* (reedition). Paris: La Découverte.

Farkas, J., and J. Schou. (2018). Fake news as a floating signifier: Hegemony, antagonism and the politics of falsehood. *Javnost - The Public* 25(3):298-314.

Fawcett, L. (2000). Ethical imagining: Ecofeminist possibilities in environmental learning. *Canadian Journal of Environmental Education* 5: 134–149.

Ferguson, J. (2010). The uses of neoliberalism. *Antipode* 41: 166-184.

Ferguson, J. (2015). *Give a man a fish: Reflections on the new politics of distribution.* Durham, NC: Duke University Press.

Fernández Gónzalez, J. (2013). *Caracterización de las Comarcas Agrarias de España.* Madrid: Provincia De Zamora.

Fernández-Gil, A., J. Naves, A. Ordiz, M. Quevedo, E. Revilla, and M. Delibes. (2016). Conflict misleads large carnivore management and conservation: Brown bears and wolves in Spain. *PLoS ONE* 11(3): 1–13.

Fischer, J., G.D. Peterson, T.A. Gardner, L.J. Gordon, I. Fazey, T. Elmqvist, A. Felton, et al. (2009). Integrating resilience thinking and optimisation for conservation. *Trends in Ecology and Evolution* 24(10): 549–554.

Fletcher, R. (2009). Ecotourism discourse: Challenging the stakeholders theory. *Journal of Ecotourism* 8(3): 269–285.

Fletcher, R. (2011). Sustaining tourism, sustaining capitalism? The tourism industry's role in global capitalist expansion. *Tourism Geographies* 13(3): 443–461.

Fletcher, R. (2014a). Orchestrating consent: Post-politics and intensification of NatureTM Inc. at the 2012 World Conservation Congress. *Conservation and Society* 12(3): 329–342.

Fletcher, R. (2014b). *Romancing the wild: Cultural dimensions of ecotourism.* Durham, NC: Duke University Press.

Fletcher, R. (2017). Connection with nature is an oxymoron: A political ecology of 'nature-deficit disorder'. *The Journal of Environmental Education* 48(4): 226–233.

Fletcher, R., and J. Breitling. (2012). Market mechanism or subsidy in disguise? Governing payment for environmental services in Costa Rica. *Geoforum* 43: 402-411.

Fletcher R., and B. Büscher. (2017). The PES conceit: Revisiting the relationship between payments for environmental services and neoliberal conservation. *Ecological Economics* 132: 224-231.

Fletcher, R., and B. Büscher. (2018). Neoliberalism in denial in actor-oriented PES research? A rejoinder to Van Hecken et al. and a call for justice. *Ecological Economics* 156: 420–423.

Fletcher, R., and B. Büscher. (2020). Conservation basic income: A non-market mechanism to support convivial conservation. *Biological Conservation* 244: 108520.

Fletcher, R., B. Büscher, K. Massarella, and S. Koot. (2020). 'Close the tap!': COVID-19 and the need for convivial conservation. *Journal of Australian Political Economy* (85): 200–211.

Fletcher, R., W. Dressler, Z. Anderson, and B. Büscher. (2019). Natural capital must be defended: Green growth as neoliberal biopolitics. *Journal of Peasant Studies* 46(5): 1068-1095.

Fletcher, R, W. Dressler, B. Büscher, and Z. Anderson. (2016). Questioning REDD+ and the future of market-based conservation. *Conservation Biology* 30(3): 673-675.

Fletcher, R., K. Massarella, A. Kotahri, P. Das, A. Dutta, and B.E. Büscher. (2020). A new future for conservation: Setting out the principles of post-growth conservation. *Progressive International Blueprint*, August 10. Online at: https://progressive.international/blueprint/e6e09a90-dc09-410d-af87-5d3339ad4ed3-fletcher-et-al-a-new-future-for-conservation/en (accessed 21 April 2021).

Fletcher, R., and S. Toncheva. 2021. The political economy of human-wildlife conflict and coexistence. *Biological Conservation* 260: 109216.

Folke, C., R. Biggs, A.V. Norström, B. Reyers, and J. Rockström. (2016). Social-ecological resilience and biosphere-based sustainability science. *Ecology and Society* 21(3).

Formo, R.K. (2010). *Power and subjectivation: The political ecology of Tanzania's Wildlife Management Areas*. Masters Thesis, Norwegian University of Life Sciences, Oslo, Norway.

Fossey, D. (1974). Observations on the home range of one group of mountain gorillas (*Gorilla gorilla beringei*). *Animal Behaviour* 22: 568–581.

Frank, B. (2016). Human–wildlife conflicts and the need to include tolerance and coexistence: An introductory comment. *Society & Natural Resources* 29(6):738-743.

Frank, B., and J.A. Glikman. (2019). Human-wildlife conflicts and the need to include coexistence. Pp. 1-19 in *Human-wildlife interactions: Turning conflict into coexistence*, B. Frank, J.A. Glikman, and S. Marchini (eds.). Cambridge, UK: Cambridge University Press.

Frank, B., J.A. Glikman, and S. Marchini (eds.). (2019). *Human–wildlife interactions: Turning conflict into coexistence*. Cambridge, UK: Cambridge University Press.

Franks, P., and M. Twinamatsiko. (2017). *Lessons learnt from 20 years of revenue sharing at Bwindi Impenetrable National Park, Uganda*. London: International Institute for Environment and Development.

Fraser, N. (2009). *Scales of justice: Reimagining political space in a globalizing world*. New York: Columbia University Press.

Freire, P. (1987). *Literacy: Reading the word and the world*. Westport, CT: Bergin and Garvey.

Friedman, M. (1962). *Capitalism and freedom*. Chicago: University of Chicago Press.

Frosch, C., A. Dutsov, D. Zlatanova, K. Valchev, T.E. Reiners, K. Steyer, M. Pfenninger, and C. Nowak. (2014). Noninvasive genetic assessment of brown bear population structure in Bulgarian mountain regions. *Mammalian Biology-Zeitschrift für Säugetierkunde* 79(4): 268–276.

Fuentes, M.C., M.P. Otón, F.J.A. Quintá, and X.C.M. Arce. (2011). The Natura 2000 network in Spain and its lack of protection. *European Journal of Geography* 1: 1-11.

Fujimura, J.H. (2010). Crafting science: Standardized packages, boundary objects, and 'translation'. Pp. 168-212 in *Science as practice and culture*, A. Pickering (ed.). Chicago: University of Chicago Press.

Fusch, P.I., and L.R. Ness. (2015). Are we there yet? Data saturation in qualitative research. *The Qualitative Report* 20(9): 1408.

Gadgil, M., F. Berkes, and C. Folke. (1993). Indigenous knowledge for biodiversity conservation. *Ambio* 22(2/3): 151–56.

Galtung, J. (1969). Violence, peace, and peace research. *Journal of Peace Research* 6(3): 167–91.

Galtung, J. (1990). Cultural violence. *Journal of Peace Research* 27(3): 291–305.

García, E.J., M. Martín, V. Palacios, and L. Llaneza. (2011). *Aspectos sociales en la gestión y conservación del lobo en el Parque Nacional de los Picos de Europa 2008–2010*. Seguimiento de las poblaciones de cánidos del Parque Nacional de los Picos de Europa, 2011-2012.

Garcia, S. N.O. (2009). El desafío bioético de la era planetaria: La convivencialidad. *Revista Latinoamericana de Bioética* Julio-Diciembre: 42-61.

Gartzke, E., and A. Weisiger. (2014). Under construction: Development, democracy, and difference as determinants of systemic liberal peace. *International Studies Quarterly* 58: 130–45.

Gelpi, C.F., and J.M. Grieco. (2008). Democracy, interdependence, and the sources of the liberal peace. *Journal of Peace Research* 45(1): 17–36.

Ghimire, K.B., and M.P. Pimbert. (2013). *Social change and conservation*. Oxfordshire: Routledge.

Giarracca, N. (2010). 'Espacios de esperanza' y 'buen vivir'. Online at: https://www.biodiversidadla.org/Noticias/Espacios_de_esperanza_y_buen_vivir (accessed 23 March 2021).

Gill, V. (2019). Rhino release: Endangered animals despatched to Rwanda. *BBC News*, June 25. Online at: https://www.bbc.com/news/science-environment-48691443 (accessed December 10, 2020).

Gintis, H. (1972). Towards a political economy of education: A radical critique of Ivan Illich's Deschooling Society. *Harvard Educational Review* 42(1): 70-96.

Gliessman, S.R. (2021). *Package price agroecology: The ecology of sustainable food systems* (3rd ed.). Boca Raton, FL: CRC Press.

Glikman, J.A., B. Frank, and S. Marchini. 2019. Human-wildlife interactions: Multifaceted approaches for turning conflict into coexistence. Pp. 439-452 in *Human-wildlife interactions: Turning conflict into coexistence*, B. Frank, J.A. Glikman, and S. Marchini (eds.). Cambridge, UK: Cambridge University Press.

Goldman, M. (2003). Partitioned nature, privileged knowledge: Community-based conservation in Tanzania. *Development and Change* 34(5): 833–862.

Goldman, M. (2009). Constructing connectivity: Conservation corridors and conservation politics in East African rangelands. *Annals of the Association of American Geographers* 99(2): 335-359.

Goldman, M.J., J. Roque De Pinho, and J. Perry. (2010). Maintaining complex relations with large cats: Maasai and lions in Kenya and Tanzania. *Human Dimensions of Wildlife* 15(5): 332-346.

Goldman, M.J, J. Roque De Pinho, and J. Perry. (2013). Beyond ritual and economics: Maasai lion hunting and conservation politics. *Oryx* 47(4): 490-500.

Gómez-Baggethun, E., and V. Reyes-García. (2013). Reinterpreting change in traditional ecological knowledge. *Human Ecology* 41(4): 643–647.

González, J., C. Montes, and D. Rodríguez. (2008). Rethinking the Galápagos islands as a complex social-ecological system: Implications for conservation and management. *Ecology and Society* 13(2): 41-53.

Gonzalez-Vicente, R. (2020). The liberal peace fallacy: Violent neoliberalism and the temporal and spatial traps of state-based approaches to peace. *Territory, Politics, Governance* 8(1): 100–116.

Goodall, J. (2015). Caring for people and valuing forests in Africa. Pp. 21-26 in *Protecting the wild: Parks and wilderness, the foundation for conservation*, G. Wuerthner, E. Crist, and T. Butler (eds.). London: Island Press.

Government of Uttarakhand. (2010). Forest and environment Section-2, Notification. Online at: https://ntca.gov.in/tiger reserves/#tiger-reserves-2 (accessed December 4, 2020).

Graham, W., and F. Cruz. (2007). *Galápagos at risk: A socioeconomic analysis.* Puerto Ayora, Galápagos, Ecuador: Charles Darwin Foundation.

Green, K.E. (2016). A political ecology of scaling: Struggles over power, land and authority. *Geoforum* 74: 88-97.

Green, K.E., and W.M. Adams. (2015). Green grabbing and the dynamics of local-level engagement with neoliberalization in Tanzania's wildlife management areas. *Journal of Peasant Studies* 42(1): 97-117.

Gregg, M., and G.J. Seigworth (eds.). (2010). *The affect theory reader.* Durham, NC: Duke University Press.

Grenier, C. (2007). *Conservación contra natura: Las islas Galápagos.* Quito: Editorial Abya Yala.

Guerrini, G. (2021). Looking for the *Terra di u Cumunu*: Genesis, evolutions and perspectives of the collective lands of the Corsican Mountain. *Journal of Alpine Research* 109(1): 1–12.

Gupta, D., S. Lele, and G. Sahu. (2020). Promoting a responsive state: The role of NGOs in decentralized forest governance in India. *Forest Policy and Economics* 111: 102066.

Gupta, J., and C. Vegelin. (2016). Sustainable development goals and inclusive development. *International Environmental Agreements: Politics, Law and Economics* 16(3): 433-448.

Gurney, G.G., S. Mangubhai, M. Fox, M.K. Kim, and A. Agrawal. (2021). Equity in environmental governance: Perceived fairness of distributional justice principles in marine co-management. *Environmental Science & Policy* 124: 23-32.

Gustafsson, K.M. (2013). Environmental discourses and biodiversity: The construction of a storyline in understanding and managing an environmental issue. *Journal of Integrative Environmental Sciences* 10(1): 39-54.

Gustavsson, M., L. Lindström, N.S. Jiddawi, and M. de la Torre-Castro, M. (2014). Procedural and distributive justice in a community-based managed marine protected area in Zanzibar, Tanzania. *Marine Policy* 46: 91-100.

Guzmán, J.C., and J.E. Poma. (2013). Bioagriculture: An opportunity for island good living. In *Galapagos Report 2013-14.* Fairfax, VA: Galapagos Conservancy.

Gwaravanda, E.T. (2019). Ubuntu environmental ethics: Conceptions and misconceptions. Pp. 79-92 in *African environmental ethics: A critical reader*, M. Chemhuru (ed.). Cham, Switzerland: Springer Nature.

Hajer, M.A. (1995). *The politics of environmental discourse: Ecological modernization and the policy process*: Oxford: Clarendon Press.

Hajer, M., and W. Versteeg. (2005). A decade of discourse analysis of environmental politics: Achievements, challenges, perspectives. *Journal of Environmental Policy & Planning* 7(3): 175-184.

Hajjar, R., J.A. Oldekop, P. Cronkleton, P. Newton, A.J.M. Russell, and W. Zhou. (2021). A global analysis of the social and environmental outcomes of community forests. *Nature Sustainability* 4: 216-224.

Hall, S. (1992). The west and the rest: Discourse and power. Pp. 85-94 in *Race and racialization: Essential readings*, T. Das Gupta, C.E. James, C. Andersen, G.-E. Galabuzi, and R. C. A. Maaka (eds.). Toronto: Canadian Scholars.

Hall, S. (2014). Akagera celebrates 80 years of conservation in 2014. *African Parks News* (blog), January 14. Online at: https://www.africanparks.org/newsroom/press-releases/akagera-celebrates-80-years-conservation-2014 (accessed January 6, 2021).

Haller, T. (2019). Towards a new institutional political ecology. Pp. 90-120 in *The commons in a glocal world*, T. Haller, T. Breu, T. De Moor, C. Rohr, and H.T. Znoj (eds.). London: Routledge.

Haller, T., G. Acciaioli, and S. Rist. (2016). Conditions for crafting local ownership of institution-building processes. *Society & Natural Resources* 29: 68–87.

Haller, T., A. Zangger, and S. Weissman. (2020). *Convivial constitutionality: human-predator interrelations in complex social-ecological systems*. Research proposal, Swiss National Science Foundation.

Hamilton, L., and N. Taylor. (2017). Listening for the voices of animals. Pp. 51-67 in *Ethnography after humanism*, L. Hamilton and N. Taylor (eds.). London: Palgrave Macmillan.

Hanlon, J., D. Hulme, and A. Barrientos. (2010). *Just give money to the poor: The development revolution from the Global South*. West Hartford, CT: Kumarian Press.

Haraway, D.J. (2008). *When species meet*. Minneapolis, MN: University of Minnesota Press.

Haraway, D.J. (2016). *Staying with the trouble: Making kin in the Chthulucene*. Durham, NC: Duke University Press.

Harcourt, W., and I. Nelson (eds.). (2015). *Practicing feminist political ecologies: Moving beyond the 'Green Economy'*. London: Zed.

Harris, L. (2015). Hegemonic waters and rethinking natures otherwise. Pp. 157-181 in *Practicing feminist political ecologies: Moving beyond the 'Green Economy'*, W. Harcourt and I.L. Nelson (eds.). London: Zed Books.

Hart, I. (2001). Deschooling and the web: Ivan Illich 30 years on. *Educational Media International* 38(2-3): 69-76.

Hartel, T., I. Dorresteijn, C. Klein, O. Máthé, C.I. Moga, K. Öllerer, M. Roellig, M., H. von Wehrden, and J. Fischer. (2013). Wood-pastures in a traditional rural region of eastern Europe: Characteristics, management and status. *Biological Conservation* 166: 267–275.

Hartel, T., T. Plieninger, and A. Varga. (2015). Wood-pastures in Europe. Pp. 61-76 in *Europe's changing woods and forests: From wildwood to managed landscapes*, K.J. Kirby and C. Watkins (eds.). Wallingford: CABI.

Hartel, T., B.C. Scheele, A.T. Vanak, L. Rozylowicz, J.D.C. Linnell, and E.G. Ritchie. (2019). Mainstreaming human and large carnivore coexistence through institutional collaboration. *Conservation Biology* 33(6): 1256-1265.

Harvey, D. (2000). *Spaces of hope*. Berkeley: University of California Press.

Harvey, D. (2005). *A brief history of neoliberalism*. Oxford: Oxford University Press.

Harvey, D. (2014). *Seventeen contradictions and the end of capitalism*. London: Profile.

Hayek, F.A. (1979). *Law, legislation and liberty: A new statement of the liberal principles of justice and political economy, vol. III: The political order of a free people*. London: Routledge & Kegan Paul.

Hazzah, L., S. Chandra, and S. Dolrenry. (2019). Leaping forward: The need for innovation in wildlife conservation. Pp. 359-383 in *Human-wildlife interactions: Turning conflict into coexistence*, B. Frank, J.A. Glikman, and S. Marchini (eds.). Cambridge, UK: Cambridge University Press.

He, J., and T. Sikor. (2015). Notions of justice in payments for ecosystem services: Insights from China's Sloping Land Conversion Program in Yunnan Province. *Land Use Policy* 43: 207-216.

Heatherington, T. (2012). From ecocide to genetic rescue: Can technoscience save the wild? Pp. 39-66 in *The anthropology of extinction: Essays on culture and species death*, G. Sodikoff (ed.). Bloomington: Indiana University Press.

Heindrichs, T. (1997). *Innovative financing instruments in the forestry and nature conservation sector of Costa Rica*. Eschborn, Germany: Deutsche Gesellschaft für Technische Zusammenarbeit (GTZ) GmbH.

Henle, K., D. Alard, J. Clitherow, P. Cobb, L. Firbank, T. Kull, D. McCracken, R.F. Moritz, J. Niemelä, M. Rebane, and D. Wascher. (2008). Identifying and managing the conflicts between agriculture and biodiversity conservation in Europe: A review. *Agriculture, Ecosystems and Environment* 124(1–2): 60–71.

Hennessy, E. (2018). The politics of a natural labouratory: Claiming territory and governing life in the Galápagos islands. *Social Studies of Science* 48(4): 483–506.

Heynen, N., J. McCarthy, S. Prudham, and P. Robbins (eds.). 2007. *Neoliberal environments: False promises and unnatural consequences*. London: Routledge.

Hickel, J. (2017). *The divide: A brief guide to global inequality and its solutions*. New York: Random House.

Hickel, J. (2020). The sustainable development index: Measuring the ecological efficiency of human development in the Anthropocene. *Ecological Economics* 167: 106331.

Hicks, C.C., A. Levine, A. Agrawal, X. Basurto, S.J. Breslow, C. Carothers, S. Charnley, S. Coulthard, N. Dolsak, J. Donatuto, and C. Garcia-Quijano. (2016). Engage key social concepts for sustainability. *Science* 352: 38-40.

Hidalgo-Capitán, A.L., and A.P. Cubillo-Guevara. (2017). Deconstrucción y genealogía del 'buen vivir' latinoamericano. *Revue Internationale de Politique de Développement* 9. DOI: https://doi.org/10.4000/poldev.2517

Hidalgo-Capitán, A.L., S. García-Álvarez, A.P. Cubillo-Guevara, and N. Medina-Carranco. (2019) Los Objetivos del Buen Vivir: Una propuesta alternative a los Objetivos de Desarrollo Sostenible. *Revista Iberoamericana de Estudios de Desarrollo* 8(1): 6-57.

Higgins-Desbiolles, F. (2009). *Capitalist globalisation, corporatised tourism and their alternatives*. New York: Nova Science.

Hinchliffe, S. (2007). *Geographies of nature: Societies, environments, ecologies*. London: Sage.

Hinchliffe, S., M.B. Kearnes, M. Degens, and S. Whatmore. (2005). Urban wild things: A cosmopolitical experiment. *Environment and Planning D: Society and Space* 23: 643–658.

Hinchliffe, S., and S. Whatmore. (2006). Living cities: Towards a politics of conviviality. *Science as culture* 15(2): 123–138.

Hoang, C., P. Satyal, and E. Corbera. (2019). 'This is my garden': Justice claims and struggles over forests in Vietnam's REDD+. *Climate Policy* 19 (sup1): S23-S35.

Hodgetts, T., and J. Lorimer. (2015). Methodologies for animals' geographies: Cultures, communication and genomics. *Cultural Geographies* 22(2): 285–295.

Hodgson, I., S. Redpath, C. Sandström, and D. Biggs. (2020). *The state of knowledge and practice on human-wildlife conflicts.* Cambridge, UK: Luc Hoffmann Institute.

Hoffman, D.M., D. Fay, and L. Joppa. (2011). Introduction: Human migration to protected area edges in Africa and Latin America: Questioning large-scale statistical analysis. *Conservation and Society* 9: 1-7.

Holland, T.G., G.D. Peterson, and A. Gonzalez. (2009). A cross-national analysis of how economic inequality predicts biodiversity loss. *Conservation Biology* 23: 1304-13.

Holmes, G. (2012). Biodiversity for billionaires: Capitalism, conservation and the role of philanthropy in saving/selling nature. *Development and Change* 43(3): 185–203.

Holmes, G. (2014). Defining the forest, defending the forest: Political ecology, territoriality and resistance to a protected area in the Dominican Republic. *Geoforum* 53: 1–10.

Holmes, G., and C.J. Cavanagh. (2016). A review of the social impacts of neoliberal conservation: Formations, inequalities, contestations. *Geoforum* 75: 199-209.

Holstein, E.V. and L. Head. (2018). Shifting settler-colonial discourses of environmentalism: Representations of Indigeneity and migration in Australian conservation. *Geoforum* 94: 41–52.

Homewood, K., M. R. Nielsen, and A. Keane. (2020). Women, wellbeing and Wildlife Management Areas in Tanzania. *The Journal of Peasant Studies* 49(2): 335-362.

Honey, M. (2008). *Ecotourism and sustainable development: Who owns paradise?* (2nd ed.). Washington, DC: Island Press.

Hope, J. (2020). The anti-politics of sustainable development: Environmental critique from assemblage thinking in Bolivia. *Transactions of the Institute of British Geographers* 46(1): 208-222.

Hope, J. (2022). Globalising Sustainable Development: Decolonial disruptions and environmental justice in Bolivia. *Area* 54(2): 176-184.

Hornedo, B. (2002). Ivan Illich: Hacia una sociedad convivencial. Pp. 22-44 in *La convivencialidad*, by Ivan Illich. Barcelona: Virus Editorial.

Howitt, R., and S. Suchet-Pearson. (2006). Rethinking the building blocks: Ontological pluralism and the idea of 'management'. *Geografiska Annaler: Series B, Human Geography* 88(3): 323-335.

Hsiao, E., and P. Le Billon. (2021). Connecting peaces: TBCAs and the integration of international, social, and ecological peace. *International Journal on World Peace* 38(1): 7-40.

Humbert, M. (2017). Convivialism: Reframing society and economy. Queen Mary University of London, Second Radical Social Innovation Symposium. Online at: http://altersocietal.org/documents/convivial/princ/MH-254-Convivialism%20 Reframing-2017-pdfppt.pdf (accessed May 2, 2021).

Humphries, K. (2013). *A political ecology of community-based forest and wildlife management in Tanzania: Politics, power and governance.* PhD Thesis, University of Cambridge, Cambridge, UK.

Hurn, S. (2012). *Humans and other animals: Cross-cultural perspectives on human-animal interactions.* London: Pluto Press.

Hurn, S. (2015). Baboon cosmopolitanism: More-than-human moralities in a multispecies community. Pp. 152–166 in *Cosmopolitan animals*, K. Jones, D. Landry, M. Mattfeld, C. Rooney, and C. Sleigh (eds.). London: Palgrave Macmillan.

Hussain, S. (2019). *The snow leopard and the goat: Politics of conservation in the Western Himalayas.* Seattle: University of Washington Press.

Hutchins, F. (2007). Footprints in the forest: Ecotourism and altered meanings in Ecuador's upper Amazon. *The Journal of Latin American and Caribbean Anthropology* 12(1): 75–103.

Ibrahim, H.O. (2018). Q&A: Getting indigenous women's voices heard on the SDGs. Online at: https://www.iied.org/qa-getting-indigenous-womens-voices-heard-sdgs (accessed March 12, 2021).

Icaza, R., and R. Vázquez. (2013). Social struggles as epistemic struggles. *Development and Change* 44(3): 683-704.

ICCA Consortium. (2021). *Territories of Life: 2021 Report. ICCA Consortium worldwide.* Online at: report.territoriesoflife.org (accessed July 30, 2021).

Igoe, J. (2010). The spectacle of nature in the global economy of appearances: Anthropological engagements with the images of transnational conservation. *Critique of Anthropology* 30: 375–397.

Igoe, J. (2017). *The nature of spectacle: On images, money, and conserving capitalism.* Tucson, AZ: University of Arizona Press.

Igoe, J., and D. Brockington. (2007). Neoliberal conservation: A brief introduction. *Conservation and Society* 5(4): 432–449.

Igoe, J., and B. Croucher. (2007). Conservation, commerce, and communities: The story of community-based wildlife management areas in Tanzania's northern tourist circuit. *Conservation & Society* 5(4): 534-561.

Igoe, J., K. Neves, and D. Brockington. (2010). A spectacular eco-tour around the historic bloc: Theorising the convergence of biodiversity conservation and capitalist expansion. *Antipode* 42(3): 486–512.

Illich, I. (1971). *Deschooling society*. New York: Harper and Row.

Illich, I. (1973). *Tools for conviviality*. New York: Harper and Row.

Immovilli, M. and M. Kok. (2020). *Narratives for the 'Half Earth' and 'Sharing The Planet' scenarios: A literature review*. The Hague: The Netherlands Environmental Assessment Agency. Online at: https://www.pbl.nl/sites/default/files/downloads/pbl-2020-narratives-for-half-earth-and-sharing-the-planet-scenarios-4226.pdf (accessed March 19, 2021).

Indigenous Peoples' Major Group. (2015). Position paper on proposed SDG indicators. Online at: https://www.forestpeoples.org/sites/fpp/files/publication/2015/10/sdg-indicatorsfinal-web1.pdf (accessed January 3, 2021).

Ingold, T., and J.L. Vergunst. (2008). *Ways of walking: Ethnography and practice on foot*. London: Routledge.

Inman, P.L. (1999). *An intellectual biography of Ivan Illich*. PhD dissertation, Doctor of Education, Northern Illinois University, DeKalb, IL, USA.

Ioja, C.I., M. Pătroescu, L. Rozylowicz, V.D. Popescu, M. Vergheleț, M.I. Zotta, and M. Felciuc. (2010). The efficacy of Romania's protected areas network in conserving biodiversity. *Biological Conservation* 143(11): 2468–2476.

Iordăchescu, G. (2018). Making the European Yellowstone: Unintended consequences or unrealistic intentions? *Environment & Society Portal Arcadia* 10.

Iordăchescu, G. (2021). The shifting geopolitical ecologies of wild nature conservation in Romania. Pp. 185-210 in *Environment politics and Eastern European government*, E.K. Kovacs (ed.). Cambridge: Open Book Publishers.

Intergovernmental Panel on Climate Change (IPCC). (2018). *Global Warming of 1.5C*. Bonn: IPCC.

Intergovernmental Science-Policy Platform on Biodiversity and Ecosystem Services (IPBES). (2019). *Global assessment report on biodiversity and ecosystem services of the Intergovernmental Science-Policy Platform on Biodiversity and Ecosystem Services*, J. Settele E. S. Brondizio, S. Díaz, and H. T. Ngo (eds.). Bonn, Germany: IPBES secretariat.

Isaacson, W. (2014). *The Innovators: How a group of hackers, geniuses, and geeks created the digital revolution*. New York: Simon and Schuster.

Isquierdo Tort, S. (2018). *Payments, ecosystems and development: Payments for environmental services (PES) in the Mexican Lacandona Rainforest*. PhD thesis, University of Oxford, UK.

IUCN-WCPA Task Force on OECMs. (2019). *Recognising and reporting other effective area-based conservation measures*. Gland, Switzerland: IUCN.

Jaireth, H. (2008). Introduction to the special issue: Human-wildlife conflict and peace-building strategies. *Journal of International Wildlife Law and Policy* 11(2–3): 99–100.

Janaszek, B. (2010). Convivial software (or, why open source matters). Online at: https://www.cardus.ca/comment/article/convivial-software-or-why-open-source-matters/ (accessed February 2, 2020).

Jeanrenaud, S. (2002). Changing people/nature representations in international conservation discourses. *IDS Bulletin* 33(1): 111-122.

Jhala, Y.V., Q. Qureshi, and A.K. Nayak (eds.). 2020. *Status of tigers, copredators and prey in India, 2018*. National Tiger Conservation Authority, Government of India, New Delhi, and Wildlife Institute of India, Dehradun.

Jordan, N.R., B.P. Smith, R.G. Appleby, L.M. van Eeden, and H.S. Webster. (2020). Addressing inequality and intolerance in human-wildlife coexistence. *Conservation Biology* 34(4): 803–810.

Joshi, D. (2011). Caste, gender and the rhetoric of reform in India's drinking water sector. *Economic and Political Weekly* 46(18): 56–63.

Joshi, D. (2014). Feminist solidarity? Women's engagement in politics and the implications for water management in the Darjeeling Himalaya. *Mountain Research and Development* 34(3): 243–254.

Junta de Castilla y León (JCyL). (2014). *Informe de Sostenibilidad Ambiental*. Programa de Desarollo Rural de Castilla y León 2014-2020. Valladolid.

Junta de Castilla y León (JCyL), Consejería de Fomento y Medio Ambiente. (2018). *Plan de Conservación y Gestón del Lobo en Castilla y León*. Memoria 2017. Valladolid.

Junta de Castilla y León (JCyL), Consejería de Fomento y Medio Ambiente. (2019). *Plan de aprovechamientos comarcales de lobo en los terrenos cinegéticos situados al norte del Río Duero en Castilla y León para las temporadas 2019/2020, 2020/2021 y 2021/2022.* Valladolid.

Junta de Castilla y León (JCyL), Red de Reservas Regionales de Caza de Castilla y León. (2020). *Aguardo de Lobo.* Available at: http://www.subastasdecaza.com/en/node/24621 (accessed October 29, 2020).

Kabra, A. (2020). Caste in stone? Exploring caste and class dimensions of conservation displacement in Central India. *Journal of Contemporary Asia* 50(5): 785–805.

Kajobe, R. (2007). Nesting biology of equatorial afrotropical stingless bees (*Apidae meliponini*) in Bwindi Impenetrable National Park, Uganda. *Journal of Apicultural Research* 46(4): 245–255.

Kallis, G. (2018). *Degrowth.* Newcastle upon Tyne, UK: Agenda Publishing.

Kanyamibwa, S. (1998). Impact of war on conservation: Rwandan environment and wildlife in agony. *Biodiversity and Conservation* 7(11): 1399–1406.

Kapoor, I. (2017). Cold critique, faint passion, bleak future: Post-development's surrender to global capitalism. *Third World Quarterly* 38: 2664-2683.

Kareiva, P. (2014). New conservation: Setting the record straight and finding common ground. *Conservation Biology* 28(3): 634-636.

Kareiva, P., M. Marvier, and R. Lalasz. (2012). Conservation in the Anthropocene: Beyond solitude and fragility. Online at: http://thebreakthrough.org/index.php/journal/past-issues/issue-2/conservation-in-the-Anthropocene/ (accessed September 25, 2020).

Kasaona, J. K. (2020). From poacher's son to conservation leader: Defending Namibia's community conservation story. *Conservation Namibia* (blog), October 9. Online at: http://conservationnamibia.com/blog/b2020-poacher-conservation-leader.php (accessed February 21, 2021).

Kashaigili, J. J., R. M. Kadigi, B. A. Lankford, H.F. Mahoo, and D.A. Mashauri. (2005). Environmental flows allocation in river basins: Exploring allocation challenges and options in the Great Ruaha River catchment in Tanzania. *Physics and Chemistry of the Earth* Parts A/B/C 30(11-16): 689-697.

Kashaigili, J.J., K. Rajabu, and P. Masolwa. (2009). Freshwater management and climate change adaptation: experiences from the Great Ruaha River catchment in Tanzania. *Climate and Development* 1(3): 220-228.

Kashwan, P., R.V. Duffy, F. Massé, A.P. Asiyanbi, and E. Marijnen. (2021). From racialized neocolonial global conservation to an inclusive and regenerative conservation. *Environment: Science and Policy for Sustainable Development* 63(4): 4-19.

Keeley, A.T.H., P. Beier, T. Creech, K. Jones, R.H.G. Jongman, G. Stonecipher, and G.M. Tabor. (2019). Thirty years of connectivity conservation planning: An assessment of factors influencing plan implementation. *Environmental Research Letters* 14(10): 103001.

Kihwele, E., E. Muse, E. Magomba, B. Mnaya, A. Nassoro, P. Banga, E. Murashani, D. Irmamasita, H. Kiwango, C. Birkett, and E. Wolanski. (2018). Restoring the perennial Great Ruaha River using ecohydrology, engineering and governance methods in Tanzania. *Ecohydrology & Hydrobiology* 18(2): 120-129.

Kimenyi, A. (No Date). Clans, totems and taboos in Rwanda. Online at: http://kimenyi.com/clans.php (accessed February 21, 2021).

Kirksey, S.E., and S. Helmreich. (2010). The emergence of multispecies ethnography. *Cultural Anthropology* 25(4): 545–576.

Kisingo, A.W., and J.R. Kideghesho. (2020). Community governance of wildlife resources: Implications for conservation, livelihood, and improvement in democratic space. Pp. 113-120 in *Protected areas in northern Tanzania: Local communities, land use change, and management challenges*, J.O. Durrant, E. H. Martin, K. Melubo., R. R. Jensen., L.A. Hadfield., P.J. Hardin, and L. Weisler (eds.). Cham: Springer.

Kistler, L., S.Y. Maezumi, J.G. de Souza, N. AS Przelomska, F.M. Costa, O. Smith, H. Loiselle et al. (2018). Multiproxy evidence highlights a complex evolutionary legacy of maize in South America. *Science* 362(6420): 1309–1313.

Kiwango, W.A. (2017). *Decentralised environmental governance: An examination of its effectiveness in Wildlife Management Areas, Tanzania. Case study of Idodi-Pawaga WMA*. PhD Thesis, The Nelson Mandela African Institution of Science and Technology, Arusha, Tanzania.

Kiwango, W.A., H. C. Komakech, T. M.C. Tarimo, and L. Martz. (2015). Decentralized Environmental Governance: A reflection on its role in shaping Wildlife Management Areas in Tanzania. *Tropical Conservation Science* 8(4): 1080-1097.

Kiwango, W. A., H. C. Komakech, T. M.C. Tarimo, and L. Martz. (2018). Levels of community participation and satisfaction with decentralized wildlife management in Idodi-Pawaga Wildlife Management Area, Tanzania. *International Journal of Sustainable Development & World Ecology* 25(3): 238-248.

Kiwango, W.A., and M.B. Mabele. (2022). Why the convivial conservation vision needs complementing to be a viable alternative for conservation in the Global South. *Conservation and Society* 20(2): 179-189.

Klein, N. (2015). *This changes everything: Capitalism vs. the climate.* New York: Simon and Schuster.

Knorn, J., T. Kuemmerle, V.C. Radeloff, A. Szabo, M. Mindrescu, W.S. Keeton, I. Abrudan, P. Griffiths, V. Gancz, and P. Hostert. (2012). Forest restitution and protected area effectiveness in post-socialist Romania. *Biological Conservation* 146(1): 204–212.

Kodiveri, A. (2016). *Narratives of dalit inclusion and exclusion in formulating and implementing the Forest Rights Act, 2006.* Policy Report No. 17. New Delhi: The Hindu Centre for Politics & Public Policy.

Kolipaka, S.S. (2018). *Can tigers survive in human-dominated landscapes?* PhD thesis, University of Leiden, The Netherlands.

Komi, S. (2021). Political and symbolic wolves/Poliittinen ja symbolinen susi. *CONVIVA research blog*, December 2. Online at: https://conviva-research.com/political-and-symbolic-wolves-poliittinen-ja-symbolinen-susi/ (accessed April 14, 2022).

König, H.J., C. Kiffner, S. Kramer-Schadt, C. Fürst, O. Keuling, and A.T. Ford. (2020). Human–wildlife coexistence in a changing world. *Conservation Biology* 34(4): 786-794.

Koot, S., and B. Büscher. (2019). Giving land (back)? Indigeneity and the meaning of land in the ontological politics of the South Kalahari Bushmen land claim in South Africa. *Journal of Southern African Studies* 45(2): 357-374.

Kopnina, H., H. Washington, J. Gray, and B. Taylor. (2018). The 'future of conservation' debate: Defending ecocentrism and the Nature Needs Half movement. *Biological Conservation* 217: 140–148.

Kothari, A. (2014). Radical ecological democracy: A way for India and beyond. *Development* 57(1): 36–45.

Kothari, A. (2021). Half-Earth or Whole-Earth? Green or transformative recovery? Where are the voices from the Global South? *Oryx* 55(2), 161-162.

Kothari, A., P. Camil, and J. Brown. (2013). Conservation as if people also mattered: Policy and practice of community-based conservation. *Conservation and Society* 11(1): 1–15.

Kothari, A, F. Demaria, and A. Acosta. (2014). Buen vivir, degrowth and ecological swaraj: Alternatives to sustainable development and the green economy. *Development* 57(3–4): 362–375.

Kothari, A., and A. Neumann. (2014). ICCAs and Aichi Targets: The Contribution of Indigenous Peoples' and Local Community Conserved Territories and Areas to the Strategic Plan for Biodiversity 2011-20. *ICCA Consortium Policy Brief No.1.*

Kothari, A., C. Corrigan, H. Jonas, A. Neumann, and H. Shrumm. (2012). Recognising and Supporting Territories and Areas Conserved by Indigenous Peoples and Local Communities: Global overview and national case studies. *Technical Series No. 64.* Montreal: Secretariat of the Convention on Biological Diversity, ICC Consortium, Kalpavriksh and Natural Justice.

Kothari, A., A. Salleh, A. Escobar, F. Demaria, and A. Acosta (eds.). 2019. *Pluriverse: A post-development dictionary.* New Delhi: Tulika Books and Authorsupfront.

Krauss, J.E. (2021). Decolonizing, conviviality and convivial conservation: Towards a convivial SDG 15, life on land? *Journal of Political Ecology* 28 (1). doi: https://doi.org/10.2458/jpe.3008.

Krauss, J.E. (2022). Unpacking SDG 15, its targets and indicators: Tracing ideas of conservation. *Globalizations* 19(8): 1179-1194.

Krauss, J.E., A. Jiménez Cisneros, and M. Requena. (2022). Mapping the Sustainable Development Goal System: Connections, Eurocentric framings and equity in SDGs 8, 9, 12, 13 and 15. *Sustainability Science.* https://doi.org/10.1007/s11625-022-01112-3

Kremen, C., and A. Miles. (2012). Ecosystem services in biologically diversified versus conventional farming systems: Benefits, externalities, and trade-offs. *Ecology and Society* 17(4).

Kueffer, C., and C.N. Kaiser-Bunbury. (2014). Reconciling conflicting perspectives for biodiversity conservation in the Anthropocene. *Frontiers in Ecology and the Environment* 12(2): 131-137.

Kuijper, D.P.J., M. Churski, A. Trouwborst, M. Heurich, C. Smit, G.I.H. Kerley, and J.P.G.M. Cromsigt. (2019). Keep the wolf from the door: How to conserve wolves in Europe's human-dominated landscapes? *Biological Conservation* 235: 102–111.

Kukreti, I. (2018). Gujarat's Narmada district takes a step forward in forest governance: Down to Earth. Online at: https://www.downtoearth.org.in/news/forests/gujarat-s-narmada-district-takes-a-step-forward-in-forestgovernance-62198 (accessed June 3, 2021).

Kumar, K., and J.M. Kerr. (2012). Democratic assertions: The making of India's recognition of forest rights act. *Development and Change* 43(3): 751–771.

Kuperman, A.J. (2004). Provoking genocide: A revised history of the Rwandan patriotic front. *Journal of Genocide Research* 6(1): 61–84.

Laclau, E., and C. Mouffe. (1985). *Hegemony and socialist strategy: Towards a radical democratic politics*. London: Verso

Laidlaw, B., and T. Beer. (2018). Dancing to (re)connect: Somatic dance experiences as a medium of connection with the more-than-human. *Choreographic Practices* 9(2): 283-309.

Landolt, G. (2019). Swiss alpine pastures as common property. Pp. 233-253 in *The commons in a glocal world*, T. Haller (ed.). London: Routledge

Lang, C. (2018). Colonialism vs. conservation. *Conservation Watch* (blog), October 17. Online: http://www.conservation-watch.org/2018/10/17/colonialism-vs-conservation/ (accessed July 18, 2020).

Langdon, J. (2013). Decolonising development studies: Reflections on critical pedagogies in action. *Canadian Journal of Development Studies / Revue Canadienne d'études du Développement* 34(3): 384-399.

Lankford, B., B. van Koppen, T. Franks, and H. Mahoo. (2004). Entrenched views or insufficient science? Contested causes and solutions of water allocation; insights from the Great Ruaha River Basin, Tanzania. *Agricultural Water Management* 69(2): 135-153.

Lasgorceix, A., and A. Kothari. (2009). Displacement and relocation of protected areas: A synthesis and analysis of case studies. *Economic and Political Weekly* 44(49): 37–47.

Laso, F. (2020). Galapagos is a garden. Pp. 137-166 in *Land cover and land use change on islands*, S.J. Walsh, D. Riveros-Iregui, J. Arce-Nazario, and P.H. Page (eds.). New York: Springer.

Latimer, J., and M. Miele. 2013. Naturecultures? Science, affect and the non-human. *Theory, Culture and Society* 30(7-8): 5-31.

Latour, B. (1984). The powers of association. *The Sociological Review* 32: 264-280.

Latour, B. (1987). *Science in action: How to follow scientists and engineers through society*: Cambridge, MA: Harvard University Press.

Lätsch, A. (2019). Constitutionality and identity. Pp. 210-232 in *The commons in a glocal world*, T. Haller (ed.). London: Routledge

Laundré, J.W., L. Hernández, and W.J. Ripple. (2010). The landscape of fear: Ecological implications of being afraid. *The Open Ecology Journal* 3(3): 1-7.

Law No. 33/2010 of 24/09/2010. (2010). Establishing Akagera National Park. Government of Tanzania.

Law No. 68/2019 of 29/10/2019. (2019). Governing the Akagera National Park. Government of Tanzania.

Law, J. (2008). On STS and sociology. *The Sociological Review* 56(4): 623–649.

Law, J. (2015). What's wrong with a one-world world? *Distinktion: Scandinavian Journal of Social Theory* 16(1): 126–139.

Le Grange, L. (2019). Ubuntu. Pp. 323-326 in *Pluriverse: A post-development dictionary*, A. Kothari, A. Salleh, A. Escobar, F. Demaria, and A. Acosta (eds.). New Delhi: Tulika Books.

Le Velly, G., and C. Dutilly. (2016). Evaluating payments for environmental services: Methodological challenges. *PloS ONE* 11: e0149374.

Leach, M., and R. Mearns. (1998). *The lie of the land: Challenging received wisdom on the African environment*. London, UK: International African Institute.

Leach, M., A.C. Stirling, and I. Scoones. (2010). *Dynamic sustainabilities: Technology, environment, social justice*. Oxfordshire: Routledge.

Leal Filho, W., M. Mandel, A.Q. Al-Amin, A. Feher, and C.J. Chiappetta Jabbour. (2016). Review: An assessment of the causes and consequences of agricultural land abandonment in Europe. *International Journal of Sustainable Development and World Ecology* 24(6): 554–560.

Leal, A.P. (2007). Participation: The ascendancy of a buzzword in the neo-liberal era. *Development in Practice* 17(4-5): 539-548.

Letseka, M. (2014). Ubuntu and justice as fairness. *Mediterranean Journal of Social Sciences* 5(9): 544–551.

Li, T.M. (2007). Practices of assemblage and community forest management. *Economy and Society* 36(2): 263-293.

Liere, H., S. Jha, and S.M. Philpott. (2017). Intersection between biodiversity conservation, agroecology, and ecosystem services. *Agroecology and Sustainable Food Systems* 41(7): 723–60.

Lim, M.M.L., P.S. Jørgensen, C.A. Wyborn. (2018) Reframing the sustainable development goals to achieve sustainable development in the Anthropocene—a systems approach. *Ecology and Society* 23(3): 22. https://doi.org/10.5751/ES-10182-230322.

Linnell, J.D.C., and B. Cretois. (2018). *Research for AGRI Committee—The revival of wolves and other large predators and its impact on farmers and their livelihood in rural regions of Europe.* Brussels: European Parliament, Policy Department for Structural and Cohesion Policies.

Lischka, S.A., T.L. Teel, H.E. Johnson, S.E. Reed, S. Breck, A.D. Carlos, and K.R. Crooks. (2018). A conceptual model for the integration of social and ecological information to understand human-wildlife interactions. *Biological Conservation* 225: 80-87.

Llaneza, L., J.V. López-Bao, and V. Sazatornil. (2012). Insights into wolf presence in human-dominated landscapes: The relative role of food availability, humans and landscape attributes. *Diversity and Distributions* 18(5): 459–469.

Locke, H. (2013). Nature needs half: A necessary and hopeful new agenda for protected areas. *PARKS* 19(1): 9–18.

Locke, P. (2012). Animals, persons, gods: Kaleidoscopic ontologies in a multispecies total institution. Annual Meeting of the Association of American Anthropologists, San Francisco, CA, USA, November 14-18.

Locke, P. (2013). Explorations in ethnoelephantology: Social, historical, and ecological intersections between Asian elephants and humans. *Environment and Society* 4(1): 79-97.

Locke, P., and J. Buckingham. (2016). *Conflict, and the challenge of rethinking human-elephant relations.* Oxford: Oxford University Press.

Locke, P., and U. Munster. (2015). *Multispecies ethnography.* Oxford: Oxford University Press.

Loft, L., P.T. Thuy, and C. Luttrell. (2014). Lessons from payments for ecosystem services for REDD+ benefit-sharing mechanisms. InfoBrief no. 68. Bogor, Indonesia: CIFOR.

Loftus, A. (2012). *Everyday environmentalism: Creating an urban political ecology.* Minneapolis: University of Minnesota Press.

Long, G. (2018). *How should civil society stakeholders report their contribution to the implementation of the 2030 Agenda for Sustainable Development?* United Nations Division for Sustainable Development (UNDESA).

López-Bao, J.V., J. Bruskotter, and G. Chapron. (2017). Finding space for large carnivores. *Nature Ecology and Evolution* 1(5): 140.

Lora Bavo, P., and A. Villar Lama. (2020). Iberian Wolf and tourism in the 'emptied rural Spain'. TERRA: *Revista de Desarrollo Local* 6(6): 179.

Lorimer, J. (2008). Counting corncrakes: The affective science of the UK corncrake census. *Social Studies of Science* 38(3): 377-405.

Lorimer, J. (2010). Elephants as companion species: The lively biogeographies of Asian elephant conservation in Sri Lanka. *Transactions of the Institute of British Geographers* 35(4): 491-506.

Lorimer, J. (2011). Author's response to Jepson et al. 'Towards an intradisciplinary bio-geography'. *Transactions of the Institute of British Geographers* 36(1): 175 -177.

Lorimer, J. (2015). *Wildlife in the Anthropocene: Conservation after nature.* Minneapolis, MN: University of Minnesota Press.

Lorimer, J., C. Sandom, P. Jepson, C. Doughty, M. Barua, and K.J. Kirby. (2015). Rewilding: Science, practice, and politics. *Annual Review of Environment and Resources* 40: 39–62.

Lozano, J., A. Olszańska, Z. Morales-Reyes, A.A. Castro, A.F. Malo, M. Moleón, J.A. Sánchez-Zapata, A. Cortés-Avizanda, H. von Wehrden, I. Dorresteijn, and R. Kansky. (2019). Human-carnivore relations: A systematic review. *Biological Conservation* 237: 480–492.

Lu, F., G. Valdivia, and W. Wolford. (2013). Social dimensions of 'nature at risk' in the Galápagos islands, Ecuador. *Conservation and Society* 11(1): 83.

Lugones, M. (2010). Toward a decolonial feminism. *Hypatia* 25(4): 742-759.

Lugones, M. (2020). Gender and universality in colonial methodology. *Critical Philosophy of Race* 8(1-2): 25-47.

Lukonge, A. (2021). Ng'ombe 200 wakamatwa bonde la Ihefu. *Habari Leo*, January 26. Online at: https://www.habarileo.co.tz/habari/2021-01-2660100aa914541.aspx (accessed February 26, 2021).

Lulka, D. (2009). The residual humanism of hybridity: Retaining a sense of the earth. *Transactions of the Institute of British Geographers* 34(3): 378-393.

Lund, J.F., E. Sungusia, M.B. Mabele, and A. Scheba. (2017). Promising change, delivering continuity: REDD+ as conservation fad. *World Development* 89: 124-139.

Lunstrum, E. (2014). Green militarization: Anti-poaching efforts and the spatial contours of Kruger National Park. *Annals of the American Association of Geographers* 104(4): 816–832.

Lute, M.L., N.H. Carter, J.V. López-Bao, and J.D.C. Linnell. (2018). Conservation professionals agree on challenges to coexisting with large carnivores but not on solutions. *Biological Conservation* 218: 223-232.

Mabele, M.B. (2017). Beyond forceful measures: Tanzania's 'war on poaching' needs diversified strategies more than militarised tactics. *Review of African Political Economy* 44(153): 487–498.

Mabele, M.B. (2020). In pursuit of multidimensional justice: Lessons from a charcoal 'greening' project in Tanzania. *Environment and Planning E: Nature and Space* 3(4): 1030-1052.

Mabon, L., S.T. Nguyen, T.T. Pham, T.T. Tran, H.N. Le, T.T.H. Doan, T.N.H. Hoang, N. Mueller-Hirth, and S. Vertigans. (2020). Elaborating a people-centered approach to understanding sustainable livelihoods under climate and environmental change: Thang Binh District, Quang Nam Province, Vietnam. *Sustainability Science* 16: 221–238.

MacDonald, K., and C. Corson. (2012). TEEB begins now: A virtual moment in the production of natural capital. *Development and Change* 43(1): 159–184.

MacKillop, E. (2018). How do empty signifiers lose credibility? The case of commissioning in English local government. *Critical Policy Studies* 12(2): 187-208.

MacKinnon, J., C. Aveling, R. Olivier et al. (2016). Larger than Elephants: Inputs for an EU strategic approach to wildlife conservation in Africa. Online at: https://op.europa.eu/en/publication-detail/-/publication/d76ac7eb-bc4a-11e6-a237-01aa75ed71a1/language-en (accessed February 27, 2021).

Madden, F. (2004). Creating coexistence between humans and wildlife: Global perspectives on local efforts to address human–wildlife conflict. *Human Dimensions of Wildlife* 9(4): 247-257.

Madden, F., and B. McQuinn. (2014). Conservation's blind spot: The case for conflict transformation in wildlife conservation. *Biological Conservation* 178: 97–106.

Madden, R. (2014). Animals and the limits of ethnography. *Anthrozoös* 27(2): 279-293.

Maddox, G., J.L. Giblin, and I.N. Kimambo (eds.). 1996. *Custodians of the land: Ecology & culture in the history of Tanzania*. Dar es Salaam: Mkuki na Nyota.

Madianou, M. (2019). Technocolonialism: Digital innovation and data practices in the humanitarian response to refugee crises. *Social Media + Society*, July-September: 1-13.

Magnusson, W., C. Grelle, M. Marques, C. Rocha, B. Dias, C. Fontana, H. Bergallo, et al. (2018). Effects of Brazil's political crisis on the science needed for biodiversity conservation. *Frontiers in Ecology and Evolution* 6(163): 1–5.

Maldonado-Torres, N. (2007). On the coloniality of being: Contributions to the development of a concept. *Cultural Studies* 21: 240-270.

Maldonado-Torres, N. (2016). Outline of ten theses on coloniality and decoloniality. Fondation Frantz Fanon. Online at: http://caribbeanstudiesassociation.org/docs/Maldonado-Torres_Outline_Ten_Theses-10.23.16.pdf (accessed July 28, 2020).

Mancini, C., and J. Lehtonen. (2018). The emerging nature of participation in multispecies interaction design. Pp. 907-918 in *Proceedings of the 2018 Designing Interactive Systems Conference*, June 9-13, Hong Kong, China, ACM.

Marchesini, R. (2016). The theriosphere. *Angelaki* 21(1): 113-135.

Margulies, J.D., and K.K. Karanth. (2018). The production of human-wildlife conflict: A political animal geography of encounter. *Geoforum* 95: 153-164.

Marris, E. (2011). *Rambunctious garden: Saving nature in a post-wild world*. New York: Bloomsbury.

Marsden, K., T. Hovardas, S. Psaroudas, Y. Mertzanis, and U. Baatz. (2016). *EU platform on large carnivores: Supporting good practice for coexistence—presentation of examples and analysis of support through the EAFRD*. Platform Secretariat to DG Environment of the European Commission.

Martin, A. (2005). Environmental conflict between refugee and host communities. *Journal of Peace Research* 42(3): 329–346.

Martin, A., A. Akol, and N. Gross-Camp. (2015). Towards an explicit justice framing of the social impacts of conservation. *Conservation and Society* 13(2): 166–178.

Martin, A., M.T. Armijos, B. Coolsaet, N. Dawson, G.A.S. Edwards, R. Few, N. Gross-Camp, et al. (2020). Environmental justice and transformations to sustainability. *Environment: Science and Policy for Sustainable Development* 62(6): 19-30.

Martin, A., B. Coolsaet, E. Corbera. N.M. Dawson, J.A. Fraser, I. Lehmann, and I. Rodriguez. (2016). Justice and conservation: The need to incorporate recognition. *Biological Conservation* 197: 254–261.

Martin, A., M. Teresa Armijos, B. Coolsaet, N. Dawson, G.A.S. Edwards, R. Few, N. Gross-Camp, I. Rodriguez, H. Schroeder, M.G.L. Tebboth, and C.S. White. (2020). Environmental justice and transformations to sustainability. *Environment: Science and Policy for Sustainable Development* 62(6): 19-30.

Martínez, F.A. (2019). Wolf watching tourism in the Culebra Mountain Range. *Revista Lider* 35: 137–160.

Marvier, M. (2014). New conservation is true conservation. *Conservation Biology* 28(1): 1-3.

Marvier, M., P. Kareiva, and R. Lalasz. (2012). Conservation in the Anthropocene: Beyond Solitude and Fragility. *The Breakthrough 2*. Online at: https://thebreakthrough.org/journal/issue-2/conservation-in-the-anthropocene (accessed February 15, 2019).

Mason, V., and P.R. Hope. (2014). Echoes in the dark: Technological encounters with bats. *Journal of Rural Studies* 33: 107–118.

Massarella, K., J.E. Krauss, W. Kiwango, and R. Fletcher. (2022). Special Section: Exploring convivial conservation in theory and practice: possibilities and challenges for a transformative approach to biodiversity conservation. *Conservation & Society* 20(2).

Massarella, K., A. Nygren, R. Fletcher, B. Büscher, W.A. Kiwango, S. Komi, J.E. Krauss, M.B. Mabele, A. McInturff, L.T. Sandroni, P.S. Alagona, D. Brockington, R. Coates, R. Duffy, K. M.P.M.B. Ferraz, S. Koota, S. Marchini, and A. Reis Percequillo. (2021). Transformation beyond conservation: How critical social science can contribute to a radical new agenda in biodiversity conservation. *Current Opinion in Environmental Sustainability* 49: 79-87.

Massarella, K., S.M. Sallu, J.E. Ensor, and R. Marchant. (2018). REDD+, hype, hope and disappointment: The dynamics of expectations in conservation and development pilot projects. *World Development* 109: 375–85.

Massumi, B. (2018). *99 thesis on the revaluation of value: A postcapitalist manifesto*. Minneapolis: University of Minnesota Press.

Mawere, M. (2012). 'Buried and forgotten but not dead': Reflections on 'Ubuntu' in environmental conservation in southeastern Zimbabwe. *Afro Asian Journal of Social Sciences* 3(3.2): 1–20.

May, V. 2014. 'Speaking into the Void'? Intersectionality critiques and epistemic backlash. *Hypatia* 29(1): 94-112.

Mbaria, J., and M. Ogada. (2016). *The big conservation lie: The untold story of wildlife conservation in Kenya*. Auburn, WA: Lens&Pens Publishing LLC.

Mbembe, A.J. (2016). Decolonizing the university: New directions. *Arts and Humanities in Higher Education* 15(1): 29-45.

Mbembe, A. (2017). *Critique of black reason*. Durham, NC: Duke University Press.

MBOMIPA (Matumizi Bora ya Malihai Idodi na Pawaga). (2014). *General Management Plan 2013-2023*. Iringa: MBOMIPA.

McCauley, D.J. (2006). Selling out on nature. *Nature* 443: 27-28.

McShane, T.O., P.D. Hirsch, T.C. Trung, A.N. Songorwa, A. Kinzig, B. Monteferri, D. Mutekanga, H. Van Thang, J.L. Dammert, M. Pulgar-Vidal, and M. Welch-Devine. (2011). Hard choices: Making trade-offs between biodiversity conservation and human well-being. *Biological Conservation* 144: 966–72.

Mech, L.D. (2017). Where can wolves live and how can we live with them? *Biological Conservation* 210: 310–317.

Meijer, E. (2013). Political communication with animals. *Humanimalia* 5(9). Online at: http://www.depauw.edu/humanimalia/issue09/meijer.html (accessed November 17, 2019).

Meinzen-Dick, R., and M. Zwarteveen. (2001). Gender dimensions of community resource management: The case of Water Users' Associations in South Asia. Pp. 63-88 in *Communities and the environment: Ethnicity, gender and the state in community-based conservation*, A. Agrawal and C.C. Gibson (eds.). Rutgers, NJ: Rutgers University Press.

Menton, M., C. Larrea, S. Latorre, J. Martinez-Alier, M. Peck, L. Temper, and M. Walter. (2020) Environmental justice and the SDGs: From synergies to gaps and contradictions. *Sustainability Science* 15(6): 1621-1636.

Menzies, C.R., and C. Butler. (2006). Introduction: Understanding ecological knowledge. Pp. 1-17 in *Traditional ecological knowledge and natural resource management*, C.R. Menzies (ed.). Lincoln, NE: University of Nebraska Press.

Mert, A. (2015). *Environmental governance through partnerships*. London: Edward Elgar.

Meyer, J., and R. Land. (2006). *Overcoming barriers to student understanding: Threshold concepts and troublesome knowledge*. London: Routledge.

Meyer, S.M. (2006). *The end of the wild*. Cambridge, MA: MIT Press.

Mfune, O. (2017). Conservation narratives and contested protected areas in Zambia: A political ecological analysis. *Journal of African Studies* 7(1): 118–137.

Michel, A.C., and A. Bruggmann. (2019). Conflicting discourses: Understanding the rejection of a Swiss National Park project using data analysis triangulation. *Mountain Research and Development* 39(1): R24–R36.

Mignolo, W.D. (2011). *The darker side of western modernity: Global futures, decolonial options*. Durham, NC: Duke University Press.

Mignolo, W.D., and A. Escobar (eds.). (2015). *Globalization and the decolonial option*. London: Routledge.

Mikkelson, G., A. Gonzalez, and G.D. Peterson. (2007). Economic inequality predicts biodiversity loss. *PloS ONE* 2: e444.doi:10.1371/journal.pone.0000444.

Milich, K.M., K. Sorbello, L. Kolinski, R. Busobozi, and M. Kugonza. (2020). Case study of participatory action research for wildlife conservation. *Conservation Science and Practice* 3(5): 1–15.

Minister of Trade and Industry. (2012). *Determining the list of wild animal species concerned with the law on compensation for damages caused by animals.* Madrid: Ministry of Trade and Industry.

Ministerio de Agricultura y Pesca Alimentación y Medio Ambiente (MAPAMA). (2017). *El turismo de naturaleza en España.* Publicaciones de la SGAPC. Madrid: MAPAMA.

Ministerio para la Transición Ecológica y el Reto Demográfico (MITECO). (2020). *El borrador de la estrategia para la conservación y gestión del lobo propone su inclusión en el listado de protección especial.* Madrid: MITECO.

Ministry of Lands, Resettlement and Environment. (2003). *National strategy and action plan for the conservation of biodiversity in Rwanda.* Kigali: MINITERE.

Ministry of Natural Resources and Tourism (MNRT). (2007). *The wildlife policy of Tanzania.* Dar es Salaam: Government Printer.

Ministry of Natural Resources and Tourism (MNRT). (2012). *The wildlife conservation (Wildlife Management Areas) regulations.* Dar es Salaam: Government Printer.

Ministry of Natural Resources and Tourism (MNRT). (2013). *The wildlife sub-sector statistical bulletin.* Dar es Salaam: Wildlife Division.

Ministry of Natural Resources and Tourism (MNRT). (2018). *The 2028 Tourism Statistical Bulletin.* Dodoma: MNRT.

Minority Rights Group, Rainforest Foundation UK, and Survival International. (2020). NGO concerns over the proposed 30% target for protected areas and absence of safeguards for Indigenous peoples and local communities. September 1. Online at: https://assets.survivalinternational.org/documents/1959/final-en-ngo-concerns-over-the-proposed-30-target-for-protected-areas-and-absence-of-safeguards-for-indigenous-people-and-local-communities-200901.pdf (accessed November 18, 2020).

Mitchell, A. (2020). Revitalizing laws, (re)-making treaties, dismantling violence: Indigenous resurgence against 'the sixth mass extinction'. *Social & Cultural Geography* 21(7): 909-924.

Mkandawire, T. (2007). 'Good governance': The itinerary of an idea. *Development in Practice* 17(4/5): 679-681.

Mogashoa, T. (2014). Understanding critical discourse analysis in qualitative research. *International Journal of Humanities Social Sciences and Education* 1(7): 104-113.

Mogg, S., C. Fastre, M. Jung and P. Visconti. (2019). Targeted expansion of protected areas to maximise the persistence of terrestrial mammals. *bioRxiv*: 608992.

Mol, A. (1999). Ontological politics: A word and some questions. *The Sociological Review* 47(1): 74-89.

Mol, A. (2002). *The body multiple: Ontology in medical practice*. Durham, NC: Duke University Press.

Molefe, M. (2019). Ubuntu and development: An African conception of development. *Africa Today* 66(1): 97–115.

Molefe, M., and N.L. Magam. (2020). What can Ubuntu do? A reflection on African moral theory in light of post-colonial challenges. Pp. 285–307 in *Philosophical perspectives on land reform in southern Africa*, E. Masitera (ed). Cham, Switzerland: Springer Nature.

Mollett, C., and T. Kepe (eds.). (2018). *Land rights, biodiversity conservation and justice: Rethinking parks and people*. London: Routledge.

Mollett, S., and C. Faria. (2013). Messing with gender in feminist political ecology. *Geoforum* 45: 116–125.

Montgomery, R.A., K. Borona, H. Kasozi, T. Mudumba, and M. Ogada. (2020). Positioning human heritage at the center of conservation practice. *Conservation Biology* 34(5): 1122-1130.

Moore, J. (2016). The rise of cheap nature. Pp. 78-115 in *Anthropocene or capitalocene? Nature, history, and the crisis of capitalism*, J. Moore (ed.). Oakland: PM Press.

Moosavi, L. (2020). The decolonial bandwagon and the dangers of intellectual decolonisation. *International Review of Sociology* 30(2): 332-354.

Moraes, S.E. (2014). Global citizenship as a floating signifier: Lessons from UK universities. *International Journal of Development Education and Global Learning* 6(2): 27-42.

Mosse, D. (2004). Social analysis as product development: Anthropologists at work in the World Bank. Pp. 77-87 in *The development of religion/the religion of development*, O. Salemink, A. van Harskamp, and A.K. Giri (eds.). Delft, NL: Uitgeverij Eburon.

Mowforth, M., and I. Munt. (2016). *Tourism and sustainability: Development, globalisation and new tourism in the third world*. London: Routledge.

Moyo, F., J. Ijumba, and J.F. Lund. (2016). Failure by design? Revisiting Tanzania's flagship Wildlife Management Area Burunge. *Conservation and Society* 14(3): 232-242.

Mtahiko, M.G.G., E. Gereta, A.R. Kajuni, E.A.T. Chiombola, G.Z. Ng'umbi, P. Coppolillo, and E. Wolanski. (2006). Towards an ecohydrology-based restoration of the Usangu wetlands and the Great Ruaha River, Tanzania. *Wetlands Ecology and Management* 14(6): 489-503.

Mujuni, C.N., K. Nicholson, P. van de Kop, A. Baldascini, and S. Grouwels. (2003). Community-based forest enterprise development for improved livelihoods and biodiversity conservation: A case study from Bwindi World Heritage Site, Uganda. XII World Foresty Congress, Québec City, Canada, September 21-28.

Mukadasi, B., and M. Nabalegwa. (2007), Gender mainstreaming and community participation in plant resource conservation in Buzaya county, Kamuli district, Uganda. *African Journal of Ecology* 45: 7-12.

Murombedzi, J. (2003). *Pre-colonial and colonial conservation practices in southern Africa and their legacy today*. Gland, Switzerland: IUCN.

Murove, M.F. (2012). Ubuntu. *Diogenes* 59(3-4): 36-47.

Museka, G., and M.M. Madondo. (2012). The quest for a relevant environmental pedagogy in the African context: Insights from *unhu/ubuntu* philosophy. *Journal of Ecology and the Natural Environment* 4(10): 258–265.

Musumali, M.M., T.S. Larsen, and B.P. Kaltenborn. (2007). An impasse in community based natural resource management implementation: The case of Zambia and Botswana. *Oryx* 41(3): 306–313.

Mwamidi, D., A. Nunow, and S.H. Mwasi. (2012). The use of indigenous knowledge in minimizing human-wildlife conflict: The case of Taita Community, Kenya. *International Journal of Current Research* 4(02): 026-030.

Naicker, I. (2011). The search for universal responsibility: The cosmovision of Ubuntu and the humanism of Fanon. *Development* 54(4): 455-460.

Naidu, S.C. (2013). Legal exclusions, private wealth and livelihoods: An analysis of work time allocation in protected areas. *Ecological Economics* 89: 82–91.

Narodowski, M., and M. Botta. (2017). La mayor disrupción posible en la historia de la pedagogía moderna: Ivan Illich. *Pedagogía y Saberes* 46: 45-54.

Naude, P. (2019). Decolonising knowledge: Can Ubuntu ethics save us from coloniality? *Journal of Business Ethics* 159(1): 23–37.

Naughton-Treves, L. and A. Treves. (2005). Socio-ecological factors shaping local support for wildlife: Crop-raiding by elephants and other wildlife in Africa. Pp.252–77 in *People and wildlife: Conflict or co-existence?*, R. Woodroffe, S. Thirgood, and A. Rabinowitz (eds.). Cambridge: Cambridge University Press.

Navarro, A., and J.V. López-Bao. (2018). Towards a greener common agricultural policy. *Nature Ecology and Evolution* 2(12): 1830–1833.

Ndalu, D. (2021). Tourism earnings down as visitors stay away from Tanzania. *The East African*, February 11. Online at: https://www.theeastafrican.co.ke/tea/business/tourism-earnings-down-as-visitors-stay-away-from-tanzania-3288132 (accessed March 21, 2021).

Nelson, D., N. Adger, and K. Brown. (2007). Adaptation to environmental change: Contributions of a resilience framework. *Annual Review of Environment and Resources* 32: 395–419.

Nelson, F. (2007). *Emerging or illusory? Community wildlife management in Tanzania*: London: IIED.

Nelson, F. (2010). Introduction: The politics of natural resource governance in Africa. Pp. 3–31 in *Community rights, conservation and contested land: The politics of natural resource governance in Africa*, F. Nelson (ed.). London: Earthscan.

Nelson, F., R. Nshala, and W. Rodgers. (2007). The evolution and reform of Tanzanian wildlife management. *Conservation and Society* 5(2): 232–261.

Neumann, R. (1998). *Imposing wilderness: Struggles over livelihood and nature preservation in Africa*. Berkeley and Los Angeles, CA: University of California Press.

Neumann, R. (2002). The postwar conservation boom in British colonial Africa. *Environmental History* 7(1): 22–47.

Neumann, R. (2014). Stories of Nature's hybridity in Europe: Implication for forest management in the Global South. Pp. 31-44 in *The social lives of forest: Past, present and future of woodland resurgence*, S.B. Hecht, K.D. Morrison, and C. Padoch (eds.). Chicago: Chicago University Press.

Newbold, T., L. Hudson, A. Arnell, S. Contu, A. De Palma, S. Ferrier, S. Hill, et al. (2016). Has land use pushed terrestrial biodiversity beyond the planetary boundary? A global assessment. *Science* 353(6296): 288–291.

Nightingale, A. (2011). Bounding difference: Intersectionality and the material production of gender, caste, class and environment in Nepal. *Geoforum* 42(2): 153–162.

Nirmal, P., and D. Rocheleau. (2019). Decolonizing degrowth in the post-development convergence: Questions, experiences, and proposals from two Indigenous territories. *Environment and Planning E: Nature and Space* 2(3): 465–492.

Nixon, R. (2011). *Slow violence and the environmentalism of the poor.* Cambridge, MA: Harvard University Press.

Nkondo, G.M. (2007). Ubuntu as public policy in South Africa: A conceptual framework. *International Journal of African Renaissance Studies* 2(1): 88–100.

Noe, C. (2019). The Berlin curse in Tanzania: (Re)making of the Selous World Heritage Property. *South African Geographical Journal* 101(3): 379-398.

Noe, C., A. Budeanu, E. Sulle, M.F. Olwig, D. Brockington and R. John. (2017). Partnerships for wildlife protection and their sustainability outcomes: A literature review. NEPSUS Working Paper. Frederiksberg, Denmark: New Partnerships for Sustainability.

Noe, C., and R.Y.M. Kangalawe. (2015). Wildlife protection, community participation in conservation, and (dis)empowerment in Southern Tanzania. *Conservation and Society* 13(3): 244-253.

Noxolo, P. (2017). Introduction: Decolonising geographical knowledge in a colonised and re-colonising postcolonial world. *Area* 49: 317-319.

NTCA (2012). Gazette notification National Tiger Conservation Authority.

NTCA (2020). Project tiger. Online at: https://ntca.gov.in/about-us/#project-tiger (accessed January 1, 2021).

Nygren, A. (1999). Local knowledge in the environment-development discourse. *Critique of Anthropology* 19(3): 267–288.

Nygren, N.V., and A. Jokinen. (2013). Significance of affect and ethics in applying conservation standards: The practices of flying squirrel surveyors. *Geoforum* 46: 79–90.

Nyhus, P.J. (2016). Human–wildlife conflict and coexistence. *Annual Review of Environment and Resources* 41: 143–171.

O'Brien, K. (2012). Global environmental change II: From adaptation to deliberate transformation. *Progress in Human Geography* 36(5): 667–76.

O'Brien, K., J. Reams, A. Caspari, A. Dugmore, M. Faghihimani, I. Fazey, H. Hackmann, D. Manuel-Navarrete, J. Marks, and R. Miller. (2013). You say you want a revolution? Transforming education and capacity building in response to global change. *Environmental Science & Policy* 28: 48-59.

O'Mahony, K., A. Corradini, and A. Gazzola. (2018). Lupine becomings: Tracking and assembling Romanian Wolves through multi-sensory fieldwork. *Society and Animals* 26(2): 107-129.

Ogada, M. (2017). The Big Conservation Lie: Overview and interview with the authors. *National Geographic* (Blog). July 28. Online at: https://blog. nationalgeographic.org/2017/07/28/the-big-conservation-lie-overview-and-interview-with-the-authors/ (accessed January 13, 2020).

Ogada, M. (2019). Decolonising conservation: It is about the land, stupid! Online at: https://www.theelephant.info/culture/2019/06/27/decolonising-conservation-it-is-about-the-land-stupid/ (accessed January 13, 2020).

Ogden, L., N. Heynen, U. Oslender, P. West, K.A. Kassam, and P. Robbins. (2013). Global assemblages, resilience, and earth stewardship in the Anthropocene. *Frontiers in Ecology and Environment* 11(7): 341–347.

Ogunniyi, M.B. (2020). Tapping the potential of Ubuntu for a science that promotes social justice and moral responsibility. Pp. 157–176 in *Nature of science for social justice*, H.A. Yacoubian and L. Hansson (eds.). Cham, Switzerland: Springer Nature.

Ojeda, D. (2012). Green pretexts: Ecotourism, neoliberal conservation and land grabbing in Tayrona National Park in Colombia. *The Journal of Peasant Studies* 39(2): 357–375.

Okereke, C., and M. Charlesworth. (2014). Environmental and ecological justice. Pp. 123-147 in *Advances in international environmental politics* (2nd ed.), M.M. Betsill, K. Hochstetler and D. Stevis (eds.). London: Palgrave Macmillan.

Oldekop J.A., G. Holmes, and W.E. Harris. (2016). A global assessment of the social and conservation outcomes of protected areas. *Conservation Biology* 30(1): 133–141.

Olvera, R., and J. Márquez. (No Date). Ivan Illich – Su vida. Online at: https://www. ivanillich.org.mx/Illich-Antologia.pdf (accessed May 9, 2020).

Oneal, J.R., F.H. Oneal, Z. Maoz, and B. Russett. (1996). The liberal peace: Interdependence, democracy, and international conflict, 1950-85. *Journal of Peace Research* 33(1): 11–28.

Opincaru, I.S. (2020). Elements of the institutionalization process of the forest and pasture commons in Romania as particular forms of social economy. *Annals of Public and Cooperative Economics* 92(1): 101–118.

Oppie, T. (2021). New Idaho law calls for killing 90% of the state's wolves. *NPR*, May 21. Available at: https://www.npr.org/2021/05/21/999084965/new-idaho-law-calls-for-killing-90-of-states-wolves?t=1628160390745 (accessed September 8, 2021).

Ospina, P. (2001). Identidades en Galápagos. Consejo Latinoamericano de Ciencias Sociales.

Ospina, P. (2003). Ética ambiental y actores sociales en Galápagos: Apuntes sobre las relaciones entre naturaleza y sociedad. *Ecología Política* 25: 111–19.

Ostrom, E. (2008). Institutions and the environment. *Economic Affairs* 28(3):24–31.

Ostrom, E., J. Burger, C.B. Field, R.B. Norgaard, and D. Policansky. (1999). Revisiting the commons: Local lessons, global challenges. *Science* 284(5412): 278–282.

Ostrom, E., and M. Cox. (2010). Moving beyond panaceas: A multi-tiered diagnostic approach for social-ecological analysis. *Environmental Conservation* 37(4): 451–463.

Ostry, J.D., P. Loungani, and D. Furceri. (2016). Neoliberalism: Oversold. *Finance & Development* 53: 38-41.

Otero, I., and J.Ø. Nielsen. (2017). Coexisting with wildfire? Achievements and challenges for a radical social-ecological transformation in Catalonia (Spain). *Geoforum* 85: 234-246.

Othman, N., B. Goossens, C.P.I. Cheah, S. Nathan, R. Bumpus, and M. Ancrenaz. (2019). Shift of paradigm needed towards improving human–elephant coexistence in monoculture landscapes in Sabah. *International Zoo Yearbook* 53(1): 161-173.

Otto, J., C. Zerner, J. Robinson, R. Donovan, M. Lavelle, R. Villarreal, N. Salafsky et al. (2013). *Natural connections: Perspectives in community-based conservation.* Washington, DC: Island press.

Pagiola, S., A. Arcenas, and G. Platais. (2005). Can payments for environmental services help reduce poverty? An exploration of the issues and the evidence to date from Latin America. *World Development* 33: 237-253.

Pagiola, S., J. Bishop, and N. Landell-Mills (eds.). (2002). *Selling forest environmental services: Market-based mechanisms for conservation.* London: Earthscan.

Palacios, J.F., B. Salem, F.S. Hodge, C.R. Albarrán, A. Anaebere, and T.M. Hayes-Bautista. (2015). Storytelling: A qualitative tool to promote health among vulnerable populations. *Journal of Transcultural Nursing* 26(4): 346–353.

Pan, A. (2019). Embracing difference: Towards a standpoint praxis in dalit feminism. *South Asian Review* 40(1-2): 34–50.

Pandey, A.D. (2017). The challenges of neoliberal policies and the indigenous people's resistance movement in Odisha, India. *E-Cadernos CES* 28.

Parenti, C. (2013). The environment making state: Territory, nature, and value. *Antipode* 47(4): 829–848.

Parque Nacional Galápagos. (2014). *Plan de manejo de las areas protegidas de Galápagos para el buen vivir*. Puerto Ayora: Parque Nacional Galápagos

Parthasarthy, S.K. (2015). Politics of commons: Power relations and intersecting gender, caste and tribe contestations. Pp. 71-86 in *Land Rights in India: Policies, movements and challenges*, V. Bhagat-Ganguly (ed.). Oxfordshire: Routledge.

Paulson, W. (2001). For a cosmopolitical philology: Lessons from science studies. *Substance* 30(3): 101-119.

Pearce, F. (2015). *The New Wild: Why invasive species will be nature's salvation*. Boston: Beacon Press.

Peck, J. (2010). *Constructions of neoliberal reason*. Oxford: Oxford University Press.

Peck, J., and N. Theodore. (2015). *Fast policy*. Minneapolis: University of Minnesota Press.

Peluso, N.L., and C. Lund. (2011). New frontiers and land control: Introduction. *The Journal of Peasant Studies* 38(4): 811–836.

Pena, P. (2014). *The politics of the diffusion of conditional cash transfers in Latin America*. Brooks World Poverty Institute Working Paper no. 201. University of Manchester.

Perrault, T., G. Bridge, and J. McCarthy (eds.). (2015). *The Routledge handbook of political ecology*. London: Routledge.

Persson, J., G.R. Rauset, and G. Chapron. (2015). Paying for an endangered predator leads to population recovery. *Conservation Letters* 8(5): 345–350.

Persson, U.M., and F. Alpizar. (2013). Conditional cash transfers and payments for environmental services: A conceptual framework for explaining and judging differences in outcomes. *World Development* 43: 124-137.

Peterson, M., D. Hall, A. Feldpausch-Parker, and T. Peterson. (2009). Obscuring ecosystem function with application of the ecosystem services concept. *Conservation Biology* 24: 113–119.

Peterson, M.N., J.L. Birckhead, K. Leong, M.J. Peterson, and T.R. Peterson. (2010). Rearticulating the myth of human-wildlife conflict. *Conservation Letters* 3(2): 74–82.

Peterson, R., D. Russel, P. West, and J.P. Brosius. (2010). Seeing (and doing) conservation through cultural lenses. *Environmental Management* 45: 5–18.

Pettersson, H.L., C.H. Quinn, G. Holmes, S.M. Sait, and J.V. López-Bao. (2021). Welcoming wolves? Governing the return of large carnivores in traditional pastoral landscapes. *Frontiers in Conservation Science* 2(710218).

Petursson, J.G., and P. Vedeld. (2015). The 'nine lives' of protected areas: A historical-institutional analysis from the transboundary Mt Elgon, Uganda and Kenya. *Land Use Policy* 42: 251–263.

Petursson, J.G., and P. Vedeld. (2017). Rhetoric and reality in protected area governance: Institutional change under different conservation discourses in Mount Elgon National Park, Uganda. *Ecological Economics* 131: 166–177.

Pickering, A. (1995). *The mangle of practice: Time, agency, and science.* Chicago, IL: University of Chicago Press.

Piketty, T. (2014). *Capital in the twenty-first century.* Cambridge, MA: Harvard University Press.

Pirard, R. (2012). Market-based instruments for biodiversity and ecosystem services: A lexicon. *Environ. Sci. Pol.* 19-20: 59–68.

Pitman, C.R.S. (1935). The Gorillas of the Kayonsa Region, Western Kigezi, SW, Uganda. *Proceedings of the Zoological Society of London* 105(3): 477–494.

Plumwood, V. (2003). Colonization, Eurocentrism and anthropocentrism. Pp. 51-78 in *Decolonizing nature: Strategies for conservation in a post-colonial era*, W.M. Adams and M. Mulligan (eds.). London: Earthscan.

Pooley, S., M. Barua, W. Beinart, A. Dickman, G. Holmes, J. Lorimer, A.J. Loveridge, D.W. Macdonald, G. Marvin, and S. Redpath. (2017). An interdisciplinary review of current and future approaches to improving human–predator relations. *Conservation Biology* 31(3): 513-523.

Pooley, S,, S. Bhatia, and A. Vasava. (2021). Rethinking the study of human–wildlife coexistence. *Conservation Biology* 35(3): 784-793.

Pörtner, H.O., R.J. Scholes, J. Agard, E. Archer, A. Arneth, X. Bai, D. Barnes, et al. (2021). IPBES-IPCC co-Sponsored workshop report on biodiversity and climate change. Zenodo.

Powell, N. (1998). Co-management in non-equilibrium systems. Cases from Namibian Rangelands. Agraria 138. Swedish University of Agricultural Sciences.

Pradhan, P., L. Costa, D. Rybski, W. Lucht, and J.P. Kropp. (2017). A systematic study of Sustainable Development Goal (SDG) interactions. *Earth's Future* 5: 1169-1179.

Pretty, J., B. Adams, F. Berkes, S.F. De Athayde, N. Dudley, E. Hunn, L. Maffi, K. Milton, D. Rapport, P. Robbins, and E. Sterling. (2009). The intersections of biological diversity and cultural diversity: Towards integration. *Conservation and Society* 7(2): 100-112.

Promberger, B., and C. Promberger. (2015). Rewilding the Carpathians. A present-day opportunity. Pp. 242-249 in *Protecting the wild: Parks and wilderness, the foundation for conservation*, G. Wuerther, E. Crist, and T. Butler (eds.). London: Island Press.

Prunier, G. (1995). *The Rwanda crisis: History of a genocide*. London: Hurst & Co.

Pudyatmoko, S., A. Budiman, and S. Kristiansen. (2018). Towards sustainable coexistence: People and wild mammals in Baluran National Park, Indonesia. *Forest Policy and Economics* 90: 151-159.

Quijano, A. (2000). Coloniality of power and Eurocentrism in Latin America. *International Sociology* 15: 215-232.

Quijano, A. (2007) Coloniality and modernity/rationality. *Cultural Studies* 21 (2-3): 168-178.

Rai, N.D. (2021). Human wildlife coexistence #1: Exploring 'co-existence' in wildlife habitats (webinar). Online at: https://www.youtube.com/watch?v=5548S3UnvIY (accessed February 27, 2021).

Rai, N.D., T.A. Benjaminsen, S. Krishnan, and C. Madegowda. (2019). Political ecology of tiger conservation in India: Adverse effects of banning customary practices in a protected area. *Singapore Journal of Tropical Geography* 40(1): 124–139.

Ramdas, S. (2009). Women, forest spaces and the law: Transgressing the boundaries. *Economic and Political Weekly* XLIV 44(44): 65–73.

Ramose, M. (2015). Ecology through Ubuntu. Pp. 69-76 in *Environmental values: Emerging from cultures and religions of the ASEAN Region*, R. Meinhold (ed.). Bangkok, Thailand: Konrad-Adenauer-Stiftung.

Ramsbotham, O., T. Woodhouse, and H. Miall. (2011). *Contemporary conflict resolution: The prevention, management and transformation of deadly conflicts* (3rd ed.). Cambridge, UK: Polity Press.

Ramutsindela, M., and M. Shabangu. (2018). The promise and limit of environmental justice through land restitution in protected areas in South Africa. Pp. 31-48 in *Land rights, biodiversity conservation and justice*, S. Mollett and T. Kepe (ed.). London: Routledge.

Rastogi, A., G.M. Hickey, R. Badola, and S.A. Hussain. (2014). Understanding the local socio-political processes affecting conservation management outcomes in Corbett Tiger Reserve, India. *Environmental Management* 53(5): 913-929.

Raworth, K. (2017). *Doughnut economics: Seven ways to think like a 21st-century economist*. London: Penguin.

Rear, D., and A. Jones. (2013a). Discursive struggle and contested signifiers in the arenas of education policy and work skills in Japan. *Critical Policy Studies* 7(4): 375-394.

Rear, D., and A. Jones. (2013b). Operationalising Laclau and Mouffes discourse theory as a practical method for text analysis. *Critical Policy Studies* 7(4): 375-394

Redford, K., and W.A. Adams. (2009). Payment for ecosystem services and the challenge of saving nature. *Conservation Biology* 23: 785–787.

Redford, K., C. Padoch, and T. Sunderland. (2013). Fads, funding, and forgetting in three decades of conservation. *Conservation Biology* 27: 437–438.

Redpath, S.M., J. Young, A. Evely, W.M. Adams, W.J. Sutherland, A. Whitehouse, A. Amar et al. et al. (2013). Understanding and managing conservation conflicts. Trends in Ecology and Evolution 28(2): 100-109.

Redpath, S.M., J. Young, A. Evely, W.M. Adams, W.J. Sutherland, A. Whitehouse, A. Amar, R.A. Lambert, J.D. Linnell, A. Watt, and R.J. Gutierrez. (2017). Don't forget to look down: Collaborative approaches to predator conservation. *Biological Reviews* 92(4): 2157–2163.

Resurrección, B. (2017). Gender and environmnent in the Global South: From 'women, environment, and development' to feminist political ecology. Pp. 71-85 in *Routledge handbook of gender and environment*, S. MacGregor (ed.). Oxfordshire: Routledge.

Rights and Resources Initiative. (2015). *Who owns the world's land? A global baseline of formally recognised indigenous and community land rights*. Washington, DC: RRI.

Rights and Resources Initiative. (2020). *Rights-based conservation: The path to preserving Earth's biological and cultural biodiversity?* Washington, DC: RRI.

Rio-Maior, H., M. Nakamura, F. Álvares, and P. Beja. (2019). Designing the landscape of coexistence: Integrating risk avoidance, habitat selection and functional connectivity to inform large carnivore conservation. *Biological Conservation* 235: 178-188.

Rist, G. (2007). Development as a buzzword. *Development in Practice* 17(4-5): 485-491.

Robbins, P. (2012). *Political ecology: A critical introduction* (2nd ed.). Malden, MA: John Wiley & Sons.

Robinson, M.O., T. Selfa, and P. Hirsch. (2018). Navigating the complex trade-offs of pesticide use on Santa Cruz island, Galápagos. *Society and Natural Resources* 31(2): 232–245.

Rocheleau, D. (2015). A situated view of feminist political ecology from my networks, roots and territories. Pp. 29-66 in *Practicing feminist political ecologies: Moving beyond the 'Green Economy'*, W. Harcourt and I.L. Nelson (eds.). London: Zed Books.

Rocheleau, D., and P. Nirmal. (2015). Feminist political ecologies: Grounded, networked and rooted on Earth. Pp. 793-813 in *The Oxford handbook of transnational feminist movements*, R. Baksh and W. Harcourt (ed.). Oxford: Oxford University Press.

Rocheleau, D., B. Thomas-Slayter, and E. Wangari. (1996). Gender and environment: A feminist political ecology perspective. Pp. 34-40 in *Feminist political ecology: Global issues and local experiences*, D. Rocheleau, B. Thomas-Slayter, and E. Wangari (eds.). New York: Routledge.

Rode, J., E. Gómez-Baggethun, and T. Krause. (2015). Motivation crowding by economic incentives in conservation policy: A review of the empirical evidence. *Ecological Economics* 117: 270-282.

Rodgers, W.A., R. Nabanyumya, E. Mupada, and L. Persha. (2002). Community conservation of closed forest biodiversity in East Africa: Can it work? *Unasylva* 53(209): 41–47.

Rodríguez, L.C., U. Pascual, R. Muradian, N. Pazmino, and S. Whitten. (2011). Towards a unified scheme for environmental and social protection: Learning from PES and CCT experiences in developing countries. *Ecological Economics* 70: 2163-2174.

Rodriguez, L.C., U. Pascual, R. Muradian, N. Pazmino, and S. Whitten. (2013). Unifying environmental and social protection: Learning from PES and CCT in developing countries. Pp. 120-149 in *Values, payments and institutions for ecosystem management*, P. Kumar and I. Thiaw (eds.). London: Edward Elgar.

Rodríguez, J.P., A.B. Taber, P. Daszak, R. Sukumar, C. Valladares-Padua, S. Padua, L.F. Aguirre, R.A. Medellín, et al. (2007). Globalization of conservation: A view from the South. *Science* 317(5839): 755-756.

Rooney, T., K. Lawlor, and E. Rohan. (2016). Telling tales: Storytelling as a methodological approach in research. *Proceedings of the 15th European Conference on Research Methodology for Business Management* 14: 147–156.

Root, T. (2014). The elephant chief. *Harper's Magazine*, April 14. Online at: https://harpers.org/2016/04/the-elephant-chief/ (accessed April 14, 2016).

Rose, D. (2009). Introduction: Writing in the Anthropocene. *Australian Humanities Review* (47), N_A.

Rose, D.B. (2015). Dialogue. Pp. 127-132 in *Manifesto for living in the Anthropocene*, K. Gibson, D.B. Rose, and R. Fincher (eds.). Santa Barbara, CA: Punctum Books.

Ruano-Chamorro, C., G.G. Gurney, and J.E. Cinner. (2022). Advancing procedural justice in conservation. *Conservation Letters* 15(3): e12861.

Rubis, J.M., and N. Theriault. (2020). Concealing protocols: Conservation, indigenous survivance, and the dilemmas of visibility. *Social and Cultural Geography* 21(7): 962–984.

Rwanda Environment Management Authority. (2016). *National biodiversity strategy and action plan*. Kigali, Rwanda: REMA.

Saad-Filho, A. (2016). Social policy beyond neoliberalism: From conditional cash transfers to pro-poor growth. *Journal of Poverty Alleviation and International Development* 7: 67-93.

Sahlins, M. (2008). *The western illusion of human nature*. Chicago: Prickly Paradigm Press.

Sajeva, G., G. Borrini-Feyerabend, and T. Niederberger. (2019). Meanings and more. Policy Brief of the ICCA Consortium Policy Brief no. 7. ICCA Consortium in collaboration with Cenesta. Online at: https://www.iccaconsortium.org/wp-content/uploads/2019/11/ICCA-Briefing-Note-7-Final-for-websites.pdf (accessed December 8, 2020).

Salleh, A. (2016). Climate, water, and livelihood skills: A Post-development reading of the SDGs. *Globalizations* 13(6): 952-959.

Salzman, J., G. Bennett, N. Carroll, A. Goldstein, and M. Jenkins. (2018). The global status and trends of Payments for Ecosystem Services. *Nature Sustainability* 1(3): 136-144.

Samojlik, T.. I.D. Rotherham, and B. Jędrzejewska. (2013). Quantifying historic human impacts on forest environments: A case study in Bialowieza Forest, Poland. *Environmental History* 18(3): 576–602.

San Miguel, A., S. Roig, and R. Perea. (2016). The pastures of Spain. *Revista de Pastos* 46(1): 6–39.

Sanchez. (2010). Galápagos sale de la lista en peligro. *El Comercio*, July 29. Online at: http://www.elcomercio.com/tendencias/galapagos-sale-lista-peligro.html (accessed November 4, 2020).

Sandbrook, C. (2015). What is conservation? *Oryx* 49: 565–566.

Sandbrook, C., J.A. Fisher, G. Holmes, R. Luque-Lora, and A. Keane. (2019). The global conservation movement is diverse but not divided. *Nature Sustainability* 2(4): 316-323.

Santander, T., J.A. González Novoa, W. Tapia, E. Araujo, and C.M. del Olmo. (2009). *Tendencias de la investigación científica en Galápagos y sus implicaciones para el manejo del archipiélago*. Puerto Ayora: Parque Nacional de Galápagos. Online at: https://repositorio.uam.es/handle/10486/3209 (accessed January 1, 2021).

Santos, B. (2018). *Decolonising the university: The challenges of deep cognitive justice*. Cambridge: Cambridge Scholars Publishing.

Sarin, M., N.M. Singh, N. Sundar, and R.K. Bhogal. (2003). *Devolution as a threat to democratic decision-making in forestry? Findings from three states in India*. London: ODI.

Schilthuizen, M. (2018). *Darwin comes to town: How the urban jungle drives evolution*. London: Quercus.

Schleicher, J., J.G. Zaehringer, C. Fastré, B. Vira, P. Visconti, and C. Sandbrook. (2019). Protecting half of the planet could directly affect over one billion people. *Nature Sustainability* 2: 1094–96.

Schlosberg, D. (2004). Reconceiving environmental justice: Global movements and political theories. *Environmental Politics* 13(3): 517-540.

Schulz, K. A. (2017). Decolonizing political ecology: Ontology, technology and 'critical' enchantment. *Journal of Political Ecology* 24(1): 125-143.

Scoones, I. (2007). Sustainability. *Development in Practice* 17(4-5): 589-596.

Scoones, I., M. Edelman, S.M. Borras Jr., R. Hall, W. Wolford, and B. White. (2018). Emancipatory rural politics: Confronting authoritarian populism. *The Journal of Peasant Studies* 45(1): 1–20.

Scott, J. (1998). *Seeing like a state: How certain schemes to improve the human condition have failed*. New Haven and London: Yale University Press.

Secretariat of the Convention on Biological Diversity. (2020). *Global Biodiversity Outlook 5*. Montreal: CBD.

Seiler, N., and M.M. Robbins. (2016). Factors influencing ranging on community land and crop raiding by mountain gorillas. *Animal Conservation* 19(2): 176–188.

Sen, A., and S. Pattanaik. (2019). The political agenda of implementing Forest Rights Act 2006: Evidences from Indian Sundarban. *Environment, Development and Sustainability* 21: 2355–2376.

Servicio Público de Empleo Estatal. (2018). *Informe del Mercado de Trabajo de Zamora*. Datos 2017. Madrid: Servicio Público de Empleo Estatal.

Sevilla. (2007). Las islas Galápagos, en peligro. *ABC*, April 11. Online at: https://www.abc.es/internacional/abci-islas-galapagos-peligro-200704110300-1632475630188_noticia.html (accessed January 1, 2021).

Shackeroff, J., and L. Campbell. (2007). Traditional Ecological Knowledge in conservation research: Problems and prospects for their constructive engagement. *Conservation and Society* 5: 343-360.

Shaw, I.G., and M. Waterstone. (2019). *Wageless life: A Manifesto for a future beyond capitalism*. Minneapolis: University of Minnesota Press.

Shizha, E. (2016). African Indigenous perspectives on technology. Pp. 47-64 in *African Indigenous knowledges and the sciences: Journeys into the past and present*, G. Emeagwali and E. Shizha (eds.). Rotterdam: Sense Publishers.

Shrestha, G., and F. Clement. (2019). Unravelling gendered practices in the public water sector in Nepal. *Water Policy* 21: 1017–1033.

Shrivastava, A., and A. Kothari. (2012). *Churning the earth: The making of global India*. New York: Penguin.

Siegel, P.E. (2018). *Island historical ecology: Socionatural landscapes of the eastern and southern Caribbean*. New York: Berghahn Books.

SIGTIERRAS. 2014. *Censo aropecuario 2014*. Quito: MAGAP.

Sikor, T. (2004). The commons in transition: Agrarian and environmental change in Central and Eastern Europe. *Environmental Management* 34(2): 270–280.

Singh, N.M. (2015). Payments for ecosystem services and the gift paradigm: Sharing the burden and joy of environmental care. *Ecological Economics* 117: 53–61.

Singh, N. (2018). Introduction: Affective ecologies and conservation. *Conservation and Society* 16(1): 1–7.

Sirima, A., and K.F. Backman. (2013). Communities' displacement from national park and tourism development in the Usangu Plains, Tanzania. *Current Issues in Tourism* 16(7-8): 719-735.

Smit, B., and J. Wandel. (2006). Adaptation, adaptive capacity and vulnerability. *Global Environmental Change* 16(3): 282–292.

Smith, L.T. (1999). *Decolonizing methodologies: Research and Indigenous Peoples.* London: Zed.

Sodikoff, G. (ed.). 2012. *The anthropology of extinction: Essays on culture and species death.* Bloomington: Indiana University Press.

Soutullo, A., M. Ríos, N. Zaldúa, and F. Teixeira-de-Mello. (2020). Soybean expansion and the challenge of the coexistence of agribusiness with local production and conservation initiatives: Pesticides in a Ramsar Site in Uruguay. *Environmental Conservation* 47(2): 97–103.

SPANEST (Strengthening the Protected Area Network in Southern Tanzania). (2016). *Ecological baseline study Greater Ruaha-Rungwa and Greater Kitulo-Kipengere Landscapes.* Iringa: Tanzania National Parks.

Spann, M. (2017). Politics of poverty: The post-2015 Sustainable Development Goals and the business of agriculture. *Globalizations* 14(3): 360-378.

Spinage, C.A., and F.A. Guinness. (1971). Tree survival in the absence of elephants in the Akagera National Park, Rwanda. *Journal of Applied Ecology* 8(3): 723–28.

Srinivasan, K. (2019). Remaking more-than-human society: Thought experiments on street dogs as 'nature'. *Transactions of the Institute of British Geographers* 44(2): 376-391.

Staddon, S. (2021). Conservation's all about having a blether and getting people on board: Exploring cooperation for conservation in Scotland. *Conservation and Society* 19(3): 161-71.

Stahl, H. (1998). *Contribuţii la Studiul Satului Devălmaş.* Bucureşti: Cartea Romaneasca.

Standing, G. (2017). *Basic income.* New York: Penguin Books.

Star, S.L., and J.R. Griesemer. (1989). Institutional ecology, 'translations' and boundary objects: Amateurs and professionals in Berkeley's Museum of Vertebrate Zoology, 1907-39. *Social Studies of Science* 19(3): 387-420.

Stem, C., L. Lassoie, D. Lee, and D. Deshler. (2003). How 'eco' is ecotourism? A comparative case study of ecotourism in Costa Rica. *Journal of Sustainable Tourism* 11: 322-347.

Stevens, S. (2014). *Indigenous peoples, national parks, and protected areas: A new paradigm linking conservation, culture and rights.* Tucson: University of Arizona Press.

Stevens, S., T. Jaeger, and N.P. Broome. (2016). ICCAs and Overlapping Protected Areas: Fostering Conservation Synergies and Social Reconciliation. *Policy brief of the ICCA Consortium No. 4.* Tehran: ICCA Consortium.

Stiglitz. JE. (2012). *The price of inequality: How today's divided society endangers our future.* New York: WW Norton & Co.

Strier, K.B. (1993). The animal boundaries of anthropology, or why don't all anthropologists consider themselves primatologists? *Reviews in Anthropology* 22(3): 165-174.

Stronza, A. (2007). The economic promise of ecotourism for conservation. *Journal of Ecotourism* 6(3): 210–230.

Suchet-Pearson, S., S. Wright, K. Lloyd, L. Burarrwanga, and B. Country. (2013). Caring as country: Towards an ontology of co-becoming in natural resource management. *Asia Pacific Viewpoint* 54(2): 185–197.

Sullivan, K. (2014). Akagera Park's 80 years of ups and downs. *The East African*, August 22. Online at: https://www.theeastafrican.co.ke/tea/magazine/akagera-park-s-80-years-of-ups-and-downs--1327502 (accessed February 13, 2021).

Sullivan, S. (2009). Green capitalism, and the cultural poverty of constructing nature as service-provider. *Radical Anthropology* 3: 18-27.

Sullivan, S. (2018). Making nature investable: From legibility to leverageability in fabricating 'nature' as 'natural capital'. *Science and Technology Studies* 31(3): 47–76.

Sultana, F. (2011). Suffering for water, suffering from water: Emotional geographies of resource access, control and conflict. *Geoforum* 42: 163–172.

Sultana, F. (2021). Political ecology I: From margins to center. *Progress in Human Geography* 45 (1): 156-165.

Sundar, N. (2001). Is devolution democratization? *World Development* 29(12): 2007–2023.

Sundberg, J. (2004). Identities in the making: Conservation, gender and race in the Maya Biosphere Reserve, Guatemala. *Gender, Place & Culture* 11(1): 43-66.

Sungusia, E., J.F. Lund, and Y. Ngaga. (2020) Decolonizing forestry: Overcoming the symbolic violence of forestry education in Tanzania. *Critical African Studies* 12(3): 354-371.

Survival International (2018). Colonialism vs. conservation [Video]. Online at: https://vimeo.com/295143710 (accessed February 23, 2020).

Svarstad, H., and T.A. Benjaminsen. (2020). Reading radical environmental justice through a political ecology lens. *Geoforum* 108: 1-11.

Swanson, H.A. (2017). Methods for multispecies anthropology: Thinking with salmon otoliths and scales. *Social Analysis* 61(2): 81-99.

TallBear, K. (2011). Why interspecies thinking needs indigenous standpoints. *Cultural Anthropology* 24: 1-8.

Tallis, H., J. Lubchenco, and 238 co-signatories. (2014). Working together: A call for inclusive conservation. *Nature* 515(7527): 27-28.

Tamale, S. (2020). *Decolonization and Afro-feminism*. Ottawa: Daraja Press.

Tanzania Broadcasting Corporation (TBC). (2017). Magembe dissolves MBOMIPA board. Online at: https://www.youtube.com/watch?v=gVA4zF7BTRg (accessed September 4, 2021).

Tauli-Corpuz, V. (2010. Indigenous peoples' self-determined development: Challenges and trajectories. Pp. 1-78 in *Towards an alternative development paradigm: Indigenous people's self-determined development*, V. Tauli-Corpuz, L. Enkiwe-Abayao and R. de Chavez (eds.). Philippines: Tebtebba Foundation.

Tauli-Corpuz, V., J. Alcorn, A. Molnar, C. Healy, and E. Barrow. (2020). Cornered by PAs: Adopting rights-based approaches to enable cost-effective conservation and climate action. *World Development* 130(March): 104923–36.

Tavernaro-Haidarian, L. (2018). Deliberative epistemology: Towards an Ubuntu-based epistemology that accounts for a priori knowledge and objective truth. *South African Journal of Philosophy* 37(2): 229–242.

Temper, L. (2019). Blocking pipelines, unsettling environmental justice: From rights of nature to responsibility to territory. *Local Environment* 24(2): 94-112.

Temper, L., and D. Del Bene. (2016). Transforming knowledge creation for environmental and epistemic justice. *Current Opinion in Environmental Sustainability* 20: 41-49.

Temper, L., M. Walter, I. Rodriguez, A. Kothari, and E. Turhan. (2018). A perspective on radical transformations to sustainability: Resistances, movements and alternatives. *Sustainability Science* 13(3): 747-764.

Terblanché-Greeff, A.C. (2019). Ubuntu and environmental ethics: The West can learn from Africa when faced with climate change. Pp. 93-110 in *African environmental ethics*, M. Chemhuru (ed.). Cham, Switzerland: Springer Nature.

Thomas, C. (2017). *Inheritors of the earth: How nature is thriving in the age of extinction*. New York: Allen Lane.

Thomas, C.D., A. Cameron, R.E. Green, M. Bakkenes, L.J. Beaumont, Y.C. Collingham, B.F. Erasmus, M.F. De Siqueira, A. Grainger, L. Hannah, and L. Hughes. (2004). Extinction risk from climate change. *Nature* 427: 145.

Tiger Conservation Plan. (2015). *Core zone*. Corbett Tiger Reserve, NTCA.

Tlostanova, M., and W. Mignolo. (2009). Global coloniality and the decolonial option. *Kult 6* 130-147.

Toncheva, S., and R. Fletcher. (2021). From conflict to conviviality? Transforming human–bear relations in Bulgaria. *Frontiers in Conservation Science* 2: 682835.

Toncheva, S., and R. Fletcher. (2022). Knowing bears: An ethnographic study of knowledge and agency in human-bear cohabitation. *Environment and Planning E: Nature and Space* 5(2): 901-923.

Toomey, A.H. (2020). The making of a conservation landscape: Towards a practice of interdependence. *Conservation and Society* 18: 25-36.

Toporek, R. (2013). Social class, classism, and social justice. Pp. 21-35 in *The Oxford handbook of social class in counselling*, W.M. Liu (ed.). Oxford: Oxford University Press.

Torralba, M. N. Fagerholm, T. Hartel, G. Moreno, and T. Plieninger. (2018). A social-ecological analysis of ecosystem services supply and trade-offs in European wood-pastures. *Science Advances* 4(5): eeaar2176.

Trajce, A. (2017). *The gentleman, the vagabonds and the stranger: Cultural representations of large carnivores in Albania and their implications for conservation.* Ph.D. thesis, University of Roehampton, London, UK.

Tran, T.C., N.C. Ban, and J. Bhattacharyya. (2020). A review of successes, challenges, and lessons from Indigenous protected and conserved areas. *Biological Conservation* 241: 108271.

Treves, A., and K. Karanth. (2003). Human-carnivore conflict and perspectives on carnivore management worldwide. *Conservation Biology* 17: 1491–1499.

Treves, A., L. Naughton, D. Bantlin, N. Kimambo, J. Olson, and J. Karama. (2019). *Socioeconomic and ecological dimensions of restoring Akagera National Park, Rwanda*. Rwanda: University of Wisconsin-Madison and Akagera Management Company.

Trueman, M., and N. d'Ozouville. (2010). Characterizing the Galápagos terrestrial climate in the face of global climate change. *Galapagos Research* 67 (October): 26–37.

Tsai, Y.L., I. Carbonell, J. Chevrier, and A.L. Tsing. (2016). Golden snail opera: The more-than-human performance of friendly farming on Taiwan's Lanyang Plain. *Cultural Anthropology* 31(4): 520–544.

Tuck, E. and K.W. Yang. (2012). Decolonization is not a metaphor. *Decolonization: Indigeneity, Education and Society* 1(1): 1-40.

Tucker, M., K. Böhning-Gaese, W. Fagan, J. Fryxell, B. Van Moorter, S. Alberts, A. Ali, et al. (2018). Moving in the Anthropocene: Global reductions in terrestrial mammalian movements. *Science* 359(6374): 466–469.

Tumusiime, D.M., and P. Vedeld. (2012). False promise or false premise? Using tourism revenue sharing to promote conservation and poverty reduction in Uganda. *Conservation and Society* 10(1): 15-28.

Turnhout, E., C. Wateron, K. Neves, and M. Buizer. (2013). Rethinking biodiversity: From goods and services to 'living with'. *Conservation Letters* 6(3): 154–161.

UNESCO. (2007). *State of conservation Galápagos islands (Ecuador)*. Paris: UNESCO.

United Nations (UN). (2014). *Millennium Development Goals update 2014*. New York: United Nations.

United Nations (UN). (2015). *Transforming our world: The 2030 Agenda for Sustainable Development*. New York: United Nations.

United Nations (UN). (2018). Global indicator framework for the Sustainable Development Goals and targets of the 2030 Agenda for Sustainable Development. Online at: https://unstats.un.org/sdgs/indicators/Global%20Indicator%20Framework%20after%20refinement_Eng.pdf (accessed December 14, 2020).

United Nations Environmental Programme-World Conservation Monitoring Centre (UNEP-WCMC). (2011). *Bwindi Impenetrable National Park Uganda: Protected Areas and World Heritage*. Nairobi: United Nations Environment Program.

United Nations Environmental Programme-World Conservation Monitoring Centre (UNEP-WCMC) and IUCN. (2016). *Protected Planet report 2016*. Cambridge, UK: UNEP-WCMC and IUCN.

United Republic of Tanzania (URT). (2015). *National Biodiversity Strategy and Action Plan 2015-2020*. Dar es Salaam: Vice President's Office.

United Republic of Tanzania (URT). (2016). *The National Five Year Development Plan 2016/2017-2020/2021: Nurturing Industrialization for Economic Transformation and Human Development*. Dar es Salaam: Ministry of Finance and Planning.

United Republic of Tanzania (URT). (2020). *The written Laws (miscellaneous amendments) (No 2) Act, 2020*. Dodoma: Government Printer.

Upadhyay, V. (2019). 24 villages with 'van gram' status threaten to boycott polls. *Times of India*, April 1. Online at: https://timesofindia. indiatimes.com/elections/ lok-sabha-elections-2019/uttarakhand/ news/24-villages-with-van-gram-status-threaten-to-boycott-polls/articleshow/68660646.cms (accessed May 25, 2020).

U.S. House of Representatives. (1984). *The human rights situation in South Africa, Zaire, the Horn of Africa, and Uganda*. Washington, DC: U.S. House of Representatives.

van der Duim, R., C. Ampumuza, and W.M. Ahebwa. (2014). Gorilla tourism in Bwindi impenetrable national park, Uganda: An actor-network perspective. *Society & Natural Resources* 27(6): 588–601.

van der Duim, R., C. Ren, and G.T. Jóhannesson. (2013). Ordering, materiality, and multiplicity: Enacting actor–network theory in tourism. *Tourist Studies* 13(1): 3–20.

Van Dooren, T. and D.B. Rose. (2016). Lively ethography storying animist worlds. *Environmental Humanities* 8(1): 77–94.

Van Dooren, T., E. Kirksey, and U. Münster. (2016). Multispecies studies cultivating arts of attentiveness. *Environmental Humanities* 8(1): 1-23.

Van Parijs, P., and Y. Vanderborght. (2017). *Basic Income*. Cambridge, MA: Harvard University Press.

Van Valkenburgh, B., and R. Wayne. (2010). Carnivores. *Current Biology* 20(23): 21–57.

Varga, A., and Z. Molnár (2014). The role of traditional ecological knowledge in managing wood-pastures. Pp. 203-220 in *European wood-pastures in transition*, T. Hartel and T. Plininger (eds.). London: Routledge.

Vasile, M. (2015). The role of memory and identity in the *Obștea* Forest commons of Romania. Pp. 1-15 in *Patterns of commoning*, D. Bollier and S. Helfrich (eds.). Amherst, MA: The Commons Strategies Group.

Vasile, M. (2018). Formalising the commons, registering rights: The making of the forest and pasture commons in the Romanian Carpathians. *International Journal of the Commons* 12(1): 170–201.

Vasile, M. (2019). *Forest and pasture commons in Romania: Territories of life, potential ICCAs: Country Report*, No. 53. Online at: https://doi.org/10.13140/ RG.2.2.32592.05127/1 (accessed February 19, 2021).

Vasile, M., and L. Mantescu. (2009). Property reforms in rural Romania and community-based forests. *Sociologie Romaneasca* 7(2): 95–113.

Vatn, A. (2015). Markets in environmental governance: From theory to practice. *Ecological Economics* 105: 97–105.

Vicente, J.L., M. Rodríguez, and J. Palacios. (2000). Gestión del lobo ibérico (Canis lupus signatus Cabrera, 1097), en la reserva regional de caza 'Sierra de Culebra' (Zamora). *Galemys* 12(1): 181–199.

Vizenor, G.R. (1998). *Fugitive poses: Native American Indian scenes of absence and presence.* Lincoln: University of Nebraska Press.

von Essen, E., and M.P. Allen. (2018). Taking prejudice seriously: Burkean reflections on the rural past and present. *Sociologia Ruralis* 58(3): 543–561.

von Hagen, L. (2020). Earth Live Lesson with Lynn Von Hagen: Human to elephant coexistence [recorded lecture]. Online at: https://www.youtube.com/watch?v=fi0LFk6Vp5g&t=1066s (accessed July 10, 2020).

Wa Ngugi, M. (2012). *Rethinking the Global South.* The Global South Project. Online at: http://www.globalsouthproject.cornell.edu/rethinking-the-global-south.html (accessed March 8, 2020).

Waghid, Y., and P. Smeyers. (2011). Reconsidering Ubuntu: On the educational potential of a particular ethic of care. *Educational Philosophy and Theory* 44(S2): 6–20.

Waldron, A., V. Adams, J. Allan, A. Arnell, G. Asner, S. Atkinson, A. Baccini, J. Baillie, A. Balmford, and J. Austin Beau. (2020). *Protecting 30% of the planet for nature: costs, benefits and economic implications: Working paper analysing the economic implications of the proposed 30% target for areal protection in the draft post-2020 Global Biodiversity Framework.* Campaign for Nature: http://pure.iiasa.ac.at/id/eprint/16560/.

Walker, S., A. Brower, T. Stephens, and W. Lee. (2009). Why bartering biodiversity fails. *Conservation Letters* 2: 149–157.

Walker, J., and M. Cooper. (2011). Genealogies of resilience: From systems ecology to the political economy of crisis adaptation. *Security Dialogue* 42(2): 143–160.

Walsh, M. (2000). The development of community wildlife management in Tanzania: Lessons from the Ruaha Ecosystem. In *Proceedings of the Conference on African wildlife management in the new millennium,* organised by the Mweka College of African Wildlife Management (CAWM), Moshi, CAWM, December 13-15.

Walsh, M. (2012). The not-so-Great Ruaha and hidden histories of an environmental panic in Tanzania. *Journal of Eastern African Studies* 6(2): 303-335.

Walsh S.J., L. Brewington, F. Laso, Y. Shao, R.E. Bilsborrow, J. Arce Nazario, H. Mattei, P.H. Page, B.G. Frizzelle, and F. Pizzitutti. (2020). Social-ecological drivers of land cover/land use change on islands: A synthesis of the patterns and processes of change. Pp. 63–88 in *Land cover and land use change on islands: Social and ecological interactions in the Galapagos islands*, S.J. Walsh, D. Riveros-Iregui, J. Arce-Nazario, and P.H. Page (eds.). New York: Springer.

Walwa, W.J. (2020). Growing farmer-herder conflicts in Tanzania: The licensed exclusions of pastoral communities' interests over access to resources. *The Journal of Peasant Studies* 47(2): 366-382.

Wark, M. (2015). *Molecular red: Theory for the Anthropocene*. London: Verso.

Watson, J., N. Dudley, D. B. Segan, and M. Hockings. (2014). The performance and potential of protected areas. *Nature* 515(7525): 67-73.

Watson, J., D. Shanahan, M. Di Marco, J. Allan, W. Laurance, E. Sanderson, B. Mackey, et al. (2016). Catastrophic declines in wilderness areas undermine global environment targets. *Current Biology* 26(21): 2929–2934.

WCED. (1987). *Our Common Future – Report by World Commission on Environment and Development*. Oxford: Oxford University Press.

Weaver, D., and L. Lawton. (2007). Twenty years on: The state of contemporary ecotourism research. *Tourism Management* 28: 1168–1179.

Weber, H. (2017). Politics of 'Leaving No One Behind': Contesting the 2030 Sustainable Development Goals Agenda. *Globalizations* 14 (3): 399-414.

Weeratunge, N., A. Agrawal, S. Gururani, K. Milton, J. Schrijvers, J. Spencer, and N. Weeratunge. (2000). Nature, harmony, and the Kaliyugaya: Global/local discourses on the human-environment relationship. *Current Anthropology* 41(2): 249-268.

Weichselgartner, J., and I. Kelman. (2015). Geographies of resilience: Challenges and opportunities of a descriptive concept. *Progress in Human Geography* 39(3): 249-267.

Welch, J.R., E.S. Brondízio, S.S. Hetrick, and C.E.A. Coimbra Jr. (2013). Indigenous burning as conservation practice: Neotropical Savanna recovery amid agribusiness deforestation in central Brazil. *PLOS ONE* 8(12): e81226.

Weldemichel, T.G. (2020). Othering pastoralists, state violence, and the remaking of boundaries in Tanzania's militarized wildlife conservation sector. *Antipode* 52(5): 1496-1518.

Wells, M., and T.O. McShane. (2004). Integrating protected area management with local needs and aspirations. *Ambio* 33(8): 513–519.

West, P. (2006). *Conservation is our government now: The politics of ecology in Papua New Guinea*. Durham, NC: Duke University Press.

West, P. (2016). *Dispossession and the environment: Rhetoric and inequality in Papua New Guinea*. New York: Columbia University Press.

West, P., and J.G. Carrier. (2004). Getting away from it all? Ecotourism and authenticity. *Current Anthropology* 45(4): 483–98.

West, P., J. Igoe, and D. Brockington. (2006). Parks and peoples: The social impact of protected areas. *Annu. Rev. Anthropol.* 35: 251-277.

West, S., L.J. Haider, S. Stålhammar, and S. Woroniecki. (2020). A relational turn for sustainability science? Relational thinking, leverage points and transformations. *Ecosystems and People* 16(1): 304-325.

Western, G. (2019). Conserving human-wildlife coexistence in Kenya [recorded lecture]. Online at: https://www.youtube.com/watch?v=EQ59RX0MtDY&t=1206s (accessed August 15, 2020).

Western, G., D.W. Macdonald, A.J. Loveridge, and A.J. Dickman. (2019). Creating landscapes of coexistence. *Conservation & Society* 17(2): 204-217.

Wezel, A., H. Brives, M. Casagrande, C. Clément, A. Dufour, and P. Vandenbroucke. (2016). Agroecology territories: Places for sustainable agricultural and food systems and biodiversity conservation. *Agroecology and Sustainable Food Systems* 40(2): 132–44.

White, B., S.M. Borras Jr, R. Hall, I. Scoones, and W. Wolford. (2012). The new enclosures: Critical perspectives on corporate land deals. *The Journal of Peasant Studies* 39(3-4): 619–647.

Widenhorn, S. (2013). Towards epistemic justice with Indigenous Peoples' knowledge? Exploring the potentials of the convention on biological diversity and the philosophy of Buen Vivir. *Development* 56(3): 378-386.

Wild Europe. (2018). *Old Growth Forest Protection Strategy Outline*. Brussels: Wild Europe. Online at: https://www.wildeurope.org/wp-content/uploads/2019/10/old-growth-forest-protection-strategy-outline.pdf (accessed May 30, 2020).

Wild Europe. (2019). New initiatives from a decade of progress: A conference for an action plan to protect and restore wilderness and old growth/primary forest in Europe, Bratislava, November 20-21.

WILD10. (2015). *A vision for a wilder Europe* (2nd ed.). Online at: wild10.org (accessed February 19, 2021).

Wilebore, B., M. Voors, E.H. Bulte, D. Coomes, and A. Kontoleon. (2019). Unconditional transfers and tropical forest conservation: Evidence from a randomized control trial in Sierra Leone. *American Journal of Agricultural Economics* 101(3): 894-918.

Wilkinson, R., and K. Pickett. (2010). *The spirit level: Why more equal societies almost always do better*. London: Penguin Books.

Wilshusen, P.R., S.R. Brechin, C.L. Fortwangler, and P.C. West. (2002). Reinventing a square wheel: Critique of a resurgent 'protection paradigm' in international biodiversity conservation. *Society and Natural Resources* 15(1): 17–40.

Wilson, E.O. (2016). *Half-earth: Our planet's fight for life*. New York: WW Norton & Co.

Wily, L.A., and S. Mbaya. (2001). *Land, people and forests in eastern Africa at the beginning of the 21st century: The impacts of land relationship on the role of communities in forest future*. Nairobi: IUCN–EARO.

Wittemyer, G., P. Elsen, W.T. Bean, A.C.O. Burton, and J.S. Brashares. (2008). Accelerated human population growth at protected area edges. *Science* 321: 123-6

Woolgar, S., and J. Lezaun. (2013). The wrong bin bag: A turn to ontology in science and technology studies? *Social Studies of Science* 43(3): 321–340.

Woolgar, S., and J. Lezaun. (2015). Missing the (question) mark? What is a turn to ontology? *Social Studies of Science* 45(3): 462–467.

World Bank. (2015). *The state of social safety nets 2015*. Washington, DC: World Bank.

Wuerthner, G., E. Crist, and T. Butler (eds.). (2014). *Protecting the wild: Parks and wilderness, the foundation for conservation*. London: Island Press.

Wuerthner, G., E. Crist, and T. Butler (eds.). (2015). *Keeping the wild: Against the domestication of Earth*. London: Island Press.

WWF. (2018). *Living Planet Report 2018*. Gland: WWF.

Wyborn, C. (2015). Connectivity conservation: Boundary objects, science narratives and the co-production of science and practice. *Environmental Science & Policy* 51: 292-303.

Wyborn, C., J. Montana, N. Kalas, F. Davila Cisneros, S. Clement, S. Izquierdo Tort, N. Knowles, E. Louder, M. Balan, J. Chambers, L. Christel, A. Deplazes-Zemp, T. Forsyth, T. Henderson, G.M. Lim, M.J. Martinez Harms, J. Merçon, E. Nuesiri, L. Pereira, V. Pilbeam, E. Turnhout, and S. Wood. (2020). *Biodiversity revisited: Research and action agenda for sustaining diverse and just futures for life on Earth*. Cambridge, UK: Luc Hoffmann Institute.

Yeo, J.H., and H. Neo. (2010). Monkey business: Human-animal conflicts in urban Singapore. *Social and Cultural Geography* 11(7): 681–699.

Zafra-Calvo, N., and R. Moreno-Peñaranda. (2017). Exploring local people's views on the livelihood impacts of privately versus community managed conservation strategies in the Ruvuma landscape of North Mozambique-South Tanzania. *Journal of Environmental Management* 206: 853–862.

Zafra-Calvo, N., U. Pascual, D. Brockington, B. Coolsaet, J.A. Cortes-Vazquez, N. Gross-Camp, I. Palomo, and N.D. Burgess. (2017). Towards an indicator system to assess equitable management in protected areas. *Biological Conservation* 211: 134-141.

Zaid, G. (2011). Illich el removedor. Online at: https://www.letraslibres.com/mexico-espana/illich-el-removedor (accessed January 11, 2020).

Zanotti, L., C. Carothers, C. Aqpik Apok, S. Huang, J. Coleman, and C. Ambrozek. (2020). Political ecology and decolonial research: Co-production with the Iñupiat in Utqiaġvik. *Journal of Political Ecology* 27(1): 43-66.

Zhang, W.E.I., and S. Pagiola. (2011). Assessing the potential for synergies in the implementation of payments for environmental services programs: An empirical analysis of Costa Rica. *Environmental Conservation* 38: 406-416.

Zia, A., P. Hirsch, A. Songorwa, D.R. Mutekanga, S. O'Connor, T. McShane, P. Brosius, and B. Norton. (2011). Cross-scale value trade-offs in managing social-ecological systems: The politics of scale in Ruaha National Park, Tanzania. *Ecology and Society* 16(4).

Zimmermann, A., B. McQuinn, and D.W. Macdonald. (2020). Levels of conflict over wildlife: Understanding and addressing the right problem. *Conservation Science and Practice* 2(10): e259.

Zlatanova, D. (2010). *Modelling the habitat suitability for the bear (Ursus arctos), the wolf (Canis lupus) and the lynx (Lynx lynx) in Bulgaria.* PhD thesis, Sofia University, Sofia, Bulgaria.

Zurba, M., K.F. Beazley, E. English, and J. Buchmann-Duck. (2019). Indigenous protected and conserved areas (IPCAs), Aichi Target 11 and Canada's Pathway to Target 1: Focusing conservation on reconciliation. *Land* 8(1): 10.

Георгиева, И. (1993). Българска народна митология. 2 издание. София: Наука и изкуство.

Гоев, А. (1981). Леене на куршум за страх. Българска етнология 3-4: 57–63.

Дуцов, А. и др. (2012). План за действие за кафявата мечка в България. Министерство на околната среда и водите.

Index

A

academics, 18, 172, 175–76, 179–81, 183–87, 189–91, 341

access, 320, 324–25, 331, 334–36, 340
  elite, 54, 80–82
  and equity in conservation, 11
  to land ownership, 336

accumulation, 58, 94

activists, 41, 175, 178, 184–87, 190–91

activities, human, 18, 73, 104, 148, 301, 367

actors
  local, 28, 62, 65, 166, 245
  nonhuman, 36

Adams, William, 73, 78, 101, 115, 122, 194, 271, 375

affect, 254–57, 263–64, 349

agency, 60, 130, 149, 197, 250, 252, 254, 264, 312, 323, 332
  non-human, 254

agriculture, 7, 22, 144, 150, 152–53, 158–61, 163, 165, 229, 327, 350
  marginal, 349–50

Akagera Management Corporation (AMC), 299, 304–5, 307

Alaska Permanent Fund (APF), 277

Ampumuza, Christine, 26–27, 29–30, 32–38, 40, 96, 98, 104, 106, 115, 136, 220

Anthropocene, 15, 22, 41–43, 46–49, 70, 73, 100, 132–33, 219–20, 251, 265

approaches, 21, 24–25, 28, 41, 190
  capitalist, 321–22
  conceptual, 194–95
  culture-based, 317
  non-human, 251
  sustainable, 95

areas
  conservation, 51, 269, 272, 282, 361
  human, 144, 156, 160
  natural, 203, 220

assets, natural, 235

assumptions, 24, 102, 105, 150, 157, 172, 188, 251–52, 306

attacks, 107–9, 205, 207, 233, 278

B

Batwa, 26, 32, 96, 98, 101, 103–16

bear, 32, 78, 225, 229–34, 240, 242–43, 260–61
  hide, 233, 236–40, 243

beings
  human, 75, 83, 85, 93, 184, 368
  more-than-human, 250, 254
  non-human, 86, 248, 250, 253, 256

beliefs, 45, 86, 102, 105, 109, 111, 147, 153, 223, 232–33, 308

benefits
  direct, 213, 239
  economic, 32, 223, 238–40
  significant, 132–33

Berkes, Fikret, 58, 145, 148, 223, 249, 374

biodiversity
  crisis, 49, 367–68, 375
  hotspots, 139, 283, 344–45, 355, 357
  loss, 18, 26, 62, 64, 100, 103, 119, 136, 140, 145–46, 367–69
  offsetting, 270
  protection, 226, 270, 346

biologists, 152, 263–64, 357

Bocci, Paolo, 7, 9, 22, 27–28, 31, 36–37, 39–40, 144, 154, 162, 165

bodies, 97, 102, 109, 112, 256–58, 271, 282

Boonman-Berson, Susan, 27, 30, 34–36, 38, 40, 222–23, 231, 242, 247, 253, 259–60

borders, 159, 259, 262, 342

boundaries, 50, 52, 82, 96, 105, 109, 223, 231–32, 243, 248, 262
  fenced, 307
  planetary, 42

breeding, 227

Brockington, Dan, 47, 73–74, 76–77, 79, 81, 96, 134, 346, 367–68, 373, 375

buen vivir, 28, 39, 89, 127–28, 144–45, 153, 156–57, 184

buffer zones, 203, 211, 302, 327, 372

Bulgaria, 7, 27, 29, 31, 218, 226–27, 229, 236, 240

Büscher, Bram, 20–25, 28–33, 41–43, 79–80, 82–84, 98, 129–31, 133–35, 137–38, 171–74, 214, 220–23, 247–49, 268–71, 293–95, 321–23, 342–43, 345–48, 363–64, 366–69

business, 7, 22, 47, 169, 333

buzzwords, 28, 40, 169, 171–75, 177–79, 186–89

Bwindi, 97, 99, 101, 103–7, 110–11, 115
    Forest, 7, 22, 96, 109

Bwindi Impenetrable National Park (BINP), 26, 104

bylaws, 356, 358–59, 363

C

capacity, 134, 140, 144, 149, 161, 227, 255–56, 312, 345, 354

capital, 56–58, 61, 162, 224, 274, 310, 325
    logics of, 61
    natural, 47, 51, 57, 67, 270

capitalism, 34, 40, 47, 56, 58–59, 70–71, 94, 292

capitalist, 48–50, 80, 249, 293, 295
    system, global, 62–64

care
    household, 330–31
    mutual, 27, 37, 295, 298, 314–15

carnivores, 193–95, 214
    large, 12, 27, 170, 180, 195, 212, 214–15, 372

cash transfer program (CTP), 269, 273–79, 281–82, 284–86, 361
    conditional, 273–75, 281
    unconditional, 273, 275–76

caste, 30–31, 38, 319–20, 324–26, 331, 337, 339–40

categories, 62, 64–65, 68–69, 114, 220, 230, 251, 324, 330, 371, 373–74

Centre for International Forestry Research (CIFOR), 280

change
    ecological, 158, 160, 296
    environmental, 11, 128, 137, 142, 294
    anthropogenic, 296

ethics of, 90

colonization, 113, 121–22, 142

commodification, 26, 32, 38, 56, 224, 243, 271, 285–86, 310, 315, 348

commoners, 344, 354–56, 358–59, 362

commoning, 347, 351, 364–65

common pool resource (CPR), 221

commons, 8, 23, 325, 341–42, 344, 347, 351–52, 354–65

communication, 55, 259–61, 265

communities
agricultural, 197, 301
disrupted, 291, 317
epistemic, 174, 187–89
human, 162, 203
indigenous, 32, 99, 149
rural, 9, 32, 204, 332, 362
target, 283, 285
tribal, 325–26, 337
village, 325

community-based conservation (CBC), 32, 47, 96, 132–34, 148, 181, 256, 367

concept, threshhold, 36, 38, 249, 253–54

conditions, dehumanising, 87–88

conflict
management, 222
mitigation, 181–82, 184
resolution, 10, 310
human-wildlife. *See* human-wildlife conflict
human-carnivore, 176, 219

connectedness, 99, 103–4, 107–8

conservation
activities, 155, 370
actors, 67, 124, 344, 360–61
approaches, 26, 81, 290, 348, 369–70
convivial, 24, 38, 41, 69, 142, 265, 338
equitable, 342, 365
fortress, 25, 370

analysis, 172–73, 177

displacement, forced, 292, 295, 310–11

dispossession, 33, 65, 113, 196, 325–26

disruption, socionatural, 291, 296–98, 317

distribution, uneven, 30

diversity, biocultural, 37, 57, 195–96, 216

Driessen, Clemens, 98, 220, 250, 261, 265

Duffy, Rosaleen, 19, 47, 51, 54, 79, 96, 123, 135, 151, 224, 298

Dunlap, Alexander, 21, 100, 271–72

E

earth, 18, 46, 56, 108, 114, 132–33, 289, 292–93, 295, 298, 368

ecology, 51, 77, 92, 98, 148, 155, 163, 183, 238, 294
    social, 177–78

ecosystems, 42, 46, 54, 73, 76, 119–20, 140, 145, 148, 155–56, 297, 313, 370–73

ecosystem services, 132–33, 148, 150, 157, 269–70, 279, 286, 367. *See* also services, ecosystem

ecotourism, 181–82, 218, 223–25, 235–36, 239, 241–43, 327–28, 332, 337, 340, 346, 348

elephants, 79, 99, 108, 180–82, 256, 308–12, 315, 372

elites, 63–64, 83, 124, 132–34, 136, 337

embodiment, 36, 126, 253–54, 256–59, 264

encounters, 108, 229–31, 233, 255

energy, 45, 68, 110, 350

engagement, 21, 28–29, 37–39, 54, 56, 65, 67–68, 161, 224, 254–57, 323

environmental education, 285, 315

environmentalism, everyday, 55, 98, 112, 130, 347

epistemologies, 26, 36, 91, 123, 266

equity, 11, 50, 88, 128, 146, 249, 269, 319, 321, 341, 351

Escobar, Arturo, 25, 39, 74, 101–2, 122, 224

ethics, 85–87, 90, 93–95, 127, 266, 295

networks, 44, 78, 96, 165, 183, 198, 335, 349, 362

new conservation. *See* conservation, new

Nightingale, Andrea, 149, 324

Nixon, Rob, 294, 312

O

objects, boundary, 172, 174–75, 179, 188–89

observations, 83, 111, 114, 199, 202–3, 226, 236, 262

Ogada, Mordecai, 19, 26, 73, 81, 113, 118–19, 123, 171

ontologies, 36, 91, 94, 99, 102–3, 112–15
    Indigenous, 99, 102–3, 112
    multiple, 100–101, 112
    western, 91, 102

organizations, 44, 47, 50, 61, 69, 176, 179–80, 182, 186–87, 352. '
    non-governmental (NGOs), 58, 63, 67–68, 106, 176, 189, 208, 215, 364. *See* also
    conservation non-governmental organizations

Other Area-based Conservation Measures (OECMs), 351–53, 363

P

Pandya, Revati, 27, 30–31, 33, 36, 38–40, 136, 319

park, 104–5, 146–47, 158–61, 289, 291, 298–302, 304–9, 311–12, 314–15, 371–72, 375
    authorities, 306, 309, 314, 375–76
    lands, 304, 309, 317
    park management, 292, 300, 305–6, 308

Parque Nacional Galápagos, 144–45, 155–57. *See* also Galápagos National Park

participants, 15, 110, 146–47, 176, 200, 238, 240, 250, 329

participation, 25, 28–30, 37, 132–33, 136, 146–53, 157, 161, 221, 225, 261, 264–65
    local, 145–47, 149, 151, 153, 166, 214, 325

participatory, 25, 37, 117, 124, 128, 131, 137, 142, 148
    conservation, 148–49

pastures, 77, 105, 164, 203–4, 347, 354–56, 359, 364
    woody, 354–55

patterns, 121, 148, 177, 189, 225, 263, 286–87, 313, 324

payment for ecosystem services (PES), 148, 269–70, 279–83, 287. *See* also services,
    ecosystem

payments, 67, 132–33, 148, 207–8, 269, 273, 277–78, 280–86, 288
  direct, 32, 355–56, 361

peace, 10, 289–91, 293–95, 305, 317
  ecological, 290–91, 293, 295–99, 316–17
        negative, 295–98, 304–6, 309–10, 312, 315
        positive, 30, 290–91, 295, 297, 299, 304, 306–8, 310, 313, 315–18
  liberal, 293–94, 315, 317
  negative, 290–91, 293–95, 313, 315, 317
  positive, 290–91, 293–94, 299, 315–16

peacebuilding
  ecological, 23, 289
  environmental, 10, 295

people
  dehumanized, 88
  local, 28–29, 64–65, 67, 224, 228, 239, 242, 256, 314–15, 345, 347
  marginalized, 66, 265

perspectives, nonhuman, 29–30, 38

Pettersson, Hanna, 27, 29, 34–35, 37–38, 40, 193

philosophy, 74, 76–79, 85–86, 88, 93–94, 113, 127, 262

planet, 18, 42, 44, 47, 80, 94, 139, 220, 265

plans, 144–46, 151, 153, 156–57, 226, 364

plants, 104, 159, 229, 250, 252, 255, 296
  invasive, 158

policies, 12, 24, 58, 67, 84, 90, 118–19, 174–75, 271–72, 367, 375

political ecology, 11, 15, 43, 101, 117–18, 149, 172, 178, 185, 249, 319

political economy, 44, 49, 191

politics, 22, 25, 43–45, 49, 65, 70–71, 145, 147, 156–57, 324, 331

Pooley, Simon, 41, 169–70, 188–90, 194–95, 197, 215–16, 223

populations, 150, 165, 202, 216, 227–28, 236, 240, 243, 310, 332
  increasing, 183, 302
  local, 75, 224, 228, 238–39, 241, 244

positionality, 119, 142, 225, 329

poverty, 49, 70–71, 141, 274, 350
  alleviation, 281–82

gorilla, 102, 104
    in protected areas, 368
    nature, 209, 370
    nature-based, 364
    photographic, 371, 374
    wolf, 208, 210

tour operator, 236–38, 241, 243

traditional ecological knowledge (TEK), 26, 35, 97, 99, 223, 296–97

transformation, 18, 24–25, 50, 60, 87, 91, 169, 172, 175, 190, 249
    axial, 19–20

U

Ubuntu, 7, 22, 26, 39, 73–75, 83–95, 112, 127–28, 137, 139, 184

Uganda, 7, 22, 29, 32, 96–98, 186, 301, 311

United Kingdom (UK), 176, 178, 180, 258

universal basic income (UBI), 214, 269–70, 276–79, 282–83, 285–87

V

value, 57, 130

villagers, 212, 230–32, 235, 314–16, 331, 333, 335, 337
    revenue, 331, 336

villages
    forest, 326, 328–38, 340
    revenue, 328, 331–34, 337–38

violence, 66, 121, 135, 291, 293, 296, 312
    direct, 293–94, 296, 306
    slow, 33, 294, 312
    structural, 290, 293, 295, 308–9

visitation, engaged, 31, 56, 80, 132–33, 357

W

water, 160, 162, 164, 183, 256, 372

wealth, 58, 94, 114, 146, 205

wellbeing, 272, 274, 296, 315, 347, 361
    non-human, 296, 364

wetlands, 140, 313, 327, 347, 376

www.ingramcontent.com/pod-product-compliance
Lightning Source LLC
Chambersburg PA
CBHW050641270326
41927CB00012B/2829